Industrializing American Shipbuilding

New Perspectives on Maritime History and Nautical Archaeology

UNIVERSITY PRESS OF FLORIDA

Florida A&M University, Tallahassee
Florida Atlantic University, Boca Raton
Florida Gulf Coast University, Ft. Myers
Florida International University, Miami
Florida State University, Tallahassee
University of Central Florida, Orlando
University of Florida, Gainesville
University of North Florida, Jacksonville
University of South Florida, Tampa
University of West Florida, Pensacola

New Perspectives on Maritime History and Nautical Archaeology
James C. Bradford and Gene A. Smith, Series Editors

This series is devoted to providing lively and important books that cover the spectrum of maritime history and nautical archaeology broadly defined. It includes works that focus on the role of canals, rivers, lakes, and oceans in history; on the economic, military, and political use of those waters; and upon the people, communities, and industries that support maritime endeavors. Limited neither by geography nor time, volumes in the series contribute to the overall understanding of maritime history and can be read with profit by both general readers and specialists.

Maritime Heritage of the Cayman Islands, by Roger C. Smith (1999; first paperback edition, 2000)

The Three German Navies: Dissolution, Transition, and New Beginnings, 1945–1960, by Douglas C. Peifer (2002)

The Rescue of the Gale Runner: *Death, Heroism, and the U.S. Coast Guard*, by Dennis L. Noble (2002)

Brown Water Warfare: The U.S. Navy in Riverine Warfare and the Emergence of a Tactical Doctrine, 1775–1970, by R. Blake Dunnavent (2003)

Sea Power in the Medieval Mediterranean: The Catalan-Aragonese Fleet in the War of the Sicilian Vespers, by Lawrence V. Mott (2003)

An Admiral for America: Sir Peter Warren, Vice-Admiral of the Red, 1703–1752, by Julian Gwyn (2004)

Maritime History as World History, edited by Daniel Finamore (2004)

Counterpoint to Trafalgar: The Anglo-Russian Invasion of Naples, 1805–1806, by William Henry Flayhart III (first paperback edition, 2004)

X Marks the Spot: The Archaeology of Piracy, edited by Russell K. Skowronek and Charles R. Ewen (2006)

Life and Death on the Greenland Patrol, 1942, by Thaddeus D. Novak, edited by P. J. Capelotti (2006)

Industrializing American Shipbuilding: The Transformation of Ship Design and Construction, 1820–1920, by William H. Thiesen (2006)

Admiral Lord Keith and the Naval War against Napoleon, by Kevin D. McCranie (2006)

Commodore John Rodgers: Paragon of the Early American Navy, by John H. Schroeder (2006)

Borderland Smuggling; Patriots, Loyalists, and Illicit Trade in the Northeast, 1783–1820, by Joshua M. Smith (2006)

Brutality on Trial: Hellfire Pedersen, Fighting Hansen, and The Seamen's Act of 1915, by E. Kay Gibson (2006)

Crisis at Sea: The United States Navy in European Waters In World War I, by William Still (2006)

Uriah Levy: Reformer of the Antebellum, by Ira Dye (2006)

Industrializing American Shipbuilding

The Transformation of Ship Design
and Construction, 1820–1920

William H. Thiesen

Foreword by James C. Bradford and Gene A. Smith, Series Editors

University Press of Florida
*Gainesville · Tallahassee · Tampa · Boca Raton
Pensacola · Orlando · Miami · Jacksonville · Ft. Myers*

Copyright 2006 by William H. Thiesen
Printed in the United States of America on recycled, acid-free paper
All rights reserved

11 10 09 08 07 06   6 5 4 3 2 1

A record of cataloging-in-publication data is available from the
Library of Congress.
ISBN 0-8130-2940-6

The University Press of Florida is the scholarly publishing agency
for the State University System of Florida, comprising Florida A&M
University, Florida Atlantic University, Florida Gulf Coast University,
Florida International University, Florida State University, University
of Central Florida, University of Florida, University of North Florida,
University of South Florida, and University of West Florida.

University Press of Florida
15 Northwest 15th Street
Gainesville, FL 32611-2079
http://www.upf.com

Contents

List of Figures vii

Series Foreword ix

Acknowledgments xi

1. The Origin of Practical Shipbuilding Methods 1

2. The Growth of Scientific Shipbuilding in Great Britain 16

3. Practical Shipbuilding Develops in the United States 44

4. The Golden Era of Urban American Shipbuilding 59

5. Building Iron Ships in a Wooden Shipbuilding Culture 80

6. A Clash of Cultures: The Failure of Theory in a Practical Shipbuilding World 113

7. An American Naval Renaissance and the Introduction of Theoretical Ship Design to the United States 140

8. The New American Style of Shipbuilding 169

Conclusion: Building an American Ship in the Twentieth Century 213

Notes 219

Bibliography 269

Index 293

Figures

1. Axemen at a shipyard 8
2. Small wood shipyard 11
3. Hauling a mast timber 12
4. Trunnels fastening hull planking 13
5. Trunnel-making machine 68
6. Timber-bending machine 70
7. Wooden dry dock 72
8. Iron shipbuilding magnate John Roach 85
9. Early iron shipbuilding patent 87
10. Ironworkers fashioning an iron keel 89
11. Ironworkers bending a ship's frame 100
12. Erecting an iron ship's frames 102
13. Yard workers hauling iron plate 105
14. Steam boiler being lowered into a ship 110
15. Wooden side-wheel steamer under construction 114
16. Royal Naval constructor William H. White 150
17. HMS *Leander* and USS *Chicago* 154
18. Model ship basin at the Washington Navy Yard 163
19. Naval constructor David W. Taylor 165
20. Hydraulic-punching machine 176
21. Early pneumatic field riveter 180
22. Machine shop in a midwestern shipyard 189
23. Mold loft for patterns and templets 197
24. Parts and subassemblies in a World War I shipyard 207
25. Aerial view of a World War I shipyard 210

Foreword

Water is unquestionably the most important natural feature on earth. By volume the world's oceans compose 99 percent of the planet's living space; in fact, the surface of the Pacific Ocean alone is larger than that of the total land bodies. Water is as vital to life as air. Indeed, to test whether the moon or other planets can sustain life, NASA looks for signs of water. The story of human development is inextricably linked to the oceans, seas, lakes, and rivers that dominate the earth's surface. The University Press of Florida's series New Perspectives on Maritime History and Nautical Archaeology is devoted to exploring the significance of the earth's water while providing lively and important books that cover the spectrum of maritime history and nautical archaeology broadly defined. The series includes works that focus on the role of canals, rivers, lakes, and oceans in history; on the economic, military, and political use of those waters; and upon the people, communities, and industries that support maritime endeavors. Limited by neither geography nor time, volumes in the series contribute to the overall understanding of maritime history and can be read with profit by both general readers and specialists.

Industrializing American Shipbuilding: The Transformation of Ship Design and Construction, 1820–1920 describes the development and evolution of American shipbuilding from the early nineteenth to the early twentieth century. Between those dates, skilled craftsmen constructed ships from wood using designs and methods that changed little over time. But marked changes occurred during the century examined in this work. Wood gave way first to iron and then to steel as the main construction material; formally trained naval architects who based their designs on principles developed by engineers replaced craftsman who depended on tradition for their plans; steam engines replaced sails to power the new vessels; steam-powered machinery operated in large shipyards by semiskilled laborers or ones who specialized in only a small component of the shipbuilding process replaced the small, often family-run shipyards that depended on master craftsmen, their apprentices and journeymen using hand tools to construct the ships of the new machine age.

Beginning in seventeenth-century France and becoming increasingly professionalized in nineteenth-century England, naval architecture gradually evolved from wooden sailing vessels to steam-powered iron/steel ships.

Design and shipbuilding advanced from practical design methods to designs based on complicated laws, theories, experimentation, and abstract mathematics. And this technological evolution greatly impacted the urban landscape, as shipyards required more space and new technology to build the iron behemoths; construction tasks also became more specialized and labor gangs ultimately became proficient in only one part of the larger overall production process.

The late nineteenth-century arms race ultimately brought the British system of theoretical ship design to the United States. American naval officers, who became the conduit of technological transmission, gathered and disseminated intelligence on new warship construction, and many of them began teaching theoretical design in American universities. Efficiency experts streamlined the shipbuilding process, reorganized navy yards, and rebuilt shipyards based on scientific management principles. These changes permitted the United States to build ships quickly and efficiently—the country had successfully carried through the rationalization of the shipyard to the ultimate expression. And these changes permitted the United States to emerge as the preeminent shipbuilder in the world by the beginning of the twentieth century, just as the country emerged as the most powerful industrial nation in the world.

James C. Bradford and Gene A. Smith
Series Editors

Acknowledgments

There are too many people who have aided me in this work to identify all of them by name. Some individuals, however, have been of great help to me, and I thank them. Arwen Mohun of the University of Delaware's Hagley Program advised me throughout the writing of this work. Cathy Matson, Peter Kolchin, Reed Geiger, George Basalla, and Pat Orendorf of the Department of History at the University of Delaware were also of great help to me. I would also like to thank Ritchie Garrison of the University of Delaware's Department of Art History and Roger Horowitz of the Hagley Center in Business History for their assistance. Eugene Ferguson, professor emeritus with the Hagley Program, also provided me with very useful advice. Delaware Valley historian Paul Schopp provided me with a wealth of ideas and research leads. This book is much richer for his assistance. My Maine friends George and Georgene Allen and Bill Brown gave me my start in wood shipbuilding and are partly to blame for my writing this book. I am grateful to them for it. I would like to thank the supportive staff and volunteers at the Wisconsin Maritime Museum. I greatly appreciate the support of the New Perspectives on Maritime History and Nautical Archaeology Series' editors, Gene Smith and Jim Bradford. I also thank Susan Albury and Meredith Morris-Babb at the University Press of Florida for their kind assistance.

Last, but most important, I am grateful to my wife, Mary. This book would only have been possible with her support.

1

The Origin of Practical Shipbuilding Methods

> *I tell this tale, which is strictly true,*
> *Just by way of convincing you*
> *How very little since things was made*
> *Things have altered in the shipwright's trade.*
>
> Rudyard Kipling, "A Truthful Song"

Kipling's quote testifies to how slowly and gradually shipbuilding methods changed in the years leading up to the nineteenth century.[1] At a time when there existed little time and money to undertake large construction projects, building a wooden ship represented a considerable investment. Shipbuilders did their best to ensure that their products were swift and seaworthy. They relied on time-tested craft methods, their aesthetic judgment, and contemporary examples of the best sailing ships as models for their own work.

This conservative approach to shipbuilding had been passed on for generations in shipyards throughout Europe. In the Anglo-American shipbuilding community—that is, shipbuilders located in Britain and the North American colonies before the Revolution—the craft of shipbuilding evolved gradually. The relatively diminutive size of ships, the use of wood, and the risks inherent in building experimental vessels ensured that Anglo-American shipbuilders would not introduce revolutionary shipbuilding methods. Anglo-American shipbuilders on both sides of the Atlantic adapted craft methods based on technological antecedents or a combination of antecedents.[2] As technological improvements occurred in one region, they spread to other locations. This transfer of technology occurred through worker migration and knowledge transmitted through newly constructed ships visiting foreign seaports. During the seventeenth and eighteenth centuries, shipbuilders adapted and modified craft methods of design and construction to suit their needs.

Throughout much of recorded history, the ship has remained one of the largest and most technologically sophisticated machines built by man. It often required immense amounts of material, labor, and financing for its manufacture. Furthermore, shipbuilders have always faced the complexities involved in a vessel that is influenced by forces under water, on the water's surface, and in the atmosphere. An unsuccessful experimental ship could prove a disaster to a small builder that had little time and money to develop better ships. In the face of these complexities, the prospect of building an experimental vessel or untried design remained the privilege of wealthy or state-funded shipbuilders, who tended to practice the high art of shipbuilding. Most Anglo-American shipbuilders were small-scale craft workers trying to earn a living. They relied on past experience for building copies of a successful prototype rather than risking precious time and money on new designs. They could spin off numerous ships from one model that proved successful.[3]

English ship design included both a "high art" and a "folk art."[4] The high art had its roots in the Renaissance, when Venetian and French shipbuilders incorporated the use of drawing and mathematics in the design process. This more scientific approach will be presented in detail in the next chapter. The folk art of ship design represented the more conservative of the two traditions, or the craft of shipbuilding.

One part of this conservative folk art was modeling the ship's hull after forms found in nature. Through the eighteenth century, Anglo-American ship designers failed to fathom the principles of hydrodynamics. Rather than spending large amounts of time and money on building failed experiments, they tried to assure their chances of success by adopting the lines of natural underwater forms. The immersed lines of a swimming duck, with the form full forward and fine to the rear, became especially popular. For years the duck form was believed to be the most stable, efficient, and seaworthy because it copied a form perfected by nature itself. Anglo-American shipbuilders believed the underwater lines of a ship could resemble forms of aquatic creatures, such as dolphins, which were thought to afford the greatest speed. The depiction of a fish superimposed on the ship's hull in a drawing found in Baker's *Fragments of Ancient English Shipwrightry* indicates how Elizabethan shipwrights perceived this notion.[5] Through the mid-1800s, shipbuilders adhered to the rule of a "cod's head and mackerel tail" hull form, meaning a bluff bow and a narrow stern, to provide the adequate seaworthiness.[6]

Many construction methods adopted by English shipbuilders had the result of standardizing vessels produced by England's small shipyards. These small builders used primitive templates, "ribbands," and "whole molding" to do this. Archaeologists have found evidence to indicate that English shipbuilders used frames and structural timbers from disassembled ships as templates to model structural parts for later vessels. The ability to standardize their products may have been one reason for the development of using skeletal framing in ships since the use of molds seems to date back to the time when skeletal framing first emerged in the Mediterranean, some time between the late Roman period and the early Middle Ages.[7]

Even if these shipbuilders had erected only the stem, sternpost, and the mid-ship frame, where the ship is widest, they could establish the contours of the rest of the ship using ribbands. They did this by running wooden battens, or ribbands, from the stem to the sternpost around the mid-ship frames. The shipwrights could run these ribbands as full or narrow as their eye for hull forms dictated, taking care to attach one at the bottom, another at the deck level, and some in between. By using ribbands they could see a rough outline of the hull in three dimensions before they began shaping hewing frames or planking, and they could ascertain the contours of any frame before shaping it.[8]

Another method employed by medieval shipwrights has been termed "whole molding." This method probably appealed to provincial builders because it required very little calculation or drawing. All they needed to begin was the length and breadth of the ship under construction. Employing the early whole-molding technique, shipwrights used the mid-ship frame profile as a jig for the rest of the frames. They had to take care that the frame replicas of the mid-ship became smaller and to extend the lines upward so that the hull's lines faired into the stem and stern. All that was necessary was to reuse the shape of the mid-ship frame only with diminishing beam toward the stem and stern. This method gave uneducated shipwrights a rote method of design and construction that eliminated guesswork and intricate calculation. After the late seventeenth century, shipbuilders continued to use whole molding, but they combined it with more sophisticated geometrical methods.[9]

Early English shipbuilders used little more than basic measurements to guide them in the design and construction process. Few, if any, of them are known to have used drawings or drafts to guide them in their work. They did, however, attain some level of what industrial experts term "standardization." Archaeologists have grouped together medieval ships exhibiting certain size and construction similarities as "cogs," "hulks," and "keels."[10] The fact that vessels built in northern Europe during the Middle Ages exhibited enough similarities to be categorized this way attests to a collective, albeit unconscious, effort by European shipwrights to incorporate common design and construction elements in their ships.

Another factor that led to the standardization of Anglo-American ship design was the founding and development of Lloyd's *Register of Shipping*. By issuing their requirements, or "Rules" for seaworthy vessels, Lloyd's Society had the effect of standardizing ship design and workmanship. Lloyd's Society originated from the same circumstances that led to the organization of Lloyd's of London, the marine insurance underwriters. They both formed in London late in the seventeenth century at Edward Lloyd's coffeehouse where individuals interested in shipping tended to congregate. Lloyd's Society emerged as a separate concern supported by subscribers wishing to know the seaworthiness of merchant vessels for purposes of insuring them or investing in them or their cargoes. By the early seventeenth century, "Ships' Lists," which contained profiles of insurable vessels, circulated among members at the coffeehouse. These manuscripts probably passed from hand to hand at first, but by 1726 they began to appear as printed registers. The first known publication of the *Register of Shipping*, known to subscribers as the "Green Book," began in 1760. At first Lloyd's issued the Green Book only to subscribers, but with time it became more widely circulated.[11]

While various warship types had been standardized by the English for years, the method that signaled the institutionalization of warship dimensions was the use of "establishments." Establishments prescribed the number of guns, weight, and size for various classes, or "rates," of vessels in the Royal Navy. Based on a similar set of standards found in the French Navy during the seventeenth century, the British began to use this method of standard rates in the 1670s and continued to employ the practice in revised form throughout the eighteenth century.[12]

Over the course of the eighteenth century, the Green Book served increasingly to control the construction of vessels because it classified many of them during the construction process. The Society's surveyors were skilled shipwrights, knowledgeable in matters of design and construction. They classified ship's hulls on a scale of *A*, *E*, *I*, *O*, and *U*, where *A* held the highest rating for seaworthiness and *U* the lowest. At first the surveyors rated a ship's machinery and equipment using the letters *G*, *M*, and *B* for "good," "middling," and "bad." Later they adopted the scale of one to four, with four representing the lowest class. Thus "A1" became the highest possible rating, and wooden ships built on the Thames, at the Royal Dockyards, or in India became the only ships able to achieve it. British shipbuilders bound themselves to obtain a favorable classification by Lloyd's because their clients often specified this in their contracts when ordering a new vessel.[13]

This then was the state of ship design in many of the shipyards in the Anglo-American world prior to the Revolution. It was a conservative tradition that copied the models of successful vessels and risked little in experiment. The skills of the Anglo-American shipbuilder required little theoretical knowledge—just the ability to take measurements and perhaps perform rudimentary mathematical tasks. A successful vessel could be reproduced using templates and ribbands or by reproducing frames through the use of whole molding. The master shipbuilder had the skills to carry through the entire production process from stump to ship. The master shipwright often filled the roles of owner, foreman, lumberjack, designer, bookkeeper, teacher, salesman, and, perhaps, ship owner. The small Anglo-American shipyard stood at the center of a work hierarchy, where the master shipwright labored alongside his men and had close personal contact with his workers. Instead of shipyard labor being divided into trades, it was separated more by skill level with master craftsmen at the top; journeymen in the middle; and laborers, apprentices, and boys at the bottom.

The manner that this practical design tradition spread may be found in the family-oriented and craft-based culture of Anglo-American shipbuilding. Rather than rising above their station, such workers as shipwrights maintained a certain social status that they passed along to generations of male descendants. The extended family network formed a cornerstone of the culture and trade of shipbuilding. At least as far back as the thirteenth century, documents indicate a strong family orientation toward the craft of shipbuilding. It was not uncommon in European shipyards to find dynasties where several generations of one family worked side by side as shipwrights.[14] In the Royal Dockyards, Henry VIII retained the services of master shipwright James Baker to build his warships. James's sons Matthew and Christopher carried on the family trade, and, in 1572, Matthew became the first individual officially designated a master shipwright in the service of the Royal Navy. During his service to Queen Elizabeth I, Matthew built many of the English warships that defended the realm from the Spanish Armada. Three generations of the Pett family, including father Peter, sons Phineas and Christopher, and grandson Peter, were the Royal shipwrights responsible for building up the English navy during the first half of the seventeenth century. In the preface to his 1711 work *The Shipbuilder's Assistant*, William Sutherland related that his grandfather, uncle, and "father and several of my relations" had been shipwrights in the employ of the Royal Navy.[15] Christopher Drew, founder of the American caulking tool manufacturer C. Drew & Company, traced his lineage back through six generations of shipwrights to Sir Edward Drew, knighted by Queen Elizabeth for his part in building the fleet that repulsed the Spanish Armada.[16] After Englishman Daniel Bacon established his shipyard in Salem, Massachusetts, in 1664, at least two generations of Bacon men followed him into the trade.[17]

Anglo-American shipbuilders diffused shipbuilding knowledge not only through family ties but also through craft traditions. While the European guild system never established itself in North America, American shipbuilders continued the practice of apprenticeship, the method of training young shipbuilders employed in pre-industrial Europe. As an apprentice to a shipwright, a boy found himself contracted for up to four years, usually from his mid-teens to around the age of twenty. The apprenticeship system represented a holistic approach to learning the craft where the master shipwright trained the apprentice in all of the various aspects of wood shipbuilding, such as hull construction, joinery, caulking, scraping and painting, perhaps even timber selection and rigging. The learning process was a hands-on approach based on practical experience and the implements of the trade. Apprenticeship encouraged strong bonds between the apprentices, master shipwrights, and other shipyard workers.[18]

Due to the itinerant nature of the shipbuilding trade, workers spread shipbuilding knowledge from yard to yard and continent to continent. After completing their apprenticeship, journeymen shipbuilders ventured from one shipyard to the next to gain the practical experience necessary to become a master shipwright.[19] Shipwrights frequently migrated to regions or countries that also promised better pay. For example, English shipbuilders began to migrate to North America as soon as settlement began. In 1624, Plymouth received its first documented master shipwright. In the spring of 1629, the Massachusetts Bay Company sent to Salem master shipwright Robert Molton and a gang of six shipwrights. Master shipwright William Stephens became one of many to immigrate to Salem during the 1630s, lured there by grants of free shorefront property for shipbuilding purposes. He arrived in Salem in 1637, but a year later he moved to Marblehead, and in 1642 he moved to Gloucester. Other English shipwrights emigrated as far south as Charleston.[20] Colonial shipbuilders became so efficient at their trade that they undercut the price of ships in England. The subsequent decrease in demand for ships built on the Thames forced many shipwrights to immigrate to the colonies to make a living. In 1724, the master shipwrights in the London area petitioned the Board of Trade to restrict colonial shipbuilding, claiming that half the shipwrights in Great Britain had immigrated to New England since 1710.[21]

Immigrant shipbuilders from within the colonies also spread shipbuilding methods and technology. During the pre-Revolutionary period, Massachusetts boasted the largest concentration of shipbuilding settlements in the colonies. These included the villages of Scituate, Ipswich, Beverly, Salem, Charlestown, Boston, Marblehead, and Weymouth. Many Massachusetts shipbuilders migrated to outlying settlements in Portsmouth, Newport, New London, and New Haven to establish shipbuilding industries in those communities. For example, many shipbuilders located around the mouths of such rivers as the Merrimac and Connecticut. New England seaports attracted these shipwrights by providing free shorefront property for shipyards, exempting shipwrights from militia service, and protecting stands of ship timber from unnecessary cutting.[22]

Craft knowledge was passed not only through social and cultural forces but also by technological factors. Ships usually sailed from one seaport to another. Shipbuilders needed only to stroll to the wharves near their shipyards to observe the latest in designs from foreign yards. The results of new design and construction methods used to build merchant, naval, and pleasure craft would rarely remain secret for long. Domestic shipbuilders would examine new models built abroad whenever foreign ships entered port. Naval personnel compared their warships with those of other naval powers during battle and in times of peace. During the Revolution, the Royal Navy found American naval vessels better designed than their own. The British captured and then copied the lines from the best American performers in order to reproduce the same qualities in their own ships.[23]

The craft tradition of practical shipbuilding was anchored in the tools used to build ships. To shipwrights, hand tools were much more than physical objects necessary to perform tasks and assemble wooden ships. They were an integral part of the design and construction process in Anglo-American shipbuilding. The shipwright's hand tools helped him shape the vessel in his mind as well as in the shipyard. Tools represented a repository of practical knowledge. Anglo-American shipbuilders did not need to read and write to learn their trade and practice it successfully. In a way similar to textbooks in formal education, hand tools represented a teaching aid for learning the trade of wooden shipbuilding. One historian has noted that "A great deal of the know-how which built the vessels of the past resided in the tools . . . . these artifacts constituted a continuum of inherited shipbuilding skill and knowledge whose origins were very ancient indeed."[24] Like ships, hand tools were artifacts that provided an ideal medium for transferring design and construction expertise from place to place and generation to generation.

From the Middle Ages through the nineteenth century, the shipwright's basic tool set remained little changed. A kit of shipbuilder's tools dating back to between AD 950 and 1000 included an axe, adz, chisels, augers, and handsaws.[25] Evidence from the apprentice indentures of late sixteenth-century England indicate that a typical shipwright's tool kit included an axe, adz, handsaw, chisel, gouge, shave, hammers, auger, brace, caulking irons, and caulking mallet. These tools remained the basic units of the shipwright's tool kit through the nineteenth century.[26]

Figure 1. Axemen wielding broad axes in an American shipyard. *Harper's New Monthly Magazine* 24 (April 1862).

The most basic part of a wooden shipbuilder's set of tools has always been edge tools, and the most important tool of the shipwright's kit was the axe. Wooden shipwrights relied upon more than one kind of axe for building a ship. In medieval France and Italy, shipwrights were even referred to as "masters of the axe."[27] Those shipwrights who ventured into the woods for timber took along a felling, or pitching, axe to cut down trees. This axe had a blade over a foot long with a thin edge weighted heavily so it could penetrate into the tree farther than other blades.[28] The axe most commonly associated with wooden shipbuilding has been the broad axe. Shipwrights used it for shaping and finishing timbers, such as those used for frames, keel, stem, masts, spars, and sternpost. The broad axe has a short handle offset to one side by a few inches so the knuckles of the axe man can clear the timber being hewed. It evolved into this form after the thirteenth century. With the short handle and long heavy head, the broad axe is ideally suited to hewing and shaping timbers rather than removing large quantities of wood. It has remained a fundamental tool for wood shipbuilding well into the twentieth century.[29] Shipwrights also used a hand axe, a multipurpose one-handed axe. The hand axe was considerably lighter and smaller and meant to be used with less force than a felling axe. This axe is most commonly found on shipwrecks because it became the primary axe for ship carpenters onboard vessels.[30]

The second-most important tool in the kit was the adz. The adz is an edge tool that has been a part of the Mediterranean shipbuilding tradition since the Egyptian civilization. It is shaped like a common garden hoe with a nine-inch blade weighing five to six pounds and a handle up to three feet long depending upon the height of the adz man. A pin poll usually projects on the side opposite the blade, so woodworkers can drive spikes and nails under the wood's surface and avoid striking them.[31] Throughout its history, the adz has been employed for finishing off wood surfaces that have proved too awkward or irregular for the broad axe. The adz is manipulated like a garden hoe to chip off the wood by raising it up in front and swinging it down toward one's feet. While some adz men bragged that they were accurate enough to split the sole of their shoes without cutting either the wood or their feet, one can well imagine why foot and lower leg lacerations became the most common injuries in wood shipyards.[32]

Another basic part of the shipbuilder's tool kit was the saw. Like the adz, the handsaw had figured prominently in Mediterranean shipbuilding since the late Bronze Age. The early use of the tool in the Mediterranean may have been due to the prevalence of soft woods easily cut by primitive saw blades. Even though the early Middle Ages saw the introduction of handsaws to northern Europe, the axe proved more effective in the dense hardwoods of the region, rather than early forms of the saw. By the fifteenth century, however, two-man crosscut saws became durable enough to cut down trees in northern Europe.[33]

Along with the adz and broad axe, the two-man frame saw became one of the tools characteristic of shipbuilding. By the late thirteenth century, the frame saw developed into the primary tool for cutting out planks. By that period, framed plank saws began to appear in pictorial material of northern Europe. Archaeologists in Germany and Denmark have located shipwrecks made with planks having saw marks, indicating that the plank saw had begun to make its appearance in northern Europe by the thirteenth century.[34] The frame saw represented a faster and less labor-intensive method for producing planks than earlier methods, so when saw blades tough enough to rip through hardwoods became available, northern shipbuilders began to use them.[35]

Once the two-man frame saws became durable enough to produce large quantities of plank, sawyers became an important part of the shipbuilding workforce. Many men associated with wooden shipbuilding made their living strictly as sawyers. They would set a log horizontally over a pit in the ground, or across a pair of heavy-duty trestles, and use a frame saw or whip saw to cut out timbers. In more recent times, the men standing on top of the log were referred to as the "top sawyers," and the men on the ground as the "pit men." Looking something like gymnasts, the top sawyer pulled up on the saw while the pit man pulled down on it. The teeth of the saw were set pointing to the ground so the cut would benefit from gravity on the down stroke. Pitmen often required the use of a broad-brimmed hat to prevent sawdust from drifting into their shirts. Because the two-man plank saw was commonly used in association with a pit, it came to be known as a pit saw. The use of pit saws continued into the twentieth century and may yet be found in use in the developing world.[36]

Boring tools of greater variety and sophistication became a part of the wooden shipbuilder's tool kit. The auger originated in northern Europe, where tougher hardwoods required muscle to bore and vessels were built heavier to withstand harsher wind and water conditions. The chest or breast auger, like the pit saw, was a tool uniquely associated with wooden shipbuilding and appears to have been developed by shipwrights. Pictures in the *Bayeux Tapestry* of 1085 indicate that the tool began to see service in European shipyards by the nineteenth century. Braced against the shipwright's chest and equipped with projecting arms for rotating it, the chest auger allowed shipwrights to apply more pressure to the auger and cut larger holes. This allowed shipwrights to drill harder and heavier planking and made possible the use of larger treenails for fastening planking.[37]

The Mediterranean had a different tradition of boring tools in lighter twist drills. The Ancient Egyptians used a sophisticated bow drill for boring wood. Northern Europeans failed to benefit from the small lighter drills until the fifteenth century, when they began to employ the brace, a hand-powered twist drill. The wooden brace failed to hold up under great pressure as well as the chest auger. It was better suited to drill small holes and could make pilot holes for larger augers faster and more accurately than an auger.[38]

The use of caulking in shipbuilding predates the seventh century, and evidence indicates that the Romans may have caulked their ships. Caulking consists of cotton or oakum, which is hammered into the seams between planks. Caulking tools include the beetle, a specialized mallet for driving the caulking irons. Beetles are made of hardwood, and their heads, measuring up to sixteen inches in length, are banded with steel rings for added reinforcement. With the impact brought to bear by beetles, the irons produce enough pressure to wedge the materials into the seams. Professional caulkers often suffered deafness from the high-pitched ring caused by the beetles striking the caulking iron.[39]

Figure 2. A small American wood shipyard during the nineteenth century looks much as it would have a century earlier. Wisconsin Maritime Museum Collection. By permission of the Wisconsin Maritime Museum, Manitowoc.

Few if any records remain to document the layout of the colonial shipyard. Records are unnecessary, however, to determine the layout of the small pre-industrial shipyard. It was common for colonists to establish shipyards in sheltered water near a plentiful supply of wood. Any shoreline with adequate depth for launching at high tide and an inclination of no more than eleven degrees supplied the necessary surroundings for a colonial shipyard. The technology early shipbuilders relied on remained medieval and the motive power for the work was animal and not machine. Shipwrights and joiners were responsible for owning and maintaining their own hand tools and transporting them to work every day.[40]

With the exception of the owner's house, few major structures stood in the pre-industrial shipyard. Each yard had at least one set of shipways upon which to build each vessel. Some yards had two or three sets of ways depending on their output. Some shipyards also had a wharf extending into the water for fitting out hulls after launch. The largest structures commonly found in wooden shipyards were storage sheds to house costly items, such as pit saws and crosscut saws, spars, cordage, or blocks. The yard might also have a steam shed for cooking planks to fit around sharp lines of the hull. These sheds, or steam boxes, included a trunk of up to thirty feet long, into which planks were inserted; a firebox underneath; and a boiler to supply the steam. The plank steamer could explode if not handled properly and often required the constant attention of an unskilled laborer or boy. The first recorded use of them was 1736, but they probably were used much earlier.[41]

Figure 3. A team hauls a mast timber to a shipyard much as the task had been performed for centuries. Wisconsin Maritime Museum Collection. By permission of the Wisconsin Maritime Museum, Manitowoc.

Shipyards performed materials-handling tasks in the form of lifting and carting by using manpower or livestock, such as oxen, mules, or horses. Livestock also supplied the power for pulling large loads and logs. To haul trees out of the forest or around the yard, shipbuilders used a two-wheeled timber carriage or cart, which held the sticks between its oversized wheels. After dragging trees from the forest, shipbuilders "limbed" them, at which point they referred to them as "sticks." They then cut the sticks in their sawpits, although some yards relied on local water-driven saw mills.[42]

Anglo-American shipbuilders employed the same methods used by medieval shipwrights. Having some knowledge of the vessel's dimensions, the shipbuilder would venture into the woods to select trees of appropriate size and cut and transport them from the forest with the aid of a team of oxen. Shipbuilders prized native white oak for building vessels. Its strength and durability made it ideal for plank and frame stock.

Laying the keel was the first step in assembling a wooden hull. Before the keel could be laid, stocks had to be set in the ground to provide a straight inclined platform for the ship. The keel was usually the largest piece of timber incorporated in the vessel. In the early days, when smaller vessels were built, one large tree could be used for the entire keel. As ships became larger and suitable trees became scarcer, large timbers had to be scarphed together like puzzle pieces using large metal rods or drifts as fasteners. Early on, ships' frames were also built out of solid pieces of wood, but as time went on, the frames began to be assembled from smaller pieces like the keel. To build one frame, smaller timbers, or "futtocks," would be assembled in the shape of the frame. Sets of two frames were partnered together using treenails, or "trunnels," to increase the strength of the entire frame unit. The frames of the hull were sandwiched in between the keel on the bottom and the keelson on top. The keelson ran the length of the keel but was usually of smaller proportions. The base of each frame would lie across the keel, and the keelson would be placed over the frames and secured with bolts or drifts to keep the frames in place.

The planking began once the keel had been laid and frames erected. Shipwrights fastened planks to the ship's hull, beginning with the heavy-duty garboard strake at the very bottom. Top timbers were then fastened to the

Figure 4. A wooden ship being planked showing all of the trunnels fastening the planks to their frames. Desmond, *Wooden Ship-Building* (New York, 1919). By permission of Vestal Press, Inc.

tops of the frames to provide stanchions for railings. The shipbuilders fashioned trunnels from boards of oak by splitting off square pieces roughly two feet long and over an inch across. Workers in wood shipyards produced circular rod-shaped trunnels with a shave, plane, and hand axe at night or in the winter off-season. Using an auger, a hole would be drilled through the plank and the frame, and the slightly oversized trunnel driven into the opening. Excess wood was cut off on either end of the trunnel and a small oak wedge driven into each end to secure it. The trunnel's diameter had to be oversized or the fastener would leak. The trunnel could not be too wide, or it would check and split the wood surrounding it when water expanded its diameter.

The final touches to the ship included decking, joinery, caulking, and painting. With its heavy beams and wooden planking, the deck formed the topmost support of the ship's skeletal frame. It not only closed off the ship's interior from the elements, it also prevented the hull from collapsing in upon itself. Shipwrights covered the interior of the frames with "ceiling." Similar to planking attached to the inside of the frames, ceiling provided additional structural support and protected the frames and exterior planking from exposure to shifting cargo. The ceiling usually ran from the bilge to just below the deck where shipwrights left airspace for ventilation. Next, the shipwrights began the inside joiner work, including building cabins, ladders, stairs, companionways, and so on. Outside joiner work included rough carpentry, such as laying decks and building deckhouses. After planking the hull, shipwrights drove oakum into the plank and deck seams, making the hull watertight and considerably stiffer. Finally they scraped and smoothed the hull and tarred or painted it.

A concept found in anthropology termed the "stock of knowledge" is useful for studying the development of shipbuilding technology through time. This term refers to the tools and methods used by workers and the spatial organization of those tools to "facilitate the goal orientation of work and the accomplishment of desired ends."[43] In shipbuilding, these tools included physical objects, forms of technical knowledge, and the way shipbuilders transmitted expertise throughout the shipbuilding community. This system of mental and physical tools included design and construction technology. Anglo-American shipwrights were responsible for overseeing the entire shipbuilding process, including these essential elements of production. This Anglo-American stock of knowledge of craft methods and traditions evolved gradually over time.

Throughout the nineteenth century, the size of ships would increase, the process of ship design would grow more complex, and the craft of ship construction would undergo industrialization. These factors would transform the shipbuilding industries in Great Britain and the United States in different ways. The early introduction of iron to British shipbuilding and the influence of state support for theoretical ship design would push the development of British shipbuilding in one direction. American shipbuilders would be pushed in a different direction by the country's plentiful supply of wood. In the United States, shipbuilders would adapt and modify Anglo-American tools and methods to their needs. They would develop these methods to the level of a fine art, fashioning products that would become very popular during the first half of the nineteenth century.

2

The Growth of Scientific Shipbuilding in Great Britain

> *"Science" has been defined to be "Knowledge reduced to a system"; if, therefore, we aim at Science in the Construction of ships, it is not a question whether theoretical and experimental knowledge should be collected and arranged with the utmost regard to method; but the inquiry is—how is it to be effected?*
>
> British naval shipbuilder Henry Chatfield, 1832

Prior to the American Revolution, British and American ship design methods remained tied to the practical methods that had been used since medieval times.[1] By the beginning of the nineteenth century, however, social and technological factors steered British ship design on a different course than that in the United States. British shipbuilders began to rationalize a process that had for centuries relied on intuition, aesthetics, and practical experience. Men such as Chatfield also began to associate the term "science" with shipbuilding.[2] Scientific shipbuilding did not represent the introduction of principles from the natural sciences but rather a conscious effort to base naval architecture on the rationalism of system and mathematics. Chatfield claimed that the "*purely scientific* part of the subject consists in . . . the rules of arithmetic, the principles of geometry, the doctrine of curves, the laws of gravitation, the nature of fluids, &c."[3] Scientific shipbuilding did differ greatly from the intuitive or craft-based methods of practical shipbuilding that prevailed in most American shipbuilding firms through the early nineteenth century.

While practical shipbuilding methods based on wood continued to predominate in American shipyards, iron laid a foundation for Britain's scientific shipbuilders. The growing scarcity of wood pushed Britain's shipbuilding industry to rely increasingly on iron. The introduction of iron to shipbuilding reinforced the scientific shipbuilding movement by drawing civil engineers to the industry. These engineers brought with them a desire to replace craft methods with rational mathematically based techniques. They became working intellectuals who used design tools, such as model ship basins, mechanical calculators, and drafting. They employed abstract mathematics to codify their knowledge and books, treatises, and professional journals to disseminate it. These individuals institutionalized their work by establishing schools of naval architecture and forming associations and societies devoted to their profession.

Some of the impetus for scientific shipbuilding came from Great Britain's need to control the ocean lifelines that supported its economy. The island nation required a merchant fleet to supply its needs and a powerful navy to protect its supply lines. The British movement to rationalize the craft of shipbuilding might not have taken place had it not been for the intervention of the state, and in particular the Royal Navy. Postal subsidies and naval subventions, supported primarily by Admiralty, aided in the construction of numerous passenger liners and freighters. Iron warship production had the most noticeable impact on the development of naval architecture, but state support for scientific shipbuilding came in the form of technical and moral assistance as well. The founding of schools, establishment of professional societies, publication of theoretical works, and the undertaking of experimental research all had ties to naval shipbuilding.

One of the most important factors pushing British shipbuilders toward a "scientific," or theoretical, approach to shipbuilding was the introduction of iron to the industry. It took some time for scientific shipbuilding to become fully established, but the introduction of iron materials to shipbuilding expedited the process. The conversion to iron did not revolutionize the methods of British naval architects, but it did draw in individuals from fields that had been alien to the shipbuilding community. Primarily civil engineers, these individuals brought to shipbuilding new ideas and institutions from their own area of expertise. Well after this transformation of British shipbuilding took place, American marine engineer Horace See pinpointed the source of change as an "awakening" that "was first manifest abroad, where a new order of things had been created, where the engineer, through his connection with the building of the metal vessel, founded the new order of naval architecture in place of the old-time one where wood was the basis."[4]

The supply of shipbuilding materials, or lack thereof, had an important impact on the design of British ships. England had experienced shortages of shipbuilding timber as early as the sixteenth century. The lack of suitable shipbuilding wood became even more acute during the late eighteenth century. A timber survey in 1783 showed only 50,000 loads left, and it took 2,000 loads to build a ship-of-the-line.[5] By 1817, a Plymouth shipbuilder claimed that "the whole of the royal forests do not *now* furnish annually more oak timber than will build a single 74-gun ship."[6] As domestic supply became scarcer, naval and civilian shipbuilders had to obtain wood from as far away as Asia, Africa, and North America.[7]

Iron failed to revolutionize British shipbuilding during the eighteenth century because it took time to produce it in a form that could be used to construct steam boilers and ship hulls. In 1784, Englishman Henry Cort devised the process for rolling wrought iron and earned himself a government pension and great fame. By 1786, the British had applied iron plate to the manufacture of boilers, and within a year machinist and ironworker John Wilkinson had fabricated the canal boat *Trial*.[8] In 1818, shipbuilders on the Clyde, in Scotland, had constructed the first iron sailing vessel, *Vulcan*. In 1822, the British first realized the advantages of steam power and iron construction in the first iron steamer, *Aaron Manby*.[9] Pioneer iron shipbuilder John Laird established his iron yard at Birkenhead in 1825, and by the early 1830s iron shipyards could be found on the rivers Thames, Mersey, and Clyde. By 1855, iron shipbuilding had supplanted wood on the Clyde.[10] Statistics show that the number of commercial iron vessels built in Great Britain surpassed wooden ship construction by 1865, a feat unequaled in the United States for another fifty years.[11]

By the mid-1800s, the British had an extensive history of iron shipbuilding, but it would be misleading to indicate that all Britons embraced iron shipbuilding from the very beginning. Initially iron shipbuilding was adopted reluctantly because of a certain cultural resistance. British shipbuilders could not fathom a change from "the materials of which Noah built the ark, namely, pine and pitch," to "a material that will not float, that is eight times heavier than water, and that quickly sinks to the bottom of the sea."[12] To traditionalists, the idea that a material heavier than water could "swim" seemed inconceivable, even "contrary to nature."[13] Allegedly, workers burned to the ground one of the first iron shipbuilding firms established in Britain because they opposed the use of iron in shipbuilding.[14] The Royal Navy resisted the incursions of iron warships into its fleet of wooden warships.[15] According to early iron shipbuilder John Grantham, the Royal Navy had "but one obstacle to the general introduction of iron in ship-building . . . which in this country it will be always difficult to overcome,—namely *national prejudice*. We cannot easily bring our minds to relinquish the 'wooden walls of old England.'"[16]

One of the many cases of iron vessels surviving grounding that he put forward was that of *Garry Owen*. The first iron steamer to incorporate watertight bulkheads, Laird's of Birkenhead launched *Garry Owen* in 1834. On January 6, 1839, a storm drove the 130-foot vessel ashore on the relatively smooth mouth of the Shannon River along with over two dozen wooden craft. The wooden craft were destroyed or severely damaged, while experts found *Garry Owen* damage-free after refloating her. This episode became the first public demonstration of the merits of iron ships relative to wooden ones.[17]

Men such as John Grantham, William Fairbairn, I. K. Brunel, and John Scott Russell helped establish a ship design elite based upon the use of iron and theory. John Grantham, referred to at times as both a mechanical and a civil engineer, became one of the earliest advocates of using iron for building ships. Little is known of Grantham's early life, but his father, John Grantham Sr., built one of England's first iron steamers. The senior Grantham built the steamer in 1825 at the Horsley Company, in Staffordshire, where the iron components for *Aaron Manby* had been fabricated in 1821. John Grantham Jr. became president of the Polytechnic Society of Liverpool by the 1840s and, through lectures and publications, became an active promoter of iron shipbuilding during the mid-1800s.[18]

William Fairbairn became one of the first reputable iron shipbuilders in England. Born in 1789, Fairbairn spent much of his early career as a millwright and machine builder in Manchester. In 1835, he established a shipyard at Millwall, on the Thames near London, in partnership with Andrew Murray, his former pupil and later noted author on shipbuilding. The firm produced up to a dozen high-quality iron ships per year for clients such as the Peninsular and Oriental Lines, the Royal Navy, and the East India Company.[19] Unfortunately, the Millwall yard proved to be a financial disaster because of the expense of London's labor, its great distance from the source of iron, and the mysteries of building ships with a new material.[20]

In addition to the shipyard at Millwall, Fairbairn involved himself in the production of a myriad of iron products. Fairbairn's operations produced iron cranes, boilers, locomotives, millworks, and waterwheels. Indeed, if he had not been proprietor of a cotton mill in Manchester, he could never have paid off the debts associated with the shipyard. During the twelve years Fairbairn ran the Millwall concern, he invested £50,000 in capital improvements, but he realized only £12,000 from the shipyard's sale in 1848. His son Robert claimed that Fairbairn lost £100,000 to the firm over the course of its existence.[21] In conjunction with Robert Stephenson, Fairbairn also superintended the construction of the Britannia Bridge over the Menai Straits. Fairbairn brought a wealth of experience in iron shipbuilding to this project, which paid off in a bridge design based on wrought-iron girders.[22]

Fairbairn has been strongly identified with iron shipbuilding by historians, but he should be remembered as one of that class of engineers who successfully applied iron to the production of numerous technologies. After building the iron steamer *Lord Dundas* in 1831, Fairbairn became interested in experimenting with iron. In 1835, the British Association for the Advancement of Science gave the task of investigating the properties of cast iron to Fairbairn and Eaton Hodgkinson, England's foremost authority on the properties of cast iron at that time. They carried out experiments with cast iron for a number of years at Fairbairn's industrial facilities. Between 1845 and 1847, Fairbairn came together with Hodgkinson once again to test the structural strength of wrought iron at the Millwall shipyard and determine the best forms and dimensions for the tubes of the Conway and Britannia bridges. The results of Fairbairn and Hodgkinson's tests were widely circulated and made both men famous.[23] In 1861, Admiralty appointed Fairbairn to its Special Committee on Iron, which over the course of the next four years determined the most suitable iron armor for British warships.[24] These experiments and others formed the basis of information for Fairbairn's nearly eighty articles, papers, and books related to the mechanical properties of iron and its application to civil engineering and naval architecture. This work included papers presented before the Royal Society, British Association for the Advancement of Science, and Institution of Naval Architects, as well as books such as *An Account of the Construction of the Britannia and Conway Tubular Bridges* (1849); *On the Application of Cast and Wrought Iron to Building Purposes* (1854); *Useful Information for Engineers* (1856); and *Treatise on Mills and Millwork* (1861–63). As Sir William stated: "I could not . . . suppress the desire I always had of giving to the world such information as I had collected in the varied forms and pursuits of my profession."[25] Dismayed by the lack of knowledge and guiding principles determining the use of iron, Fairbairn began testing its properties in the mid-1830s, devoted much of the rest of his life to investigations linked to iron in all its forms, and became largely responsible for popularizing the use of wrought iron in building bridges and ships.

During iron shipbuilding's early years, Grantham and Fairbairn defended the use of iron for shipbuilding by criticizing those vessels built poorly and pointing out cases of well-constructed iron ships that performed better than wooden vessels. Fairbairn claimed that "The iron ship, when well built, is indeed stronger, safer, and more durable than any other."[26] In 1842, Grantham presented a lengthy apologia for iron as a shipbuilding material before the Polytechnic Society of Liverpool entitled "Iron, as a Material for Shipbuilding." In it, Grantham pointed out that only iron ships built poorly suffered loss, while those constructed well outlasted the best wooden vessels.

The introduction of iron to shipbuilding brought with it the methods of engineering. Iron drew in civil engineers just as it had drawn such men into the railroad-building industry. Iron ships represented a similarly romantic form of technology and on the same grand scale. The engineers brought to the industry their expertise in the use of iron and their knowledge of the material's characteristics. They also transferred useful knowledge from other fields, such as bridge building. Despite their claims to "scientific" methods, their approach remained largely empirical. The most notable case of a British civil engineer adopting the shipbuilding industry as his own was Isambard Kingdom Brunel.

Other iron ships helped to dispel doubts about the feasibility of iron as a shipbuilding material. The next to do so after *Garry Owen* was the product of the genius of I. K. Brunel, a designer of railways and bridges, who began to apply himself to ship design by supervising the construction of the wooden paddle wheeler *Great Western*. As superintending engineer for the Great Western Railway Company, Brunel convinced the board of directors to extend that line, which ran from London to Bristol, across the Atlantic through regular transatlantic service. Brunel built *Great Western* at a time when British navigation experts still believed it impossible to reach America on steam power alone. The launch in 1837 of the largest vessel of its day drew a crowd of 50,000 spectators. *Great Western* established the first regular transatlantic passenger service in April 1838, and like Brunel's later ships, it captured the imagination of the public.[27] A London *Times* correspondent referred to it as a "majestic vessel," stating that "nothing could exceed the beauty of her appearance as she gallantly breasted the waves"; while a *New York Enquirer* reporter called it an "immense moving mass," and, upon viewing it, the public mind "became almost intoxicated with delight."[28]

Brunel's next ship, *Great Britain*, went well beyond *Garry Owen* to convince the British public about the durability and strength of iron hulls. Brunel intended his second ship to fulfill the same function as the first, but by employing as yet untested technology. In 1840, he completed Admiralty-funded tests of *Archimedes*, fitted with Francis Pettit Smith's screw propeller. As a consequence of these tests, the Royal Navy adopted screw propulsion and Brunel altered the design of *Great Britain*, which had been originally projected as a paddle wheeler. Completed in July 1843, *Great Britain* became the first transatlantic steamer made of iron and propelled by a screw propeller. Considered by some historians as the first modern ship, she was the largest ship of her day in the 1840s—one-third again as long as the largest warship—and came to be known as the "Mammoth." Prior to sailing for New York, *Great Britain* was thrown open to thousands of visitors in several cities throughout England.[29] The famous New York diarist Philip Hone noted in his journal on August 11, 1845: "The great iron steamer *Great Britain*, the leviathan of steam, the monster of the ocean, and unquestionably the largest and most magnificent specimen of naval architecture that ever floated, arrived here yesterday."[30]

It was a disaster that befell *Great Britain* that dispelled the doubts that many Britons harbored concerning the application of iron to shipbuilding. Due to navigational error, the vessel went aground on the beaches of Dundrum Bay, south of Belfast on the Irish coast, in September 1846. After remaining exposed to ocean surf for eleven months, *Great Britain* was refloated and found to have sustained little hull damage save a few punctures from rocks. Salvaging the vessel forced the Great Western Railway Company into bankruptcy, but it had the side effect of demonstrating in a convincing fashion the durability of large iron-hulled ships.[31] James Laing, originally a wooden shipbuilder from the river Wear, resolved to convert to iron shipbuilding after visiting the beached vessel. He built his first iron ship in 1853. Passenger lines, such as the Inman Line, began to order iron ships for their fleets.[32]

Construction of *Great Eastern*, Brunel's third and final ship, became the crowning achievement of his prolific career as a civil engineer. In 1852, Brunel teamed up with iron ship builder John Scott Russell to build the ship, but Brunel retained overall responsibility for design and construction. Brunel and Russell had the benefit of their own collective shipbuilding experience, the accumulated wisdom of thirty years of iron shipbuilding found in published papers and treatises, and a staff of expert consultants, such as civil engineer William Froude and Astronomer Royal George Airey.[33] One historian has referred to *Great Eastern* as "the ultimate expression of the iron shipbuilding ambitions of the engineers of early Victorian times," but Brunel simply called it "the machine."[34]

Like Brunel's *Great Western* and *Great Britain*, his *Great Eastern* became another sensational representation of the technological progress achieved during Britain's industrial revolution. Designed to carry her own coal for the round trip between England and India, the passenger liner became the largest ship ever built of iron and one of the largest structures of any kind built of iron. At a time when passenger vessels such as the Cunard liners averaged less than 4,000 tons displacement, *Great Eastern* displaced 18,000 tons. As a cable-laying vessel in the early 1870s, she displaced nearly 33,000 tons. The enormous vessel foiled Brunel's attempts to launch her, and an additional £120,000 and two-and-a-half months had to be spent to get her off of the Thames shoreline.[35] *Great Eastern* soon became a symbol of Britain's technological progress after becoming the subject of articles in the London *Times* and *Illustrated London News* and commemorative books such as *A Pictorial History of the Great Eastern*. The shipbuilders employed a new form of technology, photography, to record construction and admitted thousands of fee-paying visitors to help fund construction.[36]

Great Eastern was broken up for scrap in 1889, but *Great Britain* served the transatlantic route, Australian route, and as a coal hulk in the Falkland Islands. She has been restored and is now on display in the Bristol graving dock where she was built over 150 years ago.[37] The nervous strain on Brunel during the construction of *Great Eastern* proved unbearable for him, and he died on September 15, 1859, shortly after the vessel left on its trial trip. Russell built few ships after completing *Great Eastern*, but he did continue to play an important part in encouraging Britain's scientific shipbuilding movement.[38]

In a society still tied to the custom of class distinction, these engineers came to represent an elite group closely associated with technological development. Some established wood shipbuilders, such as the Napiers, Ingliss's, and Lairds, made the transition from wood to iron shipbuilding; however, the design and construction of iron vessels came to be dominated by professional engineers. It was apparent to engineers that iron had made the advancement in shipbuilding possible. John Scott Russell expressed the notion in this way: "We have parted the work of the ship-builder from that of the naval architect by the same broad line which separates the profession of civil architecture from that of mere house-builder."[39]

With examples of such ships as Brunel's, it is not surprising that iron vessels took their place alongside steam engines, steam locomotives, and iron bridges as symbols of Britain's industrial revolution. Brunel's magnificent vessels came to represent technological progress to the British. The construction of iron ships moved engineer William Fairbairn to write that "Among the many and mighty inventions . . . which have contributed to make this country and this age famous, a conspicuous place must be given to the application of iron to shipbuilding." English poet William Morris referred to iron ships as the "Cathedrals of the Industrial Age."[40]

To compete with wooden ships, iron shipbuilders had to manufacture vessels that were safe and economical to build and maintain. Wood had been used for centuries as a building material and yielded results that shipbuilders could predict well enough by rule of thumb. Iron shipbuilders tried to develop a knowledge base related to wrought iron's stress and strength tolerances and the best ways to design a ship hull using the new material. British shipbuilders gained some of this knowledge through trial and error, but some knowledge was gained through research and experimentation.

During the 1830s, scientific shipbuilders began experimentation to develop a knowledge base upon which to develop laws and principles for building iron ships. Even though these individuals began to use experimentation extensively to learn more about the things they built, it must not be assumed that this knowledge in all cases contributed to the theory behind ship design. In some cases it failed to do so. In other words, the so-called scientific approach did not always lead to sound mathematical theory. No matter whether their research led to sound naval design theory, the scientific shipbuilders held a view to their profession entirely at odds with the cultural view of their American counterparts. They saw themselves as working intellectuals rather than practical mechanics. As a historian of engineering noted: "Engineering knowledge takes various forms, and we must continually remind ourselves that knowledge does not necessarily require or even imply theory."[41]

By turning shipbuilding into a science, nineteenth-century shipbuilders increased the number of subspecialties within the field of naval architecture. These fields of inquiry included hull design, fluid resistance, the material science of iron, and the stability and displacement of hulls. The experimentation and theories developed within these fields became some of the tools associated with the scientific shipbuilders and the profession of naval architecture.[42] These tools were part of a new stock of knowledge representing a different method than practical shipbuilding because it approached design problems differently and the knowledge acquired in these fields was disseminated in a different manner.

Despite Britain's early experience with iron shipbuilding and material testing, poor design and construction plagued its iron ships through the mid-1800s. The loss of *Titanic* in 1912 was not the first tragic loss of life from the wreck of a metal passenger liner, but one of the last in a long line of disasters to plague iron and steel ships. Indeed, the wrecks of passenger vessels became the most public demonstrations of the effectiveness of iron as a shipbuilding material during the nineteenth century. The design of iron ships became failure-driven because these disasters attracted great media attention. Consequently, public pressure was brought to bear on shipbuilders to design and construct safer passenger and cargo vessels.

Throughout the nineteenth century, iron ships became more common in Great Britain. This was due in part to state funding. Beginning in 1830, the British government began to pay postal subsidies to shipping lines, such as the Peninsular and Oriental, Inman, Cunard, and White Star, that could provide regular transatlantic service. These subsidies guaranteed a minimum income for overseas carriers regardless of the number of passengers they carried on their vessels. The postal subsidies had the effect of expanding the iron shipbuilding industry rather than the wood shipbuilding industry.

This is because British steamers of the day were traditionally constructed of iron.

Greater numbers of iron ships wrecked as more and more were built. It was discovered that while they could beach without damage, iron ships were just as likely to break apart when run on the rocks. During the 1850s, a large number of iron vessels wrecked with heavy loss of life. Many of these losses were newly built ships such as *Queen Elizabeth* and *Victor Emmanuel*, which went down with nearly all hands; and *Connaught*, which sank on her maiden voyage. Lacking the requisite hull strength to endure grounding, ships like the *Metropolis* grounded and broke up under the weight of the hull and cargo.[43] Another iron vessel, *Birkenhead*, ran upon the rocks and had one watertight compartment after another break off and sink as each filled with water.[44] Early iron shipbuilder William Fairbairn bemoaned the sad state of early iron shipbuilding: "of those disasters to which all seagoing ships are exposed . . . the most destructive and appalling have occurred in iron bottoms, I need only call to mind the wreck of *Birkenhead* . . . which within the last few days has carried sorrow and anguish into hundreds of homes."[45]

Through the 1850s, iron ships continued to suffer major losses sensationalized by the British press. The loss of an iron passenger ship a year prior to the inaugural meeting of the Institution of Naval Architects dramatized this point. Similar in build to but lacking the steam power of the successful *Great Britain*, *Royal Charter* went ashore in a gale near Liverpool on October 25, 1859, after a two-month voyage bound from Melbourne, Australia. Rather than settling on the rocks, she suddenly split in two, killing over 450 passengers and crew. Eyewitness accounts of the wreck in the media and the heavy loss of life in the *Royal Charter* disaster horrified the public and foreshadowed the sensation caused by *Titanic* fifty years later.[46] These wrecks forced their builders and owners to reevaluate the methods employed for building and maintaining iron vessels.

At the Institution of Naval Architects' 1860 meeting, the wreck of *Royal Charter* and the consequent loss of confidence in iron passenger vessels reopened the subject of iron's suitability as a shipbuilding material. Papers presented at the meeting included two on the strength of iron ships, one on the progress of mathematical theory in naval architecture, and several on new methods for building iron vessels.[47] Two papers appeared on iron ship design and the benefits improved methods could bestow on iron ship construction. William Fairbairn, the day's leading authority on the strength of wrought iron, wrote one of them. Iron shipbuilding champion John Grantham wrote the other as an apologia defending the use of iron. In it he proclaimed: "The art of iron-shipbuilding may now be fairly ranked as a science, the elements of which have firmly taken root, and its full growth only requires the fostering care of those who have already nursed it in its infancy."[48]

The *Royal Charter* disaster raised other questions at the 1860 Institution of Naval Architects meeting. During the storm, the vessel parted both of her anchor chains, dooming the underpowered *Royal Charter* to wash up on the rock-bound Anglesea shore. G. W. Lenox, of the firm Brown, Lenox, and Company, presented a paper on the strength of iron chains and pointed out that *Great Eastern* had ridden out the same storm near the wreck site using only one anchor cable. Lenox ended his presentation calling for stricter standards to regulate the manufacture of chain cable.[49]

The 1860 Institution of Naval Architects meeting also began a debate over the restricting influence of Lloyd's over hull design, which would continue for decades. Due to her leaky hull, *Royal Charter* had put into Plymouth before sailing for Australia, and two ship surveyors noticed that an iron plate had worn so thin that a bar of gold bullion had shifted in the cargo and pierced the iron. Even though *Royal Charter* had been built too early to come under the influence of Lloyd's "Rules for Iron Ships," Institution members used the 1860 meeting as a forum for discussing the influence of marine insurer Lloyd's Society on iron ship production.[50] In their papers on the strength of iron ships, both John Grantham and William Fairbairn complained that Lloyd's rules were too restrictive and that the Society should cooperate with industry leaders to work out more lenient ones. The discussion after the papers became lively, with one Lloyd's surveyor labeling Grantham and Fairbairn "fault finders," and another surveyor complaining that iron shipbuilders had produced vessels without industry standards or "uniform practice in any part of the country."[51]

The history of Lloyd's as an insurer of iron ships extends back to the 1830s. In 1836, Lloyd's had begun the practice of including iron ships in the *Register*, but not classifying them. Most received the simple rating of "Built of Iron."[52] By the mid-1840s, the number of iron vessels had increased to the point that Lloyd's canvassed the British shipbuilding community for their standards so the Society could compile a set of rules for iron vessels. The response was poor because few standards then existed and they varied with each builder.[53] One iron shipbuilder answered Lloyd's questionnaire that he had "the most earnest desire to see Iron Ships built on the strongest and most scientific principles." Later he indicated that he could not "see any way of filling up your Questionnaire satisfactorily, as I consider the subject so involved with practical difficulties that it would be impossible to make Rules to meet the different cases honestly."[54] Rather than rely on the shipbuilding community, the Society started examining the plans and specifications for each new iron vessel to determine the ship's classification.[55]

During the early 1850s, the rate of iron ship construction accelerated, so Lloyd's had to develop a set of standards for iron ships. In 1853, the Society established a committee to formulate rules to classify iron ships. Lloyd's principle surveyors toured the country's most prominent iron shipyards. The committee collated a set of rules from this fact-finding mission, and they drafted them in 1854. The first Rules for Iron Ships appeared in the Green Book for 1855. These rules proved conservative because the committee remained uncertain about the properties of iron. For example, to receive an A1 classification, a vessel of only 3,000 tons required iron plating one inch thick and frames spaced only sixteen inches apart.[56]

As Lloyd's gained greater experience with and knowledge of the new material, it revised its required scantlings for iron vessels. In 1857, the Society began testing wrought-iron plate and riveting methods and expanded the rules as a consequence; however, the basic 1855 Rules for Iron Ships served the Society until 1863. In that year, debate between iron shipbuilders and the staff at Lloyd's led to a complete revision of the Rules.[57] The Society amended the Rules once more in 1870, but the modifications were minor. During the 1870s and 1880s, Clyde shipbuilder William Denny carried on the struggle against the "paralyzing" influence of Lloyd's. In the late 1870s, Denny presented two papers that supported Grantham and Fairbairn's contention that Lloyd's Rules for Iron Ships were too restrictive and argued for modifying them to take into greater consideration a ship's displacement rather than just its dimensions. This ongoing debate led to acrimonious discussions during the 1870s and 1880s but not to fundamental changes in the 1870 Rules.[58] Revision of the Rules for Iron Ships indicate the learning process that took place through testing iron and surveying iron vessels in the decades between 1830 and 1870. Through debate, testing, and development of specifications for safe iron ships, Lloyd's helped British shipbuilders surmount the many uncertainties associated with iron. Between Lloyd's and engineers such as Fairbairn and Hodgkinson, research on iron material properties had flourished. By 1875, American shipbuilder John W. Griffiths wrote that British shipbuilders had become "abundantly supplied with volumes containing information on all metals."[59]

Through a process of experimentation, application, and revision, the various parts of the iron hull became more uniform. The cumulative effect of this process of development came to be a more standardized hull form for naval vessels and for a variety of merchant vessels.

Fairbairn's experience with iron shipbuilding and construction of the Britannia Bridge led him to become one of the earliest theorists in the design of iron bridges and ships. His theories were published in his books and by such associations as the Royal Society and the Institution of Naval Architects from the late 1840s to the mid-1860s. Fairbairn's papers—such as his 1850 contribution to the Royal Society, "The Strength of Iron Ships," and his 1860 contribution to the Institution, "Strength of Iron Ships"—elucidated his ideas on the use of wrought iron in the construction of ships. In the latter paper, he applied his knowledge from designing the Britannia Bridge to develop a formula based on the assumption that ships in a seaway experience strains similar to heavily loaded iron bridges. He developed the equation $W = adc/l$, where a equals the surface area of the hull, d equals its effective depth, c equals a constant dependent on the method of riveting, and l equals the length of the ship.[60] By using this basic formula, Fairbairn tried to give a quantitative value to an iron hull's maximum strength. In 1865, he collected all of his ideas and theories on iron and iron shipbuilding and published them in a book entitled *Treatise on Iron Shipbuilding: Its History and Progress*. Fairbairn first suggested the use of a "hollow girder" analogy of a bridge structure for the longitudinal design of iron frames that ran the length of the ship. Previous to the introduction of iron, material could not be found that was strong enough to support ships in such a way.[61]

Fairbairn had not been the first and certainly was not the last to look at the mathematics that underlay the structural strength of ship hulls. This aspect of ship design for the length of a ship versus its beam had increased in the period spanning the mid-1700s to the mid-1800s from a ratio of one to three to one to nine.[62] In papers presented to the Institution of Naval Architects in the early 1860s and later in his book *Shipbuilding, Theoretical and Practical*, Scottish mathematician and civil engineer William J. M. Rankine extended and refined Fairbairn's girder theory. Rankine showed that hulls encounter their highest load stresses in two hypothetical extremes: when supported on either end or in the middle. Ships built of wood with the traditional arrangement of a keel and laterally positioned frames were especially vulnerable under these conditions. Rankine's principles for extreme stresses on ship hulls proved useful to ship design for generations.[63]

Brunel's *Great Eastern* incorporated most of the innovations in iron shipbuilding learned through experimentation and trial and error since the 1830s. Many of these innovations owed their existence to the lessons learned from construction of the Britannia Bridge in the late 1840s. Brunel and Russell based their longitudinal system of hull design on Fairbairn's "hollow girder" theory, which went against the traditional transverse design of a keel with lateral frames. In the longitudinal system, thick iron stringers supported the hull along its length with ten bulkheads spaced every fifty feet to provide transverse support.[64] Russell began to employ longitudinal design to ship design by the mid-1830s; however, his design failed to become popular because it cut down on interior cargo space. This longitudinal design later became the basis for capital warship design; came to be known as the "Isherwood System" in the twentieth century; and was subsequently adopted to strengthen oil-tanker hull design.[65] The two engineers also incorporated the cellular double-bottom system based on Fairbairn's design of the iron tube used to span the Britannia Bridge, where the ship incorporated a second bottom to protect against grounding. In fact, *Great Eastern* experienced an accident similar to *Titanic*'s, when uncharted rocks off of New York harbor ripped a hole in her outer skin eighty feet long and ten feet wide. The ship proceeded to New York without incident, her passengers unaware of the damage experienced by the vessel.[66] Brunel and Russell's design for the *Great Eastern* excluded the use of a keel altogether because it did not require the additional support, and he saw keels as a dangerous protrusion if the vessel ever rested unsupported on solid ground. Indeed, while *Great Eastern* proved to be a commercial failure, it had a significant influence on the development of British ship design.[67]

Of the new fields of scientific inquiry, the two most researched aspects of naval architecture became hull resistance to water as well as ship stability. The theoretical knowledge behind the fluid resistance of the ship allowed naval architects to render accurate estimates of power necessary to propel a ship at its desired speed, to determine how changes in the hull design altered performance, and to select underwater forms best suited to the conditions in which the vessel had to perform. Civil engineers John Scott Russell, William J. M. Rankine, and William Froude became the foremost researchers in this field.

During the 1830s and 1840s, scientist, engineer, and iron shipbuilder Russell observed the behavior of canal boats to devise laws necessary to determine the proper form and length of hulls. Most prominent among his laws was the "wave-line" principle, which he described in papers presented before the British Association for the Advancement of Science and later to the Institution of Naval Architects. In them, he explained the resistance of a ship as the force employed in "excavating" so many tons of water per hour as the hull cut a channel through the water it traversed. The quantity of a ship's resistance could then be determined by the ship's displacement and its rate of speed.[68] Russell used the theory as the basis for designing his iron ships of the 1830s. To lessen resistance, ships based on his wave-line theory had sharp bows, narrow beams, and lengthy hulls. Despite Russell's systematic approach to research in hydrodynamics, his theories had a questionable mathematical basis. Armed with more sophisticated mathematical models, later naval architects and researchers discarded the wave-line theory in favor of more accurate mathematical models.[69]

Fellow Scotsman Rankine's theory replaced Scott Russell's as the most widely accepted. Rankine was an able mathematician, but he is best known for his professional accomplishments in engineering. He introduced the "streamline" theory of resistance in one of his many contributions to the *Institution of Naval Architects Transactions*. In his theory, a streamline surface, such as a ship, traverses any number of streamlines causing unequal pressures, similar to a wing surface that develops uneven pressures in the surrounding airstreams. Ship resistance was based on surface friction, not hull volume, so it was proportional to the hull's wetted surface.[70] The treatise *Shipbuilding, Theoretical and Practical*, which he edited and to which he contributed chapters, was considered one of the most important contributions to the field of naval architecture in the late nineteenth century.[71] In 1868, the British Association appointed him, Lord Kelvin, and a special committee to study "The Stability, Propulsion and Sea-going Qualities of Ships"; the committee reported on experiments to determine hull resistance at various speeds. The committee found that resistance tests could best be carried out using full-sized vessels, because it determined that models made bigger waves and the viscosity of water might inhibit the velocity of models more than their full-scale counterparts.[72]

Another member of the committee, William Froude, embraced Rankine's streamline theory. He believed that the resistance depended on the skin friction of the wetted surface of the hull at low speeds, but that at higher speeds it also included the energy consumed by the ship producing waves and eddies on the water's surface.[73] Froude, however, dissented from Rankine's opinion as well as Russell's that only the observation of actual ships rendered trustworthy information concerning resistance, claiming "experiments on the resistances of models of rational size, when rationally dealt with, by no means deserve the distrust with which they are usually regarded, but, on the contrary, can be relied on as truly representing the resistances of the ships of which they are the models."[74] An Oxford graduate, Froude had a connection to experimental naval architecture that began in 1856, when Brunel hired him as an assistant in the design of *Great Eastern*. In the 1860s, Froude began experiments in hull behavior, mainly rolling, using a small model basin in his home at Torquay, near Portsmouth. Part of Froude's great success in naval architecture experiments stemmed from his skill in building accurate measuring devices, such as resistance-recording apparatus, machines to measure towrope strain in full-sized ship trials, and dynamometers. A friend of Froude's from Oxford claimed, "His [Froude's] hands were as skillful as his creative brain was active."[75] Froude convinced the Royal Navy's chief constructor, Edward J. Reed, of the importance of model testing to warship design. In 1871, with the aid of Reed's influence, Admiralty financed construction of the world's first model basin for Froude's experiments. The theories of pure mathematicians such as Bernoulli had suffered from the lack of any real-life verification, but the employment of Froude's model basin allowed Admiralty to test and refine mathematical theories more cheaply and efficiently than employing full-size vessels. Froude's arrangement with Admiralty began Froude's intimate working relationship with the Royal Navy.[76]

Froude did resort to towing a full-sized vessel to verify his methods. For six weeks in 1871 he oversaw the towing of HMS *Greyhound*, 160 feet long and displacing 1,150 tons, by a larger naval vessel to confirm his Law of Comparison. The Law of Comparison, or Froude's Law, was a specific application of Newton's general law of mechanical similitude. During the trials, Froude paid attention to such details as the measurement of air resistance on the vessel's hull, a factor shown to be appreciable on a windy day.[77] The results recorded by Froude's automatic measuring devices showed substantial agreement with those calculated through the use of a ten-foot model *Greyhound* replica tested at the model basin in 1872. Froude presented the results in his Institution of Naval Architects paper "On Experiments with H.M.S. *Greyhound*," which vindicated the Law of Comparison and is considered by some to be his most important contribution to naval architecture. In the paper, Froude claimed "the experiments with the ship, when compared with those tried with her model, substantially verified the law of comparison which has been propounded by me as governing the relation between the resistances of ships and their models."[78] In his Law of Comparison, Froude said: "I shall show in fact that if the velocities of the ship and model are as the square roots [of their dimensions], then these excesses of resistance—(those due to surface waves)—will be as the cubes of the dimensions."[79] After the results became known, Admiralty made model tests mandatory for all new warship designs.[80]

During his lifetime, Froude presented numerous theoretical papers to such learned groups as the British Association for the Advancement of Science and the Institution of Civil Engineers and published often in the Institution of Naval Architects' *Transactions*. Most of these concerned the hydrodynamics of hull forms, and many of them were published in the twilight years of his life. Some historians of technology consider Froude's paper "On the Stability, Propulsion, and Sea-going Qualities of Ships," which he presented before the British Association for the Advancement of Science, one of the most important nineteenth-century contributions to the theory of naval architecture.[81] British naval constructor Sir William H. White stated in 1912 before the Institution of Civil Engineers that Froude's methods were an "illustration of the modern method in which mathematics and experimental research are associated in the solution of engineering problems which would otherwise remain unsolved."[82]

Many scientific shipbuilders sang the praises of Froude, but another Scotsman and prominent Clyde shipbuilder, William Denny, became the most ardent follower of Froude's methods. In one of his many letters to Froude, Denny wrote: "Without compliment and with only truth I can say you have made my views on design."[83] In 1881, Denny demonstrated his faith in Froude's methods by building his own model basin at the family's Leven Shipyard in Dumbarton. With the aid of Froude's son Robert E., and Froude's former assistant F. P. Purvis, Denny completed the basin in 1883.[84] After using the tank for a decade, Denny became convinced that it saved many costly errors made by practical shipbuilders. Denny's shipbuilding firm actually lost some contracts because the firm was thought too scientific to produce high-quality ships.[85] Model test basins became recognized tools of naval architecture. In 1885, Admiralty opened a modern facility at Haslar to replace the original model basin in Torquay. In 1900, the Scottish shipbuilder John Brown completed his own model basin. Most major naval powers completed their own facilities during the late nineteenth century. By 1900, there existed model basins in England, Scotland, Italy, Russia, Germany, and the United States.[86]

Ship stability, the ability of a vessel to remain upright, also became a matter of intense scrutiny because the seaworthiness and consequently the safety of passengers and cargo depended upon it. Ship stability is a complex matter because it depends upon a hull's displacement in the water, freeboard (the shortest distance up the side of the hull between the waterline and the deck), and ballasting. The construction of unstable ships plagued the British shipbuilders throughout much of the nineteenth century. Some of the earliest iron ships were so top-heavy that they capsized upon entering the water. One practice to prevent early iron merchant and naval vessels from "turning turtle" was to line their hull interiors with brick walls.[87]

During the 1850s, the subject of ship stability came under greater scrutiny by scientific shipbuilders. During the mid-1800s, the theoretical work of Henry Moseley and naval constructor Frederick K. Barnes became the basis of the accepted methods for establishing stability. During his tenure as Dockyard School superintendent between 1848 and 1853, Moseley presented an important work on the stability of ships before the Royal Society that enabled naval architects to accurately calculate the stability of ships. His paper "On the Dynamical Stability and on the Oscillation of Floating Bodies" appeared in the Society's 1850 volume of *Philosophical Transactions* and became the basis for later theoretical work in the field.[88] In 1853, after HMS *Perseverance* capsized at its dock, naval constructor Frederick Barnes was called in by Admiralty to conduct inclining experiments on warships to determine their stability. Barnes became the foremost authority on the subject during the 1860s, presenting a paper on inclining experiments at the first Institution of Naval Architects meeting. At the second, he presented another paper describing the latest method of calculating stability. Barnes's work became the basis for theoretical work on stability in the 1870s, when it became a matter of intense scrutiny by naval and civilian shipbuilders.[89]

Sensational disasters once again influenced the direction of ship design research. Despite the attention naval architects had lavished on ship stability since the 1850s, the matter remained an important one for the theoreticians. The capsizing of newly constructed HMS *Captain* in 1870 brought the matter of stability to the forefront of British shipbuilding in a very public way. Up through the 1850s, stability of ships had not posed a problem because most vessels were high-sided and therefore stable enough at large angles of inclination to remain upright. After 1860, the freeboard designed into vessels, particularly in warships, began to shrink. Turreted sailing warship *Captain* had only six feet of freeboard and capsized in high winds while she was on station in the Bay of Biscay. She took her designer and over 450 crew to the bottom.[90]

During the Institution of Naval Architects' 1871 annual meeting, ship stability became the center of attention, especially for Admiralty designers Nathaniel Barnaby, William H. White, and William John. The papers of these individuals were largely an expansion and extension of Barnes's work.[91] Rankine submitted important data on stability to the Committee on Designs for Ships of War, established after the loss of *Captain*. Having served as an assistant to the naval constructor in charge of building *Captain*, assistant overseer Francis Elgar had to prepare further evidence submitted to the committee. This committee involvement motivated Elgar to continue experiments on the subject for some time and become a leading authority in the field. The *Captain* wreck also prompted Barnaby and White, the individuals in charge of the Royal School of Naval Architecture, to require students to carry out elaborate calculations for the stability of specific ships or ship designs. In his 1871 paper on stability, White claimed that the subject of stability "remained in comparative obscurity until the loss of the *Captain* forced it into painful prominence" and that the disaster marked "an epoch in the science of naval architecture."[92] After the *Captain* disaster, Admiralty required stability calculations for all new warship construction programs, and for many decades the design of *Captain* remained a lesson for naval architecture students on how not to construct ships.[93] Such disasters as those documented above led American shipbuilder J. W. Griffiths to believe that engineers had left behind the principles of their profession to "scramble for a contract to rivet iron plates together, to coffin confiding ocean-travelers ... without a basis of principles."[94]

In the early 1880s, Elgar also examined and reported on the shocking loss of the new passenger liner *Austral*, which capsized in Sydney Harbor, and the 1883 sinking of *Daphne*. The *Daphne* disaster drew much attention to the problem of stability. In the summer of 1883, Alexander Stephen and Sons of Scotland rushed construction completion of the 1,000-ton steamer in time for display at the local Glasgow Fair. In an attempt to save time, over one hundred workers remained onboard the vessel during the late-July launch and continued working. Upon entering the water, *Daphne* suddenly capsized and sank in a few minutes, trapping and drowning the workers onboard. *Daphne*'s builders were exonerated. An inquiry into the matter found that no private firms had made stability calculations for their vessels. The shipbuilders lacked the time and personnel skilled enough in theoretical mathematics to ascertain a ship's correct stability. Stability measurements had been calculated for only one merchant vessel previous to the *Daphne* disaster. That work had been conducted in 1883 for a vessel that had capsized in a similar fashion to *Daphne*.[95]

With the exception of work by Rankine and shipbuilder William Denny of Dumbarton, Scotland, Admiralty conducted most of the research on stability. After the *Daphne* disaster, however, "Stability became everything. The technical papers were full of it, the scientific societies were full of it; budding naval architects spoke of little else."[96] Naval architects and theoreticians presented an unusually high concentration of seven papers on calculating stability at the 1884 Annual Meeting of the Institution of Naval Architects. Among them, Denny prepared a paper that put forth a more reliable method for determining the stability of a ship before it touched the water. So important did the topic of stability ultimately become that entire books were devoted to the subject.[97]

What proved remarkable about the 1884 annual meeting was not only the high concentration of articles on calculating stability but also that most of the articles promoted the use of a mechanical calculator called the Amsler integrator.[98] The beauty of the integrator was that it could quantify the values necessary for stability and required little time or skill. Calculating the stability curves for *Captain* without an integrator took two trained specialists a month. It took an untrained apprentice a little over ten days to make a similar calculation using the integrator. Some experts argued that they could do similar work in less than half the time. Invented by a Swiss mathematician, the first integrator was imported to Great Britain in 1878. A paper presented to the Institution of Naval Architects brought it to the attention of shipbuilders that same year. By the mid-1880s, many of the major British shipbuilders employed the mechanical integrator to determine various sailing qualities in their ships. The integrator proved of great importance to scientific shipbuilders in predicting the stability of vessels during the design stage.[99]

The one factor that provided a rationalizing influence in British ship design was the use of drawing. In the opinion of design philosopher J. Christopher Jones, the design process changed from "craftsmanship to draftsmanship"[100] by transferring the trial-and-error aspect of the craft process onto paper. While craft workers relied upon rule-of-thumb methods and design and construction took place simultaneously, drawing separated design from construction and designers from builders.[101] Similar to the way that experiments and research later provided the basis for extrapolating theories and formulas, drawings allowed ship designers to experiment and manipulate their designs with ruler and compass before they even laid down the keel. Drawings provided the basic dimensions of a ship so its smaller features could be extrapolated. Drawings also made possible weight determination and the application of mathematical theory to ship design.[102] By the eighteenth century, drafts of naval vessels became common and British shipbuilding treatises began to appear that showed readers the best methods for drawing ships. By the nineteenth century, drafting had become the "*lingua franca* of the dockyards."[103] In 1861, iron shipbuilder John Scott Russell recounted how a British shipbuilder taught him the use of the drafting board by instructing him to lay down ships' "water-lines one way, and then another, and then another, and when you have done bring your drawings to me, and I will see what blunders you have made."[104]

The development of modern naval architecture methods by scientific shipbuilders mentioned above by no means exhausts the examples that took place during the mid- to late nineteenth century. They merely characterize the importance to scientific shipbuilders of determining iron's material properties, developing theoretical ship design methods, and in general, transforming iron shipbuilding into a science. By the 1860s, a basic understanding of iron's material properties had been achieved thanks to Fairbairn, Lloyd's, and others. Even though strict industry standards for iron ship construction still proved elusive at this time, the guidelines for insuring iron ships developed by Lloyd's in the 1850s provided the basis for such standards. By the late 1800s, British naval architects had developed a stock of hydrodynamic and material science theories based on years of experimentation.[105]

While no nineteenth-century naval architect succeeded in convincing members of the ship design community that there existed one set of rules that could account for all of the particulars necessary to design a ship's hull, the net effect of the theoretical contributions made to ship design by the Institution of Naval Architects' numerous specialists had a similar outcome. A perusal of the papers presented at the annual meetings of the Institution of Naval Architects indicates the intense scrutiny given every aspect of the ship, from its keel to its superstructure. Through the decades of the Institution's existence, the best practices for designing and building every piece of a vessel received close attention.

While the development of British naval architecture in the mid- to late 1800s could not be entirely characterized as a science, it certainly had become far more rational than at any time in its history. The ship design community had at its disposal experimental research, theoretical principles, drawing, and even Lloyd's standards for determining the proper shape and material strength of ship hulls. All it lacked was a way to transmit these methods from one member of the community to another. The aristocratic nature of the scientific design community prevented it from relying upon the traditional practices of apprenticeship and employing journeymen. Instead, British shipbuilders began to share knowledge through social institutions, where groups of individuals could learn a standard canon of rational methods. The need to establish a technological dialogue between individuals in the industry also fostered the publication of ideas in trade journals and technical treatises. By employing these various methods of idea exchange, British ship designers became working intellectuals who could exchange ideas rapidly without ever meeting one another.

Individuals concerned with maritime matters shared their ideas not only through education but also through scientific and common-interest societies. Associations concerned with ship design and construction had formed as early as 1796, when the Society for the Improvement of Naval Architecture was established to help improve the design of British warships. During the nineteenth century, societies of a more professional, and in particular engineering, nature began to proliferate. Early nineteenth-century shipbuilders and naval architects, such as I. K. Brunel, John Scott Russell, John Grantham, and William Fairbairn joined the Institution of Civil Engineers in the years following its founding in 1818. The Institution's 1828 charter even mentioned the promotion of "the art of navigation by artificial power for the purposes of commerce."[106] Scottish engineers founded the Institution of Engineers in Scotland in 1857 and the Scottish Shipbuilders Association in 1860. The two institutions amalgamated later in 1865 as the Institution of Engineers and Shipbuilders in Scotland. In 1884, British shipbuilders from Newcastle and other northeastern shipbuilding centers formed the Northeast Coast Institution of Engineers and Shipbuilders. Finally, members of the Institution whose interests identified them more closely to marine engineering set up their own Institution of Marine Engineers in 1889.[107]

By 1860, naval architects and shipbuilders had already decided to found their own institution and joined members of Admiralty and Lloyd's Registry to establish the Institution of Naval Architects. Shipbuilders and designers were well represented among the membership of the fledgling society, while associate members came from a variety of fields tied to ship construction, including marine engineering, the Royal Navy, and shipping. While the 1860 membership list did not distinguish between members and associates, the 1861 list showed 65 members and 390 associates. This list included the nation's leading private shipbuilders, the principal surveyors of Lloyd's Register of Shipping, and nearly all of the leading officials in the Shipbuilding Department at Admiralty.[108]

The Institution of Naval Architects provided an ideal forum for builders, engineers, scientists, and educated naval officers to debate the merits of materials, construction, machines, and the theory behind the construction of naval and civilian ships. It did this, as William White claimed, by "acting as a centre where valuable information could be collected, and whence it could be distributed for the general benefit of the profession."[109] As time passed, it became clear that the Institution played an important role in the ongoing technological dialogue between shipbuilders concerning ship design and construction. So important did this association become to contemporary naval architecture and marine engineering that the professional membership grew steadily. As the membership increased and papers and discussions grew increasingly focused on technical aspects of naval architecture, the associate membership declined due to its lack of technological expertise and interest.[110] At the 1897 annual meeting, Sir Edward J. Reed applauded the Institution of Naval Architects for spreading ship design knowledge, stating: "Before this institution existed, there was a danger that much of what was being done was not known—not merely that it was not applied, but that it was not known. . . . There is not the same risk now."[111]

Admiralty played a significant role in the founding and support of the Institution. Eleven of the eighteen founding members had close ties to Admiralty as students of its naval architecture schools, staff, and naval contractors. Sir John S. Packington, later Lord Hampton, who had just retired as First Lord of Admiralty, became the first president.[112] Every chief naval constructor of the Royal Navy from 1860 to World War I had been a member of the Institution and played a leading role in its business. During the Institution's lean times, when it failed to raise the funds necessary for its own support, Admiralty supplied the balance of money.[113] Retired chief naval constructor William H. White believed that Admiralty's support of the Institution had been beneficial for British naval development, claiming that since the INA's "commencement have been held debates on warship construction far more valuable than any discussions in Parliament could possibly be." He further believed that "From the very outset the Institution was chosen as the place whereat the constructive policy of the Admiralty for the time being should be explained and discussed."[114]

The primary reason for forming the Institution had to do with the introduction of iron to shipbuilding in general and its influence on warship construction in particular. During the Naval Panic of 1859–60, it was felt that the introduction of steam power and iron armor to naval construction erased the Royal Navy's supremacy, especially since the French had begun building ironclad batteries in 1854 for the Crimean War.[115] The construction of French ironclads such as *La Gloire* in the late 1850s and American ironclads such as the USS *Monitor* in the early 1860s heightened concerns of a nation whose imperial ties and very survival rested upon ocean commerce and control of the seas. In the Institution's inaugural address, Sir John Packington referred to the arms race between France, Russia, the United States, and Great Britain by saying: "What is the real object of this Institution? the answer would be, 'It is to take care, as we are bound as Englishmen to take care, that beyond all question England shall win that race.'"[116] Even though shipwrecks and the safety of iron ships became the topic of discussion for the inaugural meeting, the debate centered on the design and construction of ironclad warships in 1861.[117]

The Institution became part of a naval-industrial network that tied ship designers to naval arms manufacturers as well as Admiralty. The strongest of these ties bound Admiralty to ordnance and warship manufacturer William Armstrong and Company. Between 1883 and 1914, all of the Royal Navy's chief constructors came from Armstrong's, including Sir William H. White, Sir Philip Watts, and Sir Tennyson d'Eyncourt. Other naval arms manufacturers, such as Vickers and Cammell-Laird, had their share of representatives working for Admiralty or employed influential individuals who had served there. This cadre of public-private warship designers represented the elite of Britain's naval architects and included such men as Sir Edward J. Reed, Sir John H. Biles, Sir Nathaniel Barnaby, and the men mentioned above.[118]

Admiralty also played a major role in establishing formal naval architecture education in Britain. Admiralty's desire to emulate the theoretical methods of the French led to the establishment of a school of naval architecture in Portsmouth in January 1811. Conditions of admission included a working understanding of the first six books of Euclid's Elements and the ability to read French since so many theoretical works on naval architecture were written in that language. Subjects of study included drawing, differential and integral calculus, mechanics, and hydrostatics. Forty-one students received training in Portsmouth before Admiralty closed it in 1832. It did this because the conservative First Lord of Admiralty, Sir James Graham, saw technical education as too impractical. Alumni of this program included the Royal Navy's first chief naval constructor, an engineer-in-chief of the Royal Navy, and a chief surveyor for Lloyd's Society.[119] In 1843, Admiralty opened a small school in each of its dockyards to supplement the practical training that its apprentices received. In 1848, Admiralty founded the Central School of Mathematics and Naval Construction at the Portsmouth Dockyard to educate the highest achievers from each of the dockyard schools. Under the guidance of Dr. Joseph Woolley, a product of the first naval architecture school, the institution accepted eight pupils per year from the branch schools. From that school's select group of naval architects came two future chief constructors—Sir Edward J. Reed and Reed's successor, Sir Nathaniel Barnaby—and several distinguished civilian shipbuilders.[120] When Graham returned to the post of First Lord, he closed the second school in 1853, explaining that "there was too much of science and too little of practical knowledge creeping into the Navy."[121]

At the 1863 Institution of Naval Architects Annual Meeting, shipbuilder and experimental engineer John Scott Russell raised the question of founding a British school of naval architecture in his paper "Education of Naval Architects in England and France."[122] The response from the membership was overwhelmingly in favor of founding such a school. A year later the Institution of Naval Architects and Admiralty cofounded the Royal School of Naval Architecture and Marine Engineering in South Kensington, London. Dr. Woolley became the school's director of studies. To become a graduate as an "Associate," students had to pass examinations in elementary mechanics, hydrostatics, and ship drawing, while a "Fellow" had to qualify in the principles of ship design, advanced mathematics, applied mechanics, and the properties of metals. Voluntary subjects for special certification included dynamics and hydrodynamics, strength of materials and structures, theory of marine propulsion and fluid resistance, theory of waves and behavior of ships, the relation of heat to marine engines, and the laws behind steam power.[123]

Through the 1880s, Admiralty-supported schools provided for the demands of trained professionals for the Royal Navy and Lloyd's Society. The shipbuilding industry, however, remained tied to the tradition of training its ship designers in the shipyard and sent few students to the school. Between its founding in 1864 and 1873, only 24 of 119 students came from private shipbuilders, the remainder coming from Admiralty and foreign governments. Finally, in 1873, the Royal Naval College at Greenwich absorbed the Royal School at South Kensington and focused the curriculum on warship design. Admiralty had to take this measure to ensure a steady supply of educated naval constructors for Royal Navy service.[124]

With the increased ship production and demand for competent merchant ship designers in the second half of the nineteenth century, however, more naval architecture programs emerged in private schools. In 1884, Glasgow University received an endowment for a chair in naval architecture, as did Armstrong College, in Newcastle, in 1890, and Liverpool University in 1908. One would-be benefactor even attempted to endow a chair in naval architecture at Cambridge but withdrew the offer after school officials insisted that students become proficient in Greek.[125]

These schools came to provide a method of selection for Britain's shipbuilding industry. Only the best academic performers qualified as the nation's civilian and military ship designers. For example, to qualify for a position in the "drawing-office" at the Leven shipyard of the Denny Brothers, one of the most reputable shipbuilding firms on the River Clyde, candidates had to have attended the school at South Kensington for two years and have passed their elementary stages of examination in naval architecture. They also had to pass a competitive examination, which included arithmetic; plane, solid, and Euclidean geometry; algebraic equations and logarithms; theoretical mechanics; and freehand and mechanical drawing.[126]

Professional literature such as manuals, treatises, textbooks, magazines, professional journals, and published lectures represented a third important method to disseminate information concerning the design and construction of ships. While most British works written on shipbuilding up until the early 1800s had been practical works aimed at apprentices, journeymen, or any shipwright who might wish to buy a reference work on his trade, later publications on shipbuilding increasingly took the form of textbook or treatise written for classroom instruction, or technical and theoretical literature written for publication in professional journals and magazines.

There existed a strong relationship between education and the spread of naval architecture know-how through treatises, manuals, and articles written on the subject. Many notable works on practical shipbuilding had been written during the seventeenth and eighteenth centuries, but these books focused on problems faced by the shipwright in the shipyard and not on mathematical and theoretical problems. It was only after the establishment of formal schools of naval architecture, that experts such as instructors began to write textbooks to fill the void of theoretical works written in English. After the 1811 founding of the first School of Naval Architecture at Portsmouth Dockyard, Principal James Inman translated naval architect Fredrik Henrik af Chapman's *Treatise on Shipbuilding* from French and published it in 1820. In addition to Inman's translation, students also studied *Introductory Outline of the Practice of Shipbuilding* and *On Masting Ships and Mast Making*, written by instructor John Fincham.[127] The Royal Navy's Central School of Mathematics and Naval Architecture, founded in 1848, relied on superintendent Henry Moseley's *Mechanical Principles of Engineering and Architecture*. Moseley's book was the first to introduce British engineers to the French theory of beams to resist the bending of vertical loads and was translated into German.[128] The school also relied on a second edition of Fincham's *Outline of Shipbuilding* as a textbook. Fincham had become an examiner at the second school and managed to publish his *History of Naval Architecture* before Admiralty closed the institution in 1853. The second school's principal and teacher, Dr. Joseph Woolley, published a treatise entitled *The Elements of Descriptive Geometry* in 1850. Woolley also wrote a companion volume on the application of descriptive geometry to ship construction prior to the school's closure, but it was never published.[129] Many works followed on the heels of the establishment of the Royal School of Naval Architecture in 1864. This flourish of important treatises included William Fairbairn's *Treatise on Iron Shipbuilding*, John Scott Russell's *Modern System of Naval Architecture*, William J. M. Rankine's *Shipbuilding, Theoretical and Practical*, naval constructor Edward J. Reed's *Shipbuilding in Iron and Steel*, and William H. White's *A Manual of Naval Architecture*.[130]

The volume of published material generated on ship design and construction also grew in proportion to the proliferation of professional shipbuilding societies. Beginning in 1841, shipbuilders in the I.C.E. could content themselves by publishing their papers in the *Minutes of Proceedings*. The Institution of Naval Architects began issuing its *Transactions* in 1860. A perusal of *Transactions* for the years immediately following its first year of publication shows how frequently the industry's leading theoreticians, such as Fairbairn, Russell, Froude, and Rankine, contributed papers to the Institution. William White claimed that "Owing to the rapid advances constantly being made in both the science and the practice of the profession, the 'Transactions' have come to be the chief text-books available ... [and] ... now everything worth preservation naturally finds its way to the 'Transactions.'"[131] Other important associations, including the Institution of Engineers and Shipbuilders in Scotland, the Northeast Coast Institution of Engineers and Shipbuilders, and the Institute of Marine Engineering, published their annual proceedings and provided another forum for the exchange of ship design knowledge. The primary objective set forth by the founding members of the Institution of Naval Architects included "the bringing together of those results of experience which so many shipbuilders, marine engineers, naval officers, yachtsmen and others acquire, independently of each other ... [that] ... tend much to improve our navies when brought together in the printed Transactions of an Institution."[132]

In addition to professional journals and the proceedings of engineering societies, popular magazines devoted to engineering began to appear in Great Britain in the 1820s. These periodicals published numerous articles on ships and shipbuilding, a major preoccupation of an island nation such as Great Britain. First published in 1823, *Mechanics' Magazine* catered to the interests of engineers, builders, and mechanics of all sorts. It remained in publication for seventy years, the last twenty under the title of *Iron*. During the 1850s and 1860s, the number of competing magazines grew. This number included the *Engineer* and *Engineering*.[133] Established in 1872 by former chief constructor of the Royal Navy and one-time editor of *Mechanics' Magazine* Edward J. Reed, *Naval Science* claimed as its goal the promotion "of naval architecture, marine engineering, steam navigation, and seamanship."[134] The volume of published material related to shipbuilding led Thomas F. Rowland, builder of John Ericsson's *Monitor*, to state before Congress in 1870 that "The English never learned anything without immediately running to some printing office and publishing it all."[135]

British theoreticians and scientists realized the importance of transmitting knowledge through associations as far back as the formation of the Royal Society, and by the beginning of the nineteenth century, shipbuilders and naval experts had also appreciated the necessity of sharing knowledge this way. It was not until the 1860s, when military necessity stepped in once again, that this rapid transmission of industry knowledge became a reality. Instructors, experimenters, industrialists, and professionals actively participated in this information exchange through publication, education, and professional societies. In fact, these three professional institutions formed a mutually reinforcing triangle of learning and knowledge transmission.

By the early nineteenth century, the way the British designed and built their ships had begun to change. Britain's shipbuilders might have continued to use practical methods had it not been for its reliance on iron and proactive naval establishment. With the depletion of ship timber reserves, the British resorted to building iron ships. With iron came a new kind of shipbuilder, one with an engineering background. Britain's scientific shipbuilders received the technical, moral, and financial support of the state to establish their profession. The British government nurtured the new scientific approach through its navy, which supported the establishment of professional societies, schools of naval architecture, and research of and experimentation into better design.

Encouraged by state support, Britain's elite shipbuilders became a kind of aristocracy of the industry, boasting specialized knowledge and control over the design process. By the 1870s, British shipbuilders had become an elite group of wealthy and well-educated men with increasingly little in common with practical shipbuilders. Learned men with an education in theoretical mathematics, the physical sciences, or engineering became specialists in the field. Other experts came from wealthy shipbuilding families that owned their own yards. By the late nineteenth century, the membership of professional shipbuilding societies listed wealthy shipbuilders, academics and researchers, elite engineers, naval experts, and nobility; in short, an aristocracy of the shipbuilding industry.

By the second half of the nineteenth century, this shipbuilding elite felt they had developed naval architecture to the level of a science. In 1865, John Scott Russell noted that:

> The forms and proportions of ships, prescribed by traditional knowledge, and universally employed in the early part of this century, have either ceased to exist, or are preserved as relics. . . . New forms and new proportions have taken their place, and these are determined by principles not known before the present century. Naval architecture has taken a higher and nobler place, and, having abandoned mere tradition, has become a positive science.[136]

Through years of research and application and numerous failure-driven developments, scientific shipbuilders had accumulated a stock of knowledge that addressed nearly every aspect of iron ship design.

3
Practical Shipbuilding Develops in the United States

Their strictly Puritan origin; their exclusively commercial habits; even the country they inhabit, which seems to divert their minds from the study of science, literature, and the arts; [and] the [in]accessibility of Europe . . . have singularly concurred to fix the mind of the American on purely practical objects.

Alexis de Tocqueville, 1832

In the lines above, social commentator Tocqueville indicates a distinctively American disposition toward technology during the nineteenth century.[1] Cultural and environmental influences on industry help explain why American shipbuilders adopted a "practical" style of shipbuilding by the nineteenth century. The American shipbuilder's view of practicality rested not only on his ability to build marketable ships but also on his ability to employ efficient methods and technology. While other cultures spent time and money studying the theoretical and scientific ramifications of their products, Americans focused on perfecting products that would sell, such as finely crafted wooden ships. Practical shipbuilders prided themselves on adhering to the simplest, most efficient methods for building ships.

If an Anglo-American shipbuilder had been transported by a time machine to a nineteenth-century wood shipyard in the United States, he would have recognized nearly everything in it. The methods employed by America's practical shipbuilders evolved little from those employed during the colonial era. Practical shipbuilders held a philosophical bias against the analytical and deductive style of ship design beginning to emerge in Great Britain. Instead, they held a bias in favor of an empirical, inductive style.[2] One of the only changes instituted in the United States that might elude the Anglo-American shipbuilder is the way practical shipbuilders designed their vessels. They used a three-dimensional half-hull model that was foreign to previous shipbuilding practice. Anglo-American shipwrights, however, would have easily grasped the way in which nineteenth-century Americans used the half-hull model to design their ships. In most other respects, the methods used in nineteenth-century American shipbuilding resembled those used during the seventeenth and eighteenth centuries.

The development of practical shipbuilding had its origin in economic as well as social factors specific to the United States. The plentiful supply of timber allowed methods similar to those used by Anglo-American shipwrights to survive in America throughout the nineteenth century. The untapped stands of virgin forest extending beyond the East Coast ensured a long-term supply of ship timber, and the high cost of iron in the United States encouraged Americans to produce wooden ships throughout the nineteenth century. That wood shipbuilding enjoyed such a lengthy existence in the United States should not be construed as a sort of cultural resistance to the adoption of new technology. Rather, Americans continued to work in the material that they knew best and built the cheapest.

The use of wood supported a uniquely American socio-technical system. One historian has coined the term the "wooden age"[3] to describe the reliance American mechanics placed on wood for producing manufactured products throughout the nineteenth century. Americans used wood for building roads, wagons, canals, clocks, bridges, scientific instruments, early machine tools, and technology of all kinds. They did so because North America's stands of timber seemed limitless and American mechanics were experts at working with wood. Even when other materials could have better satisfied Americans' needs, they continued to use wood due to their intimate knowledge of the material, how it suited their purposes, and the working conditions it could withstand.[4] America's practical shipbuilders stubbornly held to the conviction that "in a wooden country like this, years must elapse, and generations pass away, before wood, as a material for constructing vessels, will be abandoned."[5]

Wood-based shipbuilding methods and technology found in post-Revolutionary America closely resembled those found in Anglo-American shipyards. The tools used and skills employed remained very similar to those traditionally employed in eighteenth-century Europe and the North American colonies. The early American shipyard still formed the basis for a production process based on close interpersonal work relationships, training through practical experience, and knowledge based on the "art and mystery" of the craft. The tightly knit American shipbuilding community and the way it disseminated technological knowledge supported a practical shipbuilding tradition.

The methods and institutions that underlay ship construction in early nineteenth-century America changed gradually from their Anglo-American predecessors. The American wood shipbuilding community represented an exclusive and conservative work culture characterized by intermarriage, shared work ethic, and close ties between builders and workers. Bound to unspoken rules of work etiquette, such as the clothes they wore and the particular tools they used, shipwrights and their families lived in close proximity to the shipyard and formed a cohesive work society.[6]

During the early nineteenth century, the American approach to shipbuilding retained most of the trappings of the earlier Anglo-American tradition. Only two significant features changed: how the Americans perceived themselves and the way in which they designed their vessels. The changes in design methods adopted by the Americans will be discussed later. The new incarnation that American shipbuilders adopted for themselves could be seen in nineteenth-century shipbuilding literature. They referred to themselves as "practical shipbuilders," not to be confused with theoretical ones. Lauchlan McKay, shipwright and brother of famed clipper-ship builder Donald, referred to himself as a "practical shipbuilder."[7] Clipper-ship designer John W. Griffiths considered himself a practical shipbuilder, a term that he later defined as a shipwright "who had passed through, and graduated in all the successive stages of mechanism in a ship-yard, and learned the art of building ships by practical application."[8] McKay and Griffiths were not the only ones to use the term "practical"; it may be found throughout contemporary literature describing not only shipbuilders but also other American mechanics, such as machinists.[9]

An important part of practical shipbuilding was a basic set of hand tools that had been a traditional part of the trade for centuries. Inventories found in account books and probate records from the nineteenth century indicate that edge tools, augers, and saws still formed the basis of the shipwright's tools as they had in Anglo-American shipbuilding.[10] Beginning in the late eighteenth century, American manufacturers became expert at making the hand tools necessary for building wooden ships. For edge tools, the tool manufacturer of L. and I. J. White of Buffalo, New York; D. R. Barton of Rochester, New York; and the Campbell Axe Company of St. John, New Brunswick became preferred brands. The Connecticut firm of Collins Axe and Tool Company became one of the most acclaimed axe and adz manufacturers during the nineteenth century.[11] Philadelphia's Henry Disston and Sons became one of the most respected of the major saw makers in nineteenth-century America. Stanley Rule and Level Company of New Britain, Connecticut, became one the better-known American manufacturers of planes, rules, and small edge tools. C. Drew and Company of Kingston, Massachusetts, became renowned for manufacturering caulking tools.[12]

Certain tool-use etiquette came to be observed by practical shipbuilders. After the apprentice shipwright completed his term, he often was given his first set of tools, and it was not uncommon to present him with a new set of the finest brand.[13] If a shipwright "bummed" tools, failed to care properly for the ones he owned, or stole those of others, he could lose the respect of fellow shipwrights at the very least and lose his job in extreme cases.[14] As a boy in Philadelphia, Charles H. Cramp witnessed a breech of etiquette in his family's shipyard. When a group of new employees began hewing a large timber with the wrong type of axe, an experienced shipwright noticed the faux pas, and "he immediately dropped his tools, put them in his box, and, shouldering it, started out of the yard at a rapid gait."[15]

Practical shipbuilding was a family-based trade established on work-oriented family networks. Families, such as the Webbs of New York, established dynasties in large family-operated shipyards. Other such families included the Browns and the Berghs of New York City and the Hartts and Pooks from Boston. In Wilmington, certain wood shipbuilding families carried on the trade for well over a century. Four generations of the Harris family carried on the business from the mid-1700s until after the Civil War.[16] For over seventy-five years, the name Enoch Moore remained a prominent one in Wilmington's shipbuilding industry as Enoch Moore, Enoch Moore Jr., and Enoch Moore III took on the trade.[17] In Philadelphia, the Vaughan, Lynn, Birely, and Cramp families dominated the local shipbuilding industry for well over a hundred years.[18] On the Jersey Shore, several generations of the Van Sant family served in the trade for nearly two hundred years. In rural Delaware, practically every nineteenth-century shipyard employed a member of the Lank family. The many generations of the Abbott, Deputy, Carlisle, and Black families were also well represented in rural Delaware's shipyards.[19] Charles Cramp's father, grandfather, uncles, and great-uncles had built ships in Britain and then in Philadelphia.[20] Charles Cramp described what it was like to grow up in a shipbuilding family: "It was my father's profession and that of five great-uncles and a grandfather; and having had the words 'master builder' drummed into my ears from early childhood by my mother, grandmother, and all of my aunts, it is no surprise that I was so inclined."[21] The U.S. Navy also encouraged the dynastic tradition in bequeathing the family trade from one generation to the next. What had been practiced unofficially for centuries was institutionalized by a general order in 1868, which gave preference for apprenticeship positions to the children of mechanics employed in navy yards.[22]

Craft knowledge and skills were spread not only through family networks and shipbuilding culture but also by the institution of apprenticeship. America's practical shipbuilders differed with Britain's scientific shipbuilders with respect to the spread of design and construction knowledge. The dissemination of technological knowledge in scientific shipbuilding rested on formal education, professional associations, and publication. Practical builders believed shipbuilding skills could be imparted only through the guidance of a shipwright and practical experience in the yard, not in a classroom.[23] As John W. Griffiths claimed: "There is no royal road to practical knowledge. The student in the school of technology can not acquire experience in any of the mechanical arts from the study of books, illustrated by exercises on the blackboard; the hand must be educated as well as the head."[24]

Unlike British shipbuilders, Americans relied very little on books and periodicals to disseminate shipbuilding knowledge. Dozens of manuals, treatises, pamphlets, and papers concerning the art and science of shipbuilding had been printed in England between 1600 and 1830, but according to contemporary sources, American shipbuilders read few of these publications.[25] British shipbuilding books remained inaccessible to American shipwrights due in part to their extraordinarily high cost. For example, *Elements and Practice of Naval Architecture*, by British shipbuilder David Steel, sold for the extraordinarily high price of forty-two dollars in 1844. Shipbuilder Leonard H. Boole searched the bookstores of New York and Brooklyn in the mid-1840s and could find nothing on shipbuilding, except for a British work costing forty-five dollars.[26]

British books were not only expensive but also difficult to understand. Noted maritime historians have pointed out that American shipbuilders made few references to using British shipbuilding texts.[27] If an ordinary master shipwright found a way to acquire one of these books, he found it so theoretical as to be "mystifying" and "unintelligible."[28] Shipbuilder John W. Griffiths admitted that during the early 1800s a number of works on naval architecture had been printed in Europe, "but there were but two, if, indeed, there was more than a single copy of these works in the United States; and these, not being adapted to the American need, were of little use to ship-builders."[29] Practical shipbuilders, especially in rural areas, were often uneducated mechanics. They saw the drawings and mathematical formulas used by British builders as unnecessary and time-consuming. As New York shipbuilder Lauchlan McKay observed in his 1839 book *The Practical Shipbuilder*: "The publications of other countries have been large and expensive, full of intricacy, scientific rather than practical, and consequently of little use to the uneducated mechanic."[30] Even after the Civil War, American naval constructor William H. Varney stated that: "these works [British], from the depth of mathematical knowledge required for their perusal, and from the expense involved in their purchase, are sealed sources of information to the practical shipwright."[31]

Much like Anglo-American shipbuilders, practical shipbuilders spread knowledge through apprenticeship. Practiced in private and navy yards, this system taught promising young men specialized skills in the design and construction of wooden ships. Builders believed such skills could be imparted only by their guidance and through practical experience in the yard, not in a classroom.[32] Apprentices spent every day in the shipyard learning to build vessels through practical experience with hand tools. John W. Griffiths briefly described the typical apprenticeship experience:

> The boy, at perhaps the age of sixteen, is apprenticed to a ship-builder to learn the art; time rolls on, he obtains the use of tools, learns to edge and bevel plank, fay a knee, and perhaps take the spiling of a piece of plank shear [sic]; and if he is what is commonly called smart, he may learn to fit a breast-hook or any other difficult piece of timber at the first cut. He goes into the loft, and by the time he has filled the measure of his servitude, he is recognized as a mechanic of the first water.[33]

The apprenticeship system encouraged shipbuilding families to bequeath the skills, and often the family shipyard, from one generation to the next.[34] When asked by the Czar of Russia where he had attended naval architecture school, Charles Cramp replied, "Sire, I am a graduate of my father's shipyard in Philadelphia."[35] It also encouraged strong bonds between the apprentices, the master shipbuilders, and shipyard workers. Two out of the ten young men Delaware shipwright John Harris apprenticed married into his family.[36] Bonds with builders were often so strong that the apprentices occasionally named their children for them.[37]

Two of the best-known New York builders to apprentice aspiring young shipwrights were Henry Eckford and Isaac Webb. Eckford was an early nineteenth-century patriarch of New York's shipbuilding community. Among his many apprentices were prominent shipbuilders Isaac Webb and Stephen Smith. Like his mentor, Webb apprenticed some of the most famous builders of the nineteenth century, such as his son William, John W. Griffiths, and Donald McKay.[38] Through his apprentices, Eckford helped New York become the world's center of the wooden shipbuilding.

Shipbuilding knowledge was diffused not just through apprenticeship but also through the itinerant nature of the trade. Shipbuilding has historically been one of the most peripatetic trades of all, and these traveling shipwrights spread their knowledge wherever they worked. American shipbuilding benefited greatly from the influx of immigrant shipbuilders after the Revolution.

For example, naval constructor Josiah Fox had begun his career working in British dockyards before building American warships. Prominent American shipbuilder Henry Eckford was born in Scotland and served his apprenticeship with his uncle in Canada before settling in New York. Donald McKay and his brother Lauchlan moved from Nova Scotia to serve their apprenticeships in New York. Prominent New York shipbuilder Christian Bergh hailed from Canada.[39]

Practical shipbuilding knowledge diffused naturally through the tradition of journeying the trade. After completing their apprenticeship, journeymen shipwrights often ventured from one shipyard to the next to gain the practical experience necessary to become a master shipwright.[40] To this day, the few workers remaining in the wood shipbuilding business travel from one job to the next to ply their trade. Subcontractors also traveled with their gangs of workers to complete jobs in various locations. This meant moving from yard to yard in one region or even from state to state.[41]

The ebb and flow of migrant shipwrights followed the whims of the market for wooden ships. Shipwrights also traveled to where the wages were higher, the wood was cheaper, or historical events dictated. During the War of 1812 and for years afterward, hundreds of shipwrights migrated to the Great Lakes.[42] Henry Eckford led a large crew of shipwrights to Lake Erie to build the warships for the U.S. Navy's Great Lakes fleet. After the war had ended and he returned to New York, Eckford received a tempting offer to build warships for Turkey. He moved there a year later with a crew of shipwrights. John Englis also moved from New York to Lake Erie and back. Many more Canadians moved to New York during the 1820s, when the city experienced a shortage of skilled shipwrights.[43]

Many shipwrights moved from small towns to the big city in search of employment. During the nineteenth century, many shipwrights from small towns on the Delmarva Peninsula, such as Milford and Milton, left their homes and families for better wages in the cities. For example, William Lank and his friends left their families in Milton to join the army of well-paid shipwrights assembled in Philadelphia to fill contracts for military and civilian vessels during the Civil War. After the war, many shipbuilders from these small towns moved to Wilmington, Philadelphia, and Camden, New Jersey, where the business of building and repairing wooden ships was often brisk and always better paid.[44]

Many northeastern builders who received their training in the East Coast shipyards traveled south and west where there existed cheaper ship timber and a chance to make a better living. New York builder Jacob Westervelt moved to Savannah before returning to become one of New York's most prominent shipbuilders. Some New Yorkers moved to the Delmarva Peninsula, where plentiful supplies of white oak still existed before the Civil War.[45] Most migrant shipbuilders saw greater promise out West, where timber and orders for river and Great Lakes steamers were plentiful. Two branches of New Jersey's Van Sant family of shipbuilders moved to the Midwest, one to the Cincinnati area and another, John W. Van Sant, to Rock Island, Illinois. John's son, Samuel, later became a two-term governor of Minnesota. The shipbuilder for whom John Van Sant originally worked in Illinois, Jonathan Zebley, hailed from Wilmington, Delaware.[46] Carter Van Duesen took a crew of forty men with him from New York to Louisville, Kentucky, to build a steamboat, before returning to his hometown. Daniel French, successful New York steamboat builder and inventor, moved his family to Jeffersonville, Indiana, to build river steamboats.[47] Some shipwrights left the East Coast during the California Gold Rush, some to ply their trade and others to try their luck. In 1848, shipbuilder William Hanscom solicited the Pacific Mail Steamship Company for free passage to San Francisco to establish a shipyard there. George K. Stevenson set himself up as a shipwright in Valparaiso, Chile. In 1860, journeyman Philip Hichborn sailed from Boston to San Francisco to become a naval constructor at the Mare Island Navy Yard.[48]

After the Civil War, those workers who could afford to move traveled to Maine to start over. Other American builders, such as Lauchlan McKay and Henry Warner, moved to Canada, where labor and timber costs remained relatively low. At the same time, American shipyards in the Great Lakes region lured lower-paid Canadian workers from Quebec and Montreal to work for them.[49] In some cases, urban shipbuilders moved from one city to the next. Camden, New Jersey, builder David Corson moved his yard to Chester, Pennsylvania. Shortly thereafter, builder Joseph Burk of Wilmington moved his construction and repair business from Wilmington to Camden.[50] An examination of the historical record indicates that skilled workers involved in the shipbuilding trade remained at the mercy of the market and highly mobile.

In addition to being highly transient, America's practical shipbuilders also developed the craft of wooden shipbuilding into a fine art. While British shipbuilders conducted tests and generated theories and turned increasingly toward engineering and research to design their ships, Americans relied on more practical methods. The Anglo-American tradition of standardization remained an important part of sailing ship design, and American shipbuilders gained their knowledge of ship performance from full-size ships. Practical shipbuilders experimented with actual vessels to determine the best hull characteristics, and they relied on scale half-hull models to represent their vessels during the design process.

The unconscious pursuit of standardization found in Anglo-American shipbuilding remained an element of American shipbuilding and still does today. Nineteenth-century sailing ships, for example, have been grouped into vessels of similar construction, such as sloops, coasting schooners, packets, clipper ships, and so on. American shipbuilders spun off numerous copies of an original model that proved to be a good performer. This not only saved the builder time and money, since the molds for parts of the hull had already been produced, but ship owners would often purchase ships whose prototype had proven successful. Other builders simply modified a good model according to the preferences of the ship owner.[51] The institution of apprenticeship contributed to the standardization of ship design as well. Shipbuilder John W. Griffiths claimed that the apprentice "builds a vessel, just as he learned from his tutor. His models have a striking similarity to those of his former master, and why should it be otherwise, his eye drank in all the peculiarities of his tutor's forms, he has become wedded to them from necessity."[52]

Practical shipbuilders did try to improve the design of each successive vessel they built through gathering data on vessel performance, but they usually began with a standard model or prototype. A successful model of clipper ship or packet might be altered only slightly when building the next vessel of similar proportions. Merchants and other clients often specified the construction of a vessel on similar lines to a proven ship design.[53] One group of Staten Island builders bought a successful pilot boat from Baltimore and reproduced pilot boats of the same lines for New Yorkers. The unpublished results of a study of a Camden, New Jersey, builder indicates that he produced numerous schooners based on one or two models.[54] Details as to how closely ship designers adhered to previous successful models remain unclear. The opinion of wood shipbuilders of the day indicates that anything of an experiment in new ship design represented a grave risk that they could ill afford. One failed vessel design could result in diminished demand for their ships and potential financial ruin. In defining the methods of a practical shipbuilder, John Griffiths explained that "comparison" was one of the most important design techniques. Griffiths described comparison as the way an American shipbuilder "takes up the model of some previous ship that he has built . . . he knows the good and bad qualities before him . . . such as instability, bad sailing qualities, &c., &c., and he avoids committing the same error over again."[55]

Standardization has always been an important part of naval ship construction. The U.S. Navy standardized warships since its original warship construction programs. In 1797, for example, the famous superfrigates *United States, President,* and *Constitution* were laid down from the same set of plans. Throughout the nineteenth century, specific naval construction programs produced classes of vessels from one set of plans. During the Civil War, American naval constructor John Lenthall designed a class of "90-Day Gunboats," to speed up production of warships for military service.

Beginning in the eighteenth century, certain British experimenters began to focus their attention on the resistance of different shapes to water by using primitive model test basins. Many American builders were aware of the frictional resistance of different forms to water, but they did not see the relevance of pulling miniature wooden shapes through a pond of water.[56] Out of six articles published on fluid resistance in the *Journal of the Franklin Institute* during the 1830s, all had to be reprinted from British sources except one found in *Silliman's Journal*, an American scientific periodical.[57] The first serious American treatment of fluid resistance and its influence on ships appeared as a chapter of civil engineer John W. Nystrom's *Treatise on Screw Propellers and Their Steam Engines*, published in 1852. No other publications dealt with the subject until late in the nineteenth century.[58] Practical builder David Brown, of the New York shipbuilding firm of Brown and Bell, summed up the prevailing American attitude in an 1850 letter to John W. Griffiths: "It is not in the power of an experimenter, with cut blocks, in a pond of smooth water, and with artificially applied forces, to determine the best model for a given end."[59]

The practice of observing ship design and behavior was an important part of the American design process. Certain builders would inspect ships newly arrived in port with notebook and pencil in hand and record any design innovations they could find.[60] While many European experimenters began to test ship hydrodynamics using model test basins, American builders believed that the best test tank was the ocean and the best way to ascertain a ship's sea-keeping qualities was to observe its performance at sea.[61] To do this, they drew on the expertise of those individuals who understood the behavior of ships, their masters. New York builder Henry Eckford greeted returning ship masters on vessels he had built to ascertain performance characteristics and make adjustments in future models. Joshua Humphreys, designer of the USS *Constitution*, and his son, naval constructor Samuel Humphreys, wrote naval captains, requesting information on the sailing qualities of the warships they had built.[62] Many shipbuilders owned the vessels they built or had shares in them, and sailed them or employed family or friends to sail them.

Through firsthand or secondhand information, these builders could determine the problems with each model and alter future vessels accordingly.[63] Shipbuilder David Brown believed that the best "experiments" were "with the ships themselves; and the only fair scene of experiment is the ocean upon which those ships are to sail, and to whose accidents they are liable."[64]

While incremental change of proven models provided a mainstay of sailing ship design, empirical experimentation represented an important element of the nascent wooden steamboat–building industry. Beginning with Robert Fulton, American shipbuilders designed wooden steamboats through trial and error. The earliest wooden steamers resembled their sailing counterparts, but to determine the best hull form for a steamer, their builders would alter and modify their hulls for maximum performance. For example, Fulton's original *Clermont* was cut down the center and widened, while steamer *New World* simply had greater width added to her sides. The builders usually finalized the lines of steamers after their trial trip rather than before launching.[65] A British observer, civil engineer David Stevenson, noted that few of the steamboats built to ply the Hudson River "have attained the age of six months without undergoing some material alterations."[66] During his travels throughout the United States, Stevenson inspected the *Swallow*, a steamer originally considered inferior in terms of speed. The vessel underwent considerable alterations to her hull and was one of the fastest American steamers in 1837.[67] The breadth of the beam, length of the keel, and shape of the bow of steamboats were commonly altered to increase their performance. Between 1820 and 1830, American shipbuilders became the world's finest builders of river steamers, increasing their ships' speed from five knots to over twenty. Some believed that steamboat construction had reached the level of a science while others considered this trial-and-error design method rather rudimentary. After surveying the products of American steamship builders, most of whom also built sailing vessels, Stevenson found it "impossible to trace any *general* principles which seem to have served as guides for their construction." Stevenson went on to report that each American steamboat builder held his own unique methods, which were not founded "on theoretical principles, but on deductions drawn from a close examination of the practical effects of the different arrangements and proportions adopted in the construction of different steam-boats."[68] The success of American steamboats during the nineteenth century indicates that America's practical shipbuilders developed their trade into a fine art.

Practical shipbuilders relied not only on experience and empiricism to design their vessels but also on aesthetics and their eye for hydrodynamic forms. Throughout the nineteenth century, American master builders such as Henry Eckford, Isaac Webb, Donald McKay, and John W. Griffiths relied on their artistic skills to sculpt three-dimensional wooden models to design their vessels. They used half-hull models that measured from four to five feet in length depending on the scale.[69] Rather than using them in test tanks like the British, the American builders "whittled" them by hand according to their experience and eye for hull forms. These half-hull models represented only half of the hull and were used to produce lines for the ship and to determine its displacement.[70] This method eliminated the need for abstruse mathematical formulations to design the hull. In 1861, a British shipbuilder reported the results to his colleagues of a visit to American shipyards. Rather than draw out the line of the ship on paper as did most British shipbuilders, the Americans carved a half-hull model. The British visitor stated that one of the American shipbuilders told him, "We can most of us whittle better than we can draw."[71]

Although the exact origin of the half-hull model is not known, its use in North America dates back to the early eighteenth century. The custom of carving half models probably came across the Atlantic from Scotland, a region known for model carving during the eighteenth century. Half-hull model making for design purposes did exist in England during the nineteenth century, but prior to that time there is no record of its existence. A significant influx of Scottish shipbuilders to America began in the late eighteenth century. Many of these immigrants located in Canada, but some also made their way to the United States.[72] The half-hull model became very popular among American shipbuilders and came to characterize the practical methods they employed during the nineteenth century. As John W. Griffiths put it, "The model is an American invention and is a proud emblem of American genius."[73]

By 1820, shipbuilders in New York City began to boast that they had invented the half-hull model.[74] While the facts accumulated from artifacts and documents remain sketchy, they indicate that the technique originated overseas and first saw use somewhere in New England or the Canadian Maritime Provinces before finding its way to points along the mid-Atlantic United States. The oldest American half-hull model thought to exist has been tentatively dated at around 1765. It is a "lift" model of a colonial warship named the *Sylvester Hull*, which came from a shipyard in Clinton, Connecticut, on the Indian River. Although no earlier models have been positively dated, it is believed that "sectional" half-hull models became popular before the lift model. This indicates that sectional models had been in use before the *Sylvester Hull* was carved in the mid-1700s.[75] The Peabody-Essex Museum, in Salem, Massachusetts, holds the next oldest model known to exist, that of the ketch *Eliza*, built by Enos Briggs in Salem in 1794. The New York Historical Society holds a lift model carved by Orlando Merrill of Newburyport in 1796.[76]

American shipbuilders used two kinds of half-hull models to set down the lines of their vessels. The earliest form of model they made is referred to as a "sectional" model. Shipbuilders sculpted this model from a solid block of wood and then cut vertical cross sections equidistant along its length. Each cut provided a transverse section that could be used to trace miniature frame outlines onto paper and extrapolated to full scale. Sectional models were somewhat awkward to use because the hull sections were difficult to secure through the length of the model, so pieces could be easily lost. Only a few examples of this kind of model have survived into the twentieth century.[77]

The second type of half-hull model, referred to as the "wave-line," "slip," or "lift" model, became increasingly common by the nineteenth century. Rather than cutting cross sections from a solid block of wood, shipbuilders sandwiched together uniformly thin horizontal boards, or lifts. These lifts ran parallel to the model's waterline. Model makers used square wooden pegs, treenails, or lengthy wood screws to secure the lifts together.[78] Builders usually preferred making their models of softwood, such as pine, because they could shape and smooth it easier than a hardwood, such as oak. While many builders relied only on pine for the model, it became increasingly customary in the nineteenth century to alternate dark woods with the light-shaded pine lifts. These dark woods included mahogany, walnut, and cedar. Once these lifts were assembled and locked into position, the designer shaped the wooden mass into the half hull.[79]

After sculpting the model, the shipbuilder could determine the ship's dimensions. The most important facts that had to be derived from the model were the displacement, the center of flotation, and the dimensions of the frames, or offsets. Finding the displacement and the center of flotation allowed the shipwright to determine the ship's draft, cargo capacity, and waterline. The shipbuilder took the lines off of the models by disassembling the lifts and drawing them in profile so that the parallel lines of each lift could be seen in outline. Next, the model had to be traced from an overhead view with each layer drawn individually, resembling something like a topographic map of the hull. These two views, usually drawn on the same sheet of paper, rendered the figures for the center of flotation and displacement. The approximate displacement could also be found quickly by depressing the half-hull model in a tub of water, and multiplying the water's spillover by its scale.[80]

Next, the model builder got the offsets, the same cross sections that were obtained with the sectional model. Once a table of the model's offsets had been recorded, the shipwright was ready to lay down the full-scale frames.[81]

By the mid-1800s, the use of half-hull models had become common practice in most American shipyards. In 1839, Lauchlan McKay claimed that American vessels were "almost universally built from models."[82] Their experience with models allowed Americans to rely even more on their own instincts and eye for hull forms rather than copy shapes of fish and waterfowl as had their Anglo-American predecessors. John Griffiths explained: "the analogy in form, that should exist between the ship and the fish . . . I cannot discover any farther analogy in their required forms for velocity, than what may be derived from their both navigating the same element."[83] The American clipper bow, for example, defied the traditional "cod's head and mackerel tail" formula, and yet it proved swifter and more seaworthy than older forms.

The half-hull model grew in popularity for a variety of practical reasons. Few American mechanics during the early nineteenth-century had the training necessary to read scale drawings, so it is likely that even fewer of them could read drawings during the eighteenth century.[84] Half models provided a useful three-dimensional tool for designing ships and training apprentices. It could be whittled more quickly than drafts could be drawn.[85] As John Griffiths claimed in an 1844 lecture before New York's American Institute, "there is no calculation rendered necessary that cannot be made from the model with more precision and in less time than from the draft."[86] Using the model, the master shipwright and his workers could estimate the lumber necessary to build the ship, the layout of the ships' rigging, and the initial plank layout of the hull. Due to their numerous responsibilities, practical builders valued the added convenience and time savings provided by the model, and shipwrights with a demonstrated skill in making good half-hull models became highly sought after by shipbuilding firms.[87] Drafting failed to emerge as an important shipbuilding skill until the mid-1800s, and it did not completely supplant model making until the end of the nineteenth century.

The use of half-hull models for design purposes made building a ship much easier and more accessible to American shipwrights. Relying on their practical experience, eye for hydrodynamic shapes, and sense for the sea conditions the ship would face, practical shipbuilders relied on a simple pocketknife, or jack knife, to "whittle" their models. Rural shipbuilder Israel Smith of Atlantic County, New Jersey, carved a new model for every ship he built.[88] Walter Bassett Van Sant of southern New Jersey described the preferred method of his ancestors for making a half-hull model:

They were made with thin boards fastin togather [sic] so they could be taken apart easily. After they were shaped up, they scraped and smothed [sic] them with broken glass. After they were completed and ready to use they would start from the keel and take off one board at a time to get measurements and shap [sic] they needed for the ribs or sides of the boat.[89]

Half-hull models characterize the object-oriented manner that American mechanics and inventors used to approach their work during the nineteenth century. Later in the nineteenth century, such inventors as Samuel Morse, Thomas Edison, Alexander Graham Bell, and Elmer Sperry embraced the use of models to conceptualize the designs of their inventions. The United States Patent Office required three-dimensional models of their patent applications to supplement written specifications and drawings.[90]

American shipbuilders continued to build wooden vessels throughout most of the nineteenth century. They became renowned for producing high-quality wooden sailing vessels and steamers at low prices. From the War of 1812 until the Civil War, low production costs and a reputation for quality workmanship pushed American shipbuilders above the rest of the world's leading producers. America's wooden ship production continued to exceed its iron ship production for the rest of the nineteenth century due to the unnaturally high cost of tariff-protected iron, the country's plentiful supply of shipbuilding timber, and the immense capital costs required to establish an iron shipyard.[91] Even in Pittsburgh, center of the country's greatest iron and coal reserves, wooden vessels could be built for half the price of comparable iron ships for most of the nineteenth century.[92]

America's practical shipbuilders embraced a stock of knowledge that was accessible to all individuals wishing to enter the trade. They relied on a simple set of hand tools, practical experience, and the sculpting of models for design purposes. These methods proved far more accessible to American mechanics and craft workers and appealed to their largely democratic notion of work and its socio-technical basis. Practical American shipbuilders disliked elements of British shipbuilding such as abstruse mathematical theory and expensive technical books. They saw the profession of naval architecture as antidemocratic and intended to make shipbuilding inaccessible to all but the best educated in society. While British shipbuilders developed an approach based on mathematical theory and elitist social and intellectual institutions, America's practical builders proudly continued the age-old traditions of craftwork.

4

The Golden Era of Urban American Shipbuilding

> *The traveller who sailed down the East River and saw the spacious yards that lined the New York shore, the noble vessels on the stocks, the thousands of busy workmen, and the huge collections of timber . . . might have been pardoned for supposing that Manhattan Island was the head-quarters of the ship-building of the world; for such indeed it was.*
>
> "The Old Ship-Builders of New York," Harper's Magazine, 1882

As this passage reflects, New York's East River became one of early America's most important shipbuilding centers.[1] On the Manhattan side, immense shipyards crowded side by side. Each of these firms employed hundreds of workers and had multiple sets of shipways. A wooden sailing ship or steamer in some stage of completion occupied each set of ways. On the Brooklyn side of the river sat the New York Navy Yard, one of antebellum America's largest industrial sites. On both sides of the river one could see the city's large marine engine-building firms and signs advertising every sort of ancillary maritime trade imaginable. These trades included marine hardware retailers, sail makers, ship joiners, caulkers, and hand tool makers. Scenes such as this could be found in many of the major seaports of the East Coast.

During the years leading up to and including the Civil War, urban American shipbuilders became the world's leaders in developing wooden shipbuilding, and the urban shipyard provided the nexus of technological change. Between 1820 and 1865, the shipbuilders of such cities as Boston, New York, Philadelphia, and Baltimore adapted to meet greater demand. They became masters at designing the world's best wooden steamers and sailing vessels. They expanded production by employing greater numbers of workers. They divided the responsibilities once held by the master shipwright into subspecialties and delegated those tasks to subcontractors. They rationalized production as much as contemporary technology allowed through mechanization and systematic organization of work. The wood shipyards of America's coastal cities became the nineteenth century's ultimate expression in wooden ship production.

The U.S. Navy participated in the industrialization of wood shipbuilding by embracing much of the latest shipbuilding technology. The navy yard system faced a unique set of circumstances, however. Due to political conventions of antebellum America, they were normally overstaffed with unskilled political appointees. As a result, the navy yards were equipped with structures to house their workforce as well as important technology to administer to the fleet. The navy yards led civilian shipyards in the adoption of many forms of technology, but they had little need for laborsaving devices and adopted them at a later date.

The urban shipyards of the American East Coast represented a unique form of practical shipbuilding. Despite the industrialization of urban shipbuilding that took place in the years leading up to the Civil War, American shipbuilders remained tied to many of the methods and techniques used during the eighteenth century. So, while the British developed theoretical ways to design their ships, urban American shipbuilders retained some of the trappings of Anglo-American craft methods. The urban American yards did, however, adopt industrial methods for building their vessels. Consequently, they came to represent a unique transitional stage between craft methods and the technology of Anglo-American shipyards as well as modern industrial methods and the technology found in American shipyards at the end of the nineteenth century.

After 1820, a succession of events ensured the demand for vessels manufactured by urban shipbuilders. During the 1820s, American roads remained primitive and railroads did not yet dominate American transportation. Navigation continued to be the most important way of moving cargo and passengers between points along the coasts and inland waterways. During the 1830s and 1840s, immigration from Europe to the United States encouraged the demand for large passenger vessels. Shipbuilding and repair contracts also increased during the war with Mexico to serve the transportation needs of the U.S. Army. From the late 1840s through the mid-1850s, the California Gold Rush supported the demand for large wooden vessels. This demand collapsed in the late 1850s, at the conclusion of the Crimean War, when the British merchant marine was unleashed on the Atlantic trade. Within a few years, however, the Civil War had revived the demand for American-made vessels. The demand for wooden vessels failed to outlast the war; however, iron vessels became increasingly popular in its aftermath.[2] This transition from wooden to iron shipbuilding provides the subject matter for the following chapters.

The market for all kinds of vessels grew during the early nineteenth century. In the eighteenth century and early nineteenth century, American yards had specialized in packet ships, large merchant sailing vessels able to stow great quantities of cargo. In the period between 1820 and 1860, however, urban yards began to branch out into producing various kinds of sailing and steam-powered vessels. Some yards specialized in building smaller steamers and ferries for navigation along the inland and coastal waters of the East Coast, while others built oceangoing steamers for long passages to Europe or the West Coast. Other yards focused on building swift clipper ships for the trade routes to the Pacific.

Not only did the variety of ships increase, but so did their size. Between 1830 and 1850, the average tonnage of wooden cargo vessels built in the United States tripled in size from about 500 tons to over 1,500 tons.[3] By the 1850s, the size of vessels actually exceeded the ability of wood to support the weight of the hull. Urban shipbuilders developed new ways to counter the effects of age, gravity, and storms, which wracked and twisted lengthy wooden hulls. These new reinforcement techniques included double-planking the hull and increased framing. Urban builders also introduced iron structural reinforcement using iron bulkheads, iron keelsons, and iron truss work sandwiched in between the frames and planking.[4]

Urban American shipyards grew to an immense size during the mid-1800s. Due to increased production, some of them expanded their workforce to include hundreds of men, many on a full-time basis. For example, some New York builders employed up to four hundred workers in 1850. This represented a large workforce for a firm at that time.[5] Market demands and the concentration of workers in the major seaports facilitated this growth of urban shipyards. The big cities had a greater supply of skilled mechanics and hosted numerous ancillary maritime industries. European immigration to the United States, the Gold Rush, trade with the Far East, and various wars created this great demand for American-built ships.

Urban American shipyards represented the cutting edge in wooden shipbuilding methods and technology. The goal of reducing the cost of skilled labor had been a characteristic of American industry since the early nineteenth century. Shipbuilders first dealt with this problem through labor division and subcontracting. Early industrialization of shipbuilding also included expanding the use of cost-effective pay systems such as job work and piecework. Shortly before the Civil War, American shipbuilders began to adopt mechanization and materials-handling equipment and to improve yard layout. In their efforts to produce increasingly large vessels as cheaply as possible, American shipbuilders began to innovate new shipbuilding technology and develop laborsaving machines and apply them to their industry. This kind of "American system" of shipbuilding could be found in both civilian shipyards and government navy yards.

With the advent of large urban shipyards, the wood shipbuilding industry could take advantage of economies of scale and begin to systematize shipyard labor. Urban shipyards began to industrialize through labor division; job work and piecework; and subcontracting jobs to task-specific gangs. The greater size of plant, product, and labor force in urban yards spelled the end of the multiskilled master carpenter and the beginning of the division of labor into specialized trades at every level. This alteration of work practices changed the way craft knowledge was transmitted and decreased the control of skilled labor over the production process.

The proprietors of urban shipyards in East Coast seaports required greater productivity, and division of labor supplied the necessary efficiency. As the demand for larger ships grew, urban builders pursued labor specialization and division of the master shipwright's responsibilities into specific trades.[6] Unskilled laborers carried and sorted timber; liners marked out the shape and position of timbers and planks; and molders marked out the lines on timber and plank stock; hewers shaped the ship timbers, while dubbers faired them up using broad axe and adz; borers drilled the holes for fasteners; trunnelers produced trunnels to fasten together the wooden parts of the ship, and fasteners used the treenails to secure the planks to the ship. Once the hull had been assembled, caulkers caulked the seams between the planks using oakum and pitch; while "inside" joiners installed cabinetry, furnishings, and finish work inside the hull; and "outside" joiners finished the deck and the hull. Painters usually finished the process by scraping and painting the finished hull. By the end of the Civil War, wood shipbuilding included such specialists as bolt-drivers, bolt-cutters, and hammer-runners. This introduction of industrialized labor to shipbuilding marked the final days of the master craftsman in American shipyards. It also marked the beginning of what one historian terms "bastard artisanship," or the assignment of craftsmen to one of the sequence of tasks required to make a product.[7]

To increase efficiency and cut costs, urban shipyards turned increasingly to job work and piecework. Both of these payment systems had appeared in the United States during the eighteenth century, but their popularity grew during the nineteenth century.[8] Job work involved payment for fulfilling a specific task to complete part of a ship. The subcontractor would negotiate with the proprietor or master builder for a specific price to perform one job or complete one section of the ship. In the record books of Baltimore shipbuilder James J. Williams may be found a number of job work contracts, including the following with "Mr. G.":

Baltimore Feby 1832
Job Work
Mr. G

New Ship the Keel Stern Frame and Stem to be put togather the apron harse pieces. And dead wood forehead and Aft facing on the Keel. the Ship to be praised compleate ready for receiving the floors. fore one hundred and Sixty Eight dollars.[9]

Piecework became especially popular with tasks amenable to large quantities of standardized items, such as fastening planking or sawing. Plank gangs were often paid by every thousand treenails driven into the hull, while sawyers were paid by the board foot sawed. Under the heading for the bark *Julia Rollins* in Baltimore shipbuilder William Skinner's account book may be found an example of a job contracted by piecework:

July 15th 1884

John Sermans Agrees to treenail the New Bark now Building for Thornton & Others for the Sum of Fifty Dollars per one thousand ($50.00) he to bor, Drive & Wedge in Side and out Side finish the job Complete We are to furnish all material

note: 11888 treenails drove in the Bark 1 1/4 $594.40[10]

Piecework allowed shipwrights to work in more than one yard at the same time, and it saved master builders money by encouraging yard workers to work more efficiently; however, the practice appears to have been a uniquely American solution to managing the production process in shipyards. Piecework was relatively unknown in British shipyards until later in the nineteenth century. The first recognition of the use of piecework in any industry came with James Whitworth's 1851 Committee on Machinery, which observed the method in the United States and recommended its use in establishing the Enfield rifle works in England. Piecework was instituted in British shipyards in the 1870s. The method may have been employed later in Britain because of labor resistance to its use.[11]

The use of job work and piecework systems and the increased subdivision of the production process may not have led directly to the use of subcontracting, but they certainly encouraged the practice. During the eighteenth century, trades allied with shipbuilding—sawyers, blacksmiths, riggers, rope makers, block makers, and spar makers—had already served as subcontractors to the shipbuilder. The earliest gangs subcontracted to perform parts of the shipwright's trade failed to specialize in one particular task. Rather, these gangs consisted of master or journeymen shipwrights that subcontracted to do any part of the construction process previously carried out by full-time master shipwrights. This method lent itself to either job work or piecework, for the same gang could contract to build one part of a ship at one yard and then move on to perform some other task at another yard.[12] The practice of subcontracting various parts of the construction of a ship became common in larger yards by the nineteenth century.[13]

Subcontracting accelerated the trend toward specialization and deskilling, and it required a great deal of coordination on the part of the master builder superintending construction. "Gangs" were organized around specialized tasks, such as planking, joinery, and caulking. The size of a gang could range from three men for joinery to ten for a planking gang. Where the master carpenter had been considered the "boss" in smaller yards, workers referred to the subcontractor as the boss of the work gang.[14] In his Census Report on the shipbuilding industry, Henry Hall described the subcontracting "system" as follows: "The labor is divided among men skilled in their respective branches, and is thus more quickly and efficiently performed."[15]

By the mid-1800s, the production process in larger yards had become so divided and specialized that workers employed in subcontractors' gangs required fewer skills than the master shipwright. Subcontractors, or "lumpers," as they came to be known in New York, often hired lower-skilled workers. Meanwhile the subcontractor's profit margin increased by hiring unskilled labor from the hinterland, such as those referred to as "Hoosiers" within the Philadelphia shipbuilding community.[16] In an article written in 1856, John W. Griffiths described how subcontractors used unskilled and underskilled workers: "These sub-copartnerships are usually confined to two or three persons, and the remainder of the company, consisting of from ten to sixteen, is made up of pupils [apprentices] and journeymen who have passed through this season of hasty probation."[17] The numbers of shipwrights employed in one New York shipyard between 1842 and 1843 demonstrate how subcontracting replaced the practice of employing large numbers of skilled shipwrights. In 1842, the yard had employed seventy-nine shipwrights, but by 1843 the yard had hired eight subcontractors to do the work and retained only twelve shipwrights.[18]

The trend toward specialization and labor division marked the decline of apprenticeship in the wood shipbuilding industry. The fact that formal craft guilds never existed in America as they had in Europe meant that apprenticeship practiced in the United States fell short of the rigidly held practices found overseas.[19] English observer George Wallis wrote in his report to the House of Commons that "there is no apprenticeship system, properly so called [in America]."[20] Urban business practices that altered the institution of apprenticeship did not meet with stubborn resistance by American mechanics as it might in Europe.

Subcontracting parts of the process to gangs meant that apprentices learned only one part of the larger shipbuilding process. Subcontractors indentured apprentices for planking gangs or caulking gangs; however, apprentices had to take the initiative to study other aspects of the trade on their own time if they wished to learn other parts of the trade. In this way, the skills necessary to produce a commodity from raw material to finished product, often associated with a master craftsman, had begun to decline in the large urban yards well before the Civil War. The larger builders, such as Jacob A. Westervelt and John W. Griffiths, bemoaned the trend toward deskilling in the urban shipbuilding industry.[21] In an 1856 article, Griffiths described how apprentices were employed during their entire "pupilage upon only one kind of work, such as framing, or planking, or lower deck and ceiling."[22]

The labor division and deskilling found in many mass-production industries of the nineteenth century had finally found its way into the shipbuilding industry. An unfortunate side effect of the labor division found in urban shipyards and subsequent loss of apprenticeship was the reduction in upward mobility for those wishing to establish their own shipyard. Those unskilled laborers and apprentices who learned little more than how to bore a trunnel hole or caulk a seam lacked the skill necessary to oversee their own shipbuilding firm.

Many mechanics, such as Griffiths, foresaw the deskilling of American shipbuilding and did their best to forestall its approach. From the 1830s through the 1850s, Griffiths pursued a campaign to educate American shipbuilders by contributing articles to periodicals, presenting public lectures, establishing trade journals, and publishing a number of books. He began writing articles on the subject as early as 1836; while a young shipwright at the navy yard in Portsmouth, Virginia, Griffiths began writing articles on ship design for the *Portsmouth Advocate*.[23] His campaign really got under way in New York City in September 1844, when he gave the first formal lecture on shipbuilding ever delivered in America. Entitled "Marine and Naval Architecture," it was the first in a series of lectures he gave on shipbuilding before New York's American Institute.[24] Griffiths lectured in other cities, such as Baltimore. Reporting on his lectures at the Maryland Institute, the magazine *Scientific American* stated that "There were a great many ladies present, who were exceedingly pleased, for Mr. Griffiths is a practical mechanic, understands his subject well, and a man who does this can render his subject plain."[25] He established a "marine architectural institute" in New York in 1847, where students gained instruction in ship design methods such as model making and drafting. Unfortunately for Griffiths and his students, the institute folded after only two years.[26] In 1845, he established the *United States Nautical Magazine and Naval Journal* "to advance the knowledge and prosperity of . . . every class of our fellow-citizens whose pleasure, wealth, or security is enlisted in the excellence of our shipping, and the elevation of our maritime renown."[27] Griffiths acted as editor and contributed most of the *Journal*'s articles. In April 1856, Griffiths wrote a piece for his journal on the decline of apprenticeship in which he described published lessons as "the means of remedying this manifest defect [decline of apprenticeship]." He proposed to write on the subject in his magazine, "and shall give such lessons in practical mechanism as will combine subjects of interest with those of instruction."[28] The Panic of 1857 and the consequent decline in demand for ships, however, forced Griffiths to give up publication of his journal. Griffiths concluded the final installment of his magazine in September 1857 by writing that "the history of ship-building in New York, and indeed in every part of our country, will be best gleaned by the future historian, from the pages of this Magazine. We therefore leave the subject here."[29] Ironically, Griffiths's efforts to educate apprentices and mechanics through books and periodicals may have speeded the decline of apprenticeship. His publications probably lessened the need for training provided by a master shipwright.[30]

Not only did urban shipyards represent the latest trends in labor efficiency, they were also examples of the American will to achieve commercial success by applying the latest technology. These shipbuilding firms adopted some of the most advanced production technology available to wood shipyards. No civilian yards had railway networks or specially designed drying sheds like the navy yards, and only a few had the space for their own mold loft. They did, however, incorporate as much laborsaving technology as possible. Economic conditions in urban shipyards were different than for navy yards; the navy yards were frequently used by the administration as a preserve for workers faithful to the political party occupying the White House. Consequently, there usually existed a wealth of unskilled labor in the navy yards. In rural areas there could be found much cheaper labor than in the cities, but relatively little capital existed in rural areas for investing in improvements. Urban shipyards paid their skilled labor high wages, but investors could be found to underwrite laborsaving improvements to cut costs and maximize profits.

In the early nineteenth century, urban shipbuilding firms began to introduce steam-powered woodworking machines in the urban yards of the East Coast. Urban firms adopted steam power for sawmills between 1820 and the Civil War. By the early 1820s, New York shipbuilder Noah Brown had his own steam sawmill. It was lost in a fire in 1824. The first steam sawmill erected in the Philadelphia area was completed in 1822. Their numbers grew during the 1830s. It was said that local sawyers bitterly opposed their construction because the mills dispensed with the sawyers' services.[31] By the 1840s, steam-powered sawmills with tilting blades began to eliminate much of the handiwork of sawyers and adz men. As Henry Hall stated in his Census Report several years later: "hard-wood timber as is utilized is sawed to the proper shape by a steam jig-saw which will tilt to any angle and cut the timber of any bevel, two men doing the work more rapidly than a dozen men with axes."[32] Clipper-ship builder Donald McKay embraced new technology early in his career. By 1845, he had several machines erected in his East Boston yard, including derricks and steam-powered iron shears. His most important machine was a saw that could make vertical cuts or change angles during operation to saw difficult beveled frames.[33] By the early 1850s, the Currier and Townsend yard in Newburyport, Massachusetts, had built a three-story structure to house steam-driven vertical and circular saws and machines for producing treenails and wedges. Most of the powered sawmills built through the mid-1800s were sash saws held in a frame that cut the wood using a simple up-and-down motion. The circular saw did become more popular beginning in the mid-1800s.[34] Those shipbuilders that did not own their own sawmill could purchase sawed timber from local lumber dealers; more likely they relied upon the traditional pit saw and hand labor. Pit saws remained in use in some urban yards into the twentieth century despite their ancient origin.[35]

The work formerly supplied by hand labor began to be replaced by machines in other ways. Treenails, or "trunnels"—the rod-shaped wooden pieces used to fasten planks to frames—had traditionally been cut and shaved with a drawknife by shipwrights on rainy days or at night. Measuring two feet in length and an inch around, trunnels functioned like wooden rivets. Shipwrights hammered them through holes drilled through plank and frames and pounded a wooden wedge into each end to expand their diameter. By 1838, a power lathe had been invented to mass-produce trunnels. Donald McKay was one of the first to adopt the use of this machine.

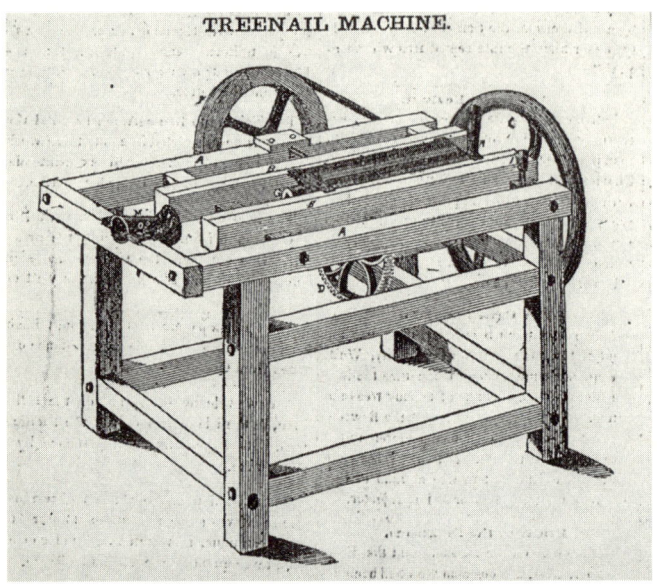

Figure 5. This trunnel-making machine eliminated the time and labor spent carving trunnels by hand. *Scientific American* 3 (November 27, 1847).

By the 1840s, the trunnel lathe had been perfected, and by the mid-1850s the Jersey City Tree-nail Factory had been established to supply the needs of the larger yards of New York City shipyards.[36] Machine planers—used to finish off planks, boards, and timbers—became second in importance as a woodworking machine only to steam-powered saws, and they generally followed sawing in the processing of wood. The development of power planers continued through the antebellum years, until the 1850s when there existed a variety of different models adapted to supply the needs of America's shipbuilding needs.[37] As the editors of the *U.S. Nautical Magazine and Naval Journal* claimed: "At least two-thirds of the drudgery of axe, adz, maul, and plane, may be performed better and cheaper by steam."[38]

Urban shipbuilders employed steam in other ingenious ways. The steam chest remained a regular fixture in urban shipyards. When a deadly fire broke out in William Webb's New York shipyard in 1848, the first thing he saved was the steam chest because the loss of it would slow later production considerably.[39] In 1836, Philadelphia's Byerly and Van Dusen shipyard installed a three-horsepower steam engine to pump water and run a grindstone for sharpening edge tools. Builders in New York set up steam-powered water pumps to see how tightly the seams had sealed by pumping water inside the hull. Most small yards had to forego this service unless they could enlist the local fire company to do it.[40]

Another tool put to use in the cities was a machine developed to bend large pieces of steamed wood to provide knees used to build the hull structure. The knee—an L-shaped piece used to support beams within the ship's hull—was commonly cut from the tree where branches and roots attached to the trunk. Inventor and shipbuilder Thomas Blanchard patented the first device for bending timbers into knees and irregular shapes desired by shipbuilders. Blanchard set up his steam-bending machinery near the New York Navy Yard, but his machine failed to make a profit.[41]

In the 1850s, clipper-ship builder John W. Griffiths began to promote a timber-bending machine based on a different patent than Blanchard's. Bent timbers from Griffiths's machine found their way into several ships during the 1850s and 1860s. Griffiths even managed to sell a complete timber-bending apparatus to the navy, which it installed at the Boston Navy Yard. The timber-bending machine never became popular, however, because wooden-ship construction had become less profitable by the time Griffiths perfected the machine, and the cost of the apparatus proved too high for most wood shipbuilders.[42]

During the antebellum period, ship repair became one of the most profitable aspects of the shipbuilding industry. In fact, shipyards often made greater profits from repairing wooden vessels than from building them. With the increased demand for ship repairs in the seaports, the physical plant of the typical civilian shipyard changed. Up to the early nineteenth century, large sailing vessels had been careened by sealing up the ship's portals, removing any heavy objects such as cannon and ballast, and pulling the vessel over on its beam ends. This exposed the hull below the waterline for cleaning, repair, and coppering. This process, however, proved costly, time-consuming, and labor-intensive. In America, the first marine railway appeared in Salem, Massachusetts, in 1824. Others were built in the East Coast's major seaports during the late 1820s and 1830s. Private shipyards began to build marine railways that could haul out large vessels on cradles using horse-powered windlasses and later steam-driven ones.[43]

In addition to the marine railway, the harbors of the East Coast began to see the appearance of various forms of dry docks. This craze also began in the 1820s. In New York, the first screw dock ever built began operation in 1827. Screw docks incorporated a wood platform able to support a sizable vessel and iron screws as large as four to five inches in diameter. The vessel needing attention would be floated over the submerged platform and a gang of men would be employed to turn the screw apparatuses until the

Figure 6. John W. Griffiths designed this timber-bending machine to bend frames and knees for wooden vessels. "Bent Timber Ships and Universal Wood Bending Machinery" (New York, 1876).

vessel had been hoisted out of the water. In this fashion it took a half hour to lift a 200-ton vessel out of the water. Other screw dry docks were established in Baltimore and Philadelphia. An attempt to build a floating dry dock in New York was begun in 1834. The state legislature incorporated it as the New York Marine Dry Dock Company; however, nothing ever came of the venture. In 1835, a hydraulic dock with an 800-ton capacity built for Ring and Company began service by lifting the famous ocean steamer *Great Britain* out of the water in forty-five minutes. A floating dry dock was successfully built in 1839, however, for the New York Floating Dry Dock Company. By 1847, it was observed that New York had eleven establishments of various kinds able to haul out vessels for repair, but the increasing size of oceangoing steamships required yet more dry-docking facilities. Beginning in 1840, New Yorkers began to build balance dry docks able to support larger payloads. The largest of these floating dry docks was the "Big" Balance Dry Dock built by William H. Webb in 1854 with dimensions of 325 in length and 100 feet in width, large enough to hold the biggest oceangoing steamers of the day.[44]

To improve ship production through the winter months, some urban shipyards began building immense ship houses during the 1820s. Poor weather provided one of the greatest hindrances to productivity in yard work, so these shelters became second only to steam power in their importance to increased productivity. Ship houses could be built large enough to enclose hulls of the largest vessels then known. One ship house in Medford stood 100 feet high and had two berths to house vessels side by side. The New York firm of Brown and Bell had one of the first of these structures in the city, but it burned in 1824 along with two steamers housed inside of it. These structures increased production by allowing shipwrights to work in all weather. Those employed in yards that relied on old methods wasted a great deal of time climbing up and down the staging to get tools and materials. Galleries built into the walls of the sheds allowed mechanics to keep these items near at hand and bosses could observe the work better.[45]

Where heavy lifting had originally been carried out by manpower, derricks powered by livestock and later steam engines came into greater use. The earliest lifting technology found in American shipyards was a form of simple block and tackle suspended from pole and powered by animal or human power. This basic form evolved into two kinds of derricks, the pole derrick for lifting loads in the yard and the shear leg derrick for lifting heavier loads onboard docked vessels. The wooden pole, or gaff-rigged derrick utilized a gaff attached to a heavy mast or pillar standing straight upright. These derricks were designed to revolve so they could place their load on a

Figure 7. This wooden dry dock is very similar to those that saw service during the heyday of the America's urban wood shipyard. Wisconsin Maritime Museum collection. By permission of the Wisconsin Maritime Museum, Manitowoc.

cart or conveyor of some sort. The earliest of these derricks were powered by manpower and animal power; however, many were adapted to steam power by 1860. Such was also the case of the shear leg derrick, which remained in use well into the twentieth century. A lofty lifting mechanism used for installing masts and placing heavy machinery onboard ships, the shear leg was normally located at the edge of a fitting-out wharf.[46]

Animals and livestock generally replaced manpower for materials handling in larger yards. In smaller shipyards lacking the luxury of livestock, all hands had to be called away from their work to shoulder large pieces of timber from one side of the yard to another. Larger yards used oxen and mules to move heavy loads throughout the yard. Less reliance on manpower accelerated production because shipwrights and other workers no longer had to quit their activities for a half hour to help carry a plank or timber through the yard.[47]

By the post–Civil War period, much of the wood shipbuilding process would be mechanized except for hull assembly. In 1875, shipbuilder John

W. Griffiths foresaw that American shipbuilding would become even more mechanized, and he envisioned a sort of assembly line production in a shipyard that could "receive the timber for a frame in at one end of a building, and, after passing through the various manipulations, should be ready to be put out from the opposite end of the building a complete frame, with beams, knees, and floor all on and fastened ready to go across the keel."[48] By 1880, yards would exist that used steam power in almost every facet of the processing of timber, including materials handling, sawing, planing, and lifting. This mechanization cut expenses, particularly labor costs.[49]

Unlike private shipyards, U.S. navy yards enjoyed the financial support of the federal government, so they became the biggest and most highly capitalized American shipyards, representing state-of-the-art shipbuilding facilities in many ways. Much of the shipbuilding process in the navy yards was housed inside roomy, well-ventilated buildings. Where civilian builders had to season and dry their timber in the open, the navy yards were often equipped with timber sheds with doors and vents along their length to promote air circulation and more efficient seasoning. After the Civil War, some yards were even equipped with an experimental drying system called the Buckley patent dryer, which used iron buildings for optimum performance.[50] In addition to timber sheds, the navy yards normally had an oakum loft, spar and boat shop, joiner shop, block shop, blacksmith shop, and plumber shop. The navy yards typically had a mold loft, a large, well-lighted interior space in which to draw the ship frames and structural pieces at full scale. Usually these rooms were located on the second floor of a large building or as part of a mold shop in which frame patterns were stored on the first floor. Wherever they were located, mold lofts usually required flat pine floors hundreds of feet long to allow space for the large patterns laid down on their floors.[51]

The U.S. Navy was probably the first institution to incorporate the use of ship houses in its yards to facilitate year-round construction. The first one was built at the Portsmouth Navy Yard in the fall of 1814, but their numbers grew rapidly in the 1820s, spreading south to other navy yards along the East Coast. Some of these ship houses stood as high as 100 feet and had windows that penetrated the walls at all levels along their entire length and rows of skylights in the roof to let in as much light as possible. Tiers of galleries built into the walls at different heights benefited the workers by granting them additional work space, benches, access to the hull, and storage area for their tools. Foremen used them to observe and supervise the work. Some of these structures housed machines necessary for hull construction, such as steam chests and steam-powered grindstones on which shipwrights could sharpen their edge tools.[52] *Niles' Register* described one of these structures at the Boston Navy Yard, measuring eighty feet high and covering nearly eight acres, as having "probably the most capacious interior of any edifice in the union [*sic*]."[53]

The navy required docking and repair facilities at its yards. As a result, marine railways and dry docks were also introduced at an early date in the navy yards. One of the first marine railways built in the nation was designed and constructed by Commodore John Rodgers at the Washington Navy Yard. The experiment was not repeated, however, in any of the other navy yards.[54] As a wave of ship house construction overtook the yards in the early 1820s, a trend of dry dock construction took place in the early 1850s. One was built in New York for the Portsmouth Navy Yard. When British visitors came to survey the major industrial plants of the United States in 1854, they were favorably impressed by the sectional dry dock in Philadelphia. It had been newly completed in 1851 at a cost of over $800,000. They, however, found the land-based dry dock at the New York Navy Yard most impressive. It took ten years to complete it in 1851. They probably found the capacity, Gothic design of the fixtures, and $2 million price-tag akin to the monumental public works built in their own country.[55]

Other advanced technology was introduced into the navy yards to increase efficiency and productivity. Railway networks began being introduced to the navy yards during the 1850s. These railways did not necessarily rely on steam locomotives. They did, however, increase the efficiency of materials handling in the navy yards by doing away with the two- and four-wheeled carts previously used. Masting shears—A-frame devices with only two legs that were used to hoist masts and heavy devices into vessels—were also in evidence in the navy yards, where few private builders could afford them.[56]

The navy yards did not, however, represent the cutting edge in the application of steam power. More than likely the abundance of unskilled civilian workers appointed for political reasons made mechanization less necessary. In 1837, the navy did install some of the first steam machinery at the Boston Navy Yard for pumping its dry dock and manufacturing cordage.[57] Equipping the navy yards with steam sawmills, however, began in the 1850s. A Navy Department survey indicated that by 1860 only two out of five of the navy yards had converted from pit saws to steam-powered sawmills. During the Civil War, however, steam-powered machinery all but replaced sawing and lifting devices that had relied on animal, human, and water power in urban civilian and government yards. By 1862, a report from the Mare Island Navy Yard, near San Francisco, could boast "a well-arranged sawmill, provided with planing, tongue and grooving, tenoning, morticing, and the various other labor-saving machines."[58] A survey of the navy yards in 1869 showed all but the destroyed Norfolk Navy Yard equipped with masting shears, rail track systems, woodworking machinery, dry docks, and ship houses.[59]

The growth of plant, product, and labor force in America's urban yards forced a division of the design and construction elements of shipbuilding. With the growth of urban shipyards came greater administrative duties than a traditionally trained master shipwright could provide. Often it required proprietors—who had to land new contracts and take care of bookkeeping and financial matters—to act as ship designer, foreman, salesman, and accountant. The fact that separate gangs under the supervision of subcontractors were delegated specific tasks within the shipyard required greater coordination by the mechanical head of the firm. Furthermore, the yard foreman had to make certain that supplies arrived on time so that each task was performed at the proper time in the production sequence. John W. Griffiths, who contracted with the federal government to build a wooden gunboat in Portsmouth, New Hampshire, was thrown off schedule due to the tardy delivery of copper spikes. The vessel lay idle on the stocks for weeks with 300,000 holes bored in her wooden hull.[60]

The 1830s and 1840s saw the proliferation of partnerships and the incorporation of sons into shipyard administration. Simple proprietorships could no longer satisfy the demands of greater mechanical and administrative duties. Philadelphia's Cramp Shipyard became so large that its founder, William Cramp, eventually handed over administrative duties to his sons while he returned to the yard to supervise men in the field. At Smith and Dimon in New York, one partner handled business matters while the other served as ship designer and foreman. Such partnerships as Brown and Bell of New York, and John Birely and Son and Vaughn and Lynn of Philadelphia had similar executive arrangements.[61]

The increased need for administrative specialization meant that the partners responsible for the mechanical side of the work became even more proficient at ship design than master shipwrights. Urban builders such as William H. Webb and Donald McKay took extended trips to Europe to observe the latest developments in foreign shipyards.[62] Others like Samuel H. Pook and John W. Griffiths became such bookish specialists in naval architecture that their practical skills atrophied. A colleague of Pook's claimed Pook failed to understand the first thing about handling shipwright's tools and "had a good deal of cheek, but very little experience or practical ability."[63] Griffiths even built a primitive model test basin for design purposes. By 1840, he had constructed a tank for testing fluid resistance, perhaps the first such tank built in America.⁶⁴ A master shipwright called to testify before Congress described Griffiths as "a fine fellow and has a good deal of theory, and understands draughting; but when it comes to the practical part he knows nothing about it."⁶⁵ A U.S. Census Bureau expert on the shipbuilding industry later described the urban trend toward design specialization: "The period from 1815 to 1850 was thus one of study, experiment, and discussion, especially in the large cities: and, in consequence, there grew up a race of acute and daring shipbuilders, whose achievements were the wonder of the world."⁶⁶

Some members of this urban shipbuilding elite became scholars of American ship design methods. Donald McKay's brother and fellow builder, Lauchlan, produced the first American work of any consequence on shipbuilding in 1839, entitled *The Practical Shipbuilder*. In his book, McKay presented material on how to design and construct a vessel in a way that was "plain and intelligible" to practical shipbuilders.⁶⁷ George W. Rogers published *The Shipwrights' Own Book* in 1845 and *Shipbuilding Made Easy* in 1865, and Leonard Boole published *The Shipwright's Handbook and Draughtsman's Guide* in 1858. Boole came to have the title "doctor" affixed to his name after publishing his book.⁶⁸ In 1866, Samuel Moore Pook, naval constructor and father of famous clipper-ship designer Samuel Hartt Pook, published a book on drafting and laying down ship lines.⁶⁹ Master builders Henry Eckford and Donald McKay also compiled manuscripts on shipbuilding for publication, but their books were never published.⁷⁰

Of all the nineteenth-century American shipbuilders, John W. Griffiths did more than any other builder to champion American shipbuilding methods. An experimenter, an advocate of formal ship-design education, and a working intellectual, Griffiths proved to be the most remarkable of America's nineteenth-century shipbuilders. He became the most prolific writer on American shipbuilding in the nineteenth century. His 1844 lecture before the American Institute developed into the first important American treatise on ship design and construction, entitled *A Treatise on Marine and Naval Architecture, or Theory and Practice Blended in Ship Building*.⁷¹ By the mid-1850s, Griffiths's book had become popular in Britain and had been translated into Dutch. Shortly after the publication of his *Treatise*, he produced the two-volume *Ship-Builder's Manual, and Nautical Referee*. He later wrote more books and established two different nautical periodicals.⁷² Griffiths believed that "the press [is] the only legitimate means by which nautical mechanism may be raised from its low position as a compound of crude notions, to the altitude of a science."⁷³

Certain urban shipbuilders became adept at drafting. Many of them probably learned drafting skills through family connections and work experience. By 1850, Samuel Hartt Pook had established himself in Boston as an independent naval architect and went on to design such vessels as the clipper ship *Red Jacket*. Pook took on William Varney as an associate in his naval architecture firm, but both draftsmen had to become naval constructors at the conclusion of the Civil War, when the bottom fell out of the market for their services.[74] Wood ship designer Leonard H. Boole trained famous yacht builders Robert Center and A. Cary Smith, who designed the first racing yacht designed entirely on a drawing board. Boole's sister Albenia married Donald McKay and, according to his biographer, taught him the art of drafting.[75] George Steers, designer of *America*, the famous schooner that brought the America's Cup to the United States in 1851, learned drafting while working for shipbuilder William Hathorne, a man considered "one of the most expert draughtsmen of New York."[76] Scale drawings made possible the construction of larger ships because they enabled builders to manage greater complexity and provide precise dimensions, measurements, and graphic representations for larger numbers of workers.

The shipbuilders above represent a minority of American master builders of their day. While the trade of drafting had paved the way for future naval architects, these men could not be compared to those we refer to as naval architects today. They had little engineering knowledge. They retained an intuitive knowledge of the shape of a hull, and their approach to ship design relied on the same instincts as practical builders throughout the rest of the United States. In his *Treatise on Marine and Naval Architecture*, published in 1850, John Griffiths could still claim with confidence that "Few vessels are built in the United States from the draught."[77]

New York builders became skilled at designing ships through the use of half-hull models much like ship designers in other parts of the country. The practice of using half-hull models began to catch on in the New York area around 1815. New York builder Isaac Webb's models date back to this period. Stephen Smith, an apprentice under the supervision of Henry Eckford at the time, built the model of the 74-gun warship *Ohio*, which was begun in 1817. Several shipbuilders have been credited with introducing the use of the model to the New York shipbuilding community.[78] No matter who introduced the half-hull model, its use grew to be "universal" in the New York area and spread to many other American shipbuilding regions between 1820 and 1850.[79] The model grew in popularity because it provided a useful tool for training apprentices and required far less time to produce than drawings.

Due to their numerous responsibilities, urban builders valued this added convenience and time savings.[80]

A combination of historical events and economic factors caused the decline of large wood shipbuilding yards during the late nineteenth century. The events that had sustained the industry in the past—the massive influx of European immigrants, the Gold Rush, and the demands of the war with Mexico and the Civil War—no longer existed. The railroads had captured the imagination of Americans, and investment fled shipping for the burgeoning railroad industry. While federal legislation favored the railroads with every incentive for growth, Congress granted the American shipping industry little market protection or any financial subsidy. Shipyards had produced vessels as fast as possible during the Civil War, but the end of hostilities brought a surplus of ships to glut the market. Meanwhile, the war had driven hundreds of American ships to neutral flags and handed the dominant position in shipping and shipbuilding to the British.

The post–Civil War period saw a shift in the industry away from big urban shipyards to rural ones. Yards located where labor and materials remained relatively inexpensive managed to survive the hard times after the Civil War. In such areas as the Great Lakes, Canada, the Delaware Valley, and Chesapeake Bay, smaller shipyards remained profitable. A few yards in cities with access to timber supplies and a lower cost of living such as Wilmington, Delaware; Camden, New Jersey; Portsmouth, New Hampshire; and some towns near Boston also managed to survive. The most prosperous of the postwar shipbuilding regions became coastal Maine. In Maine, the construction of schooner-rigged and square-rigged oceangoing freighters flourished to such an extent that the state became the chief source of large sailing vessels during the nineteenth century, producing 80 percent of the United States' total output of these vessels. In fact, when Donald McKay closed his shipyard in 1869, he sold his steam-powered woodworking tools Down East to a firm in Bath, Maine.[81]

Between 1820 and 1865, there had emerged a greater demand for large American-built sailing ships than at any time in American history. East Coast seaports became major centers of transportation and commerce and the locus of technological change in the wood shipbuilding industry. To cope with the market demands placed on them, urban shipbuilders developed more sophisticated design and construction methods. They mechanized and expanded yards to increase production. The greater size of these yards and the larger volume of ships they produced required the introduction of cost-cutting efficiency measures. These measures could be seen mainly in the adoption of new shipbuilding technology, dividing the labor force into specialties, and the expanded use of the piecework system and subcontracting. The changes in the way urban shipyards functioned reflected the contemporary trend of American entrepreneurs to find more efficient production methods, and it pushed wooden ship production as far as it could go technologically.

The advent of the large urban shipyard had a major impact on the craft traditions that had supported the trade since ancient times. This was found in the way technical know-how was passed from one generation of shipbuilders to the next. The institution of apprenticeship, which had been the basis for training generations of practical shipbuilders in the "art and mystery" of shipwrightery, began its decline. The trend toward greater efficiency and volume of production led to division of labor, specialization, and deskilling that effectively ended the control of skilled labor over production. In essence, the expansion of the shipbuilding industry in urban yards marked the decline of the craft of wood shipbuilding and the growth of shipbuilding as a heavy manufacturing industry. The large urban yards of the nineteenth century represented a transition between the craft methods and technology of Anglo-American shipbuilding and the modern industrial methods and technology found in American shipyards at the end of the nineteenth century. As the wood shipbuilding industry began its post–Civil War decline, iron shipyards adopted as many of the methods and technology from their urban wood counterparts as they could.

5

Building Iron Ships in a Wooden Shipbuilding Culture

> *The established shipbuilding interests refused, for the most part, to take any part in the construction of iron ships. Indeed, they rather despised such vessels, and with some justification. The early builders of iron vessels were, therefore, usually boiler makers, iron founders, and machinists.*
>
> John G. B. Hutchins, 1941

In his exhaustive study on American maritime industries, *The American Maritime Industries and Public Policy*, economic historian John G. B. Hutchins argued that iron shipbuilding represented a complete departure from the methods and technology of America's wood shipbuilding industry.[1] David B. Tyler, in his work concerning iron shipbuilding on the Delaware River, posited a similar argument, asserting that the shift from wood to iron shipbuilding emerged unaided from America's boiler-making industry.[2] These scholars believed that American iron shipbuilding began in the machine shops and engine-building establishments of the East Coast with little assistance from wood shipbuilders and the expertise they had amassed from centuries of crafting wooden vessels.

A cursory survey of firms that built iron ships during the nineteenth century might lead historians to assume that there existed little in common between wood and iron shipbuilding establishments. Closer study of the transition from wood to iron shipbuilding, however, shows that in many ways, wood and iron shipyards shared more characteristics than had been previously believed. For example, many of the workers involved in America's iron shipbuilding industry began their careers in the wood shipbuilding industry. These converts ensured a continuity of methods and technology between wood and iron shipyards.

The iron shipbuilding industry did not emerge unaided from the American engine and boiler-making industry, nor did it just borrow methods and technology from overseas. It developed on the basis of previous knowledge, experience, and techniques. Many of these methods and much of the technology came from the traditions of practical shipbuilding found in the urban wood shipyards often located near iron shipyards. The development of the industry took place in a gradual, evolutionary manner. In the nineteenth century, the large-scale introduction of iron may have fueled American industrialization, but it did not have the revolutionary effect on the U.S. shipbuilding industry.

In the United States, as in Great Britain, it was the private sector that pioneered the use of iron in shipbuilding. The iron shipbuilding industry developed primarily in the mid-Atlantic states. During the antebellum period, New York machine shops like the Novelty Iron Works and the Delameter Iron Works built a number of iron steamers and canal boats. By the end of the Civil War, however, expensive waterfront real estate, New York's specialization in inefficient paddle-wheel technology, and the city's high labor costs led to the decline of its marine engineering and shipbuilding industries. Iron shipbuilders in the Boston area constructed a handful of iron vessels during the 1840s and 1850s and a number of Civil War monitors and iron warships. Boston failed, however, to experience the success enjoyed by the mid-Atlantic region because of its distance from a reliable source of raw material. The American iron shipbuilding industry found its most productive region in the Delaware Valley.

To best understand the introduction of iron to American shipbuilding requires a brief sketch of the industry's development. In the early nineteenth century, many Americans had serious reservations about building ships from iron. These included their skepticism of its buoyancy and durability. When asked about the introduction of iron to naval shipbuilding, Secretary of the Navy George Bancroft disdained its use for constructing warships because such "doubtful novelties, especially such as conflict with the known laws of mechanical forces, should be disregarded."[3] In 1834, the launch of the iron vessel *John Randolph*, fabricated in Britain and assembled in Savannah, Georgia, "attracted very considerable attention and curiosity" because local residents considered such a ship too heavy to float.[4] At the 1839 launch of some iron canal boats in New York City, for example, a large crowd gathered at the waterfront expecting to see them sink under their own weight. The mob wandered away bewildered when the craft floated. This reaction to the use of iron in building vessels was not uncommon in the early days of iron shipbuilding.[5] Those gathering on shore to witness the iron ships sink failed to realize that an airtight vessel built of iron could float even though the new building material by itself could not.

Many saw iron shipbuilding as a curious practice, but there exists no record of open hostility toward, or resistance to, the introduction of iron to shipbuilding. Americans gradually accepted iron as a shipbuilding material for a number of reasons. Iron and steam power converged to mutually reinforce each other in the iron ship as they did in other forms of nineteenth-century technology. Steamships would not have developed so rapidly without this newly introduced material because propeller and paddle-wheel shafts, steam engines, screw propellers, rivets, and the machines used to produce them could not have been manufactured without it. Iron hulls promoted the use of steam by providing the rigidity and durability required by their marine engines. Steam propulsion proved the undoing of wooden steamers because the constant vibration from running the engines loosened the fastenings in wooden hulls. Furthermore, the heat produced by their boilers accelerated dry rot in the green wood often used to build new wooden steamers.[6]

Iron also provided the rigidity necessary in a hull to prevent propeller shaft misalignment. Lack of torsional hull strength in wooden hulls and "hogging" (the drooping or settling of bow and stern in older wooden ships caused by the stress of weight and motion) took a heavy toll on the drive trains in wooden steamers. Unlike iron vessels, wooden ships frequently developed leaks or even sank when a large swell wracked their hull structure. Stormy seas also misaligned propeller shafts in wooden vessels, preventing the use of their propulsion at a time of the ship's greatest need for power. Whenever wooden steamships entered a dry dock, the repair crew had to slacken the bolts securing the engine to the bedplate. This precaution prevented the sort of damage caused to propeller shafts thrown out of alignment when the flexible hull settled on its keel. It was not uncommon for the bow and stern of a 270-foot wooden ship to sit over five feet lower in the water than the midsection. One advantage of side-wheel steamers is that they suffered less from misshapen wooden hulls than did screw propeller steamers. By the 1850s, shipbuilders began to reinforce wooden ships of all kinds with iron keels and frames, and iron strapping attached along the outside of the framing, but these devices still failed to match the rigidity afforded by an iron hull.[7]

In addition to promoting the use of steam, iron improved the durability of ships. The three worst threats to the survival of a wooden ship were fire, grounding, and collision. Wood, canvas, pitch, and hemp combine to make wooden ships extremely flammable, especially when dried out by salt and sun. Onboard sailing vessels, the threat of fire had always been great, but the enclosure of fire-heated boilers inside wooden steamers increased the potential for a conflagration. Few wooden vessels survived grounding. Many fell apart in rough surf, while others suffered mortal damage when salvers attempted to tow them off of rocks or reefs. The danger of grounding proved far less catastrophic to an iron ship, particularly if it had been designed with a double bottom. The incorporation of watertight compartmentalization in iron hulls limited fire and flooding to one section of the ship, and collision bulkheads, located farthest forward, reduced losses caused by collision.[8]

During the early stages of iron shipbuilding development, most naval establishments had some sound technological reasons for reluctantly adopting the use of iron. Barnacles and sea growth fouled iron hulls more rapidly than coppered wooden hulls, thereby decreasing an iron warship's speed. Before compass correction had been devised, the magnetic effect of an iron hull could have catastrophic effects on navigation. Certain naval personnel preferred wooden warships to iron ones because the shrapnel caused by projectiles penetrating an iron hull proved deadlier to the crew than splinters flying from a shattered wooden hull. In addition, the record of early iron vessels remained spotty because the poor-quality plate iron found in them corroded quickly in salt water.[9]

During the years leading up to the Civil War, the Delaware Valley emerged as the nation's iron shipbuilding center. The Delaware Valley's proximity to the nation's largest concentration of iron rolling mills, in eastern Pennsylvania, and its faith in screw-propeller technology helped it surpass New York and Boston as the nation's most productive iron shipbuilding region. Labor costs in Philadelphia were lower than in New York. Wages in outlying cities, such as Camden, New Jersey; Chester, Pennsylvania; and Wilmington, Delaware were still lower than in Philadelphia.[10] By the postwar era, the Delaware River would earn the appellation of the "American Clyde," a favorable comparison to Great Britain's iron shipbuilding hub on the River Clyde.[11]

Delaware Valley mechanics had been the earliest ones to embrace the use of iron for building ships. In 1816, Dr. Charles Lukens had produced America's first wrought-iron boiler plate in rural Coatesville, Pennsylvania. Less than ten years later, mechanic John Elgar, of York, Pennsylvania, bought Lukens's plate iron to build *Codorus*, the nation's first documented iron steam vessel.[12] Elgar probably received the plates by wagon since no railroads or water transportation existed between the two towns at that time. Designed with a stern paddle wheel, *Codorus* began plying the shallow rocky waters of the Susquehanna River in 1825. The diminutive steamer proved a commercial failure, and Elgar was forced to sell it to investors in North Carolina. Elgar gave up iron shipbuilding and moved to Baltimore to work in that city's steam locomotive building industry. Elgar's *Codorus* became the nation's first example of an iron vessel, and it was the only one built outside of an industrial center.[13]

The Delaware Valley's earliest iron shipbuilding establishments began in the industrial cities of Philadelphia and Wilmington, Delaware, where the iron rolling mills of eastern Pennsylvania commonly shipped their products by rail. The Starr family, boilermakers and ironworkers of Philadelphia and Camden, New Jersey, became one of the earliest groups to produce iron ships. In 1829, ironworker Jesse W. Starr built the second documented American iron vessel, a canal boat for carrying coal on the Lehigh River. By the early 1840s, the Starrs had expanded their work into tugboat and steamboat construction.[14]

The encouragement of iron shipbuilding in the Delaware Valley came not only from a reliable source of raw materials but also from the local development of the screw propeller. The Stevens family of Hoboken, New Jersey, had a lot to do with the region becoming the focus of screw-propeller experimentation. Colonel John L. Stevens tested screw-propeller boats from 1801 to 1806. Industrial facilities necessary to manufacture adequate steam machinery did not exist in New York that time, so he failed to develop and patent his propeller.[15] He did, however, establish a highly profitable transportation network between New York and Philadelphia based on the Delaware and Raritan Canal. Stevens's sons took over operation of the canal and established canal boat and steamer repair facilities near each end of the canal, one at Hoboken and the other at Bordentown, New Jersey, on the Delaware River. The Stevenses likely built screw-propelled steamers for a number of reasons. For example, paddle wheels disturb the water's surface more than screw propellers, thereby incurring greater maintenance costs due to erosion of canal banks. Furthermore, paddle wheels are bulkier and less efficient than screw propellers, especially if they are fitted as side wheels.[16]

The Stevens family favored the mechanics from points south rather than rely on shipbuilding talent from New York City. For example, to assist them in constructing their canal boats and steamers, they hired such Philadelphians as master shipwright John Bennett and his sons. By employing the labor and inventive genius of Philadelphia's mechanics, the Stevenses helped diffuse screw-propulsion development to the Delaware Valley. New York had its own early promoter of the screw propeller in John Ericsson, but the wood shipbuilding industry in that city favored the use of the paddle wheel. Ericsson found himself forced to award many of the contracts for his screw-propelled vessels to Delaware Valley builders, including the contract for the world's first screw-propelled warship, the USS *Princeton*.[17]

One-time Stevens mechanic Thomas Reaney and his business partners helped establish iron shipbuilding in Philadelphia and Chester, Pennsylvania. In 1838, Reaney founded a business that became one of the nation's first iron shipbuilding firms. He began his career working for the Stevenses' Camden and Amboy Railroad, then established a Philadelphia business re-

Figure 8. Iron shipbuilding magnate John Roach (1815–87) developed America's first major iron shipbuilding firm. Mariners' Museum Collection. By permission of the Mariners' Museum, Newport News, Va.

pairing vessels from the Delaware and Raritan Canal. Reaney took on mechanic Jacob Neafie and silent partner William Smith to form the Penn Engine and Boiler Works, later known as Reaney, Neafie, and Company.[18] By 1844, Reaney and Neafie had entered the iron shipbuilding business. Richard F. Loper, a retired ship's captain and shipping agent, patented a variation of the Stevens propeller and licensed its manufacture to Reaney and Neafie. The firm prospered by building iron vessels based on the Loper screw propeller. In 1859, Reaney quit the firm, leaving Neafie and new partner John P. Levy to form the Neafie, Levy and Company. By 1860, he had moved south to Chester and formed the even larger iron firm of Reaney, Son, and Archbold. Reaney, Son, and Archbold prospered during the Civil War, benefiting from numerous contracts for iron warships. By 1870, however, contracts dried up, and the firm sold out to New York engine builder John Roach. Roach expanded the shipyard and renamed it the Delaware River Iron Ship Building and Engine Works.[19]

Wilmington, Delaware, had become the most prolific iron shipbuilding city in the United States prior to the Civil War. In 1849, Joshua L. Pusey and John Jones opened a Wilmington machine shop to provide for the demands of local industry. By 1853, Pusey and Jones Company had moved its shops to the edge of the Christina River and constructed its first iron vessel. By 1882, Pusey and Jones had built approximately one hundred iron vessels, over two-thirds of which they sold to Latin American investors to ply the rivers and inland waterways of South America.[20]

In 1836, Samuel Harlan, Elijah Hollingsworth, and Mahlon Betts had established a shop to perform repair work for the Philadelphia, Wilmington, and Baltimore Railroad. This shop later became the Harlan and Hollingsworth Company, the most prolific iron shipbuilding firm of the early and mid-nineteenth century. As with many early shipbuilding firms, Harlan and Hollingsworth started out building and repairing steam-powered machines of all kinds, but by 1844 the firm began building iron vessels of all kinds.[21] One of the first ships, the *Bangor*, provided the earliest demonstration of an iron ship's durability in the United States. Purchased by Maine investors to ply the waters between Bangor, Maine, and Boston, the *Bangor* became America's first oceangoing iron passenger vessel. In 1845, not long after her completion, the *Bangor*'s cargo caught fire and she had to be beached on the Maine coast. Even though the fire gutted her wooden interior, her hull remained intact.[22] A group of investors rebuilt *Bangor* and, in 1846, sold her to the federal government for service in the Mexican War.[23]

This brief sketch of early iron shipbuilding in the United States would indicate that the industry emerged unaided from the machine shops of the East Coast, especially along the Delaware River. Closer scrutiny of records and contemporary accounts, however, reveals a more complex interaction between the wood and iron shipbuilding industries of the United States. The sources indicate that the iron and wood shipbuilding industries shared common methods, technology, and personnel.

The transition from wood to iron ship construction took place gradually through a kind of cross-fertilization between wood and iron branches of the U.S. shipbuilding industry. America's iron shipbuilders observed many of the wood shipbuilders' time-worn traditions. Examination of early iron shipbuilding contracts indicates that the industry's technical vocabulary for parts of the ship went largely unchanged during the transition from wood to iron. For example, a "timber"—the term used to describe a wooden frame—became known as an "iron timber."[24] A "knee"—the upside-down, L-shaped piece cut from a section of tree root and used to support load-bearing beams—was modified to "iron knee." Iron builders adopted other terms used by wood shipbuilders, such as "keel," "keelson," "stem," "sternpost," "floors," "garboard strakes," and so on.[25]

The design of iron hulls also testifies to the influence of long-held wood shipbuilding traditions. Iron shipbuilders, many of them schooled in the construction of wooden vessels, chose to base their designs on the proven

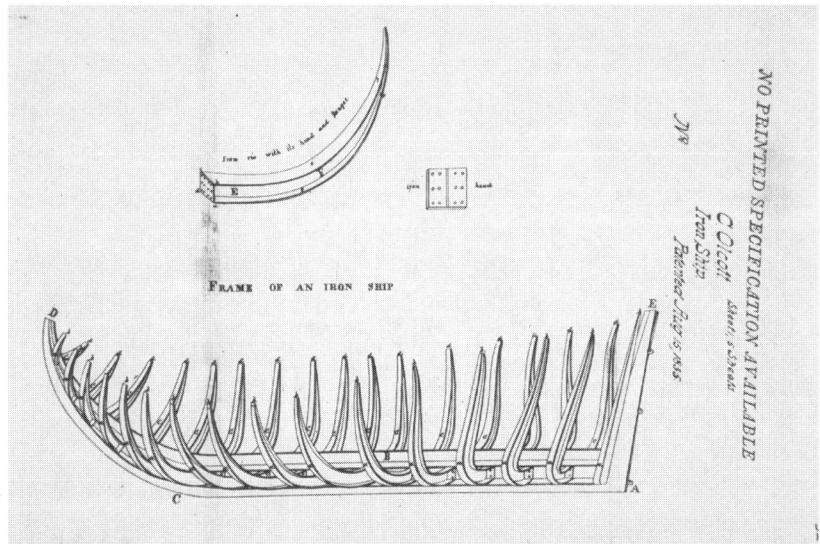

Figure 9. This early iron shipbuilding patent shows how much iron shipbuilders drew from the laterally framed hull design that wood shipbuilders had perfected since ancient times. *Journal of the Franklin Institute* (March 1836).

methods of wooden shipbuilding. The plates in iron vessels continued to have the shifting pattern of wooden planks, so that the butts of each strake never lined up vertically. The shifting-butt pattern survived into iron shipbuilding even though the haphazard pattern had no importance to the hull's strength and increased assembly time.[26] Since medieval times, practical builders had laid down their vessels using a transverse-frame design, where the keel runs the length of the hull, and riblike frames extend up and away from the keel to each side. America's early iron ship designers adhered to this system even though it did not capitalize on the superior strength of iron as did a hull designed with longitudinal ribs. The protruding keel, a design characteristic that had survived from the days of wooden sailing vessels, found its way into the hulls of iron steamships despite the fact that it failed to serve a purpose.[27] This custom of employing antecedent methods when working with a new building material was not exclusive to nineteenth-century shipbuilding. It occurred in other fields that adopted iron, such as civil engineering and architecture. As one historian of technology has noted, "given a change of material, the workers are more likely to expend extra effort to accommodate the new material to an old form."[28]

While American builders continued to replicate traditional designs, certain British designers had adopted the longitudinal hull design in the 1830s, in the early stages of British iron shipbuilding development. Larger vessels benefited from the greater support afforded by the longitudinal system that the strength of iron made possible. One of the originators of the design, Scottish shipbuilder John Scott Russell, described the conservative nature of "workers of wood":

> When iron plates were adopted for the skin of a ship, iron frames came in along with them by mere tradition. It was amusing to me to see how in early ships the copy of wood frames was carried so far that the frames were made in separate bits of angle iron, and scarphed and spliced just like [wooden] frame timbers.

Russell went on to write: "Out of these ruts it is hard to rise. I believe the way out is by the adoption exclusively of the longitudinal system, which I believe by this time would have become universal but for the precedent of timber ships."[29] While American ship designers were aware of the benefits of longitudinal design, they failed to fully embrace its use until the end of the nineteenth century. By that time it proved necessary to adapt it to support the weight of larger warships and cargo vessels, such as oil tankers and Great Lakes ore carriers.[30]

If historians consider wood shipbuilding a craft, then nineteenth-century iron shipbuilding must also be considered a craft. Into the mid-1800s, blacksmiths fabricated much of the structural iron work using an open fire and an anvil to bend pieces one at a time. Hull construction could be compared to the work of a tailor custom-fitting a suit on a client. Rather than having all the necessary parts ready to assemble at once, pieces were puzzled together one at a time. Woodworkers had planked hulls using a technique referred to as "spiling," where they made templates, or "molds," of each plank, traced the outline on wood stock, and sawed out the plank to fill the open space in the hull. There even existed specialized woodworkers called "molders," who found the appropriate plank stock and drew the plank's outlines on it. Iron platers had to fit plates by hand in a similar manner as molders because no effective system had been developed to roll prefitted ship plate until the late nineteenth century.[31] The platers "lifted" the plate's outline from its open space in the hull, using a wooden template, and traced it onto a piece of plate stock. The platers then sheared the plate to size and punched rivet holes in the machine shop. One contemporary observer referred to this as the "cut, bend and try" method.[32] Prior to the Civil War, when wood shipbuilder Charles Cramp began subcontracting his services to local iron shipyards for erecting iron hulls, his carpenters had to manhandle the ship plate between the yard and the shops to get a proper fit. Due to the great waste involved in this laborious fitting

Building Iron Ships in a Wooden Shipbuilding Culture   89

Figure 10. Ironworkers crafting a box keel out of plate iron drawn directly out of a hot furnace. *Harper's New Monthly Magazine* 56 (April 1878).

process, Cramp admitted that "in the early days the scrap heap was the largest mound in the yard."³³

Many firms in the shipbuilding industry made the transition from wood to iron by either converting their physical plant or by subcontracting to other parties. It was impossible for iron shipbuilders to make a start without the experience found in the wood shipbuilding industry. Many firms located throughout the country developed the capacity to construct ships out of both wood and iron. All of the earliest vessels built by San Francisco's Union Iron Works had been wooden steamers of various kinds. In fact, the firm experienced a great deal of difficulty in retraining its skilled mechanics to work in iron when it began producing ships out of the new material. Great Lakes firms, including two in Buffalo and another in Detroit, produced both wooden and iron vessels and utilized the same engineering talent to design them.³⁴

Similar conversions from wood to iron shipbuilding took place in New England. Bath, Maine's E. and A. Sewall switched from building wooden sailing vessels to steel ones in the 1880s.³⁵ Few historians realize that shipbuilder Donald McKay constructed iron ships as well as his famous clipper ships. In 1845, McKay had settled in East Boston, established a wood shipyard, and mechanized the process of wood shipbuilding as much as contemporary technology allowed using steam-powered woodworking machinery. With the onset of troubled financial times in 1857, McKay closed the yard. He was unsuccessful in an 1861 bid to build an ironclad for the Union navy, so he sailed to England to fill contracts with British shipbuilders for American timber. In 1863, after becoming fully versed in British ironclad construction, McKay returned to Boston prepared to embrace new technology once again.

McKay reopened his yard and established an iron shipbuilding and locomotive works with the aid of brother Nathaniel and partner George Aldus. By 1865, McKay claimed to have the best-equipped iron shipbuilding facility in the region. He and his partners built a number of iron warships and one hundred locomotives. Financial reverses forced them to close their operation in 1869.[36]

Wood shipbuilders in the mid-Atlantic states also made the transition from wood to iron shipbuilding. New York's prolific wood shipbuilder Jacob Bell built an iron vessel in 1858. In Philadelphia, wood shipbuilders experimented with iron and a few of them made a complete switch to iron shipbuilding. In 1846, the John Birely and Son shipyard built the iron ship *Mt. Vernon*. That yard's successor, the Charles Hillman Ship and Engine Company, converted completely from wood to steel ship production during the 1880s. The Cramp shipyard began building iron vessels during the Civil War after specializing in wooden ship production for thirty years. Cramp quit building wooden vessels altogether by 1870 and became one of the country's largest producers of steel ships by the end of the century. After the Civil War, Camden, New Jersey's John H. Dialogue yard produced tugboats, ferries, and other small vessels both in wood and iron.[37]

Maritime historians have implied that the conversion of the Cramp shipyard from wood shipbuilding to iron was a singular event.[38] Firms across the United States, however, experienced similar transformations. When the economic collapse of 1857 caused a rapid decline in the demand for new ships, New York's prolific wood shipbuilder Samuel Sneeden reacted by hiring Connecticut engineer Thomas F. Rowland and began constructing iron ships. Samuel Sneeden and Company, also known as Sneeden and Rowland, produced both wood and iron vessels through 1860.[39] In that year, Rowland bought out Sneeden's share of the firm and renamed it the Continental Iron Works. Rowland's firm went on to build several Civil War ironclads, including John Ericsson's famous *Monitor*. The Continental Iron Works remained in business well into the twentieth century, producing ships, machinery, and other iron products. Prior to joining forces with Rowland, Sneeden had been a partner in the firm of Sneeden and Lawrence, which built numerous wooden steamers. After they had dissolved the firm, Sneeden's former partner, George W. Lawrence, went into business for himself and built iron vessels, including warships for the Union navy.[40]

Some of the earliest iron shipbuilding firms had to adopt the methods, technology, and personnel found in the wood shipbuilding industry. Iron shipbuilding firms that began as machine shops and engine-building firms, such as Reaney and Neafie; Harlan and Hollingsworth; and Pusey and Jones, filled contracts for wooden steamers. They did this by supplying only the steam machinery and propulsion systems while local wood builders provided the wooden hulls. For example, the W. & A. Thatcher shipyard became the preferred subcontractor for building the hulls for Pusey and Jones. As these iron firms grew, they began to retain the skilled workers necessary to build their own ships, circumventing the need to subcontract hull construction to outsiders. By the 1860s, both Neafie and Levy, and Reaney, Son, and Archbold employed the skilled workers necessary to build both wood or iron ships.[41]

Not only did American shipbuilding firms have to adjust to the use of iron for construction, the workers involved in the industry had to learn to adapt as well. It would seem reasonable that few workers in wood shipyards could or would use their skills in an iron yard. Research conducted on the workers' transition from wood to iron in Bath, Maine's Bath Iron Works seems to support that view. The research found that only a few mechanics switched from ship carpentry to ironworking and riveting.[42] On the other hand, at least three out of the ten apprentices trained between 1827 and 1847 by Wilmington, Delaware's wood shipbuilder John Harris ended up in the employ of Harlan and Hollingsworth and Pusey and Jones.[43] Furthermore, contemporary observers of the industry believed that woodworkers made good iron shipbuilders. Henry Hall, a nineteenth-century government researcher on the shipbuilding industry, reported, "A ship-carpenter makes as good a man for the iron-ship yard as does the boiler-maker."[44] Theodore Wilson, chief of the navy's Bureau of Construction and Repair, agreed with Hall's assessment, claiming, "It was not an uncommon sight in this country some years ago to see a gang of shipwrights taken off a wooden ship." He even believed that the "best men that can be found in the iron-ship-building yards are those who formerly worked on wooden vessels."[45]

A complete transfer of shipbuilding talent from wood yards to iron ones probably did not take place because those skilled woodworkers who chose to become riveters or some other sort of ironworker did so in the face of lost prestige and, in most cases, lower wages. Men who had worked in wood yards, such as Charles Cramp, claimed that shipwrights considered riveting an unskilled occupation. Naval constructor Philip Hichborn testified in 1876 that "rather an intelligent set of men, ship-joiners are; different from ironworkers, boiler-makers, iron-platers, etc."[46] Wages reflected the lower esteem in which employers held riveters. At the Newport News Ship Building and Engine Works, and the Cramp and Roach shipyards, riveters earned several dollars less per week than ship carpenters and joiners.[47] Given a choice between becoming an ironworker or remaining a skilled woodworker, joiners and ship carpenters likely chose the latter. On the other hand, thousands of skilled woodworkers succeeded in making the transition. If a woodworker faced the choice between unemployment and becoming an ironworker, he probably made the transition.

Primary sources indicate that during the early days of iron ship construction, wood shipbuilders did much of the fieldwork necessary to assemble iron hulls.[48] When an iron shipyard built a vessel, it supplied the building materials and subcontracted wood builders to carve the half-hull model, lay down the hull's lines, fabricate the parts, and erect the hull. In Wilmington, Harlan and Hollingsworth subcontracted W. and A. Thatcher to design and construct its first ships. In antebellum Philadelphia, John Birely and Son, and William Cramp and Sons provided the expertise for that city's iron shipbuilders.[49] According to Charles Cramp, his men sculpted the half-hull model, laid off the lines, superintended "the bending of frames, raising them, running the ribbands, shoring and regulating them, building deck work, and finally launching the vessel. In fact the [wood] shipbuilder did all of the mechanical work except bending the frames, plates, and riveting them."[50]

The variety of trades involved in assembling an iron vessel also explains the contradiction between recent research showing a low rate of conversion and the statements of contemporary sources indicating otherwise. Most iron ships built through the Civil War incorporated numerous wooden parts, such as frames, decks, deck beams, masts, ceiling (the interior walls of a ship's hull), or deckhouses, requiring the skills of experienced joiners and shipwrights.[51] For example, the iron ship *Voyageur de la Mer*, built in Boston in 1858, incorporated locust frames to help support its iron hull. The Civil War tugboat *Pilgrim*, built by Pusey and Jones, incorporated wood in almost every part of the vessel except the hull plating and steam machinery.[52]

The "composite" ship, which combined an iron keel and frames with wooden planking, represented the ultimate expression of blending wood and iron in one vessel. In 1850, Captain Richard Loper and the John Birely and Son shipyard of Philadelphia built the world's first true composite vessel, a steamship with iron keel and frames and wooden planking.[53] The contract between Reaney, Neafie, and Company and Loper for this vessel indicates how ironworkers and woodworkers could cooperate to build a ship:

> We agree to furnish Capt. R. F. Loper with Iron of this Shape ... Drilled with holes for Four five eights Bolts, bent to Shape as per Carpenters moulds for 9 cts per lb. Bolts & nuts 10 cts per lb. Rivets 9 cts per lb. Rivetting together days work, expreßly understood the Carpenters are

to take the Timber from us stand them up in their places ready for us to Rivet at the expense of the said R. F. Loper.

Philadelphia Novr 15th 1847 Reaney, Neafie & Co.[54]

Other Philadelphia-built vessels, such as John W. Griffiths's *Pawnee* and Civil War gunboats built by John Lynn, incorporated iron parts within a wooden hull.[55]

Many of the jobs found in iron yards remained the same as those found in wood yards and the mechanics that specialized in those tasks often switched directly from one industry to the next. Nearly all iron yards had departments dedicated to woodworking, such as those for ship joiners and ship carpenters. As with wood yards, the construction process began in the mold loft. After a master shipwright determined the location of the frames and hull plates using a half-hull model, ship carpenters laid off the iron frames full scale on the immense floor space of a mold loft. From the full-scale drawings of the frames, these carpenters fashioned wooden templates with which to bend and shape the frames.[56] Iron yards had to keep on hand a crew of woodworkers to construct and maintain the wooden staging and scaffolding on which riveters and other ironworkers stood when assembling the ship's hull. Furthermore, the carpenters took responsibility for erecting the iron hull's framework and maintaining its proper alignment from start to finish. The job of the "inside" ship joiner, the individual responsible for building a ship's interior, changed little because nineteenth-century iron builders preferred to outfit their ships with wooden interiors. Records from Harlan and Hollingsworth, Pusey and Jones, and the Cramp shipyard indicate that carpenters' and joiners' departments represented some of the larger ones in iron shipyards. Shipwrights also carried out the important task of launching hulls in iron shipyards.[57]

Iron shipyards recruited a significant number of the supervisory personnel from the wood shipbuilding industry. Superintendents like Roach's Leonard H. Boole, Newport News's Sommers N. Smith, and Cramp's Charles H. Cramp had been brought up in the wood shipbuilding tradition before joining the iron shipbuilding industry. Launching iron vessels differed little from launching wooden ones, and those responsible for managing this important task, such as master shipwright John Fountain of Roach's shipyard, had learned their skills while serving in wood shipyards. John Bennett and his sons helped build the ironclad "Stevens Battery." William Rowland had run his own ship joinery subcontracting business in New York City before heading up his own department at Roach's yard.[58] In 1870, James Dickie emigrated from Scotland to San Francisco and, with his older brother John, established the wood shipbuilding firm of Dickie Brothers. In 1884, the Union Iron Works appointed James superintendent of shipbuilding and began constructing steel ships, such as the famous War of 1898 battleship USS *Oregon*.[59]

Many American ship designers made the transition from wood to iron shipbuilding and adapted traditional wooden ship design to iron. Naval architects, naval constructors, and yacht builders such as Samuel H. Pook, William H. Varney, brothers William and Isaiah Hanscom, and John Lenthall began their careers designing wooden vessels. Later in their careers, however, they designed iron vessels as well. Henry Steers started out as a wooden ship designer and builder in New York, but after the Civil War became chief ship designer for John Roach's Delaware River Iron Ship Building and Engine Works. Among his other responsibilities, master shipwright James Guiler carved half-hull models for ships at the Roach shipyard.[60]

Many customs found in wood shipbuilding remained important in iron shipbuilding. Early iron yards continued the practice of hiring ship captains to design and supervise the construction of their ships in a manner similar to wood yards. During the clipper-ship era, such blue-water captains as Nathaniel B. Palmer and Robert Waterman had designed and supervised the construction of wooden ships for the merchant houses in which they sailed. Captain Richard F. Loper gave up the sea altogether to become a shipping agent and general contractor of shipbuilding in Philadelphia. Captains Nathaniel R. Bensen and Alexander Kelley gave up a life at sea to become department managers at Harlan and Hollingsworth. Bensen supervised the yard while Kelley oversaw the engine-building department.[61] Loper knew Captain John P. Levy as a wealthy ship's master. In 1845, when Reaney and Neafie began to have financial troubles, Loper introduced them to Levy, whose investment capital and potential for landing shipbuilding contracts through shipping connections made him an ideal partner.[62] Captain Andrew B. Frazee commanded vessels for the Stevens family along the Delaware River and earned their confidence to the point that they employed him to inspect and supervise the vessels they had built by general contractors. Experienced shipbuilders resented the insinuation of seafarers into the production process; however, these sailors brought years of sailing experience to the design and construction process.[63]

Family networks comprised an important part of the social fabric of iron shipbuilding firms as they had in wood yards. By the Civil War, however, many iron shipyards had grown sufficiently large that the prospect of upward mobility became unlikely much as it had in large urban wood shipyards. Harlan and Hollingsworth grew from twenty employees in 1836 to 225 in 1850 to 1,000 in 1880.[64] Rather than climbing the occupational ladder, however, the families of practical mechanics of all types dispersed horizontally along the skilled trades level. During the 1880s, John B. Saylor worked as a rivet maker at Harlan and Hollingsworth, while his son Abraham worked as a laborer and his second son, Joseph, became a messenger boy and later an apprentice. Leslie Patton also began as a messenger boy while his father served as shop foreman at Harlan and Hollingsworth. Francis Vinsinger worked there as a laborer while his son started out as a messenger boy and later became a gatekeeper.[65]

In iron yards, much like urban wood shipyards, there existed a core group of skilled mechanics, mainly foremen and gang bosses, to run work in the yard, while unskilled labor provided the muscle power necessary to complete the work in this labor-intensive industry.[66] Boys and helpers comprised the more expendable part of the workforce and provided cheap labor. During the late 1800s, the Cramp shipyard employed between 100 and 500 boys.[67] They served as errand boys, janitors, and messengers. For example, the Cramp shipyard employed about 100 boys as messengers at the turn of the century. In iron yards, however, boys served most commonly as rivet heaters, fitters' helpers, and rivet passers.[68] For most iron yards, boys supplied up to 20 percent of the total workforce during the 1870s and 1880s. For example, the Cramp shipyard employed about 100 boys and 800 men in 1874, and Harlan and Hollingsworth employed 200 boys and 1,000 men in 1880.[69] Various kinds of helpers made up an even larger portion of the unskilled labor pool. These helpers and laborers provided a cheap, expendable labor supply, which was necessary in an industry where the market fluctuated periodically. Some yards, such as John Roach's, saved money by hiring immigrants at cut-rate prices to fill their labor needs. Roach testified before the Senate in 1885 that about two-thirds of his labor force was foreign born.[70] Others, like Harlan and Hollingsworth and Collis P. Huntington's Newport News shipyard, employed low-paid African-American workers. As late as 1910, two-thirds of the over 4,000 African Americans employed by the shipbuilding industry worked as laborers.[71]

Over the course of the century, deskilling increased in the iron shipyard just as it had in wood shipbuilding. In fieldwork this occurred not because of mechanization but because of the increased subdivision of the production process and the subcontracting of work to gangs. In these gangs, only the boss had enough experience to be deemed a skilled mechanic, while the gang comprised an odd assortment of unskilled helpers and boys. This could be seen, for example, in a riveting gang composed of heaters, rivet boys, and bucker ups in addition to the riveter. The preponderance of unskilled labor in these gangs may account for contemporary views of ironworkers as less skilled than woodworkers.

Much like the urban wood shipyards, iron shipyards became manufactories in which the workers performed the production process in a subdivided routine. This "bastard artisan system" cut production costs and multiplied output.[72] By the end of the Civil War, the process of iron shipbuilding had been divided into several specialized tasks that could be subcontracted to task-specific "gangs." Wood builders had separated the process of attaching the ship's skin into planking, boring, fastening, caulking, and painting. Iron builders separated construction into plating, drilling, riveting, caulking, and painting.[73] As time passed, it took an increasing number of specialists to assemble an iron hull. In the period between the Civil War and World War I, labor division for hull assembly multiplied from nine distinct occupations to forty-eight.[74]

Iron and large wood shipbuilding firms commonly subcontracted jobs to gangs that worked by the piece or by the job. For example, in wood yards, a planking gang included plank workers, liners or molders, borers, treenail shavers, fasteners, and unskilled laborers to mind the steam box, fetch tools, and handle materials.[75] In iron yards, a riveting gang included a riveter, or "striker"; and a "holder-on," or "bucker up," who applied pressure to the rivet against the hammer blows of the riveter. Rivet gangs also included a "heater," who tended the portable rivet forge and tossed the red-hot rivets to the striker. Gangs frequently had a rivet boy, however, who carried the hot rivets from the heater to the striker. It is difficult to know where the gang system originated, but this method of task specialization had been employed in American shipbuilding well before iron had been introduced to the industry.[76]

Shipyards typically paid the gangs responsible for attaching the skin of the vessel to the frames by the piecework system. Few records indicate exactly when iron shipbuilders began to rely on the piecework method, but James Whitworth, of the British Committee on Machinery of the United States, observed in 1851 that piecework had become standard practice wherever American industry could employ it effectively. Records from circa 1850 indicate that American naval officials preferred paying their ironworkers by "the pound and inch" rather than by "day's work," the contemporary term for hourly pay.[77] By the late nineteenth century, riveting was paid by every hundred rivets driven. For example, during the 1890s riveters received around three dollars per one hundred rivets hammered.[78]

Apprenticeship continued to remain a part of the shipbuilding tradition after the adoption of iron. Apprentices provided iron yards with another source of cheap labor, a way to bind the families of transient mechanics to the yard, and a potential source of skilled workers. Furthermore, experience provided the best training for ironworkers since no books or schools existed to educate them. Prior to the Civil War, ironworking mechanics underwent an apprenticeship experience similar to aspiring shipwrights. They learned how to use every tool and machine in the shop before their indenture ended. In this way, they learned the whole production process from raw material to finished product rather than specializing in one task.[79]

During the postwar period, the shipbuilding industry observed no industrywide apprenticeship standards, and the time-honored practice became another way to exploit workers and their families. Apprenticeship policies varied from firm to firm. Some yards required their apprentices to sign a formal indenture, and others did not. Harlan and Hollingsworth apprenticed about sixty boys during the 1880s, and Roach apprenticed about thirty. The shipbuilding process had become atomized into numerous subspecialties, so apprentices learned only a part of the production process. In effect, they became low-cost unskilled labor for the gangs employed in the shipyards. Shipbuilding firms encouraged the family men in their firm to apprentice their children at the yard. Whenever openings for apprentices became available, workers' children received preferential treatment. Apprenticeship provided another way for shipyards to lower costs and bind the workers' lives to the fortunes of the shipyard.[80]

Skilled mechanics in the early iron shipyards faced similar work customs as those faced by practical mechanics in wood shipyards. They had no professional societies with which to associate and discuss important trade-related subjects. There existed no professional schools that they could attend to become better educated. Even a formal trade organization that catered strictly to iron shipbuilders, such as the Brotherhood of Boiler-Makers and Iron Ship Builders of America, failed to materialize until 1893. Ironworkers had to learn through experience, so the shipyard filled the role of technical institute for novices. W. B. Harrison's *Mechanic's Tool Book with Practical Rules and Suggestions for Use of Machinists, Iron-Workers, and Others*, published in 1868, was the only notable published source of trade information that they could consult.[81] Ironworkers became proficient at measuring things and basic arithmetic; however, like their wood shipbuilding colleagues, they rarely learned abstract mathematics. For example, it took a shop machinist months to determine the efficiency of a turbine to be installed at a mill in Lawrence, Massachusetts. A mathematician appointed by the turbine builder made the same determination in a matter of minutes by employing calculus.[82] These nontheoretical ironworkers styled themselves as "practical" mechanics.[83]

While practical mechanics, tradesmen, and laborers became trapped at the blue-collar level, proprietors and executives maintained dynastic family networks at the administrative and supervisory levels. For example, six members of the Gause family held executive positions at Harlan and Hollingsworth during the 1880s. At Wilmington's Pusey and Jones Company, members of the Pusey family remained at the head of the firm from 1848 until 1906, and three generations of the Spiegelhalter family managed parts of the firm as well.[84] Four generations of the Cramp family served in executive positions at the Cramp Shipbuilding Company, while two generations of John Roach's family served at the Delaware River Ship and Engine Building Company in Chester, Pennsylvania. Proprietors and major stockholders typically groomed their sons for the executive level by giving them a sort of administrative apprenticeship. These young men served in managerial and blue-collar positions in various departments to gain a better understanding for running the company.[85]

As workers in the shipbuilding industry adapted themselves to the new order of iron, the methods and practices of wood shipbuilding were adapted to iron as well. One might tend to associate mechanization and the industrialization of the American factory with the application of iron to industrial pursuits. Industries that could produce interchangeable parts and mechanize the production process, such as textiles, guns, and sewing machines, did experience rapid increases in productivity due in part to the increased use of iron. In both wood and iron yards, however, much of the work involved in shipbuilding resisted the incursion of mechanization and had to rely on hand tools. While half-hull models of well-designed ships and insurance requirements tended to standardize the design of ships, each vessel built in the nineteenth century remained a custom-built product. As with wooden ships, each iron vessel had to be assembled piecemeal from the keel up, so workers still fit each part individually.[86]

Nineteenth-century wood and iron yards assembled their ships in similar surroundings. Typically, these shipyards added new equipment on a case-by-case basis without the aid of a systematic or predetermined plan. In both iron and wood shipyards, hulls grew from the keel up with wooden staging emerging on either side to grant workers access to the hull at ever higher levels. Shipyard workers built a wide ramp up to the ship so men and materials could find their way into the hull's interior or onto the staging on either side. These ramps were designed to meet the bow of the vessel, or to rise up on either side. The hull was constructed on top of the shipways, usually a set of heavy wooden tracks built on an inclined platform and supported by piles driven into the shoreline. Basically a ramp on which to launch the hull, the ways had to slant at an angle of approximately one inch to the foot to grant shipbuilders the aid of gravity in the launching process.[87] Materials handling in both kinds of shipyards relied on carts pulled by humans, or for heavier loads, by teams of livestock such as oxen and mules. Larger yards had a stable and hayloft to care for their teams of oxen, mules, and horses. By the post–Civil War period, some yards had begun to install rails for carts to ease the transport of materials from one point of the yard to the next. Any object too large to be carted, such as heavy boilers, had to be accommodated on a jury-rigged track of greased logs and plenty of animal power.[88] Like the larger wood shipyards, iron yards relied on wooden pole derricks powered by animal or steam power to do heavy lifting. For the largest loads, such as boilers, engine parts, and masts, shipyards used the tall A-frame-shaped shear-leg, or "stiff-leg," derrick, which was usually located on the outfitting wharf.[89]

The process of building an iron steamer may be best illustrated by traveling back in time to make a step-by-step examination of a ship under construction. In this case, we will attend the construction of the iron steamer *Saratoga* ("Job 170") at the Roach Shipyard in Chester, Pennsylvania. After a half-hull model of the ship had been fashioned, yard superintendent Leonard Boole took it to boss molder James Abrams. Abrams ran the mold shop, the longest building in the yard, which Roach had built after acquiring the shipyard in 1871. The second floor housed an immense flat pine floor, which measured about 185 feet by 65 feet. Abrams oversaw close to a dozen men on the second floor, while the first floor served as storage space for the templates his crew produced for the ship smiths. Like most men in the shipyard, Abrams's workers referred to him as the "boss." Roach employed over a dozen skilled foremen such as Abrams to run different departments within the Chester shipyard. At a time when there existed few professional managers in factories, these bosses and their assistants provided the only supervision over the work in the yard.

The smithing department came under the supervision of Boss John Paul. Paul and his wife occupied worker housing subsidized by the Roach shipyard located across Front Street from the yard. Between the angle-iron and blacksmith shops, Paul had seventy-five blacksmiths and ship smiths under his supervision. The angle-iron shed was a roofed open-air structure with a reheating furnace set in the middle. The "bending slab," an iron floor punctuated by regularly spaced holes, surrounded the reheating furnace. The furnace was driven to a white heat by blowing engines and had several openings so more than one frame could be bent at one time. By the time Abrams's carpenters had finished the templates for Job 170, angle-iron stock had arrived

Figure 11. These ironworkers are about to bend a white-hot frame in the same way as the men at John Roach's shipyard. Wisconsin Maritime Museum Collection. By permission of the Wisconsin Maritime Museum, Manitowoc.

from the local roll-ing mill. Angle-iron stock had a cross-section the shape of an *L*. Ironworkers brought the templates from the mold shop and chalked their outline onto the surface of the bending slab. Foreman William Clark supervised Boss Paul's frame-bending crew. Carters brought the iron bar to the angle-iron shed, and Clark's crew dropped pins, or "dogs," into the slab's holes along the outside edge of the curved chalk outline. Boss Clark then used a pair of tongs to extract a section of glowing angle iron from the furnace, and he and the others used leverlike irons to bend the hot iron into conformity with the pins along chalk lines.[90]

Even though iron shipbuilders tried to increase efficiency wherever possible, iron ships continued to be custom built throughout most of the nineteenth century. Rather than prefitting and prefabricating iron parts for assembly at the shipways, each piece had to be fabricated and attached to the hull in sequence as the hull grew from the keel up. For example, in addition to bending each frame into the profile of the template, Clark and his men had to bevel it to conform to the hydrodynamic lines of the *Saratoga*'s hull. Ship smiths did their best to get the curvature of the frame correct but occasionally failed to properly bevel the frame according to the lines of the hull. Once the frame had lost its rosy glow and cooled, the ship smiths numbered it to designate its location along the keel. Clark and his crew produced a set of two frames with the same curvature from each template chalked on the bending slab.[91]

Next, carters transported the frames to the plate mill. Boss Joseph Magowan, foreman of the yard's ironworkers, controlled this shop. Roach had erected the plate mill shortly after acquiring the shipyard. Its close proximity to the shipways made it convenient for processing the thousands of plates fabricated for ship hulls. It came equipped with everything necessary to shape plates and structural iron, including planing machines, punching and shearing machines, a steam "bull" riveter, and bending and straightening rolls. In the mill, ironworkers marked the newly bent frames with rings of white paint along its length to indicate the location of rivet holes. They took the frames to a punching machine where it was punched with holes on each side of the L-shaped iron. Each set of frames was marked with a number corresponding to its location along the keel and carted to storage before making its way to the shipways for erection.[92]

Not far from the plate mill, blacksmiths prepared deck beams to go into the *Saratoga*'s hull. Instead of using angle iron, the smithies used iron bar with the cross-section shape of a *T*. The smithies under Boss Paul split the ends of each beam down the middle and separated the two sides like a two-tined fork. In between the two tines, they forge-welded plate iron. When the beam ends were bent down at a ninety-degree angle, they possessed a wide flat surface to rivet to the side of the hull. Wooden shipbuilders referred to this curved support feature as a "knee." In iron ships, they were incorporated into the beam ends but still referred to as knees.[93]

Between the shops and the shoreline stood the boatyard, where all of the fieldwork involved in shipbuilding took place. Joe Mills supervised this part of the yard, including the "shipways" and the surrounding grounds where materials handling took place. The boatyard was the province of gangs of laborers, carts, and the teams of mules used to pull them. It was a cold place in the winter and muddy in the spring. The hull was constructed on top of shipways, a set of heavy wooden tracks built on an inclined platform and supported by piles driven into the shoreline. A ramp designed to use the force of gravity to launch the hull, the ways slanted at an angle of approximately one inch to the foot. Hulls grew from the keel up with wooden staging emerging on either side to grant workers access to the hull as it went higher. Ever-

Figure 12. The frames of an iron ship rise up in the same fashion as its wooden counterpart. *Harper's New Monthly Magazine* 56 (April 1878).

present ship carpenters built all the staging. They also built ramps designed to meet the bow of the vessel, or to rise up on either side, so men and materials could find their way into the hull.[94]

Materials handling at the yard relied on manpower, or animal power supplied by horses and mules. Laborers did the heavy lifting required around the shipways using wooden pole derricks equipped with a swinging gaff and a hand crank.[95] To facilitate the movement of heavy objects around the yard, Roach laid down a small network of railroad tracks that utilized gravity and the shoreward slope to coast cars through the yard. The main rail lines ran from the Philadelphia and Reading Railroad on Front Street. Feeder lines from the machine shop, foundry, and boiler shops merged with the main yard tracks running to the fitting-out piers. The rest of the yard had to rely on carts for heavy materials handling.[96]

Fieldwork in the boatyard proved to be the last ship construction process to be mechanized. In recollecting the lack of mechanization in drilling work, William Stephens, a man in his early twenties and a helper in the Roach yard's engine-erecting gang, wrote to a friend: "I never saw anything done by steam which could be done by hand." For example, portholes would be outlined by drilling holes in a circle and then cutting out the hole with a cold chisel. The Roach yard had to employ a large force of unskilled labor to aid in materials handling. Roach employed a dozen carters for hauling materials, but helpers and unskilled labor in the yard numbered seventy. Stephens complained of the continual reliance on handcars to cart heavy engine room gratings between the shipways and the foundry to get the gratings to fit. Activity in the shipyard was frequently compared to a swarm of insects due to the number of workers swirling around the grounds and buildings.[97] From the deck of a hull sitting on the shipways, one could survey the "lines of men bearing on their shoulders long bars of iron, [and] the teams coming and going in every direction with coal, wood, and metals."[98]

The construction of an iron hull in the late 1870s resembled the building of a wooden steamer in most respects except for the material that comprised it. Except for the riveting, the fieldwork still came under the control of woodworkers. Boss John Fountain oversaw this work. He was an experienced master shipwright and had been in the wooden shipbuilding business for many years before working with Roach. Many of his carpenters had learned their trade the old-fashioned way by serving an apprenticeship with a master shipwright, becoming a journeyman, and gaining enough experience to qualify as a master shipwright. In addition to building staging around the hull, Fountain and his men laid down the ships' decks and built much of the rough carpentry work not requiring the finish of joiner work.

The carpenter gang laid the foundation of the shipways, blocked and shored the hull, and launched it.

Keel and frame erection were the another responsibility of the ship carpenters. To support the iron keel, Fountain's men laid a wooden beam down the shipways on top of oak keel blocks. On top of this, they laid flat iron plates riveted together at the ends to form one continuous narrow plate the length of the hull. Riveters attached iron wings to this, forming the keel box of the vessel's hull. Using the large swiveling wooden derricks beside the shipways, the carpenters manhandled iron structural shapes into position. Each set of two frames was erected astride the keel. The carpenters had to make certain that each piece sat in its proper position, according to the number that had been painted on it in the plate mill. Once the frames stood upright at the proper angle, the men attached a long length of wood between each set of frames to maintain the proper width during hull assembly. The carpenters also ran wooden ribbands around the outside of the frames to help maintain their position during the plating process. It required great skill of the carpenters to keep the framework in its correct position throughout the process of constructing the hull. Since carpenters took so much responsibility in building the ship, they commanded some of the highest salaries in the yard.[99]

The half-hull model James Guiler had carved not only provided a way to lay down the frames of Job 170, it also served as a plate model. The draftsmen in the main office sketched the frames on the model. Next, they determined the exact length and width of the plates based on frame spacing, the width of each strake, and the staggering of the plate butts. Through this process, they ascertained the number and size of plates for the hull and placed an order with the rolling mill.[100]

Once the carpenters had erected the frames for the *Saratoga*, the plating gang took over. In the Roach yard, plate fitting comprised one of the most labor-intensive parts of the production process. Like other iron shipbuilding firms, Roach employed task-specific gangs, which worked by the piece. Plating gangs included a boss "fitter" and a crew of between four and six workers, the number of men depending on the size of the plates being worked. The gangs fitted plates in a manner similar to the way shipwrights fitted wooden planks. The fitters lifted the plate's outline from its corresponding space in the hull, made a wooden template from the outline, and traced the lines and rivet holes onto a piece of plate stock.[101]

After making a template, the fitters took the plate stock to the plate mill, where the edges were sheared to size and holes punched for riveting. The powerful punching machine could punch out a "button" with every stroke of

Figure 13. Yard workers haul iron plate for a Civil War–era vessel. *Harper's New Monthly Magazine* 25 (September 1862).

the machine. The workmen in the shop could move the plate so that twenty holes could be punched every minute. The accuracy of the holes punched depended on the skill of the fitter and his gang. Those plates requiring less dramatic curvature were bent using steam-powered rollers. Plates requiring extreme curvature were still bent and shaped by hand. Boss Paul's men put the plates in the plate-reheating furnace in the blacksmith shop. Once the plates achieved the proper heat, the men took them out and hammered them over a form built for the purpose, such as a box mold. In more extreme cases, the men secured the red-hot plate to a bending slab with dogs and pulled it into shape using a block and tackle.[102]

Plate-fitting gangs had to handle iron plate weighing up to half a ton between the shipways and the shops. Working with large iron pieces was especially undesirable during the winter months, when the cold plate sucked the warmth out of the workers' fingers. Even though most of the unskilled labor in the Roach yard was of Irish descent, workers referred to the gang that handled ship plate as the "Italian gang." Raising and lowering plates to the hull was not a work of precision, but one that caused a lot of noise and injuries. As the wooden derricks swung aloft the plates, they would often smash the side of the hull or crash flat on deck. Occasionally the Italian gang dragged a plate across the deck and knocked tools and iron pieces into the ship's hold, causing serious injuries to those working below.[103]

Before the plate could be riveted into place, it had to fit over the holes in the frames and other plates. Frequently the holes failed to line up exactly, and the gang had to use drifts, or tapered steel pins, driven into the unfair holes to pull the plate into position. If the holes proved too unfair to drift, fitters would line them up as best they could and then ream the unfair hole with a drill or a chisel. Fitters were easily identified because they often had missing fingers. Sometimes they would stick a finger in the rivet holes of overlapping plates to ascertain alignment. If the plate unexpectedly shifted, the immediate result was the loss of that appendage. Next, the fitters inserted "liners"—iron filler pieces weighing up to twenty pounds—in the space between each outside plate and its corresponding frame. These spaces resulted from the overlapping of one strake of plates upon the next. Finally, the plates had to be bolted in place in preparation for riveting. The fitters placed a bolt in every other hole because the process of riveting could not be depended upon to draw the plate surfaces together. After the plates had been fitted, drifted, reamed, supplied with liners, and bolted, they were ready to receive their rivets. Once the plates had been riveted, the bolts were removed.[104]

Riveting came next in the process. Riveting gangs in Roach's yard included a riveter, or "striker"; and a "holder-on," sometimes referred to as the "bucker up." The holder-on applied pressure to the opposite end of the rivet flattened by the hammer blows of the striker. The riveting gang's tools included a riveting hammer of between two and eight pounds, a holder-on hammer of between ten and forty pounds, and a "dolly bar" of between ten and thirty pounds used by the holder-on to secure the rivet against the blows of the striker. The heater's tools included a portable rivet forge, tongs, and a small bucket for carrying hot rivets. During the winter months, rivet forges offered the only heat for workers exposed to the elements on the uncovered shipways. On windy wintry days, the wool trousers and jacket most workers wore proved insufficiently warm, and the rivet forges became a popular place for those working on the shipways.[105]

Riveting gangs included a "heater," usually a boy, who tended the gang's portable rivet forge. Depending on the size of the gang, there might also be a "rivet passer," or "rivet boy," who carried the hot rivets from the heater to the striker. Boys were employed as rivet passers because they could fit through the narrow parts of the hull better than a grown man and they earned less money. The Chester yard employed between 50 and 100 boys. Some were used for odd jobs, such as messengers and errand boys. Most, however, were employed in rivet gangs. The Roach shipyard was never a haven of labor contentment. The rivet boys struck in March 1877, but Roach mustered enough new workers to replace them. Rivet gang size could be as large as six individuals—if it included two strikers, two rivet boys, and a heater—or as small as three individuals.[106] Riveting gangs were paid by the piece, usually by every hundred rivets driven. Rivet gangs could put in up to 250 rivets per ten-hour workday using hand tools. The pay was broken down among the gang with the striker getting the highest percentage of the total piece rate and the rivet boys the smallest.[107]

The riveting process began when the heater drove up the forge fire and put a fresh rivet in the portable forge. He put the rivet's point in the coals to keep the head cooler. When the rivet point became red-hot, a temperature close to welding heat, the heater gave it to the rivet passer, who used a small bucket to take it to the holder-on. If the gang was too small to have its own rivet passer, the heater tossed the rivet with his tongs to the holder-on, who caught it with a small bucket. Members of rivet gangs commonly suffered severe burns about the face and hands from the hot rivets they juggled and tossed on the job. They also faced a constant danger of injury or death from falling from the scaffolding on which they perched.[108] The holder-on inserted the rivet in its corresponding hole and set the head against the iron plate with a hammer. Next, the strikers formed the point on the opposite side using their rivet hammers. Finally, the holder-on held his hammer or the dolly bar against the rivet head to resist the blows of the strikers as they closed the point of the rivet against the plate. The whole process from throwing the rivet to clenching its head could take as little as a minute.[109]

The next step in iron shipbuilding involved caulking the hull and painting it. Ironworkers caulked ships differently than did wooden shipbuilders. Where caulkers inserted and pounded oakum in the cracks between planks to seal up the open spaces, ironworkers used chisels and hammers to force the exposed plate edge against the adjacent plate. Rivets closed together iron plates enough to make them air- and watertight, but caulking kept water out of the cracks and prevented rusting between plate edges. After the *Saratoga*'s hull was caulked, Boss E. W. Tibbels and his assistant Malvern Slaughter led the paint crew in applying paint and putty to the ship's interior. They also applied red lead and water-resistant paint to the hull's exterior in preparation for launching.[110]

William Rowland designed the interior joiner work for Roach's ships. He was a master at his craft. During the years up to and including the Civil War, Rowland had run his own joinery firm in New York City and subcontracted his gang to local shipyards. But when the shipbuilding industry collapsed after the war, he had few clients for his services. He signed on as head of Roach's joinery department when Roach acquired the Chester shipyard. The joiner department occupied a long building on Front Street opposite the mold shop. It had machine planers and saws and always smelled like fresh-cut wood. Two bosses directed joiner work in the yard. Josh Long was boss of the "outside" joiners, who built deck houses, companionways, hatches, windows, doors, and exterior woodwork.[111]

Boss Josiah Ross directed the work of the "inside" joiners. In terms of status and pay, inside joiners commanded the highest prestige and pay among yard mechanics. Their job required greater skill than an ordinary woodworker because they had to make the ship's interior look like a palace. They built furniture, stairways, intricate cabinetry, and interior woodwork that required carving and gilding. Job 170's staterooms and cabins were "frescoed" and finished in polished hardwood. A Roach steamer built shortly after Job 170 had an interior described as "elaborate," with "raised panels of highly polished wood and inlaid flowers and shrubbery, French plate windows, colored domes, glass sashes and other ornamental designs." Between the joiner crew and the carpenters, the Roach yard employed about two hundred woodworkers. The two boss joiners directed the work of most of these men.[112]

While the *Saratoga*'s hull was taking shape, work continued in other parts of the Chester shipyard. The largest building in the shipyard was the machine shop, which housed a profusion of machine tools. This collection included lathes, drill presses, planers, and the shafting and belting necessary to run all sorts of machinery by steam power. Here William "Scotty" Scott, a boss with a game leg, red goatee, and short temper, presided with his assistant, Bill Green. They controlled a force of two hundred machinists, helpers, fitters, and blacksmiths, busy building machines and engines for the ships.[113]

Not only were the engines of the craft built here but also the enormous propeller shafts forged for them. With the aid of a traveling crane, Scotty and a crew of twenty men wielded sections of the ship's shaft between a large reheating furnace and a steam hammer delivering blows of thirty-three tons. The steam hammer shook the entire machine shop, sent showers of iron sparks into the air, and shaped the red-hot shaft like an enormous piece of lead. After numerous heats and blows beneath the hammer, the shaft assumed the uniformly smooth shape that met the tolerance of the calipers Scotty used to measure its circumference. Sections of up to forty feet in length and two feet in diameter could be forged this way. The shop was also equipped with an enormous machine lathe, which could finish the surface of the shaft sections. After the sections had been forged and finished, they were ready to be coupled together into one full length of shafting. The whole process of producing a propeller shaft could take up to a month.[114]

There were many other departments in the Roach shipyard that contributed to the production of iron ships. John Roach made the tour of these shops every Saturday visit, inspecting workmanship, directing changes, and noting figures in his ubiquitous pocket notebook. He inspected the pattern shop, under Boss William Stikes, housed in the second floor of the machine shop. It produced the patterns for the engines that powered many of the vessels. He visited George "Coppersmith" Nessenthaler, who presided over two dozen men responsible for copper work such as ventilators, hoods, and steam piping for the ships and tubing for the boilers. Roach walked to the boiler shop, where Boss David Lewis presided over one hundred men working on boilers for steam engines as small as donkey engines and as large as ship engines. The incessant clatter of hammers emanated from all over the yard, but the din heard in the boiler shop was the worst. The foundry held special interest to Roach, who had begun his career as an apprentice molder. Boss Richard Wood had a workforce of over fifty men who produced iron castings from as small as a half pound to many tons. Most of these castings were related to the steam machinery onboard the ships. The temperatures in the foundry caused the men to break out in a sweat soon after starting work, but most of them continued to don their warm hats and caps nonetheless. Here they forged Job 170's propeller, after which it was attached to the shaft already installed in the hull on the ways.[115]

The last and perhaps most crucial step in hull construction was launching. Supervising this step had to be entrusted to a skilled shipbuilder because a poorly executed launch could seriously damage the hull. Typically, the carpenter gang under Boss Fountain took charge of this important job. They applied a coating to the shipways comprised of slippery substances like beef tallow, lubricating oil, and lard oil. Next, the crew knocked away the oak keel blocks so the vessel gradually settled into cradles seated on the shipways. Once the keel blocks had been knocked away and the cradles held the weight of the hull, all that kept the ship from taking its "slide" into the water were wooden "shoes" at the upper end of each way. Once these shoes had been sawed nearly through, they fractured with a loud popping noise, and pressure on the slick angled ways caused the hull and cradles to slide into the water.[116]

Throughout the nineteenth century, shipbuilders launched hulls void of all heavy machinery so there would be little weight to deter the launch. This meant that all the engines, boilers, and heavy equipment had to be installed after the ship floated. After Job 170 was launched, she received her official name, *Saratoga*. The yard tug *George E. Weed* intercepted the hull and pushed it to the fitting-out wharf. The wharf had a large derrick called a "shear legs," or "shears," made of tall iron tubes connected at the top to form a high, triangular form. A common lifting device in larger yards, the shears were hinged at their base and had a heavy-duty pulley arrangement at the

Figure 14. Riggers cautiously lower a new boiler into the engine spaces of a steamer. Wisconsin Maritime Museum Collection. By permission of the Wisconsin Maritime Museum, Manitowoc.

top so they could hoist heavy items onboard the empty hulls. A large steam engine provided power for the shears so it could lift the largest loads, such as wooden masts, boilers, engines, and heavy iron bed plates.[117]

Like most boatyard work, rigging had inherent dangers. The pieces of machinery hoisted onboard ships by the riggers weighed several tons and could easily crush a man. The responsibility for putting these heavy items onboard the *Saratoga* fell to Boss Joseph Bland and his rigging crew of two dozen men. The men in the rigging gang were some of the most interesting characters in the yard, many veterans of the Civil War. It was said of Joe Bland that "he used to preach to his riggers before the whistle blew and then when he had a boiler or a cylinder in mid-air he would tear his hair and curse."[118] Meanwhile Bland's assistant would nudge him aside, give an order to the hoisting engine operator, and the machinery would drop into the hull without any problem.[119]

Once the machinery had been hoisted onboard the hull, it had to be reassembled. A large part of that job came under the supervision of Boss James

Fraser, foreman of the machinery erecting department, and his assistant, Ambrose Belcher. Belcher commanded the respect of the workers through his skill and kindness. Few in the erecting gang liked Boss Fraser, however, with his scanty blond mustache and foul temper. One of his crew recalled a passage from the poet Byron when describing Fraser: "There was alluring devil in his sneer, which raised emotions both of hate and fear; and where his glance of apprehension fell, Hope withering fled and Mercy cried 'farewell.'"[120]

As with the rest of the boatyard work, steam power was employed in rigging as little as possible. Only the heaviest machinery was hoisted using the shear legs. Machinist's helper Stephens complained that "Nothing was ever hoisted aboard that could be carried, I almost wondered at times why we did not have to carry the [engine] cylinders and condensers aboard by hand."[121] Falling from great heights was not a danger reserved only for work on the shipways. The erecting gang working on the fitting-out dock also had their fears. Stephens remembered how precarious it was to manhandle heavy iron pieces onto the ships walking on narrow oak planks between the vessel and dock. He recounted that he and his fellow workers traversed these planks to carry "heavy gratings; I have often wondered which would be on top, the grating or the men, when we hit the Delaware mud."[122]

The machinery installed on the *Saratoga* included a compound steam engine with cylinders sixty inches in diameter and four boilers, each measuring eleven feet in diameter and ten feet in length. A standard tool of the machinists in the erecting gang was the "ratchet brace," which could drill a hole up to four inches in diameter.[123] The gang had to drill dozens of two-inch holes in the bedplate before it could receive the engine. Machinists used the hand-operated ratchets that required iron drill bits and a lubricant, such as soda water or soap and water, to bore the holes in the plate. The ratchet made an unmistakable high-pitched noise. One helper in the gang fondly remembered the "cricket-like chirp" of dozens of ratchets as he worked in the bowels of a ship. Working the ratchet permitted no loafing whatsoever because a boss could hear it anywhere in the ship.[124]

With all the machinery installed, a rivet gang attached the final deck plates on the *Saratoga*, and joiners put the finishing touches on its interior woodwork. The ship was ready for its trial trip to New York. John Roach tried and failed to organize his New York to Brazil shipping line in time for the *Saratoga* and her sister ship, *Niagara*, so he convinced shipping magnate James Ward to buy them and put them into service on his shipping line between New York and Havana, Cuba. The *Saratoga* ran briefly for the Ward line, but within a year it had been sold to the Russian government. The *Saratoga* was one of many ships the Russians purchased to aid them in one of their many fights against the Ottoman Turks. Little is known about the fate of the *Saratoga* after her sale to the Russians. Roach completed a second *Saratoga* in September 1878. It remained in service until 1906, when it was sent to the wreckers.[125]

Stories such as the construction of the *Saratoga* show how geography had a lot to do with the iron shipbuilding industry's development. Iron shipyards emerged in the industrial seaports of the East Coast because of the concentration of workers in those cities and the shipyard's proximity to shipping. Other factors, such as labor costs and the availability of raw materials, determined the long-term survival of the industry in different regions like the Delaware Valley. The expertise associated with marine propulsion also influenced iron shipbuilding. Firms along the Delaware River grew in part because of their adherence to screw propulsion. Meanwhile, New York builders who remained wedded to obsolete paddle-wheel technology went out of business.

The introduction of iron to shipbuilding did not represent a revolutionary change from craft-based construction techniques to new mechanized ones. Industrialization had influenced wood shipbuilding yards much as it had iron ones. During the nineteenth century, piecework and task-specific work gangs existed in wood and iron shipbuilding and many other industries. The process of fabricating the hull of a ship in both industries relied in large part on the hand tools and nonmechanized labor of the so-called bastard artisan. While tools such as rivet hammers and cold chisels certainly did originate in machine shops, the design and construction methods of America's wood shipbuilders provided an example upon which iron shipbuilders could model their own industry. American iron shipbuilding therefore represented yet another form of practical shipbuilding. It could trace its development back to urban wood shipbuilding and before that a more basic form of practical shipbuilding practiced in the smaller yards of eighteenth-century America.

6

A Clash of Cultures

The Failure of Theory in a Practical Shipbuilding World

Theory is almost despised by most practical men; not for want of value of it, but because they do not understand it. A blind man can walk on roads and streets, but when he meets an obstacle he must stop; at a ditch he may tumble down; he cannot turn off his accustomed track—such is the case with many practical and otherwise valuable men working without theory.

John W. Nystrom, 1863

The sentiments of Nystrom, a European engineer working in the United States, characterize the state of American ship design in the mid-1800s.[1] Despite repeated opportunities to adopt elements of the theoretical shipbuilding tradition found overseas, the U.S. shipbuilding industry adhered to practical shipbuilding methods throughout much of the nineteenth century. While European shipbuilders experimented with new building materials, developed new mathematical formulas, and established an engineering-based system of shipbuilding, American shipbuilders continued to rely on craft-based technologies, including hand tools, half-hull models, and knowledge passed on through experiential learning.

The lack of support for a theoretical tradition in the United States had many root causes. The inability of civilian and naval ship designers to adopt theoretical methods may have been a form of resistance to new technology or perhaps a sort of reverse progress ideology. Certainly the American shipbuilding industry had its share of Luddites unwilling to forsake traditional ways, but the concern for making money overruled most other concerns. For example, many wood shipbuilders switched from wood to iron during the Civil War, when the market for iron construction burgeoned. The fact is that a combination of economic and cultural factors prevented the American shipbuilding industry from embracing the sort of methods found in other shipbuilding countries.

Figure 15. Many practical shipbuilders still produced steamers the old-fashioned way after the Civil War. Wisconsin Maritime Museum Collection. By permission of the Wisconsin Maritime Museum, Manitowoc.

The American shipbuilding and engineering culture evolved in a different manner than in Europe. As one historian of engineering culture has pointed out, social and institutional contexts influence the technological style of every society.[2] The unique environment of political, economic, and social factors that influenced America's iron shipbuilding industry during the nineteenth century fostered a unique practical shipbuilding tradition. Many factors allowed this practical tradition to survive through much of the nineteenth century, far longer than it did in Europe. These influences included sources of raw materials, the high price of labor, lack of political support for overseas shipping, and the cultural valuation of practical work and on-the-job experience.

In America's iron shipbuilding industry, hull design required skills similar to those used in wooden ship design. By the late nineteenth century, the design of iron steamers was separated between the mold loft for the hull and the drafting room for the propulsion system and interior fittings. Displays at the 1876 Centennial Exhibition at Philadelphia characterized this division of design methods. The Navy Department's display included, among others, exhibits from the Bureau of Construction and Repair and the Bureau of Steam Engineering. The Construction and Repair display comprised wooden half-hull models of American naval vessels, while the Steam Engineering display consisted of drawings of the machinery housed within those naval vessels.[3]

American marine engineers chafed at the inaccuracy they perceived to be practiced in the design of the iron ship. Horace See, a marine engineer at the Cramp shipyard during the 1870s and 1880s, believed that there had been poor ship design practices in the industry into the 1870s because the shipyard manager typically "could not fathom a drawing but must have a working model to clear the way. I have known him to stop before a drawing board where something new was being developed and say, 'I suppose this is science.' He was continually at variance with the engineer in charge."[4] See rightfully believed that the shipbuilding industry lacked a design practice based on engineering principles and that an iron hull required more accuracy than designing by a wooden model could provide. In 1909, he complained bitterly about contemporary design practice, blaming the half-hull model, "which in many cases was obtained from the ship carpenter, following the uncertain method of whittling and sand-papering said model into such shape as pleased the eye, who did not work out the lines on the drawing board."[5]

America's iron shipbuilders did not follow Great Britain's lead into scientific shipbuilding. Instead, they adopted the practical techniques found in wood shipbuilding. The basis for the design of an iron ship remained the half-hull model and the mold loft just as it had been for centuries of wood shipbuilding. The design process began with the signing of the contract, where the investor specified the qualities he desired in his ship. Usually these requirements specified only cargo capacity, passenger-carrying space, and possibly speed. Exact dimensions and specifications were rarely given and were often left to the shipbuilding firm to determine.

Next, the iron shipbuilder began a process referred to as "scheming." Scheming was an industry term used to describe the process first used by wood shipbuilders to determine the general character of a ship before its exact design had been decided. The shipbuilder schemed the general qualities and characteristics of the vessel depending upon what the ship had to do, where it sailed and how it would be propelled. The hull characteristics varied depending on whether it was propelled by a screw propeller or paddle wheels. If the ship had to navigate the high seas, its lines had to be different than if it navigated inland waterways or sailed into shallow ports. Vessels destined to navigate warmer climates had to be designed differently from those meant to sail colder weather. If the vessel was intended for passenger service, then speed, comfort, and safety would be the most important characteristics. For example, a passenger ship would be given fine, sharp lines, a powerful engine, and plush accommodations. If schemed for carrying cargo, then the ship required maximum stowage and carrying capacity, and the power plant had to take up as little space as possible and provide good fuel economy.[6]

Prior to the introduction of experimental ship model basins in the United States, designers had to rely on their own knowledge and accumulated experience to determine the performance characteristics of the vessels they built. This rule held for iron vessels as well as for wooden ones. Once the preliminary scheming had been accomplished, the designer found an older vessel equipped in a similar manner. Using the older vessel as an example or a kind of design jig, the builder adopted those characteristics he needed in the new vessel and altered those he wanted to improve. In this way, American ship design relied on previous vessel design and evolved gradually through time.[7]

In the beginning, iron shipyards relied on wood shipbuilders to design their vessels. Wilmington's Harlan and Hollingsworth relied on wood shipbuilder W. and A. Thatcher to design its vessels. In Philadelphia, John Birely and Son provided the same services for Reaney, Neafie, and Company. William Cramp and Sons provided the design and hull-building expertise for the Philadelphia shops of Reaney and Neafie; I. P. Morris; and James T. Sutton and Company.[8]

Half-hull modeling remained the mainstay of ship design well beyond the Civil War. Through the early 1880s, John Roach's shipyard in Chester continued to design its vessels using a half-hull model. In 1878, *Harper's New Monthly Magazine* published an article describing the Roach shipyard in which it devoted two pages to the firm's half-hull model design methods.[9] The design staffs at Roach; Cramp; Harlan and Hollingsworth; and other major shipyards represented the country's most advanced iron ship builders during the nineteenth century and they relied on half-hull models as late as the 1890s. In fact, certain smaller yards continued to design by half-hull model into the twentieth century. Indeed, after the first model ship basin was opened in the United States in the first years of the twentieth century, tests showed that half-hull models shaped by eye still outperformed those designed on the drawing board.[10]

One of the most revered yacht designers of the late nineteenth and early twentieth centuries, builder Nathaniel Herreschoff, provides another case for the survival of half-hull modeling. Herreschoff used the half-hull model to create his famous iron and steel yachts during the late 1800s.[11] Herreschoff had been a student of physical sciences at the Massachusetts Institute of Technology and an engineer at the Corliss Steam Engine Company of Providence, Rhode Island, but he still relied on the time-honored ship-design techniques of practical shipbuilders. His method of design consisted of carving a half-hull model, taking off its lines once it satisfied his requirements, then determining the hull's actual displacement by depressing the half-hull model in a tub of water and multiplying the spillover according to the model's scale. Herreschoff next passed the completed half-hull model to his brother and business partner, John Herreschoff, for his approval. Although blind from childhood, John felt the half-hull model with his hands to determine whether it would become a successful yacht design. In addition to building some of the world's fastest steam yachts and torpedo boats, the Herreschoff Company designed and built all six of the America's Cup defenders between 1893 and 1920. Contemporary shipbuilders must have seen the success of Herreschoff's Cup defenders versus Britain's Cup challengers as a vindication of the half-hull model method and practical shipbuilding, as opposed to Britain's scientific ship design methods.[12]

To illustrate the typical American design process, let us return briefly to the case of Job 170 at the Roach Shipyard in Chester, Pennsylvania. The preliminaries for the *Saratoga*'s design began in 1875, when shipbuilding magnate John Roach decided to involve himself in the international shipping business. From his wood-paneled offices at New York City's Morgan Iron Works, which stretched between Eighth and Tenth streets on Manhattan's East River waterfront, Roach laid out a plan to establish a shipping line between New York and Brazil. Roach decided to begin his line with a class of two identical passenger-freighters and settled on his requirements for cargo capacity, passengers' accommodations, and maximum speed. Roach's firm specialized in this type of steamer and identified these two vessels with the production monikers "Job 169" and "Job 170." They would receive their names after they had been successfully launched.[13]

In planning the new steamers, Roach decided on the general characteristics, but his shipyard staff determined the exact dimensions and specifications required to meet his expectations. Every weekend he donned his top hat and black overcoat and rode the train from New York to Chester City to examine the work at the shipyard. On one of these visits in late 1876, he arranged a meeting with shipyard superintendent Leonard Boole, chief draftsman Edward Faron, marine engineer Thomas Main, and ship joiner William Rowland. They met in the yard's three-story office building, located in downtown Chester at 715 West Front Street. The office included a basement storeroom, with its barrels of lard and machine oil; offices for the yard superintendent, treasurer, and bookkeepers; and drafting rooms. The brick tower on its roof afforded a view of the entire shipyard, including the black slate roofs of the shops, the lofty "shear-leg" crane on the fitting-out dock, masts of ships docked on the waterfront, and the over one-mile expanse of the Delaware River.[14]

Roach presented his requirements to Edward Faron. Faron and his men schemed the ship's specifications, a profile, and a deck plan for the vessels based on conditions found in the waters between the port of New York and ports in Brazil. The ships would carry approximately 2,300 tons of cargo, an average size for a steamer of the day; accommodate sixty passengers, officers, and crew; and house low-fare passengers in steerage. The ships would be propelled by a 1,650-horsepower compound engine powered by four boilers and carry a brigantine sail rig in case of engine failure. The ships measured 292 feet in length, 38 feet maximum beam, and over 23 feet in depth.[15]

Once the overall plan of the vessels had been worked out, shipyard superintendent Boole took charge of the project. During the nineteenth century, building an iron ship, like building a wooden ship, required a sequence of tasks reliant on craft skills and hand tools. The process began when Boole delegated responsibility for carving the half-hull model to master shipwright James Guiler. Shipbuilders believed that talented model carvers were born, not made, and difficult to find, so Roach paid Guiler well to sculpt the forms of his ships. First Guiler called on the joinery department to assemble a block of wood from uniform widths of hardwood veneers. Guiler was an artist with wood. He relied on his experience, eye for hydrodynamic shapes, edge tools, and sandpaper to "whittle" the half-hull model. His models measured between four and six feet in length with a scale of a quarter-inch to the foot. He shaped the model so one could see the point where the bow plunged through the waves, the sheer of the deck, and the exact position of the propeller in the water. Through the early 1880s, the Roach shipyard continued to lay down its vessels using this age-old technique.[16]

Boole took off the half-hull model's lines to find the ship's hull characteristics. The important measurements that had to be determined from the model were the displacement, the center of flotation, and the dimensions of the frames. Boole found the displacement and the center of flotation by taking the lines off the model. He disassembled the veneers of the model and traced them so that the parallel lines of each lift could be seen in outline. Next, he traced the veneers from an overhead perspective so the final draft resembled a topographic map of the hull. Once Boole finished these two views, he could determine the figures for the center of flotation and displacement.[17] Boole determined the model's offsets, the measurements of the hull at various stations along the hull. The offsets resembled hull cross sections, which the mold loft foreman took off the half-hull model using a special measuring device.[18]

Once Boole had recorded a table of the model's offsets and determined the shape of the frames, his dozen carpenters laid off the frames full scale in the shop's second-floor mold loft. The carpenters drew full-scale outlines of the frames and various other structural parts of the ship. From these drawings, the carpenters fashioned wooden templates of each frame. The wooden pieces were sawed and braced to maintain the form of the templates, thus making full-scale patterns for the frames. From that point, the construction part of the process could begin.[19]

The half-hull model not only provided a way to lay down the frames of iron vessels, it could be used as a hull plate model. In the earliest days of iron ship design, plates were produced in the uniform size of about ten feet long by two to three feet wide. The designers took the length of the vessel and divided by the length of the plates, ten feet, and multiplied the number of strakes calculated to cover the midsection. They ordered the frame stock all of the same length as the widest part of the ship (the midsection) and trimmed off the ends of smaller frames from the standard size as needed. Due to its lack of precision, this method wasted about one-third the amount of plate ordered from the rolling mill. The additional trimmings from the frame stock made "the scrap heap . . . the largest in the yard."[20]

Employing a half-hull model to mark off hull plates—thereby allowing a three-dimensional method for representing each individual plate—helped reduce the waste found in the earliest iron shipyards. This method may have originated with Charles Cramp, who described how he laid off plates from a half-hull model during the 1840s. First, he traced each strake of plates on the half-hull model using a pen or pencil. He calculated the weight of the hull and estimated the cost of the iron necessary for building his earliest ships by using a half-hull model to estimate half of the weight of the vessel's midship section and multiplying by two to get the midship section's full weight. He then multiplied that figure by the length of the ship, without correcting for diminishing at the bow and stern, to compensate for iron wasted in the production process.[21] Such methods proved problematical at times, as in the case of a New York shipbuilder who ordered iron from the rolling mill using the same method as Cramp but failed to multiply the amount by two.[22] This practice began in the 1860s, but the use of models for laying off iron plates had become common practice by the late nineteenth century. Long after the demise of using the half-hull model for ship design, the plate model continued to find a purpose in determining the shape and location of hull plates.[23]

The practice of building iron vessels without a set of drawings remained the rule through the 1880s. At the beginning of the design process, shipbuilders relied little on drawings. The half-hull model and the specification book formed the basis of their design. In the iron shipyard's offices, the drafting room did produce drawings for machinery and fittings. Drawings for the hull, however, were often reproduced from the ship after it had been completed. During an 1877 congressional hearing, iron shipbuilder John Roach testified that to build an iron vessel, "it was not necessary that there should be a single drawing in existence to enable an intelligent man to know what he was to do except the mold-loft drawing for the framing. The specifications and this drawing were all that were required to form the shape."[24]

The number of perspective drawings, midship sections, and drafts of specific parts for each vessel grew throughout the process of construction. By the time the vessel was finished, a full set of drawings existed to represent it and its various parts. In stark contrast to the highly engineered shipbuilding of the twentieth century, most, if not all, of those drafts had not existed before the assembly of the ship. In 1866, marine engineer John W. Nystrom wrote: "We never find a complete working drawing of a steamer when its building is commenced! In some cases, and even in the navy yards, *the drawing is made after the steamer is finished*."[25]

Despite its adherence to a higher art of ship design, even the navy proved to be less than precise during the post–Civil War period. By the mid-1880s, the Navy Department provided only the general outlines of warships to its shipbuilding contractors. In 1886, Charles Cramp testified before Congress that his firm developed the general plan for a ship previous to construction, but the detailed drafts were developed one by one as parts of each vessel became necessary for assembly. Design methods had simply not developed to the point where shipbuilders could go beyond simple scheming without actually commencing the construction process. When the navy opened bids for its new ABCD Warships in 1882, it only supplied the bidders with basic drafts of the vessels.[26] This lack of precision was one factor that contributed to the bankruptcy of John Roach's Delaware River Ship Building and Engine Works. The sketches presented to the nation's iron shipbuilders convinced Roach to underbid his competitors by a significant margin. Roach's bid proved far below costs, he lost thousands of dollars, and he had to declare bankruptcy in 1887.[27]

The American shipbuilding industry had avoided the use of precise design drawings even though there had been numerous opportunities to adopt such methods since the late 1700s. Certain colonials built vessels for British clients using drafts supplied to them by their clients. The use of drafts, however, never caught on in the United States as it did in Great Britain. The U.S. Navy had modeled itself closely upon the Royal Navy example, so that each new warship proposed required an outline drawing worked up before the vessel could receive approval from the Board of Naval Commissioners. Some treatises published in Britain did make their way across the Atlantic despite their incredibly high cost. During the mid-1800s a few European marine engineers found their way to the United States and did their best to work within the practical tradition of shipbuilding found here at that time.

Those Americans who had the privilege of traveling to or living briefly in Europe tried to implement European ideas and design methods upon returning to the United States. Benjamin Franklin was one of the first to explore some of the practices of scientific shipbuilding. During his lengthy stays in Europe, Franklin became aware of the developments in shipbuilding there. He built and experimented with his own primitive ship model basin to test the resistance of models to water in shallow water. Canals had become popular in Europe by the late eighteenth century. Franklin wanted to test whether boats traveled more slowly in shallow water than in deeper water as European boatmen had pointed out to Franklin. Using his miniature canal and a model powered by a weight, string, pulley, and gravity, Franklin timed the model's passage at different water depths. He found that as the water became shallower, the model traveled more slowly.[28]

Franklin called for the design of fundamentally different hull forms for American ships and advocated better sails to catch the greatest amount of wind with the least resistance. He also advocated the use of watertight compartments to add safety to wooden vessels and to lower insurance rates. Franklin dabbled in computing the stability of ships. His mathematics led him astray, however, for he was not familiar with the mathematics necessary for determining the metacentric height of ships.[29]

Some New York shipbuilders tried to introduce the institutions of theoretical shipbuilding found in Europe. Robert Fulton was one of the first and only American shipbuilders to try to design his steamboats based on the results of the model ship tests conducted by British experimenters. Copies of the original patent drawings for Fulton's steamboat, found in England, testify to the importance of these tests for determining the lines for the hull of his *North River Steamboat*, also known as *Clermont*, and estimating the power necessary to propel the vessel.[30] New York shipbuilder Henry Eckford, who built a number of Fulton's earliest steamers, compiled a manuscript on naval architecture late in the 1820s, but the work was never published. Had it been published, Eckford's manuscript would have been the first such book produced in the United States, antedating the next such work by twenty years. By the 1820s, Eckford had become a wealthy man and proposed to endow Columbia College with $20,000 to fund a professorship in naval architecture. He even selected an individual to fill that post, but Eckford encountered financial reverses that prevented his endowing the professorship. Eckford died suddenly in 1832 while building warships for the sultan of Turkey, thereby bringing the possibility of his plans for treatises and endowed professorships to a close.[31]

The U.S. Navy could have become a leader in American theoretical shipbuilding methods. The so-called high art of ship design had originally carried over from the Royal Navy to the U.S. Navy after its formation in 1793. Most nineteenth-century civilian shipbuilders relied primarily on the use of half-hull models for design. Warships designed by naval constructors, however, normally required a scale drawing of a ship's outline to be submitted to the Board of Naval Commissioners for their inspection.[32] The navy did not become a bastion of theoretical ship design. For example, in planning the superfrigates of 1799, including the USS *Constitution*, naval constructor Joshua Humphreys used a half-hull model to conceptualize the design. It took an immigrant English shipbuilder, Josiah Fox, to transform Humphreys' three-dimensional form into the finished drafts required by the naval authorities for final approval.[33]

During most of the nineteenth century, the U.S. Navy followed the technical leadership provided by the private sector. The navy recruited its most accomplished engineers from the civilian shipbuilding industry. Draftsman William A. Dobson interviewed for a position in the Bureau of Construction and Repair after working at the Roach shipyard for over ten years. His examination to qualify for a position in the Bureau consisted of the chief asking whether Dobson wished to work for them.[34] During the 1870s, the Naval Academy began the custom of sending its naval engineering cadets on summer practice cruises to visit industrial plants along the East Coast. These inspection trips to private shipbuilding concerns proved a very educational part of the cadets' training.[35]

The great influx of money into the shipbuilding industry during the Civil War held out the possibility of reforming the way ships were designed. The capital invested in the nation's iron yards during the Civil War dwarfed the capital that had been invested in wood yards at any time. The war encouraged the building of new iron yards and the extension of old ones. Smaller machine and engine builders in Philadelphia, New York, and Boston accepted contracts to build monitors and iron gunboats for the Union. Firms in Cincinnati, Pittsburgh, and St. Louis joined established shipyards, such as

Reaney, Son, and Archbold; Harlan and Hollingsworth; and the Continental Iron Works to build still more iron warships.[36]

Foreseeing the need to supply the government with large numbers of ironclads, shipyards in the Delaware Valley built new shops and installed more machinery.[37] Harlan and Hollingsworth expanded its physical plant considerably by building new shipways on which to launch monitors; a machine shop containing iron shears, punches, planers, and drills and perhaps the world's largest plate-bending machine; a blacksmith's shop that contained twenty-four forges; and another machine shop that included a mammoth iron-planing machine.[38] A naval inspector at Harlan and Hollingsworth in 1863 wrote: "The improvements made and about to be made will give them all the facilities required for building the Hulls and machinery of the largest class [sic] vessels."[39]

Other local firms enjoyed marked growth. The Pusey and Jones yard nearly doubled in size due to improvements carried out during the war. Between 1862 and 1866, Pusey and Jones added a new machine shop, erecting shop, machine and steam hammer shop, ship joiner shop, mold loft, angle iron–bending slab, and boat shop and storage area.[40] The war was also responsible for the growth of the largest American iron shipbuilding complex of the postwar period. The company known as Reaney, Son, and Archbold began operation in Chester in 1859 and built 118 iron warships and civilian vessels by 1871. The firm also erected sixty dwellings for selected mechanics and a church that could seat seven hundred worshippers. The firm's twenty shops and industrial buildings occupied 23 acres that, according to a contemporary observer, "constituted a village in themselves." Despite the dramatic expansion of the iron shipbuilding industry, the builders interested themselves in new technology, not a new way of designing ships.[41]

In the aftermath of the Civil War, American shipbuilders began to take European tours to observe the latest in shipbuilding technology. John Roach traveled overseas and financed foreign intelligence-gathering trips for several individuals involved in his enterprises, including Thomas Rowland and Henry Steers. The Herreschoff brothers visited shipyards throughout Europe during an 1877 tour. During the following years, Charles Cramp and his chief engineer traveled to Europe, as did the head of Pusey and Jones, William G. Gibbons. The most noteworthy of these trips involved three executives from Harlan and Hollingsworth and resulted in a 200-page report on British shipyards that the firm published.[42] Again, however, these men interested themselves in the latest machinery and factory technology. These individuals represented an industry that lacked the desire and will to import the sort of educational and professional institutions emerging in Europe to support theoretical methods. The potential of transferring new methods of ship design and construction to the United States held out by industrial tours of Europe failed to be realized.

For those who admired the engineering practices of Europe as well as those who simply wanted greater precision in ship design, conditions in the industry led to frustration. There existed few of the sort of institutions that scientific shipbuilding had been founded upon in Great Britain. During the mid- to late nineteenth century, no society or association catered to the needs of iron shipbuilders. While certain shipbuilding texts from Europe were sold in the United States, there existed few domestically produced books. John W. Nystrom's book *Parabolic Shipbuilding* represented the only work on the subject written in the United States before the 1890s. Oliver Byrne's book *The American Engineer, Draftsman, and Machinist's Assistant* and Gustavus Weissenborn's work *American Engineering* focused on marine engineering, and they paid little attention to producing iron ships. These publications were aimed at a readership of machinists and steam and marine engineers, not ship designers.[43]

There existed no schools for naval architects until late in the century, so iron shipyards became the technical institutes for the industry. Shipyards did not recruit freshly minted engineers from the nation's leading schools. Instead they promoted their own personnel, such as draftsmen, from the ranks of their apprentices. For example, the Newport News Shipbuilding Company preferred to promote one of its own to the drafting room rather than hire a graduate of Cornell's Sibley College of Engineering.[44]

Young men from various parts of the East Coast sought work in the shipyards to begin a career in naval architecture or marine engineering. This could be seen at all the yards, but the custom became most prominent at the Roach shipyard, which became the nation's leading shipbuilding concern following the Civil War. The group self-described as "Roach boys" had an informal self-improvement club that met after work to discuss what they had learned in the yard that day and anything they had read or learned pertaining to the trade from outside sources. Most club members filled unskilled and semiskilled positions in the machine shop, blacksmith shop, and the boatyard, but a few found employment in the drafting room. These young men included such individuals as Washington Irving Babcock, son of the president of the Providence and Stonington Steamship Lines, and Hugh Fitz John Porter, son of the distinguished Union general Fitz John Porter.[45]

Young men brought up in this way filled the top design and engineering positions in iron shipyards during the late nineteenth century. They brought with them the skills of practical shipbuilding they had learned on the job.

Graduates of the Roach yard included naval architect William A. Dobson, who went on to become the head naval architect at the Cramp shipyard. W. I. Babcock founded and operated the Chicago Shipbuilding Company. William P. Stephens and William Gardner went on to distinguish themselves in the field of yacht design. Hugh Fitz John Porter, Frank S. Martin, and John L. Bogert moved to New York City to work as marine engineers and consultants in ship construction.[46] After the Roach yard went bankrupt in the late 1880s, the Cramp shipyard became the industry's number-one source of shipbuilding talent. During the 1880s and 1890s, Collis P. Huntington's fledgling Newport News Ship Building and Engine Works recruited most of its management staff from the Cramp shipyard.[47] Charles Cramp realized this point, claiming in 1906 that "Most of the foremen, leaders and best men, from drawing room to riveters, in all of the new shipyards have come from our place, and in that respect they might be considered branches of the old firm."[48]

The degree that the American shipbuilding industry remained tied to traditional design methods may be seen in two cases of theoretical engineers who immigrated to the United States. The first to arrive, John Ericsson, enjoyed a great deal of success in his field. His success was a function of how he worked within the American shipbuilding industry. Ericsson adapted to the industry by inventing and building technology that was useful and necessary. The particular case described below, however, demonstrates what happens when a practical builder executes the design of a theoretical builder like Ericsson. In the second case, Ericsson's contemporary, Swedish-born John W. Nystrom, strove to revolutionize the methods the shipbuilding industry used to design and build its ships. He did this by trying to introduce European-style methods and campaigning for a socio-technological system that the industry was not prepared to support.

One of the earliest events to test the mathematical and drafting skills of American shipbuilders was the Civil War. The realms of the practical shipbuilding world and the theoretical one came face to face for the first time during the war. Swedish marine engineer John Ericsson employed the theoretical methods then popular in Europe, while American naval engineers were trained as practical mechanics. Ericsson and naval engineer Alban C. Stimers became embroiled in the most notorious and costly ship design error in nineteenth-century America. Ericsson developed the design for a class of twenty warships called "light-draft monitors," while Stimers oversaw the construction of the vessels. This case of allowing a practical man to carry out the plans of a European-trained engineer resulted in a complete technological failure.

Prior to the Civil War, most iron shipbuilders, whether proprietors or supervisory staff, came from the United States. The most notable exception to this rule was John Ericsson. John Ericsson was one of the few European mechanical engineers to make his way to the United States prior to the Civil War. While Ericsson is best remembered for building the Civil War *Monitor* and triggering a new era of warship design, he was also responsible for first popularizing the screw propeller in the United States and for many other accomplishments. Ericsson was born in Sweden, west of Stockholm, in 1803. His parents saw to it that John and his older brother, Nils, received a technically oriented education from early on. Beginning at age six, he was taught at home by a governess, and by the time he was ten, he received instruction in chemistry, algebra, and Latin from the superintending constructor of the Göta Canal, on which John's father worked. Ericsson also learned to read and speak French and through his early teens continued to receive lessons in algebra and geometry from the engineers responsible for canal work. So precise were Ericsson's calculations that late in life his monitors varied in depth only a fraction of an inch from his computation of their draft.[49]

After receiving his early technical education, courtesy of the engineering talent close at hand along the Göta Canal, Ericsson and his brother became cadets in the Royal Swedish Corps of Mechanical Engineers. Ericsson remained in the Swedish army until 1826, when he moved to England to pursue development of his inventions. After Ericsson spent a dozen years in England developing steam-powered machines, American steam navigation proponents Robert F. Stockton and Francis B. Ogden convinced Ericsson to immigrate to the United States. Ericsson agreed and settled in New York City, where he threw himself into designing steamships, locomotives, and various steam-powered devices.[50]

Ericsson was a master draftsman. He depicted all of his work in scale drawings at a time when many American mechanics still relied on full-size representations to execute their work. Beginning at age six, he had received instruction from a draftsman engaged in building the Göta Canal. Ericsson took to mechanical drawing and was granted permission to practice the art in the drafting office of the Canal. When he was ten, Ericsson had mastered most of the tools and techniques of drawing. Contemporaries admired Ericsson's drawings as masterworks of precision and beauty. The precision of Ericsson's drawing allowed him to subcontract the fabrication of parts for his vessels from far-flung suppliers, control much of the production process from his drawing room, and eliminate much of the craft element from shipbuilding. These phenomena were highly unusual for shipbuilders of the mid-1800s. When a machinist called the accuracy of his drafts into question, Ericsson stood by his work. Few, if any, construction flaws are known to have resulted from mistakes in his drawings. It is a shame that Ericsson ordered all of his drawings and his personal diary destroyed at the time of his death.[51]

Ericsson's early training and his indefatigable appetite for work combined to turn him into an invention-producing machine. He socialized little and spent most waking hours in his home office working out the particulars of his inventions, often sleeping fully clothed on his worktable. He worked up to sixteen hours a day perfecting his designs. While living in England, Ericsson invented about forty machines, of which a third were patented.[52] He designed railroad locomotives, including the first locomotive built by the Baldwin Locomotive Works in Philadelphia. He developed the first commercially successful screw propeller used in the United States. In 1841, he received a gold medal from New York's American Institute for his horse-drawn steam-powered fire engine. Assistant Navy Secretary Gustavus Fox likened Ericsson's *Monitor* to "a piece of delicate, perfect mechanism." Fox considered ironclads designed by others as "the work of the blacksmith."[53] He not only designed and built the famous *Monitor*, he designed and built the USS *Princeton*, the world's first screw-propelled warship. He continued to build warships after the Civil War, both for the United States and other countries. He developed numerous devices for navigation and scientific measurement and even patented a successful solar-powered motor used for pumping and propulsion.[54]

By the middle of the Civil War, the Union navy needed an ironclad design of shallow draft that could prosecute the naval war in the sounds and inlets that dotted the South's Atlantic and Gulf coasts. The Navy Department called on John Ericsson to design these "light-draft monitors," but he was too busy on other naval contracts to take on the responsibility of designing and supervising the construction of another set of monitors. Ericsson declined to accept more work, but he did agree to plan the new class of monitors and allow the navy to employ its best naval engineers to carry out his plan. Ericsson had the training and expertise to carry out the design and construction of the iron monitors. The navy, on the other hand, had specialized in building wooden ironclads, and events would prove that its practical engineers lacked the skills necessary to produce the sort of complex naval weapons system that the iron monitors represented.

In the spring of 1863, the navy established a special subdepartment in New York to coordinate the construction and fitting-out of monitors for war duty. Naval engineer Alban C. Stimers appeared to be the best man for the job. A naval engineer with over twenty years' experience, Stimers had worked closely with Ericsson as the navy's inspector of the *Monitor*'s construction. Stimers had also distinguished himself by serving as the chief engineering advisor onboard the *Monitor* during its famous battle with the Confederate ironclad CSS *Virginia*. Along with John L. Worden and other members of the crew, Stimers enjoyed instant celebrity upon his return to the North.[55]

Stimers became the champion of the monitors. He went as far as claiming the *Monitor* had great sea-keeping ability, a statement proven wrong by the loss of the vessel in high seas off of the North Carolina coast.[56] Shortly after the *Monitor-Virginia* battle, Stimers's notoriety grew when he became embroiled in a highly publicized argument with Rear Admiral Samuel F. Du Pont on the merits of the monitors. Du Pont blamed his failure to capture Charleston in the spring of 1863 on his fleet of monitors. Stimers challenged Du Pont's claim that the monitors were to blame for the failure. The navy conducted a court of inquiry on the matter and finally relieved Du Pont. Stimers suddenly became the monitors' champion, which solidified his friendship with Ericsson.[57]

The navy assigned Stimers to direct the new office in New York responsible for overseeing construction of new monitors. Stimers began by hiring a chief and nine draftsmen and renting an office next door to Ericsson's home office. As his assistants, Stimers selected two young engineers with close ties to New York's ship and engine building industries. Theodore Allen was the nephew of the Novelty Iron Works' long-time president, Horatio Allen, and had spent much of his youth working in the machine-building industry.[58] Stimers's second choice, Isaac Newton, came from a family closely associated with shipping on the Hudson River. Newton's father, Isaac Sr., owned a line of steamers that ran from New York to Albany.[59] Stimers's own experience consisted of "engine driving" onboard naval vessels and self-study in iron shipbuilding. The only hands-on experience he had received came from working with Ericsson on the *Monitor*. The rest of Stimers's staff grew to a force of forty draftsmen, clerks, and office workers. The rapid expansion of Stimers's office brought the size of his workforce to nearly the same size as all of the navy's Washington bureaus combined. The increase in manpower forced him to vacate the old office next to Ericsson in favor of two floors of an office building elsewhere in Manhattan.[60]

One of the reasons for the failure of the light-draft monitor program is that Ericsson lost control over the design and construction process. He developed the initial plans for the vessels, but he and Stimers became estranged over an incident involving another class of monitors. Stimers ran a test of Ericsson's friction gear on the USS *Canonicus*. Stimers's test showed Ericsson's gear in an unfavorable light. Thereafter the proud Ericsson seldom volunteered information on the light-draft monitors, and the ambitious Stimers never sought out Ericsson's advice. The transfer of Stimers's office from Front Street, next to Ericsson, to Canal Street added physical distance to the barriers that already separated Stimers and his staff from Ericsson. Thereafter, the responsibility for design and construction oversight lay solely with Stimers, a man later described by Ericsson as a "charlatan engineer."[61]

The naval officials with access to Stimers had little knowledge of modern warship design. Those who did have an intimate knowledge of building such machines, like Ericsson, had little access to Stimers. With a background in practical engineering, Stimers proceeded to adopt design changes, which altered Ericsson's original conception of the light-draft monitors. Stimers drastically reduced the size of the steam engines Ericsson proposed. Stimers also redesigned the boilers, which Ericsson later claimed were twice as large as the engines required. The experience gained by monitors fighting the fortifications defending Charleston indicated that a heavily armored pilothouse should be added to the monitor design. Stimers did this and altered the design to incorporate an 18-ton base ring around the monitors' turrets. It occurred to the head of the Navy's Bureau of Yards and Docks that a set of water ballast tanks could aid the light-draft monitors in navigating the shallow inland waterways of the South. Stimers adopted the admiral's plan and ordered the contractors to add the necessary tanks, piping, valves, and pumping engines.[62] During an 1865 Senate investigation, a monitor contractor testified that Stimers "would have sunk every one of them [the monitors] by his additional alterations on alterations . . . [and] . . . the immense quantity of iron he put in them."[63] The intent behind Stimers's design changes was sound; however, the incorporation of the alterations in Ericsson's design were ill-conceived and proved disastrous.

Stimers also failed to detect a fatal mathematical error committed by his assistant Theodore Allen. Like the Civil War's other monitors, the light-draft design incorporated an immense mass of white oak to support its deck and to provide raftlike flotation under the weight of its armor. Since no seasoned white oak could be found by the last year of the war, it became common knowledge that shipbuilders had to rely on unseasoned oak stock. Theodore Allen calculated the weight of the oak deck based on the specific gravity of seasoned timber rather than the far heavier green wood used by the monitor builders. This miscalculation greatly reduced the buoyancy of a vessel that had already been reduced in power and increased in weight.[64]

The light-draft monitor contractors had to build a machine of great complexity based on only a few forms of information. Initially, Stimers's office issued only a basic midship section and vessel outline draft to the twenty contractors. His subdepartment also issued a ninety-page specification book to all the mechanics employed by the contractors, which some workers referred to as the "monitor prayer book."[65] That is all the mechanics used to begin building the warships. Throughout the construction process, Stimers made alterations to Ericsson's original plan, altering the buoyancy of the vessel in the process. In the course of the monitors' construction, Stimers's office forwarded to each contractor eighty-three different drafts of parts and perspectives and 120 letters outlining changes and alterations to nearly every part of the vessels.[66]

Defects in the light-draft monitor design had become clear in the spring of 1864, a year after contractors began building them. The situation came under Senate scrutiny, when the "Conduct of the War" committee convened to investigate such wartime cases as the Cheyenne massacre out West and the botched field campaign against the Confederates in Kentucky commanded by Union general William S. Rosecrans.[67] When the first completed light-draft monitor, the *Chimo*, slid down the ways in Boston, it nearly sank under its own weight. The *Chimo* sat in the water with only three inches of freeboard, a foot less than planned. One historian has delicately stated the case as one of "negative buoyancy."[68] All of the light-draft monitors sat dangerously low in the water, some with their decks partially submerged, and generated only enough power to propel the vessels at three knots, half the speed expected of them. The entire class proved a complete failure and cost the federal government $8 million, an incredibly large monetary loss for the time.[69]

The fault for the light-draft monitor debacle must be placed not just on Stimers and his crew, but also on the Navy Department. The Department expected too much by asking a practically trained American engineer to carry through a European design. Rather than having Ericsson oversee the production process from design through construction, the navy assigned Stimers the task. Stimers lacked the skills to manage the complexity involved in building twenty monitors. He had to oversee the operation of a large office force and construction sites spread throughout the mid-Atlantic and northeastern states. More important, he failed to recognize the effect that his numerous alterations would have on the completed monitors.

Despite his great self-confidence, Stimers conceded before the Senate committee that mistakes had been made in the construction of the light-draft monitors. Reaney, Son, and Archbold, one of the navy's contractors, attached a plaque to the light-draft monitor *Tunxis* that read that the vessel had been built from designs prepared by Stimers. Stimers took a cold chisel and proceeded to cut his name off of the plate.[70]

Once a war hero and champion of the monitors, Stimers's stature diminished rapidly, and he chose to retire from the navy after the war's conclusion. He and Theodore Allen became partners in a New York engineering consulting office for several years. In the early 1870s, they dissolved their partnership, and Stimers faded into obscurity and died of smallpox in 1876. In 1874, Allen moved to St. Louis, where he helped establish a small iron shipbuilding firm. The business continued in operation for a few years before going bankrupt. Allen worked in the field as a consultant but died at the age of fifty from a disease contracted in Texas during one of his jobs.[71] Newton went on to become a fairly successful civil engineer in New York. When the city decided to expand its water supply, it hired him to consult on the construction of the Croton Aqueduct. At the age of forty-seven, however, he went insane and took his own life.[72] Like Stimers, Allen, and Newton, the navy experienced decline after the failed light-draft monitor program. Congress refused to fund any major warship construction programs for the next twenty years.[73]

In addition to John Ericsson, fellow Swedish-born engineer John W. Nystrom suffered many frustrations trying to employ theoretical methods in an American shipbuilding world. At a time when most American shipbuilders relied on practical design methods, John W. Nystrom became a lone voice advocating theoretical ship design and the institutions necessary to support it. Nystrom was probably the most prolific writer on engineering topics in nineteenth-century America. His first significant contribution came in 1852 with *A Treatise on Screw Propellers and Their Engines, with Practical Rules and Examples to Calculate and Construct the Same for Any Description of Vessels*. This book addressed theoretical matters of mathematics, mechanical drawing, and fluid-testing techniques for hull shapes.[74] In 1854, he published the first of numerous editions of his *Pocket-Book of Mechanics and Engineering*. By far his most popular work, the *Pocket-Book* was translated into German and Japanese and proved more influential overseas than it did in the United States. Nystrom revised the eighteenth edition of this book shortly before his death in 1885.[75] In 1863, Nystrom's booklet *A Treatise on Parabolic Construction of Ships and Other Marine Engineering Subjects* became his first attempt to introduce his parabolic method of ship design to the U.S. shipbuilding industry. This work, however, failed to convince any American shipbuilders to pursue Nystrom's formulaic methods.[76] In addition to the books mentioned above, Nystrom contributed dozens of scientific and engineering articles to the *Journal of the Franklin Institute* and *Scientific American*. His other books include *A New Treatise on Steam Engineering*; *Technical Education and the Construction of Ships and Screw Propellers*; *On the French Metric System*; *A Project of a New System of Arithmetic, Weight,*

Measure, and Coins; *A New Treatise on Elements of Mechanics*; and several treatises on the subject of dynamics. Few of these works became popular with the American engineering community.[77]

During most of the nineteenth century, the use of abstract mathematics remained foreign to American shipbuilding practice. Nystrom blamed this situation on the fact that American builders had found little practical application for abstract mathematics in the design of their ships. This problem, however, he attributed not just to a lack of initiative on the part of practical builders but to the theoreticians and mathematicians who failed to point out the possible uses of, for example, calculus.[78] As Nystrom stated the problem in the introduction of his *Treatise on Parabolic Construction*: "When practical men see the poetry of the calculus, they get frightened and lay the book aside."[79] Nystrom saw the lack of abstract mathematics in the design process as a defect in American shipbuilding, but the truth was that few native shipbuilders understood calculus or, for that matter, simple algebra.[80]

Like Ericsson, Nystrom arrived in America well before the Civil War. He was born in 1824 in Atvidaberg, Sweden, received his technical training at Stockholm's Royal Technical Institute, and served three years at Sweden's largest and most respected machine shop, the Motala Engine Works. In the spring of 1847, after serving his term at Motala, Nystrom immigrated to the United States. He found employment with Richard F. Loper, who owned a majority share in the Gloucester Iron Works, of Camden, New Jersey. By 1856, Nystrom had risen to become head draftsman and superintendent of the works, which played an important part in developing screw propeller technology in the Delaware Valley. Loper had invented the popular Loper propeller, but Nystrom perfected it and made it possible to apply it to hundreds, if not thousands, of steamers, converted canal boats, barges, and sailing vessels. Nystrom was a prolific inventor, patenting several devices associated with steam engineering and marine propulsion. In 1856, he left the United States to become chief engineer of the Volga-Don Railroad and Don-Azovska Steamship Company. In December 1860, Nystrom returned to the United States and his responsibilities at the Gloucester Iron Works. He became part owner of the firm and submitted an unsuccessful bid to build an ironclad warship to the same naval board that had accepted Ericsson's proposal for the *Monitor*.[81]

Nystrom promoted the same sort of theoretical approach to shipbuilding that had gained favor in Great Britain. The debates concerning marine engineering raging between him and other engineers in the pages of the *Journal of the Franklin Institute* and the *Scientific American* testified to his orientation. While his American adversaries argued through the use of common rhetoric, Nystrom relied on mathematical proofs based on algebra and trigonometry. So while other writers concerned with marine engineering and naval architecture might explain their position using a minimum of mathematical description, abstract mathematics formed the basis for most all of the principles Nystrom promoted in the pages of scientific and technological journals.[82] Examples of Nystrom's mathematical language included his article "Stability of Vessels in Water," the first technical examination of the stability of ships published in the United States. Out of the three pages dedicated to this article, one is devoted to listing formulas, another to defining terms, and the last to working out the formulas for two different vessels.[83] In terms reminiscent of Britain's scientific shipbuilders, Nystrom claimed that when the American shipbuilding industry adopted engineering methods: "we will be able to demonstrate, record, and perpetuate through the unerring aid of mathematical formulas, a knowledge of the subject of the physical laws which relate to the subject, the accomplishment of which is now impossible."[84]

Nystrom supported the use of new tools to aid in implementing his mathematically based theoretical approach. These tools often proved necessary to compute the intricate formulations he put forward to engineer ships. Within a year of arriving in the United States, Nystrom began to promote his mathematical calculator. A metallic device that resembled a circular slide rule, Nystrom's calculator performed the simple arithmetical functions of addition, subtraction, multiplication, and division. Nystrom based the markings on the device upon logarithms, so it could also compute square roots, proportions, and trigonometric equations. In 1850, the Franklin Institute awarded Nystrom its gold medal in recognition of his calculator.[85] Nystrom was the first engineer in the United States to encourage the use of ship model basins to determine the power required to propel hulls. He did this in the pages of his 1852 work *A Treatise on Screw Propellers*, nearly a half century before most American shipbuilders realized the usefulness of experimental model basins for determining the power necessary to drive ships through water.[86] Nystrom also promoted the Amsler "planimeter," a device developed by Swiss mathematician Jakob Amsler. Nystrom became an advocate of the calculating device before it ever became a recognized tool for calculation in Europe. The planimeter resembled a drafting compass and could compute the area of most any shape drawn on a draft. Amsler also invented a calculator, called an "integrator," which greatly reduced the work necessary to carry out abstract mathematical calculations.[87]

Even though Nystrom promoted the planimeter during the Civil War, neither it nor the integrator became popular tools for American ship design until the turn of the century. It is unfortunate that American ship designers failed to realize the benefits of using the planimeter because the device drastically simplified tedious and time-consuming naval architecture problems. American ship designers avoided calculating the curves of stability for ship hulls until the late 1800s because the arithmetic involved proved far too cumbersome to be practicable. When the planimeter found wider use in the United States during the late 1890s, however, the use of abstract mathematics became more common. One naval architect familiar with the tiresome mathematical approach stated in 1907 that "Anyone that has waded through an experience of this sort can appreciate the work and headaches involved; others can thank God for Dr. Amsler."[88]

Nystrom was the first in the United States to promote a formulaic design method in the same way as iron shipbuilders in England. The purpose of developing such a formulaic approach stemmed from the desire to determine the performance of a ship before it was built. For generations, practical shipbuilders had relied on the examples of earlier vessels to design their next ship. Certain British shipbuilders had tried to alleviate the empiricism of trial and error and the custom of modeling ships on the lines of earlier vessels. This had been the driving force behind John Scott Russell's "wave-line theory." John W. Griffiths, a self-avowed practical shipbuilder, even devised a formulaic method, but it never became popular with American shipbuilders.[89]

Nystrom championed the parabolic method in several of his publications, including *The Parabolic Construction of Ships*.[90] Nystrom saw the parabolic method as a way to predict the performance of ships without recourse to trial and error or rule-of-thumb methods. He adopted a formula first proposed by eighteenth-century Swedish naval architect Fredrik Henrik af Chapman to determine the best lines for a ship. Nystrom refined the formula and developed it into a design system. He elaborated the formula into $Y = a(1-x^n/b^n)^q$ where a represents the length of the ship, and b represents the ship's midsection at the maximum breadth. The value for x represents the distance of the ordinate y from the dead flat, and the values for n and q are quantities based on the lines of previously successful vessels. Nystrom developed tables of figures to plug into n and q depending on the desire of the designer for full or fine hull lines. To aid shipbuilders in determining the best hull form, Nystrom published this formula and the necessary tables in his *Pocket Book of Mechanics and Engineering*.[91]

Like many other engineering practices and institutions Nystrom tried to introduce to American shipbuilding, the parabolic method met with a range of responses from indifference to open disparagement.[92] In a paper presented to England's Institution of Naval Architects in 1887, distinguished American mechanical engineer Robert Thurston reported that Nystrom's formula had "attracted but little attention."[93]

Nystrom had a fervent conviction that science and technologically based professional societies could promote greater understanding of physical and scientific principles. Nystrom practiced what he preached and became active in the affairs of the Franklin Institute as soon as he arrived in the United States. After residing a year in Philadelphia, he exhibited his novel calculating machine before members of the Institute. By 1851, he contributed the first of dozens of articles he wrote for the Institute's *Journal*. Nystrom also served on special committees formed by the Institute to investigate inventions and new technological developments. It is quite possible that Nystrom was attracted to Philadelphia in the first place because of the existence of the Franklin Institute in that city.[94]

Nystrom hoped to form an institution able to promote engineering education, and he made this desire clear in many of his publications.[95] He hoped that the federal government would fund a full-blown technological institute that would educate engineers and decide technological matters of great importance to the nation. In the spring of 1863, he made a presentation to the membership of the Franklin Institute concerning the benefits of a "National Technological Institute," in which he exhibited some of the tools and devices he had made while a student at the Royal Technological Institute in Stockholm. He reinforced his message by contributing an article to the *Journal* promoting a "National Technological Institute" that held strong similarities to those found in Europe and the benefits such an educational institution would provide students of engineering.[96]

Whether out of a sense of patriotism or a desire to boost his career opportunities, Nystrom tendered his services as an engineer to the Department of the Navy early in July 1864. He may have enlisted out of a sense of patriotism, for his Gloucester Iron Works could have been quite busy and profitable during the war. As later events indicate, Nystrom probably felt that from a position within the federal government he stood a better chance of reforming the way Americans designed and built their ships. By the end of July, he had received a communication from the Navy Department appointing him an acting assistant engineer in the Bureau of Steam Engineering. By early February 1865, Nystrom had already submitted his resignation to the Department citing the low pay and high cost of living in Washington. The navy apparently declined his resignation, for by July 1865, Nystrom was still in the navy and had been elevated to the post of acting chief engineer.[97]

During his term at the Navy Department, Nystrom made a theoretical study of human power. His articles on the "Elements of Physical Work" stand as an attempt to quantify work similar to the studies conducted by leaders of the "scientific management" movement fifty years later. Nystrom set as his goal the determination of the amount of energy consumed by an average worker in an eleven-hour day, a unit of energy he referred to as a "workmanday."[98] According to Nystrom, the workmanday equaled about 1,980,000 foot pounds in terms of time and space and would be useful in estimating the amount of human work necessary to build "a house, steamboat, or a bridge, digging a canal, ploughing the ground, steam-boiler and gunpowder explosions, the capacity of heavy ordnance, &c, &c."[99]

Nystrom finally resigned from the navy in the summer of 1865. He may have done so for a variety of reasons. First, the war had ended in the spring, precluding any need for him to render his services to his adopted country during a state of war. Second, since he had arrived in the United States he had participated in a running debate with the navy's engineer-in-chief, Benjamin F. Isherwood, over the theoretical principles of steam power and marine engineering. Published in the pages of technical journals such as the *Journal of the Franklin Institute* and the *Scientific American*, the debate became personal at times and may have proved an irritant during Nystrom's term of duty under Isherwood.[100] Nystrom also met with a great deal of disappointment during his service in the navy. In his resignation, he mentioned that he had "failed in bringing my attainments and qualifications to the notice and due appreciation of the Department" and that his duties were limited to "questions of simple arithmetic, which could be performed by a school boy."[101]

Nystrom met with many frustrations in the navy. He pleaded with the Department to institute his parabolic method for building ships, which the Department rejected. He insisted that naval engineers should be trained to take on the responsibilities of naval constructors and that he could teach them to do so. The Department also denied this request. In these requests, Assistant Secretary of the Navy Gustavus V. Fox explained to Nystrom that democratic governments failed to function as did monarchical ones such as Nystrom's native Sweden. In the Old World, the state supported the sort of institutions that fostered the growth of engineering practices, while in the United States such things had to come from the private sector.[102]

After resigning from the navy, Nystrom returned to work in Philadelphia. Like other firms involved in Civil War production, the Gloucester Iron Works went bankrupt. By 1866, Nystrom may have fallen on hard financial times for he found work in Peru, investigating the natural resources of the country for the Peruvian government. He studied the possibilities of mining in Cuzco and Chanchamayo and the potential for building new roads and waterways to access those minerals. He produced three publications based on his work, which he had translated into Spanish.

By 1872, Nystrom had returned to Philadelphia, where he remained the rest of his life. He worked closely with the City of Philadelphia to improve its water supply problems.[103] During the 1870s, Nystrom pushed for a national technological institute, but the federal government expressed little interest in the prospect. Frustrated by the reception of his proposal, Nystrom called on the Franklin Institute to provide the facilities for a technical school to train engineers and mechanics. In 1874, after presenting a paper entitled the "Progress and Future of the Franklin Institute," Nystrom offered a resolution that a committee be appointed to study the feasibility of turning the Institute "into an organization analogous to the South Kensington Museum in London, i.e., with a technical school for the thorough training of mechanics and others in various branches of the useful arts, and exhibitions of arts and manufactures at stated periods."[104] Nystrom's resolution was passed by the membership; however, the Franklin Institute never became the sort of national technological institute that Nystrom had envisioned.

Nystrom died in 1885 after struggling most of his professional life to introduce new methods and institutions to American industry. After his resignation from the navy, he wrote that the "prejudice against science is, in our day, a very serious evil."[105] Nystrom could see the forces supporting the practical approach opposing most all of the improvements that he had tried to foster. The debate over introducing the French metric system held at the Franklin Institute characterized the sort of resistance that Nystrom saw occurring throughout American science and industry. Nystrom recounted that at the April 1876 meeting of the Franklin Institute, "it was remarked that the majority report was *practical*, and the minority report *theoretical*." Nystrom went on to write: "The terms *practical* and *theoretical* are promiscuously used at the Institute, as a means of support to sciolism and perversion of the truth."[106] Nystrom never lived to see the introduction of a theoretical approach to American shipbuilding, but it would occur before the close of the nineteenth century.

The introduction of iron to the British shipbuilding industry had ushered in the institutions of engineering; however, in the United States, practical builders resisted their intrusion of this professionalism into the shipbuilding process. Practical builders like New York's David Brown believed that "naval architects have done all they could to mystify the theory of shipbuilding; subjects that are plain have been rendered intricate."[107] Shipbuilder and writer John W. Griffiths answered theorists like Nystrom that "Algebraic reasoning possesses no royal charter for the solution of rules, in the absence of salient facts." According to Griffiths:

> successful ship building is not secured by methods theoretically developed. This has been the bane of other nations in all the past. The world is theorized to the death in regard to ships. Papers are read up on every division of nautical engineering before juries of professors, who have never learned the first rudiments of practical science as they were applied in the ship yards of this nation.[108]

The iron shipbuilding industry's products never grew so immense that practical methods did not prove adequate to manufacture them. Even after the Civil War, the size of ships had not reached the point of complexity or scale that most practical methods would not suffice to design or build them. Both military and civilian vessels found in the United States during the nineteenth century were tiny in comparison to the seagoing vessels of today. For example, the *City of Paris* and *City of Tokio*, the largest American steamers built as of 1875, measured only 5,000 tons compared with the hundreds of thousands of tons of today's ships.[109]

Profitability and political expedience went hand-in-hand with cultural attitudes toward theoretical methods. Everywhere John Nystrom attempted to improve engineering methods, he met with resistance. Discouraged, he wrote in 1866 that "The efforts of a single individual . . . only result in perpetual and unprofitable struggles with organized interests and prejudices, and fail of their purpose through the misconceptions which are inseparable from new and original subjects."[110] Nystrom fought with federal authorities to finance a technological institute, but Congress found such a proposal frivolous. When Nystrom pleaded for some sort of instruction for naval engineers in theoretical shipbuilding, the secretary of the navy responded that it was not incumbent upon the navy to fund such things. During his service in that branch of the military, Nystrom complained that "Common arithmetic applied to dollars and cents, is all the mathematics necessary in politics, and as long as science and knowledge, are to be ruled by our present system of politics, we can expect no improvement."[111]

Nystrom and Ericsson blazed the trail for another generation of immigrant engineers. By the time both Nystrom and Ericsson had died, in the late 1880s, the flow of other Europeans increased as many crossed the Atlantic to see what the expanding American industry could teach them. They worked in an atmosphere of rapid technological change, which came too late for Nystrom to enjoy. The practical technological style of American shipbuilding, observed for centuries, survived as long as did Ericsson and Nystrom.

The irony of losing millions of dollars on poorly designed warships—funds that could have been spent to train naval engineers to build such vessels—did not escape John Nystrom. In 1866, he wrote that "the failure of the light-draft monitors affords a still stronger proof of the necessity of instructing engineers in shipbuilding."[112]

John Nystrom fought to alter the American way of designing and building ships. In a matter of years, he tried to change a practical shipbuilding tradition that had been gradually evolving for centuries. Nystrom wrote books and developed theories, but his campaign to reform American shipbuilding failed. His unceasing efforts failed to overcome a highly entrenched practical tradition, so his life's work became a footnote in the history of American shipbuilding. This man whose accomplishments should rank him as one of the preeminent experimental engineers in nineteenth-century America may not be found in any of the biographical encyclopedias such as the *Dictionary of American Biography*.

7

An American Naval Renaissance and the Introduction of Theoretical Ship Design to the United States

> *It is now thought, practically, more important for a naval officer to know how to build a gun, to design a ship, to understand the strength of materials, to observe the stars through a telescope, [and] to be wise in chemistry and electricity, than to have ingrained in him the knowledge of the laws of war, to understand the tactical handling of his weapons, to be expert in questions of naval policy, strategy, and tactics.*
>
> Captain Alfred T. Mahan, 1889

In November 1888, Captain Mahan sat down to write this letter to the *United States Naval Institute Proceedings*.[1] As president of the Naval War College, Mahan was acutely aware of the rapid technological changes taking place in the U.S. Navy. His cynical remarks indicate how naval personnel had changed with the times. The background and training of American naval officers became increasingly technical during the post–Civil War period as the U.S. Navy became more technologically sophisticated.[2]

Beginning in the 1870s, technically inclined officers and naval engineers began the process of converting warship design methods based on practical experience into an occupational system founded upon academics, applied science, experimentation, publication, and professional societies. While conservative officers from the Civil War generation resisted modernization, the postwar generation of naval officers brought to the United States the socio-technical system of theoretical shipbuilding, which the British began developing late in the eighteenth century.[3] The rejuvenation of the navy, which began during the early 1870s, fueled the acquisition of foreign technology and elevated the navy to a position of world prominence. The navy's transfer of shipbuilding technology to the United States not only changed the way American warships were designed and built, it converted the nation's shipbuilding industry from a practical style to a theoretical one.

The U.S. Navy's nineteenth-century renaissance rose from the ashes of the post–Civil War era. The period between the Civil War and 1880 represents what Robert G. Albion characterized as the navy's "Dark Ages," and other historians have referred to as the "days of our humiliation," "doldrums," and "dark years."[4] In the aftermath of the Civil War, the United States failed to remain a leading innovator of naval technology because saving money became Congress's most pressing concern. During the late 1860s and 1870s, the navy scrapped, sold, or mothballed many of its wartime fleet of 650 vessels. The navy lost the technological edge it once held over other naval powers in warship design and construction.[5] While European naval powers spent millions on costly iron warships, Congress cut the navy's budget. In the twenty years following the Civil War, the United States spent less than $5 million for new naval construction, while France, Great Britain, and Russia spent $121 million, $91 million, and $84 million, respectively.[6] Even the editors of the British journal *Engineer* acknowledged this state of affairs in 1883, stating that: "They [Americans] have practically no fleet, and are really, and to a very large extent, at the mercy of any third-rate naval Power. A couple of small ironclads could do frightful damage to the leading seaport towns of the country, as, for example, New York."[7]

One historian has pointed out that nations with a mastery of science and citizens of inventive genius tend to dominate those nations lacking such qualities.[8] The United States had these necessary ingredients but failed to capitalize on them in the field of naval technology. Some historians have argued that the 1870s was a period of material progress for the navy, but American naval technology enjoyed little progress during this period.[9] Innovation in American weaponry that did take place found its way to foreign nations seeking naval supremacy. For example, ordnance innovator Benjamin Hotchkiss established his first weapons factory in France after the navy rejected his rapid-fire cannon, while USS *Monitor* designer John Ericsson turned to European markets when the United States' postwar naval budgets began to shrink.[10]

During the 1870s and early 1880s, the navy deteriorated into an obsolete and dilapidated fleet. During 1874 naval maneuvers off of Key West, the "United Fleets" of the navy could maintain a maximum speed of only four-and-a-half knots. Commodore Foxhall Parker, overall commander of the fleet, asked, "what could be more lamentable . . . than to see a fleet armed with smoothbore guns, requiring close quarters for their development, moving at the rate of four and a half knots an hour?"[11] Before returning from the southern tip of Africa in 1877, the commander of the USS *Yantic* shipped home his gunboat's cannon because of the vessel's poor seaworthiness. By 1880, the navy maintained a fleet of 142 vessels on the books, but tugboats and old sailing vessels comprised 50 of their number.[12] The news media highlighted American naval weakness in the early 1880s by reporting on the collision of a runaway coal barge with the USS *Tallapoosa*, and the consequent sinking of the warship. In 1884, a 100-pound Civil War cannon exploded onboard the USS *Standish*, prompting the *New York Times* to report that the navy operated "vessels and guns capable of doing injury to an enemy in case they are captured."[13] In 1885, Captain Mahan referred to the fleet as a "Quaker Navy" because it reminded him of the "Quaker guns" that the Union navy improvised on undergunned warships during the Civil War by blackening wooden cylinders shaped like cannon.[14] By 1886, the House Naval Affairs Committee conceded that the navy had become weaker than the navies of any of the European powers, as well as those of Brazil, Argentina, and Chile.[15]

At the same time that the navy experienced the greatest decline in its history, political, economic, and technological changes in Europe gave rise to volatile international relations. European imperialism and a nascent European arms race increased diplomatic tensions in the Western Hemisphere and the Pacific. During the Civil War, France's failed puppet state in Mexico demonstrated that nation's designs on Central America. When famed builder of the Suez Canal Count Ferdinand de Lesseps formed the Inter Oceanic Canal Company in France and began digging a canal in Panama in 1881, it only served to confirm these designs in American minds. Germany expanded its colonial empire through acquisitions in the Western Hemisphere and the Pacific. Relations between the United States and Great Britain had remained strained for years after the Civil War due to British support of the French experiment in Mexico, complicity in the depredations on Union shipping by the Confederate raider *Alabama*, and postwar competition with the United States for naval dominance in the Pacific. In 1873, Spain and the United States nearly came to blows over the Cuban Revolution then underway. Spanish authorities in Cuba captured the gun-runner *Virginius*, which had been flying an American flag, and executed several American crewmen as pirates. Rather than risk hostilities, however, the two countries resorted to diplomacy and negotiation. Americans grew anxious about the threat posed by these events and various perceived violations of the Monroe Doctrine, as well as powerful foreign navies that could annihilate the entire American fleet in one encounter. Because of American naval weakness, public opinion began to swing behind strengthening the fleet.[16]

There was turbulence in the ranks of America's naval officer corps during the Dark Ages. The decline of the fleet following the Civil War decreased the possibility of promotion. As the number of seaworthy naval vessels shrank, the number of billets available to officers fell off dramatically. This promotion bottleneck forced many to resign their commissions and seek better prospects in the private sector. Those who could not afford to resign remained in the service as lieutenants and lower ranks despite their advancing years.

Before the 1870s, the navy's engineers and naval constructors had often taken on the trade of their fathers and learned their occupation through civilian work experience. A study of the records for the engineers-in-chief who headed the Bureau of Steam Engineering throughout the nineteenth century shows that none of them graduated from the Naval Academy. Naval engineers such as John A. Tobin worked their way into the corps after completing high school and apprenticing in a machine shop.[17] Benjamin Franklin Isherwood, chief of the navy's Bureau of Steam Engineering during the Civil War, proved an exception in that he received his education at the Albany Academy in New York under distinguished scientist Joseph Henry. After private school, Isherwood went on to serve an apprenticeship at a railroad machine shop like many other aspiring naval engineers.[18]

Naval constructors had typically taken up the trade of their shipwright fathers and received a commission after achieving some prowess in civilian shipyards as a shipwright or after apprenticing at a navy yard and rising through the ranks of navy yard mechanics. All the chief constructors of the Bureau of Construction and Repair had received this sort of training throughout the nineteenth century. Chief constructor Theodore D. Wilson had a typical background. Born into a shipbuilding family in Brooklyn, Wilson attended the local public schools and served an apprenticeship at the Brooklyn Navy Yard before becoming a naval constructor.[19] In his report to the secretary of the navy in 1881, Admiral David D. Porter explained that "We have some excellent constructors, but I am not aware that any of them lay claim to high mathematical and scientific ability, or a knowledge of those nice calculations which enter into the construction of the great war vessels."[20]

During the navy's Dark Ages, a new intellectual tradition rose phoenix-like from the remnants of America's once-proud navy. Despite the deterioration outwardly manifested by the fleet, the period following the Civil War became one of intellectual ferment for the navy. For example, changes in the how warships were designed, powered, and operated caused a rift between conservative personnel trained during the age of sail and the postwar generation of officers referred to by one naval historian as "Young Turks." These young officers supported technological and institutional change within the navy to promote their future career prospects.[21]

Meanwhile, the navy began a long-term campaign to reform itself from within by studying overseas shipbuilding technology and methods. It sent naval personnel on intelligence-gathering tours, assigned a permanent naval attaché to the embassy in London, posted naval cadets to foreign postgraduate education in naval architecture, and, in other ways, acquired foreign technology and technical know-how. This conscious, but unsystematic, effort to acquire foreign technology led to the establishment of institutions necessary to build a modern navy. In 1891, English naval architect Sir William H. White explained that the Americans "had been for years acquiring the most detailed information as to what was being done in Europe. They analysed these facts in the manner which might have been expected from their great ability and shrewdness."[22] Depending on which way the political winds blew, this campaign often had the support of the executive branch and Congress. More important, however, it had the full support of naval engineers and young officers who saw naval development as a way to improve their career prospects through fleet modernization, overseas expansion, and greater international prestige.[23]

As with other American occupational groups, naval personnel began to organize into specialized associations after the Civil War. Naval personnel founded two influential societies that aided in the development of the navy and naval technology. Formed at Annapolis in 1873, the United States Naval Institute became the first such association. Captain Stephen B. Luce and a group of fellow officers established the Institute to provide "a medium for the free interchange of serious thought and the debate of important subjects concerning naval science and practice."[24] In 1880, active and retired naval engineers such as George Westinghouse and Robert H. Thurston helped establish the American Society of Mechanical Engineers.[25]

Late nineteenth-century naval development encouraged officers and engineers to begin a dialogue on technical subjects through professional journals and popular magazines. The founding of the United States Naval Institute resulted in the publication of the *Proceedings* in 1874. The number of articles concerning inventions and new designs published in the *Proceedings* reflected the surge of interest in modern naval technology.[26] In 1879, retired naval officer Lewis B. Hamersly established the *United Service* to promote military reform, and it often included articles of a technical nature, including such titles as "Education of Naval Constructors," "The Interior Lighting of Steamers," and "The Most Efficient Battery for a Despatch-Boat."[27] Officers and naval engineers also began to write articles for the *United States Army and Navy Journal, Harper's Magazine, North American Review*, and *Scribner's Magazine*. These writers publicized the obsolescence of American naval policy and the fleet and recent advances in overseas naval technology.

To support early naval modernization, the navy sent specially qualified officers and engineers to observe developments taking place in Europe during the 1870s and early 1880s. Some civilian shipbuilders had made pilgrimages to Europe to observe design and construction methods, but none of their intelligence-gathering trips measured up to the navy's fact-finding missions.[28] The first significant trip took place in 1870, when naval constructor Theodore D. Wilson toured European dockyards. In 1873, the Navy Department first published a report compiled from an overseas assignment in a two-volume study by Commander Edward Simpson on European naval ordnance. After an 1876 inspection of foreign fleets, naval engineer James W. King submitted a report and later published it as *The Warship and Navies of the World, 1880*. From 1878 to 1879, James Russell Soley, professor at the Naval Academy and later assistant secretary of the navy, observed European naval schools to compile his multivolume *Report on Foreign Systems of Naval Education*. During the early 1880s, naval personnel also wrote such studies as naval engineer John A. Tobin's "Improvements in Naval Engineering in Great Britain" and naval constructor Philip Hichborn's "Report on European Dock-Yards."[29] These knowledgeable officers and engineers continued to play an important role in American naval development for years to come.

While these engineers played an important role in the Navy's intellectual renaissance, an important movement to provide greater technical background for officers and engineers took place at the United States Naval Academy. The Academy began to produce cadets of great distinction in science and engineering during the late 1860s. Referred to by one historian as the "Scholarly Warrior," French Ensor Chadwick (class of '64) went on to become the first, and for many years the only, naval attaché assigned to gather European naval intelligence for the Navy Department.[30] Between 1879 and 1881, explorer George Washington De Long ('65) undertook an Arctic expedition to investigate the territory north of the Bering Strait and contribute to mankind's knowledge of that inaccessible region. America's first Nobel laureate and the nation's leading physicist of the nineteenth century, Albert A. Michelson ('73), became an instructor at the Academy, conducting important experiments with light refraction and calculating the speed of light. Bradley A. Fiske, an 1874 graduate, published his important *Electricity in Theory and Practice* in 1883. By that time, Frank J. Sprague ('79) had achieved national recognition as one of the world's pioneers in electricity and had resigned from the navy to work with Thomas Edison. He developed the elevator, electrical appliances, control devices, and signals, many of which Edison branded with his name. Sprague became most famous for developing the electric trolley.[31]

Beginning in the 1860s, the Academy took responsibility for training commissioned personnel in the fields of designing and building the nation's warships. From that point on, Academy graduates took an active role in converting the old methods of shipbuilding, based on practical methods, into a socio-technical system founded upon such institutions as formal education, applied science, experimentation, publication, and professional organizations. The Annual Report of the Secretary of the Navy for 1863 included a section written by Assistant Navy Secretary Gustavus Vasa Fox recommending special education for naval engineers and naval constructors at the Academy. Congress approved the separation of the midshipmen into "cadet midshipmen" and "cadet engineers," and President Lincoln signed the congressional act into law on July 4, 1864.[32] Separation of the cadets into two factions caused trouble later when cadet midshipmen discriminated against cadet engineers, whom they derisively termed "greasers." On the other hand, the cadet engineers became proud members of the program, posing for group pictures after donning their coaling clothes and smearing their faces with coal dust.[33]

The cadet engineer program met with mixed results in the late 1860s and early 1870s. Attempts to recruit cadets with practical experience fared poorly. In 1866, the Academy began recruiting cadet engineering candidates from schools such as Harvard and Rensselaer Polytechnic Institute. The navy found these men to be too well educated and overaged to become cadets and promoted them directly into the engineering corps. The program remained something of an experiment, and an unsuccessful one at that, until 1871, when chief of the Bureau of Steam Engineering James King urged Navy Secretary George M. Robeson to adopt new regulations to rejuvenate the program. These new standards received the approval of the secretary as well as academy superintendent, and *Monitor* hero Rear Admiral John L. Worden. Congress passed the new guidelines in 1874, changing the length of the program from two years to four and setting age limits for entrance.[34]

Admission to the cadet engineering program demanded greater skill in academics than practical skill in steam engineering. The circular disseminated for the competitive examinations stated that "Candidates who possess the greatest skill and experience in the practical knowledge of machinery, other qualifications being equal, will have precedence for admission."[35] In all other respects, however, admission to the cadet engineering program favored well-to-do and well-educated candidates at the expense of the sort of practical mechanics who had comprised the naval engineering corps through the Civil War. The examinations covered such subjects as algebra, plane geometry, writing, spelling, English grammar and composition, geography, and the principles of steam power. They became so competitive that any candidate who had wasted time acquiring practical knowledge of machinery had little chance of gaining entrance. After the mid-1870s, few members of the entering classes of cadet engineers had any practical experience with steam machinery. This rigorous battery of tests served to pass only scholars, often college graduates, who had a mastery of the examination topics.[36]

The course of instruction for the cadet engineers stressed technical subjects, rather than topics necessary to command a ship. During the first year, the cadet engineers took the same courses as the cadet midshipmen, although they also received practical training in use of tools and marine engine operation. The Academy also provided the cadet engineers and cadet midshipmen with the same basic training in hard sciences, mathematics, shipbuilding, and naval architecture. As the cadet engineers progressed through their four-year term, however, their studies focused increasingly on steam engineering. By his fourth year, a cadet engineer had received formal instruction in mechanics, marine engines, fabrication and design of machinery, mechanical drawing, and physical measurements, in conjunction with training in tool use and marine engineering.[37]

The summer "inspection trip" further distinguished the cadet engineers from the cadet midshipmen and became an integral part of the cadet-engineer experience.[38] In 1872, the Academy began to send the cadet engineers on an extended tour of East Coast industrial establishments onboard iron-hulled steamers, such as the USS *Alert* or the tugboat USS *Mayflower*. Cadet midshipmen continued to make summer cruises onboard a sailing vessel. The cadet engineers' tour included shipyards and marine engine–building firms at the navy yards and privately owned plants in Boston; New York; Philadelphia; Chester, Pennsylvania; and Wilmington, Delaware. They participated in the operation of the steamer and kept detailed notes and sketches of the field trips, which their instructors inspected and graded. The annual reports of these inspection trips provide interesting accounts of the cadet-engineer experience during the 1870s.[39] The institution of inspection trips ended in 1882, when an act of Congress phased out the separate ranks of cadet engineer and cadet midshipman in favor of a standard technically trained "naval cadet" rank.[40]

The cadet engineering program nurtured some of the navy's most distinguished naval engineers, such as admirals Robert S. Griffin, Gustave Kaemmerling, and Charles W. Dyson. Other cadet engineers left the service to pursue influential careers in the private sector, including Asa M. Mattice, who later became chief engineer of Allis-Chalmers; Walter M. McFarland, who became vice president of Westinghouse and later headed the marine department of the Babcock and Wilcox Company; and William L. R. Emmet, who joined General Electric and played a critical role in developing the Curtis steam turbine and electric ship propulsion.[41]

During the late nineteenth century, the nation's industry became so highly mechanized that the federal government detailed its naval engineers to teach at American universities. The navy sent cadet engineers into the academic world to help spread technical knowledge of marine engineering throughout the nation's colleges and universities. In 1879, Congress authorized the Navy Department to assign naval engineers to teach, and it billeted them to such schools as the University of Pennsylvania, Cornell, Vanderbilt, Purdue, Johns Hopkins, and all the leading land-grant institutions. Of the forty-three naval engineers so assigned, all but five had come through the cadet engineer program. This number included 1874 class members such as Harry W. Spangler of the University of Pennsylvania; Ira N. Hollis of Harvard University, and later president of Worcester Polytechnic Institute; and Mortimer E. Cooley of the University of Michigan, who later served twenty-five years as that school's dean of engineering and architecture. In 1896, the government would finally curtail the practice of billeting engineers to colleges and universities.[42]

William F. Durand, from the class of 1880, became one of the most celebrated engineering educators produced by the cadet engineering program. The navy detailed Durand to teach at Lafayette College as well as Worcester Polytechnic Institute before he resigned in 1887 to teach engineering at Michigan State. In 1891, Durand left Michigan State to teach in a new engineering program at Cornell University then under the leadership of distinguished engineering educator and former naval engineer Robert Thurston. In 1904, after Thurston's death, Durand left Cornell to teach at Stanford University. During the next twenty years, Durand became one of the nation's highest authorities in marine engineering and aeronautics. Referred to by some engineers as the "Dean of American Engineering," Durand received honorary degrees from Lafayette College and the University of California and received a Guggenheim Medal for notable achievement.[43]

In the 1870s, the Naval Academy not only began to look toward naval engineering as a career track for its officers but to warship construction as well. The chiefs of the Bureau of Construction and Repair during the post–Civil War period had urged the Navy Department to provide better education for their corps.[44] In 1869, Commander Richard W. Meade III wrote *A Treatise on Naval Architecture and Ship-Building,* the first textbook designed specifically to supply a manual for the Academy's course on shipbuilding. Meade made a creditable first attempt to fill the need for a textbook on shipbuilding for cadets.[45]

In 1878, the Academy transferred the one-semester elective course on naval architecture from the Department of Seamanship to the Department of Mechanics and Applied Mechanics. This act proved characteristic of the navy's departure from practical shipbuilding methods to more theoretical practices.[46] That same year, naval constructor Theodore Wilson's *An Outline of Ship Building, Theoretical and Practical,* which comprised the lectures he presented as the shipbuilding instructor at the Academy, supplanted Meade's ten-year-old textbook. Neither Wilson nor Meade could write authoritatively on theoretical shipbuilding methods, so they both borrowed heavily from the published works of British marine engineers and naval architects such as William Fairbairn, William J. M. Rankine, Edward J. Reed, and John Scott Russell. Nevertheless, Wilson's book remained the Academy's textbook for years.[47]

To train future naval constructors in the latest methods, the Navy Department began to send technically inclined Academy graduates, such as the cadet engineers, overseas for postgraduate education. In 1877, the Board of Visitors—a committee of civilian experts charged with making an annual examination of the Naval Academy—suggested sending cadets of high standing to "the schools and establishments of engineering and naval architecture of Great Britain, where, in our opinion, are to be found the best establishments of that kind."[48] By 1880, the Academy began to send the graduates with the top academic ranking in their class to overseas naval architecture programs. Because of their rigorous academic background, cadet engineers tended to hold the highest academic standing in their respective classes, but cadet midshipmen occasionally achieved the top slots as well.[49] For that reason, cadet engineers usually, but not invariably, received the postgraduate training in naval architecture during the existence of the cadet engineering program. The navy sent graduates to the Royal Naval College in Greenwich, England, but it sent later students to the École Politechnique in Paris and the University of Glasgow.[50]

In addition to producing some of the navy's most distinguished engineers, the cadet engineering program also produced some of the navy's greatest naval constructors. For example, David W. Taylor came through the cadet engineering program. A farm boy from Louisa County, Virginia, Taylor entered Randolph-Macon College at age thirteen. Four years later, he entered the Academy and graduated at the head of his class in 1885. He attended

Figure 16. British Royal Naval constructor William H. White mentored many of America's best and brightest naval constructors prior to the U.S. Navy's rebirth. Manning, *The Life of Sir William White* (New York, 1923).

the Royal Naval College in Greenwich, England, from that year until 1888, graduating with the highest honors of any student up to that time. Through his experiments in marine propulsion and hull resistance, he became a pioneer of modern hull design. Between 1914 and 1922, he served as chief of the Bureau of Construction and Repair, supervising the construction of over one thousand warships and the development of America's early submarine and aeronautical development.[51]

The first naval constructor trainees sent overseas came under the tutelage of William H. White, lecturer on naval design at the Royal School of Naval Architecture and Marine Engineering. If anyone deserves credit for rebuilding the U.S. Navy, it would be White. His program not only produced distinguished naval constructors such as D. W. Taylor, but it also trained American yacht designer William Gardner and several naval architecture instructors who taught still more Americans. In 1876, White graduated Peter Jenkins, the second naval architect appointed to serve in the John Elder Professorship of Naval Architecture at the University of Glasgow.[52] William White's program also produced Danish naval constructor G. William Hovgaard. A classmate of Taylor's, Hovgaard graduated in 1886 and received the appointment as professor of naval design and construction at the Massachusetts Institute of Technology in October 1901. Hovgaard started directing MIT's warship design program after the Royal Naval College closed its program to foreigners and the Naval Academy began sending their naval constructor trainees to MIT for postgraduate naval architecture education.[53]

Sir John Harvard Biles proved to be the most prolific teacher of all of White's naval architecture students. He graduated from White's program in 1875 and assumed Glasgow's John Elder Professorship in 1891. He continued in this capacity for thirty years, combining his lecturing responsibilities with the work of designing vessels for shipbuilding firms. Biles proved just as popular with his American students as had White with his, and the pages of more than one American student's autobiography are graced with fond memories acquired while studying with Biles. Biles taught naval constructors such as Richard M. Watt, later head of the Bureau of Construction and Repair, and Homer L. Ferguson, who became the long-time head of the Newport News Shipbuilding Company. He also taught Holden A. Evans, who introduced scientific management to the navy and later headed Bethlehem Steel's immense shipbuilding operation at Sparrow's Point, near Baltimore. Biles taught distinguished American yacht designers Clinton H. Crane and C. Sherman Hoyt. He also instructed a third generation of naval architecture instructors, including professor Herbert C. Sadler, long-time naval architecture professor at the University of Michigan; naval constructor Lawrence Y. Spear, who headed the Naval Academy's short-lived warship design program in the late 1890s; and W. Selkirk Owen, who taught naval architecture at the Webb Institute of Naval Architecture.[54]

American naval constructors sent overseas returned home to influence the way ships were designed and built in the United States. In 1879, the first two Academy graduates sailed to England for postgraduate training. By 1885, the navy had sent eight cadets overseas to pursue naval architecture studies at Glasgow and Greenwich. Three of them, F. T. Bowles, Washington Capps, and David W. Taylor, would become admirals and fill the post of chief constructor of the navy. A fourth member of the group, Lewis Nixon, resigned his commission and became head of the Crescent Shipyard. In 1902 he became president of the United States Shipbuilding Company, the nation's largest shipbuilding concern at that time. Many more influential naval constructors would graduate from overseas naval architecture programs during the 1890s.[55]

The 1870s heralded the coming of naval modernization, but rebuilding the navy began in earnest in the 1880s. Congress authorized the construction of 150,000 tons of steel warships between 1880 and 1890. This represents a marked increase when compared with the construction total of less than 30,000 tons of wooden and iron warships built between 1870 and 1880.[56] These statistics indicate the dramatic shift naval modernization experienced during the decade. This rapid development would have been impossible had the navy not begun transferring to the United States a new way to design and build warships.

Navy Secretary William H. Hunt, who served from March 1881 to April 1882, contributed greatly to the modernization of the navy. His founding the Office of Naval Intelligence (ONI) marked the 1880s as a pivotal decade in American naval development. Shortly before leaving office in 1882, Hunt authorized the establishment of ONI under the Bureau of Navigation. ONI assigned Lieutenant Commander French E. Chadwick to England as its first attaché. Born in Morgantown, Virginia (later West Virginia), in 1844, Chadwick entered the Naval Academy in the first year of the Civil War and graduated in 1864. Beginning in 1870, he served as mathematics instructor at the Academy, and, in 1878, the Navy Department sent him to Europe to compile a report for the Bureau of Equipment and Recruiting entitled "Report on the Training Systems for the Navy and Mercantile Marine of England, and on the Naval Training System of France."[57]

Chadwick's responsibilities forced him to serve a dual role. He had to serve as a naval engineer as well as an officer in making detailed sketches of naval technology, inspecting ships and machinery, and assessing the monetary and technological value of information collected from sources in Britain, France, and Germany. He worked in conjunction with American naval constructors in school in Europe, who had close contact with foreign shipbuilders and warship designers within the Admiralty.[58] Chadwick also exhibited great persistence in gathering numerous drawings, reports, specifications, copies of patents, plans and photographs of ships, and so on. He sent home material items, including "sextants, spyglasses, sounding machine dials, magnetic instruments, and maps of various areas; . . . shells, and guns; models of various kinds for display at the United States Naval Academy; and halyards, clinometers, steel castings, signal lanterns, anchors, volt and ampere meters, and binnacles."[59] A letter written by William White in 1883 reflects Chadwick's aggressive nature. Sir William chided Chadwick for requesting copies of plans for foreign warships then under construction in British shipyards and declined the request on the grounds of confidentiality.[60]

The Office of Naval Intelligence gave ambitious young officers such as Chadwick a unique opportunity to witness the technological development of foreign navies. The U.S. Navy desperately needed information on naval technology from overseas, and naval attachés ensured its steady flow to Washington. This information applied to more than just technology, enabling the navy to keep informed of the latest advances associated with personnel, medicine, administration, foreign naval operations and other matters. The importance of Chadwick's service during his tenure at ONI proved of inestimable value to the navy because it came at possibly the most critical stage in the history of American naval development. Reflecting the vital importance of intelligence gathering and Chadwick's ability as an attaché, the Senate confirmed his assignment six successive years, a record that still stands.[61]

Formed by Secretary Hunt at the urging of a senior officer eager to rejuvenate the navy, the 1882 Naval Advisory Board set in motion a process that eventually led to the retooling of American navy yards from wood shipbuilding to steel, the emergence of a naval-industrial complex, and the construction of a fleet of steel warships called the "New Navy."[62] To aid this board in their deliberations, the navy detached passed assistant engineer John Tobin from duty at the Portsmouth Navy Yard in 1882 "to procure plans and specifications of the latest war ships [sic], including hulls, armament, machinery, &c., for the information of the Naval Advisory Board."[63] With the aid of United States Consul Bret Harte, Tobin toured the works of the world-famous Clyde shipbuilders, inspected the leading steel and armor plating works in Sheffield, visited the naval dockyards in London, and spent a few weeks attending Glasgow's Naval and Marine Engineering Exhibition. The federal government compiled and published Tobin's report for public consumption.[64]

The deliberations of the Naval Advisory Board produced two conflicting reports. The board was dominated by young officers such as Lieutenant M.R.S. Mackenzie, who first suggested the use of steel for naval construction, and Commander Robley D. Evans, who had personally experimented with steel to determine its properties. It also included ordnance expert Lieutenant Edward W. Very, who had recently won the gold medal in the United States Naval Institute's essay competition for his paper "The Type of (I) Armored Vessel, (II) Cruiser, Best Suited to the Present Needs of the United States."[65] The board's majority report urged the construction of steel warships as a part of an ambitious naval-production program. Filed by practical naval constructors Theodore Wilson, John Lenthall, and Philip Hichborn, and naval engineer Benjamin Isherwood, the minority report urged the construction of ironclad warships and objected to the introduction of steel in warship production.[66]

Congress agreed with the majority report and, under the Act of March 3, 1883, authorized $1,300,000 for the construction of America's first modern warships. Because the navy christened the vessels *Atlanta, Boston, Chicago,* and *Dolphin*, this group became known as the "ABCD Warships." The ABCD Warship Program became the first major naval construction program initiated since the Civil War and the first one calling for the use of domestically produced steel.[67] Previous to the ABCDs, all American warships had been

Figures 17a and 17b. Juxtaposing HMS *Leander* (*top*) and USS *Chicago* (*bottom*) shows how much influence British warship design had on American naval construction. *Scientific American Supplement* 17 (April 12, 1884) and Naval Historical Center, Washington, D.C.

made of wood or wrought iron. Ever since the ABCDs were completed, all American warships have been built of steel and have incorporated modern naval technology.

The promise of funding for the ABCD Warships in the spring of 1883 inspired innovation and invention within the Navy Department. Bradley Fiske, one of the most inventive naval officers of his day, led in this frenzy of creativity. Beginning in the early 1880s, he obtained patents on sixty devices in areas such as depth sounding, internal and external shipboard communications, navigation, range-finding, and gun direction.[68] The interest in new naval technology demonstrated by naval officers, such as Fiske and Chadwick, cadet engineers, and Naval Advisory Board members, prompted Rear Admiral Edward Simpson to write pro-naval Senator Eugene Hale in 1884 that "the age is full of progressive ideas, and we must become accustomed to departures from old forms."[69]

In 1881, naval constructors Francis Bowles and Richard Gatewood completed William White's training, returned to the United States and began influential careers in the navy's construction corps. With their appointment as assistant naval constructors, the Navy Department had initiated the custom of promoting Academy graduates to the construction corps rather than recruiting practical shipbuilders from navy yards and private shipyards. In 1882, Bowles and Gatewood submitted the design for an unarmored cruiser of 3,900 tons to a second Naval Advisory Board established to supervise the design and construction of the ABCD Warships. The board adopted their plan, stating that "The designs and specifications possess so many excellencies and such thorough study and skillful workmanship."[70] Bowles and Gatewood's design was used for the construction of the USS *Chicago*, the largest of the ABCDs. They based the *Chicago*'s design upon Britain's HMS *Leander*-class cruisers, which William White had promoted during his tenure as a member of the Admiralty staff in charge of naval design. At the time that they designed the *Chicago*, Bowles and Gatewood had access to a forty-page booklet of specifications for the *Leander* and the plans for *Leander*'s sister ship *Mersey*, which Chadwick had acquired for the navy's Bureau of Construction and Repair.[71]

Bowles went on to become a guiding force in American naval design during the 1880s and 1890s. Impressed with his performance, the navy assigned Bowles to the post of secretary of the second Naval Advisory Board. Rear-Admiral Edward Simpson, the board's president, commented on Bowles's influence, noting that "as the center figure about which the business of the board has circulated, he has shown an amount of method and system which, combined with a very retentive memory, has made him a valuable and, I may say, an unfailing reference at all times."[72] Throughout his tenure as board secretary, Bowles corresponded with White on matters concerning the design of the ABCDs.[73]

The ABCDs became a focus of political and technological controversy. The condition of the navy after the Civil War provided one of the most volatile political issues debated at a time when both Democrats and Republicans failed to retain control of the executive branch for more than a term. Any improvement of the navy could prove a political boon for one party and a blunder for the other.[74] Bowles and the Naval Advisory Board also had to contend with the conservatism found within the Bureau of Construction and Repair and outspoken veteran line officers. Put at the disposal of the Naval Advisory Board by the secretary of the navy to expedite the planning of the ABCDs, chief constructor Theodore Wilson opposed the board's plans nonetheless. Wilson saw the ten-foot freeboard and off-center main battery placement of the sister ships *Atlanta* and *Boston* and the *Chicago*'s revolutionary twin screws as very problematic and considered their designs failures. Having little knowledge of, or confidence in, the use of steel, both Wilson and naval constructor Hichborn argued for iron hulls and covering the metal hulls with wooden planks and copper sheathing.[75]

Even after completion of the controversial ABCD Warships, White's influence over American warship design remained strong. The navy reassigned Bowles to the Walker Board, named for its president, Rear Admiral J. G. Walker, and charged the board with designing the four warships to be built subsequent to the ABCDs. The board, however, favored buying the plans directly from the British. The navy purchased the plans for the protected cruisers *Charleston* and *Baltimore* from William White while he worked for English warship builder William Armstrong and Company. In 1886, it placed White's former pupil Richard Gatewood in charge of the construction of the *Baltimore* at Cramp's Shipyard in Philadelphia. The Navy Department bought a third set of plans for the battleship *Texas*, designed by White's close friend naval architect William John. The navy gave Bowles the task of supervising its construction while he directed naval construction at the Norfolk Navy Yard.[76] In 1889, Admiral Stephen Luce lamented that

> a quarter century after the "Monitor" had effected a revolution in the art of naval warfare, we find ourselves compelled to go abroad for the models of our war-ships; meanwhile having our naval constructors educated in foreign schools of naval architecture. The building of the battle-ship "Texas" from English designs marks a distinct era in the history of the United States Navy.[77]

The purchase of British warship designs produced awkward moments for both British and American naval authorities. From 1886 through 1887, newspapers on both sides of the Atlantic rumored that the Admiralty had sold military secrets to the U.S. Navy, in particular Naval Attaché Chadwick.[78] By 1888, political foes of Navy Secretary William Whitney called on him to publish the facts surrounding purchase of the designs, including their cost and funds expended by Naval Attaché Chadwick for technical information. In 1891, White found himself in the awkward position of trying to avoid commenting on his own designs at the Annual Meeting of the Institution of Naval Architects. In the discussion following a paper titled "Some Recent War-Ship Designs for the American Navy," White commented that "it is with some diffidence that I rise to speak on this paper . . . [because] . . . a number of the ships . . . described here to-day, as having been built in America, are built from my designs."[79] Chadwick did acquire a great deal of confidential material during his tenure in London, but facts show that plans for the three cruisers had been legally acquired from British shipbuilding firms, not the Admiralty.[80]

America's civilian shipbuilding industry benefited greatly by the technical data flowing freely from Great Britain. The transfer of technology to the United States in the form of warship designs had a direct impact on civilian shipyards. By building the European-style ABCD Warships, the Roach yard became the first American yard to construct seagoing steel ships. Bowles's Walker Board granted the contract for the White-designed cruiser USS *Charleston* to San Francisco's Union Iron Works, while the contract for White's protected cruiser USS *Baltimore* went to the Cramp shipyard. As a result of executing these designs, naval contractors acquired the expertise to build state-of-the-art warship hulls and propulsion systems, such as British triple-expansion engines. Other American shipbuilding firms learned a great deal by viewing the British plans available at the Bureau of Construction and Repair.[81] Even after British naval construction became a matter of great secrecy in the mid-1890s, the Navy Department continued to acquire confidential British warship designs for the benefit of the Bureau of Construction and Repair.[82]

Despite partisan bickering over naval building that had occurred early in the 1880s, political support for naval development became bipartisan by the end of that decade.[83] After the fall of President Chester Arthur's Republican administration to Grover Cleveland in 1885, the Democrat-controlled Congress threw all its support behind incoming navy secretary William Whitney and his efforts to build-up America's New Navy. The Senate created the Select Committee on Ordnance and War Ships, while the House established the Commission on Ordnance and Gunnery. During the 1880s, private contractors had built the navy's ships, but Congress authorized the navy to equip its navy yards to construct new warships in competition with private contractors. By the time Cleveland relinquished the White House to Benjamin Harrison in March 1889, Congress had authorized the construction of thirty new naval vessels.[84]

Renewed funding for naval construction in the 1880s had not only fostered invention and innovation by naval personnel, it also encouraged American industrial expansion and the development of an American naval-industrial complex. By 1888, a domestic gun-cotton industry had emerged on both coasts, and ordnance manufacturer Benjamin Hotchkiss returned from Paris to establish a Connecticut plant for producing rapid-firing guns and self- propelled torpedoes.[85] Up until the early 1880s, the primary consumer of American steel had been the railroads, but beginning with the ABCD Warship Program, the steel industry began to enjoy greater demand for rolled steel and steel armor.

Naval personnel actively participated in this industrial expansion. During the ABCD Program, the navy billeted engineers to oversee naval contract work at such firms as the Nashua Steel and Iron Works, John Roach's Morgan Iron Works, and Delaware River Iron Ship Building and Engine Works. The navy continued this policy throughout the 1880s as it relied increasingly on private military contractors.[86] For example, the navy assigned Lieutenant William Folger to the Gatling Gun Company and Simonds Rolling Machine Company. Former cadet engineer Ira Hollis served at San Francisco's Union Iron Works as an inspector of machinery for the cruiser USS *Charleston*, while naval constructor Frank L. Fernald inspected her construction.[87] Naval engineers set quality standards, rejected substandard materials, and recommended measures necessary to improve the production of military contractors. Many of these engineers resigned from the navy to pursue lucrative careers at the same shipyards where they had served as inspectors.[88]

Despite the preponderance of naval engineers and naval constructors employed by the private sector, it should not be assumed that the navy failed to employ line officers in positions requiring technical skill and knowledge. Through invention and foreign intelligence–gathering duties, such officers as Bradley Fiske and French Chadwick had brought the latest technology to the navy. Naval officers also introduced the navy to state-of-the-art warship armor technology. Lieutenant Francis M. Barber facilitated the transfer of steel-making technology from the firm of Schneider-Creusot of France to Bethlehem Iron Company, while Lieutenant William H. Jacques played the middleman between Bethlehem and the Whitworth works of England. These technically inclined officers became the exclusive agents for Schneider-Creusot and Whitworth's when they returned from training with the European steel makers. Jacques also supervised the construction of Bethlehem's first heavy-steel forging plant after scrutinizing Whitworth's steel-production facilities. Eventually, he retired from service to work for the steel industry full-time. Lieutenants C. A. Stone and John F. Meigs followed Jacques' example by learning their trade in the navy and pursuing more lucrative positions in industry.[89] By the time Secretary Whitney signed a multimillion-dollar contract for ship armor with the Bethlehem Iron Company in 1887, strong ties linked American and European steel makers, American government officials, and technically oriented naval personnel. This interdependent relationship resulted in government funding for civilian plant improvements, bonds between steel makers and government officials, and naval officers serving as industry advisors.[90]

The development of a naval-industrial complex paved the way for more systematic ship design and construction methods, including the creation of American naval architecture schools, which lagged far behind the schools founded in Europe. No American institution provided a formal education in naval architecture until the early 1890s, when naval personnel led the way once again. The Naval Academy continued to send its cadets to Greenwich, Glasgow, and Paris for postgraduate instruction in naval architecture until the mid-1890s. At that point, imperial rivalry and the naval arms race had heated up sufficiently for the British to close to foreigners the warship design program at the Royal Naval College. The Academy could still send its graduates to Glasgow and Paris, but it initiated its own postgraduate program in 1897 under the supervision of naval constructor Richmond P. Hobson. The Navy Department later detached Hobson for service in the Spanish-American War, so naval constructor Lawrence Y. Spear took over Hobson's responsibilities.[91]

Robert Thurston determined to establish the first American school of naval architecture and marine engineering. A naval engineer in the Civil War, Thurston distinguished himself in the field of engineering education, most notably at the Naval Academy and Stevens Institute of Technology, and helped establish the American Society of Mechanical Engineers. In 1883, the Navy Department had graduated cadet engineer Walter M. McFarland to Cornell University, where he served as assistant professor of mechanical engineering until 1885. McFarland's service to Cornell proved so successful that university president Andrew J. White requested an extension of his assignment. The navy reassigned McFarland to inspection duty, so White hired Thurston to direct Cornell's Sibley College of the Mechanic Arts to establish an engineering program.[92] By 1891, Thurston had hired William Durand to teach courses, and Sibley began to offer degrees in marine engineering and naval architecture. By 1895, Cornell's program had become recognized as the premier school in those fields.[93] When Thurston arrived at Cornell, Sibley had about seven faculty members and sixty students, but by the time of his death in 1903 there were forty-three faculty and 960 students. Despite its trailblazing the field and prospering for many years, Cornell's marine engineering program was closed in 1905. By then Sibley had not only lost Thurston, it had suffered two other blows. Cornell had bid against MIT in 1901 to host the navy's warship design program and lost. The final blow came in 1904, when Durand moved to Stanford University. Cornell continued to offer a naval architecture degree until 1929, when it was decided that the school's upstate New York location did not favor such a program.[94]

The Massachusetts Institute of Technology initiated a program in naval architecture in 1893, although courses in the subject had been offered since 1891. Like other engineering schools of the day, the MIT curriculum required students to take courses in the hard sciences, mathematics, and liberal arts for their first three years before specializing in a branch of engineering in the fourth year. By the turn of the century, the navy had decided to discharge its responsibility of training naval constructors to a private institution. Over the objections of some officers, the navy negotiated with MIT to initiate a program in warship design. In 1901, MIT began the warship design program, and the navy began sending its naval-constructor trainees there in 1902. To ensure the proper supervision for the program, MIT hired Commander William Hovgaard, an 1886 graduate of the Royal Naval College and distinguished naval constructor for the Danish government. Hovgaard modeled his program after the Royal Naval College example, which stressed applied mechanics, material science, laboratory work, and descriptive geometry. The Boston Navy Yard even offered its mold loft to allow the students to practice their skills.[95]

Further ship design programs emerged in the ensuing years. The Webb Academy and Home for Shipbuilders provided a home for indigent elderly shipbuilders and an education in ship design and construction for those students unable to afford tuition. Named for, and endowed by, New York's famed clipper-ship builder William H. Webb, the State of New York incorporated the Academy in 1888. Situated on the banks of the Harlem River in the Bronx, the Academy admitted its first students in January 1894. In order to qualify for admission to the Academy, each student had to demonstrate a familiarity with the metric system and pass examinations in algebra, plane and solid geometry, and plane trigonometry. Even though the Academy has moved to Glen Cove, Long Island, and changed its name to the Webb Institute of Naval Architecture. It survives to the present day.[96]

By the turn of the century, Philadelphia's Franklin Institute and New York's Columbia University offered naval architecture courses, and the University of Michigan had established its own naval architecture and marine engineering program. In 1901, naval architecture professor Herbert Sadler, another student of Sir John Biles in Glasgow, took over the Michigan program, and by 1905 it had acquired its own ship model tank. During the peak shipbuilding years surrounding World War I, other programs emerged. Lehigh University began a program, as did the University of California and the University of Washington. All of these programs closed during the 1920s except the department at the University of Michigan. By 1930, only three schools of ship design remained: MIT, University of Michigan, and the Webb Institute.[97]

Prior to the 1890s, American ship designers had few professional organizations with which to associate themselves. Professional associations related to shipbuilding remained naval-oriented, such as the United States Naval Institute. Some noted American marine engineers and naval architects, such as former engineer-in-chief of the navy Charles H. Haswell, chose to become members of Great Britain's Institution of Naval Architects. As naval rejuvenation advanced throughout the 1880s, however, fleet modernization and personnel professionalization became part of a mutually reinforcing process. The naval engineers formed an association separate from the United States Naval Institute. Led by naval engineer George W. Baird, later famous for installing electric lighting in the White House, they established the American Society of Naval Engineers in 1888. Other distinguished society members included Harvard educator Ira Hollis, the former engineer-in-chief Benjamin Isherwood, and current engineer-in-chief George W. Melville. The American Society of Naval Engineers became the seventh engineering society to be founded in the United States.[98]

Naval constructors Bowles, Taylor, and Capps championed the effort to establish an American equivalent to the Institution of Naval Architects, whose meetings they had attended while studying in Great Britain. All products of postgraduate education in Great Britain, these forward-looking naval constructors saw such an organization as a tool for promoting their profession through the exchange of technical information and career networking. In early 1893, Bowles, Taylor, and Capps hosted a dinner for a dozen naval constructors to discuss the founding of an American society for naval architects. The naval constructors convened the first meeting of the Society of Naval Architects and Marine Engineers later that year in the New York offices of the American Society of Mechanical Engineers. Taylor and Capps insisted that all members of the corps of constructors join the fledgling society. Naval officers such as Richard Meade, French Chadwick, and William Jacques became members, as did numerous civilian shipbuilders, such as William H. Webb.[99]

During the 1870s, 1880s, and 1890s, an American navalist movement had helped eliminate the culture and technology of the Old Navy, characterized by conservative line officers, age-old traditions, and wooden warships. This movement established a New Navy, led by progressive officers and engineers and embracing Mahanian-style naval policy, steel warships, and technical education. Social and technological factors played a major role in influencing this transition. Navy secretaries William Hunt and William Whitney encouraged naval development. The Academy produced technically inclined officers such as Bradley Fiske, French Chadwick, and William Jacques. British naval architects such as Sir William White and Sir John Biles educated a generation of naval constructors like F. T. Bowles and David W. Taylor, and educators such as William Hovgaard. These individuals guided the U.S. Navy through the technological transition from the nineteenth century to the twentieth.[100]

Quite fittingly, the turn of the century marked the consummation of the navy's thirty-year campaign to transfer foreign technology and technical know-how to the United States. By this time, the nation had the facilities to produce the armor and ships for a modern fleet. Domestic warship design and naval architecture programs had been established. Congress had combined the engineer corps and line officer ranks into one group. Other, less noticeable events occurred around 1900 as well. Not only would the first Academy-trained engineer take over the Bureau of Steam Engineering, but also the first Academy-educated naval constructor would take over the Bureau of Construction and Repair. At the same time, the navy erected the first model ship basin in the country. A facility that provided assistance in designing hulls, the experimental basin became an important research tool from which naval architecture theory could be derived.

Employed by British experimenters since the 1670s, the model ship basin used for design purposes came to the United States during the nineteenth century. Benjamin Franklin and clipper-ship designer John W. Griffiths previously experimented with primitive tanks for testing underwater forms. Nathaniel Herreschoff purportedly conducted towing tests by suspending pairs of models off the side of a steam yacht with the aid of a low-hanging platform. Herreschoff assumed that the model that lagged farther behind resisted the water the most of the two. None of these methods, however, com-

Figure 18. The model ship basin at the Washington Navy Yard was the first research facility of its kind in the United States. Naval Historical Center, Washington, D.C.

pared in sophistication with the experimental model ship tests conducted by pioneer William Froude.[101]

For over ten years, naval personnel urged Congress to fund a model basin facility for the navy similar to those that existed in Britain. Naval constructor Bowles tried to correct the lack of an American model test basin upon returning to the United States from postgraduate training in England. In 1883, he began his campaign by promoting the benefits of such a tool in the pages of the *United States Naval Institute Proceedings*. The next year, Bowles submitted a request to Navy Secretary William E. Chandler to establish such a facility and had the Naval Advisory Board submit another request on his behalf. Throughout the early 1890s, American navy secretaries and naval constructors continued to urge Congress to appropriate funds for the establishment of a test basin.[102]

Greatly impressed by the model ship experiments carried out in England, David W. Taylor took up the cause of the model basin before Congress and, in 1893, published the book *Resistance of Ships and Screw Propulsion*.

His book remained a standard text for naval architecture courses worldwide into the 1930s.[103] Congress finally relented to Taylor's pressure in 1896, appropriating $100,000 to build a "Model Tank for Experiments," and the navy assigned Taylor the task of designing and building the model ship basin. The Spanish-American War delayed completion of the facility for a time, but Taylor finally finished it in 1899.[104]

The nation's first model test basin bore the stamp of its designer and reflected the influence of American practicality. Taylor designed a tank 14 feet deep, 43 feet wide, and 470 feet long and incorporated the latest traveling crane technology by employing a 25-ton carriage powered by four 450-horsepower motors. This heavy carriage could tow models at speeds of up to 20 knots while providing uniformity in the rate of velocity and a platform for instruments. Taylor paid special attention to the temperature and purity of the tank's million gallons of water by adding alum to coagulate impurities, which could then be filtered out of the water supply provided by the city. Taylor even selected and trained the basin's staff. European experimenters built their ship models between 10 and 12 feet in length out of paraffin wax, while Taylor insisted that his be built 20 feet out of wood. These requirements increased the value of his tests by diminishing inaccuracies associated with heat and the scale of smaller models. To make each model, Taylor's staff built a mock-up of the projected hull. The mock-up supplied the jig for the cutting machine, similar in principle to early American woodworking machines and it cut the hull form from a chunk of laminated wood. Once the miniature hull had been painted and varnished, tests of resistance and propulsion could be carried out with the aid of a dynamometer, photographic equipment, and other measuring devices.[105]

The navy's model basin took much of the guesswork out of designing modern warships by granting naval constructors the ability to study hull-form behavior in microcosm. The days of designing ships based on practical knowledge and observation of full-scale vessels under real-life conditions had come to an end. Shortly after the navy completed its basin, private American institutions followed suit. From 1899 to 1900, William Durand designed and constructed a canal used for hydraulic experiments at Cornell University. The University of Michigan completed its own tank in 1905. These facilities followed more traditional practices, such as using paraffin models.[106]

During the 1890s, American shipbuilders began to publish more materials on their industry, and naval personnel produced a large portion of this work. With the founding of the Society of Naval Architects and Marine Engineers in 1893 began the publication of *Transactions*, which became

Figure 19. Naval constructor David W. Taylor developed the science of American naval architecture through research and application of principles to naval shipbuilding. Society of Naval Architects and Marine Engineers Transactions 48 (1940).

a vehicle for disseminating the latest information derived from the design and construction of the New Navy. During the 1890s, old naval constructors such as Theodore Wilson and Philip Hichborn published occasional papers. The bulk of the articles, however, came from former cadet engineers such as William Emmet and Walter McFarland; Academy-trained naval constructors like F. T. Bowles, Lewis Nixon, and Richard Watt; and educators like William Durand, William Hovgaard, Herbert Sadler, and even William White himself.[107]

David W. Taylor stands alone as the most prolific writer of all the earliest contributors to *Transactions*. After the founding of the Society of Naval Architects and Marine Engineers, Taylor published over twenty of his articles and three presidential addresses in *Transactions*. He also contributed numerous articles to the *Institution of Naval Architects Transactions*, *United States Naval Institute Proceedings*, and various other journals and magazines. Some of these articles harkened back to marine engineer John Nystrom's published work of the mid-1800s.[108] Most of Taylor's earliest articles resulted from the mass of data accumulated from experiments he conducted at the navy's model ship basin, as did his second book, *The Speed and Power of Ships*, published in 1910. The model basin's importance as a research tool eventually transcended its utility as a design tool. It supplied a database from which Taylor and others could derive formulas to further rationalize the ship design process, thereby eliminating the intuitive aspect of ship design relied on by countless generations of earlier shipbuilders.

The turn of the century had marked a true "changing of the guard" at the Bureau of Construction and Repair. Rear Admiral Philip Hichborn, the last of the practically trained chiefs of the Bureau of Construction and Repair, turned over his responsibilities to a formally educated Academy graduate. Despite the navy's trend toward formal education and professional societies, every man who had served as chief of the Bureau of Construction and Repair up to 1900 had learned the art of shipbuilding through the apprenticeship system. Younger officers had referred to the Bureau as the "Bureau of Destruction and Despair" because of its uneducated naval constructors.[109] In an 1894 discussion of a paper presented before the Society of Naval Architects and Marine Engineers on past practices of the Bureau of Construction and Repair, former chief constructor Theodore Wilson remarked that he "was very much pleased, although surprised, that one of the young constructors of the Navy should get up here and defend the old constructors."[110] In 1881, Bowles graduated from the Royal Naval College and was appointed an assistant naval constructor in the navy. From that day forward, naval constructors were assigned from the Naval Academy rather than being recruited from the practical shipbuilder ranks in the navy yards or private shipyards. In 1901, Bowles took over the post of chief naval constructor from Philip Hichborn, the last of the "old constructors." At the age of forty-three, he had become the youngest officer to reach the rank of rear admiral up to that time. His appointment marked the beginning of the tradition of promoting only Academy-educated naval constructors to head the Bureau.[111]

By the early twentieth century, British-trained Americans had found employment in education and yacht design and had begun to fill influential positions in the civilian shipbuilding industry. F. T. Bowles left the navy in 1903 to become head of Boston's Fore River Ship and Engine Company and served as head of the United States Shipping Board Emergency Fleet Corporation during World War I. Naval constructor Lewis Nixon retired from the navy to become general manager at the Cramp shipyard and later became president of the Crescent Shipbuilding Company. In 1902, he headed the United States Shipbuilding Company, a J. P. Morgan conglomerate comprising six of the nation's leading shipbuilding firms as well as Bethlehem Steel Company. Other British-educated naval constructors included Homer L. Ferguson, who managed the Newport News Shipbuilding Company from 1915 to 1947, and Holden Evans, who introduced scientific management to the navy before retiring to supervise Bethlehem Steel's shipbuilding operation at Sparrow's Point, Maryland. Naval constructor Joseph W. Powell resigned his commission to assist the president at the Cramp Shipbuilding Company and in 1914 became chief of the Fore River Shipbuilding Company. In 1917, he became vice president of Bethlehem Shipbuilding Corporation in charge of all new construction, and in 1921, he headed up the United States Shipping Board Emergency Fleet Corporation. By 1930, he had organized six New York shipyards into United Shipyards, Inc., and throughout most of World War II he held the post of special assistant to the secretary of the navy in connection with new warship construction.[112]

The Naval Academy and its alumni facilitated the transfer of European methods and technology to the United States. Cadet engineers became the first American shipbuilders to be educated in Europe, and they had the knowledge, skills, and technical background necessary to introduce this professional stock of knowledge to the United States. The Academy also produced line officers who helped lead the naval shipbuilding community into the twentieth century and established the basis of institutions necessary to sustain the demand for professional shipbuilders well into the twentieth century. Described by historians as a "naval aristocracy,"[113] Naval Academy graduates had the proper background to transfer or "translate"[114] the constellation of theoretical methods employed in British shipbuilding to the American shipbuilding industry. This systematic approach, which we look upon as modern naval architecture methods, did not begin as an outgrowth of American industrialization. It was a strategic response by the navy to the rapid advances in weapons technology witnessed overseas in the late nineteenth century. As French Chadwick wrote to Navy Secretary William Whitney in 1887: "All this has come into existence in Great Britain [industrialization of shipbuilding] through merchant shipping demands; it must come with us if at all through the Navy."[115]

The upper-class and upper-middle-class background of the naval aristocracy uniquely suited it to the task of introducing the aristocratic institutions of British naval architecture to America. By bringing theoretical shipbuilding to the United States, they not only incorporated an engineering echelon within the industry's shipyard hierarchy, but they eliminated the possibility of executive-level promotion previously available to practical shipbuilders. Consequently, practical shipbuilders would remain banished to the shipyard trades of the industry after the turn of the century.

Historians have characterized the period following the Civil War as the U.S. Navy's Dark Ages; however, it should also be remembered as one of intellectual and technological ferment. During this period, the increasing sophistication of foreign warship design and the deplorable state of the American fleet encouraged the navy to replace the institutions underlying the development of American naval technology. The consequent changes implemented by the navy throughout the late 1800s infused the American shipbuilding community with new professional institutions and a generation of formally educated shipbuilders. In his 1891 annual message to Congress, President Benjamin Harrison captured the spirit of the transformation that had occurred during that decade:

> When it is recollected that the work of building a modern Navy was only initiated in the year 1883, that our naval constructors and shipbuilders were practically without experience in the construction of large iron or steel ships, that our engine shops were unfamiliar with great marine engines, and that the manufacture of steel forgings for guns and plates was almost wholly a foreign industry, the progress that has been made is not only highly satisfactory, but furnishes the assurance that the United States will before long attain in the construction of such vessels, with their engines and armaments, the same preeminence which it attained when the best instrument of ocean commerce was the clipper ship.[116]

8
The New American Style of Shipbuilding

> *Nearly every one engaged in shipbuilding, or any other kind of building, prefers his own tools. He evolves them out of his own consciousness of what he wants, and while some one else may not see the conditions just as he sees them, nearly every place has some condition that influences the engineer, if he is a thinking man, as to what he wants.*
>
> George W. Dickie, Union Iron Works shipyard superintendent, 1899

As Dickie observed, American shipbuilders "evolved" new methods and technology for ship production late in the nineteenth century.[1] The American shipbuilding industry experienced some of its most dramatic technological changes during this period. American inventors and engineers developed new power sources and new ways to transmit power that promoted greater mechanization. New machines for production and materials handling, developed largely in the United States, lessened the industry's reliance on both skilled and unskilled workers and on traditional ways of building things. Industrial engineers and efficiency experts began to introduce more systematic methods to such industries as shipbuilding to streamline production and cut labor costs as never before. Even the design of ships changed from the more graceful lines sculpted by practical shipbuilders to simpler engineered forms developed in the interests of building ships quickly and cheaply. Just as personnel from the U.S. Navy had brought to America a new rational way of designing ships, engineers from American industry transferred new methods of construction to shipbuilding.

The introduction of theoretical design methods represented only one side of modern American shipbuilding. The other was the rapid advance made by American industry in producing heavy equipment and machine tools capable of reducing labor needs, increasing efficiency and thereby increasing productivity. During the latter decades of the nineteenth century, the shipbuilding industry found new sources of power and new ways to transmit that power throughout the shipyard. This meant that the fieldwork involved in building a ship could be mechanized. New and powerful machines for materials handling made obsolete the need for manpower and animal power to lift and transport items within the shipyard. The machine shops of the shipyards benefited from new technology in larger and more powerful machines.

By the end of the nineteenth century, these changes in the techniques and technology employed in shipbuilding culminated in a "rational" shipyard. The methods and technology used in this shipyard were found in civilian and naval shipyards, though few, if any, incorporated all of the latest improvements. The methods and technology employed in rational shipbuilding varied from yard to yard. Beginning in the early twentieth century, shipyards began to exhibit the latest in rational physical plant layout, materials-handling equipment, some aspect of scientific management, flow charts, prefabrication, standardization of parts and production, and, in at least one case, an assembly line. These improvements were made possible not by ship designers but by civil engineers, production engineers, and efficiency experts. These individuals became responsible for systematizing the shipbuilding process so as to make the most efficient use of new production technology.

The duties of the skilled shipbuilder, who had epitomized practical shipbuilding early in the nineteenth century, narrowed considerably by the late nineteenth century. This process accelerated, after 1880, when steel production made possible machines and structures of greater size. Modern shipyards grew dramatically, enjoying greater economies of scale and producing far larger steel ships. The new system of techniques and technology transferred control of the production process from skilled workers to engineers and management. The production process became mechanized and specialized in both the shops and the field, requiring less skill than ever before. The sense of aesthetics and judgment, which had been the hallmark of practical shipbuilding, was supplanted by a more rational engineering knowledge held by the executive staff of the shipyard.

In the United States, the development of the rational shipyard began in iron shipbuilding firms established prior to 1880. Early nineteenth-century builders of iron and wooden ships had relied upon steam and animal power and transmitted this power either directly or by mechanical means such as ropes, pulleys, and belts. Fieldworkers continued to use hand tools for fieldwork in the boatyard, and materials handling relied upon human or animal power. This paradigm of early industrial shipbuilding would become obsolete between 1880 and 1920 as new forms of manufacturing technology were invented and developed.

Industrial work in the iron yards mechanized gradually in the years prior to the Civil War. Practices for building iron hulls, boilers, engines, and other iron parts required the handiwork of workers such as riveters, blacksmiths, and foundry men. They shaped plates, hammered them together, cast engines and chipped away excess iron, and hammered out iron pieces. The first documented iron vessel built in the United States, *Codorus*, was manufactured in a rural machine shop where most parts were produced by a blacksmith. The power for the earliest operations came from water, animals, or humans. By the 1840s, most larger machine shops had converted to steam power and systems of shafts and pulleys to transmit power throughout the shop to various machines. The small Wilmington, Delaware, machine shop of Hollingsworth and Teas advertised itself as a blacksmith shop, iron boat builder, and boiler-making shop. While the shop had steam power to run its establishment, most of the processes required to build its products still relied on handwork.[2]

With the introduction of steam power, the sophistication of machine tools advanced more rapidly. In the 1820s, machine shops still required hand tool processes for most work, but in the machine shop of the 1850s could be seen many machine tools, such as lathes, boring tools, power drills, and cutting, punching and shearing machines. Boilermaker and locomotive builder Joseph Harrison claimed that during the 1820s, a "hammer, chisel, and file, hand-lathe, drill-brace, and screwstock were almost the only instruments used in working iron." By 1860, however, he believed that "machines are made to fashion iron into almost every form by other than man's power and skill—manual and even mental toil being in a great degree superseded by these machines."[3]

Certainly the machines of the early 1800s were more primitive than those used in the late nineteenth century, but most machine operators would recognize these early machines. Fieldwork in the boatyard and materials handling, however, resisted mechanization until the end of the nineteenth century.

The design and layout of iron shipyards were dictated by the application of steam power to machinery and the need to avoid damage by fire. Through much of the nineteenth century, the structures in iron shipyards were dominated by certain characteristics, such as brick buildings, gas or oil lighting, and steam power. The light in these buildings was normally supplied by sun during the day, but if the firm remained in operation after dark, then gas or oil lamps provided interior lighting. To guard against fire, buildings were usually built of brick with dirt or wood floors and wooden or iron supports.[4] The most sophisticated shipyards relied upon steam power to drive machinery in their shops, and machines tools had to be positioned in close proximity to the shafts that transmitted power from the steam engine. As late as

1896, a disgusted engineer wrote, "The ordinary machine shop of today, in its shape and size and in the general arrangement of its engines and machinery, is the slave of shafting transmission."[5]

Prior to the 1880s, iron yards were not arranged according to efficient flow of production; rather, the physical plant was laid out according to certain constraints, such as the best arrangement of steam machinery and available space within the firm's property. These constraints were more of a concern for yards located in urban areas, such as Philadelphia's Cramp shipyard; and Harlan and Hollingsworth and Pusey and Jones, both in Wilmington, Delaware, where open space came at a premium. Shipbuilders added to their industrial plant in a piecemeal fashion, when large civilian or naval contracts granted them the funds necessary to underwrite plant expansion. The Cramp shipyard, for example, underwrote costly shipyard improvements during the Civil War; at the turn of the century, when the shipbuilding industry experienced a temporary increase in merchant shipbuilding; and during World War I.[6]

The last decades of the nineteenth century represented a period in which new machines and shipbuilding tools were made possible by new materials and power sources. New energy sources such as pneumatic, hydraulic, and electric power granted a great deal of flexibility in production. New materials and new power sources made possible machines unknown prior to the 1880s and they generally made possible the development of already existing machine technology into efficient production systems. Hydraulic pressure provided steadier, more powerful machines than had steam. Pneumatic power made possible the mechanization of fieldwork, which had remained the last bastion of hand tool work in the shipyard. And electricity made possible the introduction of a system of mechanization that was far more efficient and flexible than the steam-powered shipyard.

The first shipbuilder to modernize iron shipbuilding was magnate John Roach. Roach came to America as a boy of sixteen and gradually rose through the ranks of the Allaire Engine Works in New York, buying the Etna Engine Works during the Civil War. By the end of the war he had acquired the Morgan Iron Works, one of the largest in New York City. In 1871, he added to his great engine-building interests the Pennsylvania shipyard of Reaney, Son and Archbold, renaming it the Delaware River Engine and Ship Building Works. Just two years later, Roach set up the Chester Rolling Mill, thereby securing a reliable source of iron materials for his shipbuilding interests. By 1875, Roach had the largest shipbuilding concern in the nation that could supply its own hulls, engines, and raw material without relying on other suppliers and subcontractors.[7]

In addition to assembling the first example of vertical integration in the shipbuilding industry, Roach mechanized production as far as contemporary technology allowed. After acquiring the Chester shipyard, Roach decided to cut labor costs by acquiring the most advanced contemporary shipbuilding technology available. He invested in "the most approved labor-saving machinery" to re-equip his yard.[8] Roach applied steam power to as many machines as possible, thereby reducing the plant's reliance on man and animal power. He installed a dozen steam engines totaling 700 horsepower at the Chester shipyard to power machine tools, derricks, and cranes, such as the hoisting shears on the fitting-out wharf. To facilitate the movement of heavy objects around the yard, Roach used railroad tracks and utilized the downgrade of the yard to coast cars through the yard. He also installed a telegraph system to reduce his reliance on messenger boys and facilitate communication between his operations in Chester. In the early 1880s, when new power sources were introduced to American industry, Roach incorporated much of it into his plant. In 1881, he purchased an Edison electric generating plant and installed electric lighting in shipyard buildings to replace oil lamps and permit working longer hours. He also purchased a stationary hydraulic riveting machine called a "bull riveter." Also in 1881, he acquired an air-compression system and the first portable pneumatic riveter introduced to shipbuilding, the Allen portable riveter.[9] While Roach adopted the most advanced contemporary shipbuilding technology available, he employed it in a less than systematic fashion. Systematizing heavy manufacturing had yet to become an important objective of American industrialists.

Most of the improved machine tools were simply refinements of older technology. For example, the multiple punching press did not make one hole at a time like older machines. Instead, it punched several holes at a time in ship plate at evenly spaced intervals along the plate. Employed by bridge builders early on, the multiple punch press became one of the plate machines commonly associated with the modern shipyard. It reduced the time, labor, and energy associated with punching holes in plate and facilitated the flow of prefabricated materials to the shipways.[10]

The rule of improving and developing older machines did have its exception. The joggling machine was developed late in the nineteenth century to streamline the production of steel ships. Strakes of ship plate naturally had to overlap to maintain a watertight fit. Unfortunately, the overlap of plate meant that every other strake of plates fit flush and the alternating strakes cleared the surface of the frames by the thickness of the flush-fitting strakes. Since the earliest date of iron shipbuilding, workers had fashioned "liners,"

15- to 20-pound iron spacers that filled the gap between the frames and every other strake of plates. The joggling machine was invented in the late 1890s to alleviate the need to fit and fasten liners to frames throughout the hull. The machine formed a margin along the edge of the outside plate so that it could overlap the next plate. The bend formed by this margin allowed the plate to fit flush along the frame, thereby eliminating the need for a liner, reducing the weight of the hull and its wetted surface.[11]

One example of the way machines replaced skilled labor could be seen in the new frame-beveling machine. Along with the old method of fitting plates, bending frames had been one of the most involved processes in building an iron hull, requiring great skill from the ironworker. The frames along the side of the hull that rose straight up from the keel required very little beveling, or twisting. The frames located in the stern and bow of most all iron vessels had to be bent to the contours of the hull and beveled so the outside flange of the frame fit flush against the plates. It took a great deal of skill and possibly two or three heats in the angle-iron furnace for an ironworker to get the frame bent just right and beveled at the proper angle for the frames. John Nystrom complained bitterly about the inability of ironworkers to bevel angle iron into frames. Development of the beveling machine in the 1880s put an end to beveling by eye because the angle iron could be fed through the machine while it was hot. The beveling machine eliminated the need for a worker to take responsibility for beveling the frames and marked another step in the replacement of handwork by machine processes.[12]

Steam power had remained the dominant form of energy used to power shipyards throughout most of the nineteenth century. In the 1880s, however, new ways of powering industrial plants were being developed. The greatest disadvantage of using steam was the way in which the power was transmitted. A steam engine provided the energy for the factory, but the power had to be transmitted throughout the yard by a system of shafts, pulleys, and leather belts hung from the ceilings of shops and factory buildings. The belts and shafts produced large quantities of dust and dripping lubricants, obscured overhead lighting, and required a great deal of maintenance. Some mechanical engineers saw steam-driven machinery as slow and easier to manipulate by workers wishing to control the pace of work. Another drawback of steam was that the amount its power tended to oscillate with the stroke of the steam engine, and the shafts and belts tended to transmit and magnify these power fluctuations to the machines.[13] The steam engine and its drive train represented the largest machine found in an iron shipyard and an inefficient one at that. At San Francisco's Union Iron Works, about 25 percent of the energy developed by its steam power plant was lost to transmission. At other industrial plants, the loss reached as much as 80 percent.[14]

One of the earliest of the modern power sources developed for heavy industrial purposes was the application of hydraulic power. Power supplied directly by steam was often erratic, owing to the rhythm of the steam engine and the shaft and leather belt transmission systems that drove the machines. Hydraulic appliances do not provide the original motive power of a device. In the nineteenth century, they were usually powered by steam. Hydraulic machines are powered by fluid pressurized in a cylinder forcing a piston to transmit energy in a steadier, more efficient way than force applied directly from a steam engine. In a hydraulic power system, pumps driven by steam or some other form of power run reservoirs of water, called accumulators. The pumps provide a constant supply of water for accumulators, which in turn transmit hydraulic power to machines via high-pressure water pipes. The machines have cylinders with plungers to supply power to do work. When the machines do work, the pressure in the lines drops, which causes rams in the accumulators to maintain the water pressure in the hydraulic lines. All sorts of machines were invented to employ hydraulic power, including lifting devices, heavy shop machinery and riveters, and any machinery requiring high pressure.

The British adopted hydraulic machinery early in the nineteenth century. Steam power was already known to be inefficient and lacked the power necessary for some industrial applications. Beginning in the mid-1830s, Sir William Armstrong developed a hydraulic accumulator device to supply the necessary pressure for heavy industrial machinery. The development of hydraulic power progressed rapidly during the latter half of the nineteenth century. By 1900, one British commentator reported that the "use of hydraulic riveting machines is now almost universal in Great Britain."[15] In addition to heavy machinery, the British had applied hydraulics to cranes and various forms of hoisting machinery by the 1880s. They became very successful in applying hydraulics to various industrial machines in part due to the milder temperatures in Britain and the relatively late introduction of electricity there. As a result, hydraulic power tended to dominate British heavy industrial machinery through the nineteenth and into the twentieth century.[16]

For American shipbuilders interested in expanding their business in the 1880s, hydraulic machinery appeared to be the way of the future. That is probably why San Francisco's Union Iron Works, the only major shipyard to undergo major expansion during the 1880s, proved a singular example of a shipyard to fully embrace its use. The only major nineteenth-century West Coast shipyard, Union Iron Works began the process of moderniz-

Figure 20. A hydraulic punching machine used to punch rivet holes in steel plate in an American shipyard. Kelly, *The Shipbuilding Industry* (Boston, 1918).

ing its facilities in 1883. Union was in a prime situation to do so because there existed no Panama Canal at the time and the U.S. Navy had begun to modernize its fleet. Since electricity had not been developed to a point of commercial application, Union decided to follow the British lead and install hydraulic machinery. The yard's hydraulic system supplied power to nearly all heavy machinery, such as stationary riveters, bending presses, plate planers, machine shop cranes, traveling cranes over its shipways, as well as a hydraulically powered dry dock. Throughout the late 1880s and early 1890s, Union Iron Works remained the nation's state-of-the-art shipbuilding establishment, constructing numerous capital warships, such as the famous War of 1898 naval vessels *Olympia* and *Oregon*. America's newest shipbuilding establishment, C. P. Huntington's Newport News Shipbuilding Company, followed the example of Union by installing its own hydraulic shop and overhead cranes.[17]

Union Iron Works did not remain the foremost shipyard for long, however. The hydraulic system that powered its machinery fell from favor with most American shipbuilding firms during the 1890s. American industry never embraced the use of hydraulic power to the extent of the British. While hydraulic lines and machinery suffered from few problems in the mild San Francisco climate and most parts of England, it suffered the defect of freezing up in shipyards in the important shipbuilding regions of the Great Lakes and Northeast.[18] British proponents of hydraulic machinery recommend gas heaters or replacing water with glycerin to prevent freezing of hydraulic lines. Problems with freezing, however, prevented the technology from spreading in the United States.[19] American firms confined their application of hydraulic power to large heavy machinery housed indoors, such as bull riveters, which they enclosed in towerlike structures. Hydraulic machinery also suffered from the defect of leaking considerably from the packing used to seal up the water around moving parts. Problems with inferior packing and leaking were never overcome to the satisfaction of American industrialists during the late nineteenth century.[20]

American shipyards embraced pneumatic power rather than hydraulic because pneumatic power proved better suited to American conditions and needs. The successful application of pneumatic power to industrial use began in drilling the Mt. Cemis Tunnel through the Alps between France and Italy. General Herman Haupt, the civil engineer who distinguished himself running the Union's railroads during the Civil War, promoted the use of pneumatic tools in the United States. In 1866, he employed a primitive compressor device to power rock drills to help dig the Hoosac Tunnel. Haupt went on to become a leading promoter of pneumatic rock drill technology during the late nineteenth century.[21] After their successful application to tunneling, pneumatic rock drills spread to quarrying and mining operations. By the 1880s, pneumatic tools had been employed in railroad shops because pumps used for railroad air brakes were commonly found there. During the 1880s, the use of pneumatic power tools also spread to the American bridge-building industry. Pneumatic power spread to other industries and was adapted to the use of cranes and traveling hoists, motors, presses, drills, hammers, chippers, caulkers, reamers, sanders, sand blasters, mining locomotives, pneumatic-powered naval ordnance, and so on. In fact, pneumatic power is versatile enough that it could be applied to just about any kind of device whether portable or stationary.[22] The increase in productivity enjoyed by firms that used pneumatic machines could be seen in the air-powered bolt cutter. Where one man could cut off forty-five bolts per day using a hammer and chisel, he could cut off the equivalent of 1,800 bolts per hour using a portable bolt cutter. Pneumatic power alleviated the need for the mechanical accumulators necessary to run hydraulic machinery. It also had an advantage in safety over electrical power tools in that no wiring had to be located in areas where workers might be exposed to the hazards of electrocution. By the mid-1890s, pneumatic power had proven so useful to shipbuilders for machines of all kinds, and riveters in particular, that new shipyards began to be constructed incorporating pneumatic power systems complete with compressors and underground air lines.[23]

The introduction of power riveting in the United States began in the early 1870s, but machines for riveting had been used much earlier in Europe. In England, the eminent mechanical engineer Sir William Fairbairn developed the first mechanical riveter in 1838. He did so as a way to circumvent the control that intractable riveting gangs held over production at his iron works. The French also became very interested in mechanical riveters during the 1830s and 1840s. Mechanical riveters such as Fairbairn's were powered by steam engines, but by the 1840s, power riveters had been developed that ran directly from the expansive power of steam. Finally, European machine makers began to replace steam and steam-powered mechanical riveters with hydraulic riveters.[24]

In all its portable and stationary manifestations, the hydraulic riveter became the most common form of riveting machine in Europe by the end of the nineteenth century. Ralph Hart Tweddell, a London-based engineer and its earliest developer, believed hydraulic riveting followed "as closely as may be, the method practised by hand, but instead of the countless blows of many hammers a pressure of 50 to 100 tons quietly does the work in one movement."[25] Tweddell built the first hydraulic riveter in 1865, a stationary machine that was followed by a portable version in 1871. Tweddell's "portable" riveters weighed hundreds of pounds, but the same hydraulic power used for pressure was employed to move the machines by using hydraulic hoists. The British shipbuilding industry had already adopted the use hydraulic power for heavy machinery, so it was only natural that hydraulic riveting quickly became a mainstay in the industry.[26] Hydraulic riveting even spread to the United States in the early 1870s, when William Sellers and Company became the licensed manufacturers of Tweddell riveters. Sellers's exhibit of a Tweddell portable hydraulic riveter at the 1876 Centennial Exposition in Philadelphia attracted considerable attention from American industrialists.[27]

Despite the early start of hydraulic riveters in Europe, the technology failed to take hold in the United States except in the form of the indoor stationary bull riveter. Instead, portable pneumatic riveters became popular in America. Pneumatic chippers and caulking tools had been used in shipyards since the mid-1890s, so it was only natural that a riveting hammer based on the same principle should be introduced before long. Pneumatic and hydraulic riveters worked in different ways. With hydraulic riveters, the rivets were closed with slow, steady pressure. The portable pneumatic riveter struck a succession of blows to close the rivet over the rivet hole. It could strike a rivet with as few as 600 or as many as 20,000 blows per minute, depending on the length of hammer's piston stroke. Pneumatic riveters came in different forms, such as the yoke or the horseshoe design, but the most common pneumatic riveters resembled a handgun, with a pistol grip and a finger or thumb trigger. The length of the barrel depended on the length of the piston stroke. A simple buck-up or hammer no longer served the holder-on as they had in the days of an ordinary rivet hammer. Pneumatic tools were also developed for the holder-on to resist the powerful blows delivered by the pneumatic riveters. Pneumatic riveting systems, including compressors, air lines, and portable tools, cost less than hydraulic and electric systems with similar capacity. The pneumatic riveters were portable and convenient because they could be easily transported to the work. This was a considerable advantage where a ship was far too large and cumbersome to move to the shops where a stationary riveter might be located. Portable pneumatic riveters could weigh as little as fifteen pounds, but as the size of rivet became larger, so did the weight of the riveting tool necessary to drive it.[28]

The American riveter-building industry emerged in industrial centers where the tools could be sold to nearby industries. In New York City, the Novelty Iron Works had built a steam-driven riveting machine in the 1850s. New York mechanic John F. Allen pioneered the world's first commercially successful pneumatic riveter. He began developing air-compressing and pneumatic-riveting technology in the mid-1870s and patented a pneumatic riveter in 1877 that could strike 300 blows per minute. He began marketing his product in the late 1870s under the name of the Allen Portable Pneumatic Riveting Machine Company and exhibited his machine at the 1878 Universal Exhibition in Paris.[29]

The Allen pneumatic riveter remained the only such machine on the market for nearly two decades and enjoyed moderate popularity in American industry. With an ordinary rivet gang of three men and a heater boy, 250 rivets could be driven each day; however, with the Allen pneumatic riveter, one man and a heater boy could drive between 750 and 800 rivets per day. John Roach bought an Allen pneumatic riveting system in 1881, and the machines could be found in other shipyards and factories later in the nineteenth century. While the Allen pneumatic riveter was referred to as a portable riveter, it was too heavy for a man to carry and had to be used in conjunction with a crane or hoist. For that reason, Allen's pneumatic riveter probably remained a tool for boiler making and shop use rather than fieldwork like later models of pneumatic riveters. Furthermore, it took a number of years before the

Figure 21. An early pneumatic field riveter used by Chicago shipyard field workers. *Society of Naval Architects and Marine Engineers Transactions* 6 (1898).

necessary compressor and piping technology had developed sufficiently to provide industrial plants with a reliable pneumatic power supply.[30]

Riveting-machine builders emerged in other cities where industry required their use. The Pusey and Jones Company of Wilmington, Delaware, had begun building steam-driven riveting machines in the late 1800s. Philadelphia's William Sellers and Company became a major supplier of steam-powered riveting machines beginning in the late 1860s. The firm provided stationary steam riveters to many of the local locomotive works, including the Baldwin works, and shipyards such as Cramp.[31] In Philadelphia, a number of independent pneumatic tools companies emerged in the 1890s, including the Philadelphia Pneumatic Tool Company, C. H. Haeseler Company, Thomas H. Dallett and Company, and the United States Metallic Packing Company. The great American industrialist Edward N. Hurley began his career in machine tools as a salesman for the U.S. Metallic Packing Company in 1890. By 1896, he had quit to organize the Standard Pneumatic Tool Company, one of the industry's leading firms. Standard Pneumatic became a major firm in the Chicago area and produced the very popular "Little Giant" pneumatic hammer. Chicago hosted the nation's largest pneumatic tool industry, including the Chicago Pneumatic Tool Company, manufacturer of the popular Boyer hammer, and the Q&C Company. And in Cleveland, the Cleveland Pneumatic Tool Company established a thriving business manufacturing pneumatic tools.[32] So while William Sellers's Tweddell portable hydraulic riveter had been of great interest at the 1876 Centennial Exposition, the exhibits of American pneumatic toolmakers stole the show at the 1900 Paris International Exposition. Chicago Pneumatic Tool even won a gold medal for its exhibit of men riveting together a section of a ship's hull.[33]

Shipbuilders around Chicago began to employ the new tools. Former "Roach boy" Washington I. Babcock presented papers before the Society of Naval Architects and Marine Engineers and England's Institution of Naval Architects publicizing the success experienced by his Chicago Shipbuilding Company with the new technology. Shortly thereafter, pneumatic tools use spread to other Great Lakes shipyards, some running air mains to all parts of their yards and employing dozens of pneumatic tools at one time.[34] Shipyards in other regions of the United States quickly followed suit after the successful application in the Great Lakes. Tools for light pneumatic work had been used at the Newport News Shipbuilding Company since 1896, but in 1897 the firm hired experts from the Chicago Shipbuilding Company to visit their facility and install a pneumatic system capable of supporting a yardwide pneumatic power system. By 1898, Newport News had America's largest pneumatic power network, capable of supplying power to field tools as well as shop machines. Cramp had installed a system by the turn of the century, and Camden, New Jersey's New York Shipbuilding Company installed a pneumatic power system when it was established.[35]

The introduction of pneumatic tools to the shipbuilding industry had a mixed effect on the way ships were manufactured. Industry leaders had hoped that introducing mechanical riveting machines could reduce the size of the typical rivet gang. At the 1893 Chicago Engineering Congress, one of the industry's engineers remarked that, "Among the various mechanical aids which would be of distinct value to the shipbuilder, few would stand higher or be more acceptable than one which would efficiently replace the ship-riveter's gang."[36] At best, the use of pneumatic riveters reduced the rivet gang by one man. In some cases, forge men could be eliminated and a heater boy could take over their duties. There still existed the need for a riveter, a bucker-up, and a heater boy to supply hot rivets. The need for a riveting gang would not be obviated completely until the large-scale introduction of welding after World War I.[37]

The results of introducing pneumatic power to the shipbuilding industry were largely beneficial to the industry. Pneumatic tools increased productivity by deskilling the riveting process and dramatically increased the quantity of rivets driven. Where riveting by hand could take a minute per rivet, it took a mere six to seven seconds to drive a rivet using a pneumatic hammer. In 1900, a committee of railroad bridge–building experts found that the use of pneumatic riveters had cut the time and expense of riveting in half. That same year, a locomotive shop manager reported a cost savings of two-thirds of the expense of riveting by hand.[38] The savings of machine riveting over hand-driven rivets by piecework totaled about one cent per rivet, and in 1898, a savings of one cent per rivet equaled nearly $5,000 for a 4,000-ton steamer.[39] Shipbuilders had always been concerned about the strength and quality of the rivets driven by hand and employed inspectors to check and test the rivets after a crew had driven them. Not only did pneumatic riveters increase the rate of riveting many times over, it provided the industry with consistently strong rivets. Part of the problem with hand riveting was that hot rivets often cooled before a striker could "plug" the hole. A pneumatic riveter could drive a rivet before it lost its heat, thereby granting a tight seal to the rivet hole.[40]

The introduction of machines to field riveting reduced the influence of skill on the riveting of ships. Where a well-driven rivet required the skill of a striker in the days of rivet hammers, pneumatic tools required little knowledge of how and where to strike a hot rivet. The flurry of pneumatic blows drove the red-hot rivet before any thought could be given to the question of how and where to strike it.[41] On at least two occasions, once at the Chicago Shipbuilding Company and another at the Cramp shipyard, field riveters went out on strike over the introduction of pneumatic field riveters. The firms responded by employing unskilled workers to run the riveting machines rather than rehire the striking riveters.[42] In his paper presented before the Society of Naval Architects and Marine Engineers, Washington Babcock reported one of the advantages of the portable pneumatic riveter was that "skilled labor in one of the principal departments in a shipyard, which has hitherto been indispensable and correspondingly arrogant and high handed, can be replaced by unskilled labor."[43]

Riveting gangs sustained great on-the-job health problems due to the new riveting machines. Riveters had always suffered hearing loss, but the problem grew with the increased noise caused by the high-speed hammering of the pneumatic riveting device. Some operators of portable pneumatic tools claimed a loss of feeling in their hands through continuous use, which they called "dead fingers." It is unclear whether the effects were permanent, but the U.S. Department of Labor studied the problem in 1917 and 1918 and concluded that dead fingers was only a temporary condition and that using pneumatic tools did not cause permanent loss of feeling in the hands.[44]

Along with hydraulics and pneumatics, electricity was the third new power source introduced late in the nineteenth century. The most common electrical system sported a power generator and electrical lines to supply energy to shop and field appliances. Electrical power was much more efficient than steam because electrons could be transmitted through power lines much more easily than with the shafts and belts that transmitted power mechanically through factories. Electrical networks were similar to air-powered systems in that the energy transmitted from the central power plant to appliances normally drove some sort of motor, which in turn powered the machine. Hydraulic systems, however, worked on water pressure, so cylinders with high-pressure plungers rather than motors usually drove the appliances.

Electrical tools had much to recommend them over steam-powered ones. Electrically powered plants had certain advantages, including a healthier and cleaner working environment, greater flexibility and adaptability of the power source, greater reliability, and improved order and disciplinary control over the workforce. Portable electrical tools could be used in the field, which was very useful in shipbuilding, where many of the tools and materials had to be used in the shipways. For example, the introduction of electricity allowed shipbuilders to run electric lighting onboard their vessels so workers could see below decks. Some builders also established temporary machine shops onboard the incomplete hulls to expedite work onboard, a technique unheard of with steam power.[45]

Electrical machine tools had many other advantages over steam-powered tools. Each electrical tool had its own motor and required no belts to power it. Steam-powered machines were powered by the shafts and belting characteristic of steam power. The shafting and belts produced dust and dripping oil, obscured overhead lighting, and prohibited the use of overhead traveling cranes. Steam-powered tools had to be placed where they could reach the belting of the steam-powered shafts. Arranging a shop or shipyard according to the dictates of the power plant did not make for the most efficient layout. Electrical machine tools could be placed anywhere electrical wires could run, which enabled industrial planners to arrange shop tools in accordance with production, not the demands of the power source. Furthermore, steam power was very inconvenient when it came to plant expansion. If new shops or plant buildings were erected, a new steam-power plant had to be built for them or shafts run out to the structures. And the more shafts and belting were extended from a power plant, the more inefficient the system became. Electrically powered machines allowed firms to control their operators better than steam power had. Using steam power, all machines ran at a prescribed speed; however, with individually motored machine tools, speeds could be set higher by the management.[46] In an 1896 discussion of the American Society of Mechanical Engineers paper "Electricity versus Shafting in the Machine Shop," Oberlin Smith enthusiastically described electricity as a way "to put our machines in any position; to control our power at any time, and not compel us to use it when we do not want to use it; to control our speeds, and to get such a large number of speeds on machines."[47]

During the 1880s and early 1890s, the use of electricity spread to all parts of the industrial plant. It could be used to power electrical lighting, which provided brighter and safer light than gas lamps. Electrical current could be used to power small tools such as a soldering iron or portable electrical rivet forges capable of heating 150 rivets per minute. Portable power tools reliant on electrical power were being devised to replace the use of traditional hand tools such as ratchet drills, cold chisels, scrapers, and files. Electricity was applied to nearly all heavy machinery found in the shops of a shipyard, including bending rolls; punches; planers; boring, drilling, and milling machines; cranes; derricks; lifting devices; and so on. The invention of the electromagnet saved labor by eliminating the need to unhitch loads. The magnetic grip could take hold of a heavy metal load and place it elsewhere, requiring only a crane and its operator.[48]

By the early 1890s, electricity had proven its usefulness for industrial applications. Once the depression of 1893 had run its course, older shipyards began the conversion of their plants from steam power to electricity. By 1895, the Union Iron Works had installed 400-horsepower worth of electricity-generating capacity.[49] By the mid-1890s, electricity had developed beyond the experimental stage, and new shipyards were being built that could take advantage of the application of electricity. The Cleveland Shipbuilding Company had completed a new, fully electrified shipyard at Lorain, Ohio, in 1897.[50] Powering shipyards with electricity became popular wherever conditions encouraged its use. In his 1896 comment, Oberlin Smith described the movement to electrify industrial plants, such as shipyards, as "remarkable," stating that "The whole movement is phenomenal. It is going faster than some of the most hopeful of us a year or two ago could reasonably have expected."[51] Meantime, the milder conditions in Great Britain allowed the British to remain faithful to hydraulic power for much of their machinery.[52]

By far the most ambitious application of electricity to a shipyard was the new facility of the New York Shipbuilding Company, referred to by locals as "New York Ship." Built in Camden, New Jersey, in 1898, New York Ship introduced electricity into the shipyard on a greater scale than had ever been attempted. An elaborate system for generating, transmitting, and distributing electricity had to be planned. Shafting was almost completely eliminated at New York Ship by extending the application of electricity to nearly every tool and device in the shipyard. This proved a great benefit because the shops were designed with an extensive overhead crane system that required unobstructed access to the shop floors. A writer for *Marine Engineering* reported that "Entering the Storage Shed, one obtains the first view of this immense inclosure [*sic*], and is struck by the absence of the belting and shafting in all the buildings."[53] The planners of the new yard included a powerhouse, which supplied both alternating and direct electrical current to the plant. The yard employed direct current to power the arc lamps for illuminating the shops. Direct current motors ran the numerous cranes housed within the shops, and alternating current motors drove the other machines tools employed by the firm.[54] In 1902, Scottish shipbuilder Archibald Denny described his visit to the shipyard to his colleagues, claiming that "Of all the yards I saw, I certainly think that the Camden Yard was the boldest in conception. Of course, when seeing these things, you have a regret that you do not own them."[55]

Welding also benefited from the introduction of electricity. Elihu Thompson began to develop electric welding in 1877, when he accidentally welded two copper wires together while lecturing at Philadelphia's Franklin Institute. He developed it for industrial purposes so that welding technology made its way into industrial use as the nineteenth century drew to a close. Welding by oxyacetylene gas was developed in France around 1900 and made its way to the United States by 1905. Welding proved its worth in early 1917, after the Germans ordered the destruction of its ships interned in the United States. German sailors sabotaged the power plants of their vessels, believing it would take the Americans years to repair them. The U.S. Navy employed welding to repair the vessels in record time so they could be refitted to aid in the Allied war effort. American authorities shared their knowledge with the British, and the first rivetless ship was laid down in England in 1918. Welding had the effect much sought after by shipbuilding firms of alleviating the need for riveting gangs. Using an electric welder or oxyacetylene gas, one man could attach plates to the hull as quickly as riveting gangs. While welding began to be used during World War I, its influence would not be strongly felt until the years leading up to World War II.[56]

Materials-handling work in shipyards represented the last bastion of unskilled labor found in American shipyards and many other industries.

The development of modern hoisting technology dramatically increased the profitability of ship construction by reducing the time and cost of materials handling, eliminating many of the bottlenecks in the production process, and bringing materials handling to a level in line with the mechanization experience in other parts of the shipbuilding process. It did this by eliminating many unskilled workers, livestock and stables, and reducing the time necessary for moving materials within the shipyard. Furthermore, the power of the new materials-handling machines allowed plates of greater size and weight to be used in ships. This meant that vessels could be built cheaper and stronger due to the reduced number of plates attached and rivets used to attach them.[57]

One of the most influential kinds of technology introduced to the shipbuilding industry during the late nineteenth century was the industrial crane. Materials handling had always been an important part of the shipbuilding process because of the size and weight of parts assembled in the final product. One historian of industrial history has characterized the introduction of modern materials handling, such as heavy-lifting technology, as a step "secondary in importance only to the introduction of the manufacture of interchangeable parts and specialized machine tools."[58] Prior to the 1880s, most lifting and transport activities within shipyards required a stable full of livestock, such as oxen, mules, or horses, and a fleet of carts, carriages, or wagons. The old method of materials handling was also time-consuming and labor-intensive, necessitating a small army of unskilled workers. In 1883, engineer Henry R. Towne claimed:

> In hundreds of mills and workshops heavy material is now being moved and handled by manual labor at an expense so much in excess of the cost of doing the same work far more rapidly and conveniently by cranes, that the saving effected by the latter would yield in annual profit of from twenty to fifty per cent upon their first cost.[59]

There were a number of factors that influenced the choice of a heavy-lifting device used in American shipyards. These included its design, construction, and power source. Most cranes found in American industrial establishments prior to the 1880s were made of wood. Many structures built to support more modern gantry and overhead traveling cranes in the 1880s and 1890s were also built of wood. For example, the state-of-the-art shipbuilding structures built to support the overhead traveling cranes at the Union Iron Works in 1884 had to be made of wood for lack of suitable structural steel material.[60] By the end of the century, industrialists had many lifting devices to choose from. There was the overhead traveling crane, requiring a structure to support it. There was the gantry crane, which had supporting uprights that traveled on tracks on the ground. There were cantilever cranes and stationary bridge cranes. Locomotive cranes were self-propelled hoisting devices that moved along railway tracks. Pillar cranes and jib cranes were smaller lifting devices often used in machine shops for hoisting smaller items. There were also stiff-leg cranes, which resembled elevated locomotive cranes. And finally there was the wire rope cable trolley system, which required support poles so loads could be transferred throughout the shipyard with cable hoists.[61]

Finding a reliable power source to run these cranes proved difficult at first. Prior to the 1880s, most of them not powered by man or beast had been run by steam power, and even the application of steam to lifting heavy loads was limited. Beginning in the early 1880s, American manufacturer Henry Towne of Connecticut began introducing hydraulically powered cranes.[62] Hydraulic cranes dominated the small American market for the next decade until electricity was found reliable enough to power hoisting devices. The first electrical crane was introduced in 1889. The application of electrical cranes spread slowly, in part due to their lack of a track record and the economic depression of 1893, which stifled capital investment for years. By the mid-1890s, however, electrical cranes had proven their superiority over hydraulic ones. By the late 1890s, most new industrial cranes built were electrical, while hydraulic cranes, such as those at Union Iron Works and Newport News Shipbuilding Company, were converted to electricity.[63]

By the late 1890s, electrical power had been proven enough and heavy-lifting technology had advanced sufficiently for a new shipyard to risk outfitting its entire physical plant with them. With a total of thirty-five electric overhead traveling cranes, each having a lifting capacity of between 5 and 100 tons, the New York Shipbuilding Company was the first to outfit its plant with a complete materials-handling system reliant on cranes. New York Ship's shops did not require railways because a network of thirty-five cranes handled nearly all of the materials that went into the ship. The plant's collection of cranes included unique "rubber neck" cranes, whose traveling hoists used extendible cantilevers to gain access to materials located in the galleries adjoining the main shop floor. New York Ship eliminated the need for many laborers employed for manipulating hooks, chains, and cables by employing electromagnets for lifting steel items. A skilled crane operator could lift a load of several sheets of steel and drop them one at time by quickly opening the magnetic switch and closing it before more than one plate had dropped. The immense Sellers 100-ton crane proved a spectacle to American and foreign visitors alike, especially since it could travel over all of the shipways and wet basin.[64] Scottish shipbuilder Archibald Denny observed: "The boldness with which they made the installation of cranes, especially with regard to that 110-ton crane, was remarkable. Their wet basin was . . . broad enough to hold two large steamers, but this crane spanned it entirely."[65]

The use of overhead traveling cranes became an essential feature of the modern American shipyard. Their value resided not just in cost reduction and timesaving but in the way they were employed to systematize the shipbuilding process. Engineers relied on these machines to alleviate production bottlenecks that had plagued nineteenth-century ship construction. Not only did these cranes fulfill the role of a lifting device, they also transported material to its next location along the production sequence. Without the new crane technology, new systematic methods developed to streamline production would have been impossible because the scale of material assembled in a large steel warship or merchant vessel around the turn of the century would have proved too burdensome for the technology commonly found in the nineteenth-century shipyard. Between 1880 and 1920, the size of an average hull plate tripled, from 12 feet in length to 36. And where a 100-ton crane seemed incredibly large at the turn of the century, naval shipbuilders were calling for fitting out cranes of up to 350 tons by the end of World War I.[66]

The early nineteenth-century introduction of the "American system" of manufactures to U.S. industry brought with it methods for greater efficiency, such as uniformity and standardization of tools in work shops. This was all a part of the movement to streamline production and make American industry more efficient. The efficiency craze extended to the design and construction of industrial plants, such as shipyards. Beginning with the Newport News Shipbuilding Company in 1886, shipyards began to be designed "to reduce manual labor to a minimum, and further, to handle material as little as possible."[67] This goal was not successfully achieved by Newport News, but it would become the hallmark of shipyards built thereafter.

The industrial engineer, skilled in designing industrial plants, rose to prominence during the late nineteenth century. Certain engineering firms began to specialize in shipyard design just as mill engineers, or so-called mill doctors, served in mill design and construction.[68] For example, H. I. Crandall and Son Company, which the Cramp shipyard consulted to build a new shipyard in Norfolk, Virginia, specialized in dry docks, marine railways, and shipyard structures. These engineering specialists concerned themselves with the delivery of power to machines in various parts of the shipyard and laying out tools in a rational sequence of production. As one historian has

Figure 22. The machine shop in a midwestern shipyard newly built of steel, concrete, and glass. Wisconsin Maritime Museum Collection. By permission of the Wisconsin Maritime Museum, Manitowoc.

noted, the metaphor of the factory as machine began to be used more frequently throughout the late nineteenth century.[69]

Beginning in the 1890s, shipyard structures began to depart in design and construction from the buildings found in wood and iron shipbuilding yards earlier in the century. They were designed to utilize sunlight as much as possible with the introduction of glassed-in or saw-toothed roofs for machine shops and sheds. Poured concrete or wood-blocked floors became more common in the shops and buildings found in the yards. The use of both steel and reinforced concrete grew in popularity during the 1880s and became more common by the turn of the century. When employed in combination with larger glass windows and skylights, these materials provided cleaner and brighter interiors, could support the heaviest buildings, and provided as much protection from fire as brick.[70]

The shipyard buildings constructed at New York Ship illustrated what modern energy sources and building materials had made possible by the turn of the century. Design of New York Ship's structures was guided largely by the desire to keep the shops and building ways under cover and accessible to traveling cranes. Railroad cars delivered materials to the shop buildings, but tracks were not allowed to traverse the floor space within the buildings, so cranes handled materials within the shops. The machine shop; boiler shop; blacksmith shop; frame shed; plate shop; general storehouse; brass shop; pipe shop; copper, tin, and light plate shop; mold loft; building ways; and outfitting basin were all sheltered under one roof. The interconnected buildings housing these departments covered a floor space of eighteen acres. The buildings possessed four acres of skylights and two acres of windows.[71] One British shipbuilder explained these structures to colleagues in guessing their size at "250 feet, but as a matter of fact they were 370. Everything was absolutely dwarfed by the enormous size of these sheds."[72]

The enormous ship sheds erected at New York Ship met with mixed results and failed to set a trend in modern shipyard construction. New York Ship's structures reduced the draft from winter winds. They also sheltered the uncompleted vessels from summer sun, which could heat them into frying pans for the ironworkers. On the negative side, sheds focused the noise of machines such as pneumatic tools within the enclosure, and the roof space increased the cost of plant upkeep. The comfort of ironworkers could not compete with the cost of such structures, and shipyards built or modernized after the establishment of New York Ship chose to erect uncovered crane-supporting structures over their shipways.[73] The chairman of New York Ship believed that "the covered ways do not appear to offer basic advantages sufficient to warrant their increased cost, for operations in the Middle Atlantic Coast climate."[74]

As the American shipyard grew in size and complexity, the hazards to shipyard workers increased as well. The great heights workers scaled to work increased the danger of workers falling, and the quantities of material suspended overhead increased the number of injuries in the shipyard resulting from materials falling on workers. Nineteenth-century iron yards used derricks and cranes with greater frequency because of the increased weight of the parts and pieces that went into a ship. The common use of cranes in more modern yards for materials handling meant that the frequency of injuries sustained from falling loads increased as well. Tools of various kinds also fell from ships into the holds, hitting workers on the head. At a time when workers did not commonly wear hard hats, injury from falling objects could prove serious if not fatal. Statistics on industrial accidents indicate that falls were the greatest cause of fatality in a shipyard. Falls into the holds of unfinished ships or from scaffolding along the hull to the shipways below nearly always resulted in death.[75] Most strikes undertaken by workers through 1920, however, took place not over unsafe working conditions but for higher wages and shorter hours.

Beginning with Collis P. Huntington's Newport News Shipbuilding Company, much larger shipyards began to build from the ground up, utilizing the latest technology and experience gained from the older, less efficient shipyards. Many of the older firms, such as the Roach shipyard; Harlan and Hollingsworth; Pusey and Jones; and Neafie and Levy, had added to their physical plant on an ad hoc basis as cash flow or lucrative contracts made such expansion possible. These larger shipyards required larger initial start-up costs but also promised smaller production costs and greater profits. While Roach and Cramp represented the largest shipbuilding concerns to be found in the nation through the late nineteenth century, they had been built upon a basis of older technology and expanded in piecemeal fashion. Shipyard technology experienced a sort of regeneration during the 1880s and 1890s, helping to push the United States near the top of the world's shipbuilding producers.

About the time that this new manufacturing technology emerged, a new kind of industrial movement began whose aim was greater efficiency and productivity. This trend had no formal parameters; it was simply an awareness by industrialists of the need to create greater efficiency through new technology and new methods. Many of its supporters were formally trained engineers, but many were efficiency experts without any formal education. Some of these individuals focused on production flow, some on time studies, some on cost accounting, some on standardization, others on piecework, still others on efficient arrangement of the physical plant, and so on. The efficiency craze went hand in hand with mechanization. Some of the new methods required machines for their implementation. Others required new machines to be developed before they could be successfully employed. Elements of this rational approach to production had been applied to American shipbuilding earlier in the nineteenth century, but shipbuilders failed to reform the entire production process until engineering practice became a major influence. A new generation of industrial engineers became masters of organizing the production of large, complex shipbuilding operations. One historian has referred to these engineers as "system builders."[76]

An awareness of the need to make things efficiently had begun in light industry with the development of the "American system" of manufactures during the early nineteenth century; however, the pursuit of similar objectives for heavy industry failed to take root until late in the nineteenth century. Some of the first indications of this trend may be seen in the special report compiled for the U.S. Census Office by chief special agent Professor W. P. Trowbridge. In his 1888 report entitled "Report on Power and Machinery Employed in Manufactures," Trowbridge studied the amount of system found in heavy manufacturing, the influence of uniform methods in production, and the degree to which interchangeability could be found in machine work. Trowbridge noted the rapid progress that machine tool development had experienced, claiming that "In the manufacture of small mechanism prolific output with great excellence of work has been realized through study and analysis." He believed, however, that only marginal progress in the attempts to use those tools had been made, but that "its demonstration is merely a matter of time."[77] Even though heavy industry had made little progress toward the goal of efficient production, the fact that an awareness and pursuit of rational methods of production had emerged marked a change in perspective for heavy industry in the United States.

One industry that had the greatest influence on the methods used in shipbuilding was bridge building. During the Civil War, the bridge-building industry had begun to standardize production after General Herman Haupt devised interchangeable bridge trusses for railroads carrying Union troops.[78] By 1880, the industry had already devised cost- and time-cutting measures such as printed specifications, steel structural members, material strength testing, templates for prefitted parts, prefabricated subassemblies, as well as standardized parts. During the 1890s, the industry standardized production further by applying uniform standards to such things as blueprints, order bills, eye bar heads, drift pins, turnbuckles, rivet spacing, rivet heads, the grading of steel, and dimensions for structural steel shapes.[79]

American bridge builders had increased efficiency through standardization to such a degree that their reputation won contracts worldwide. During the 1880s and 1890s, American firms mechanized production by placing greater reliance on overhead traveling cranes, multiple punching machines, and portable pneumatic riveters. These tools reduced the need for unskilled labor and increased the rate of production. Meantime, European bridge builders adhered to traditional practices of building each structure as a unique case without any attempt to apply uniformity or standardization. By the 1890s, American bridge-building firms began to challenge the hegemony of French and British firms in remote overseas locations such as Africa and the Far East. By the turn of the century, industry experts believed American bridge-building practices to be twenty years in advance of European methods.[80] An American incursion into markets traditionally held by European bridge-building firms was a sign of things to come in other American industries, such as shipbuilding.

The man who helped introduce similar changes to late nineteenth-century ship construction techniques was Henry G. Morse. Morse was born in Canton, Ohio, in 1850. His grandfather was half-owner of a fleet of thirty ships on the Great Lakes. His father was a banker who owned several money-making interests around Poland, Ohio. Morse graduated from the Rensselaer Polytechnic Institute in 1871 with a civil engineering degree. After graduation, he found employment with the Pennsylvania Railroad, building the Long Point Tunnel near Pittsburgh and supervising the construction of stone bridges over the Allegheny River at Foxburg and Parker's Landing.[81]

Morse became a specialist in the design and construction of iron bridges. In 1873, he left the Pennsylvania Railroad to begin a career in the bridge-building industry. Between 1873 and 1878, he served first as assistant and later chief engineer for the Wrought Iron Bridge Company in Canton. In 1878, he teamed up with his brother Charles to establish the Morse Bridge Works in Youngstown. He remained president of this concern until 1887, when a fire heavily damaged the works. The works were rebuilt and the firm renamed the Youngstown Bridge Works. Morse, however, moved on to begin business in Wilmington, Delaware. He organized the Edge Moor Bridge Company as a part of machine tool manufacturer William Sellers's Edge Moor Iron Works. Morse remained in charge of Edge Moor for nine years, enlarging the scope of the firm's business and increasing its output. Under Morse's guidance, Edge Moor made good use of Sellers's machine tools, such as hydraulic riveters and multiple punching machines, and he instituted the use of such methods as the prefabrication of subassemblies. Edge Moor Bridge built bridges throughout the United States and overseas during Morse's years with the firm.[82]

In 1896, Morse became president of Wilmington's Harlan and Hollingsworth Shipbuilding Company. The details surrounding his move to one of nation's largest shipbuilding firms remain veiled in mystery. He was the first president of the firm to be hired from outside of the company's personnel. The late 1890s proved a period of relative prosperity for the shipbuilding industry, so his move to the presidency was probably not tied to the need for fresh capital that he might bring to the firm. It is possible that Morse convinced the firm's directors to hire him so that he could introduce new construction methods that had proven highly effective in bridge construction. Within two years of signing on with Harlan and Hollingsworth, Morse would depart to fulfill his dream of establishing a state-of-the-art shipbuilding plant, employing the latest technology and methods.[83]

During his two-year stay at Harlan and Hollingsworth, Morse had already been developing a strategy for building the most modern shipyard in the United States. He used Harlan and Hollingsworth as a platform for testing the bridge-building techniques he had learned throughout his career. He may have even considered converting the old yard into a state-of-the-art facility. Such a plan could never have succeeded because of the confined area in which Harlan and Hollingsworth was located, the obsolete industrial plant found there, and the shallow, narrow river on which it was situated.

Morse resigned from the firm in the summer of 1898, and for the next twelve months he brainstormed the layout and technology he would incorporate in a brand-new shipyard. Between the summers of 1898 and 1899, Morse preoccupied himself with the establishment of a new shipyard. He developed floor plans, secured the necessary capital, sought a suitable location, and recruited a staff to help him build his new yard.[84]

While Morse was a capable planner and industrial designer, he surrounded himself with an informal brain trust of organizers and engineers to help him prepare to build the new yard. Andrew Mellon, future U.S. secretary of the treasury, became the firm's "organizer." Henry C. Frick, the coal and steel magnate, and his Pittsburgh friends underwrote the initial costs of the new plant. Morse's son, Henry G. Morse Jr., who had attained some note as a young architect, assisted in the design of the plant's structures, including its state-of-the-art office building. Construction engineer William B. Fortune had been associated with Morse since 1886, when both he and Morse began work at the Edge Moor Bridge Works. Fortune remained there until 1899, when he joined Morse to help supervise the construction of Morse's shipyard. After construction work at the yard had been completed, Fortune stayed on until 1909 as assistant hull superintendent. W. L. Robb, an academic specializing in electricity, served as consulting electrical engineer for planning the plant's electrification. Morse also recruited men from the shipbuilding industry such as Theodore Lucas, a noted marine engineer at the Cramp shipyard. Many other engineers would later leave Cramp to join Morse to take jobs at the Newport News Shipbuilding Company.[85] Morse's most influential advisor was Henry Lysholm, a native of Norway, who began his career in the United States at the New York bridge-building firm of Peter Cooper. During the late 1890s, Lysholm also joined Harlan and Hollingsworth, and together with Morse, instituted new shipbuilding methods at Harlan and Hollingsworth.[86]

The ultimate expression of efficiency and economies of scale came to be established in 1899 with the New York Shipbuilding Company. Morse broke ground in Camden, New Jersey, on July 3, 1899. A month later, contracts had been signed for preliminary work on the yard, and orders for plant machinery had been placed. Within a year, the first contract to build a ship had been signed. By September 1900, the plant employed 1,350 men. On November 29, 1900, New York Ship laid its first keel for the 3,000-ton tanker *J. M. Guffey*. The first of three oil tanker contracts, the *Guffey* was launched six months later and saw thirty-five years of service. By the end of 1901, New York Ship had already completed over $1 million worth of contracts and employed 2,500 men. By the time of Morse's untimely death in 1903, he had secured twenty shipbuilding contracts for his firm. Within a decade of its founding, New York Ship had won a capital warship contract from the navy for the armored cruiser *Washington*, a feat not commonly achieved by a new and relatively unknown yard.[87] Scottish shipbuilder Archibald Denny claimed New York Ship was a "revelation" and that "Two years before [1902], there was nothing there at all; this time I found all these sheds completed, the engine works and yard in full swing; they had delivered their first steamer, and there were two 370 footers under one shed."[88]

New York Ship would set the standard for all future shipyards as well as those contemplating modernization of their plant. Morse adopted so many shipbuilding innovations made possible by new technology that some have labeled him the "father of modern shipbuilding."[89] Morse designed the plant so the entire production process, from the supply of raw materials all the way to the fitting-out basin, took place under the cover of one roof. Because production was housed indoors, the work was sheltered from poor weather conditions and could be carried on around the clock if necessary. Enclosing the shops and shipways also meant that overhead traveling cranes had access to all parts of the enclosed space, alleviating the need to haul parts on the shop floor. With the aid of the comprehensive overhead crane system, subassemblies such as sterns, bridges, bulkheads, and deck structures could be fabricated in the shops and installed in the hull, cutting the time and expense of production. Despite the later impression that prefabricated shipbuilding methods were developed in World War I or even World War II, New York Ship began employing the technique in the early 1900s. Prior to the advent of heavy-duty cranes and derricks, shipyards had traditionally launched ships without any heavy machinery onboard and installed it all using the shear-leg derrick at the fitting-out dock. By using the overhead crane system, New York Ship became one of the first to install engines, boilers, and other heavy equipment in the hull before launching ships.[90]

Morse also had the foresight to plan his yard so that the buildings, machinery, and shipbuilding capacity could be expanded in time of need. This foresight paid off during both World Wars, when the shipyard was expanded considerably to fill the greater demand of wartime need. He built the yard on the site of a farm and used the farmhouse as the original office space. The yard began with 141 acres of land, far larger than the confined 30 acres of urban property that the Cramp shipyard encompassed at that time. By World War I, the yard was still located in a farming district, so real estate could be acquired for plant expansion and workers' housing. By the end of World War II, the yard had grown to fill up 200 acres with new shipways for building warships and merchant vessels.[91]

A hallmark of the new system employed at New York Ship, and one that marked a departure from traditional practical methods, had many different names. It was referred to as the "American method," the "factory principle" of shipbuilding, the "American system of building ships," the "mold system," and the "universal method." It was most commonly called the "template," or "templet," method.[92] This technique, along with prefabrication, had less to do with mechanization than it did with streamlining production. The common practice in nineteenth-century iron yards could be traced back to the wood shipbuilding method of "spiling," where shipwrights traced the outlines of a plank onto wood stock. In the case of iron shipbuilding, platers "lifted" a mold of the piece from the hull on the shipways and sent it to the shops where a plate could be fabricated. Using the new templet method, the plates were measured off in the mold loft from blueprints and the plates cut to shape without the added step of sending platers to the shipways to determine the outline of every single plate. By using templets, New York Ship set a record during World War I of just twenty-seven days to assemble a steel oceangoing ship.[93]

This new method allowed hull materials to move rapidly toward their location in the ship in contrast to the traditionally slow, time-consuming process of fitting plates. One Swedish engineer working at New York Ship observed that "a workpiece never turns back, but keeps moving on toward the building berth."[94] Where marking and shearing plates had been a labor-intensive process, it now became one of the quicker parts of the production process. With the templet method, plates and other parts were often ready for assembly weeks before the hulls were ready to receive them, and, as one observer noted, "if the work has been carefully performed no anxiety need be felt as to any parts not fitting properly."[95] One American naval architect claimed to have seen the deck plating for a vessel of over 600 feet "marked and completely machined before any deck beams were in position."[96]

Templeting rested on the basis of two important elements. First was the need for accurate drawings to aid a yard's shops or steel suppliers in fabricating ship parts that could be assembled as soon as they arrived at the shipways. The use of drawing in ship design had been gaining ascendancy over the use of half-hull models during the closing decades of the nineteenth century. Drafting still had only limited applications in American naval architecture until the templet method required accurate drawings to represent every piece of steel assembled in the hull of a ship. By World War I, hundreds of drawings were necessary to give steel fabricators accurate measurements for the parts making up the hull. By World War II, a battleship's design could consume 18 tons of blueprint paper.[97]

The New American Style of Shipbuilding 197

Figure 23. Patterns and templets were produced in the shipyard mold loft for cutting steel plate in the shops. Wisconsin Maritime Museum Collection. By permission of the Wisconsin Maritime Museum, Manitowoc.

The second factor that aided in the use of the templet method was the trend of engineering the ship to conform to efficient production rather than sculpting it according to the best form for speed and seaworthiness. Through the ages, practical shipbuilders had developed hull lines that provided ideal streamlined forms, but the new generation of shipbuilders needed designs that could be built cheaply and efficiently. It was the curved parts of the hull that required the most time and attention in the hull-building process. This meant that all unnecessary curves in the hull had to be straightened. Morse's engineers, such as Henry Lysholm, tried to straighten out the traditional hull form as much as possible so that uniform steel shapes could be used throughout the hull. This method facilitated greater economies of scale for New York Ship because the yard could lay off the plates for more than one ship using one set of templets. Engineering experts later agreed that New York Ship had begun to reinvent the process of designing ships, but they were quick to point out that Morse and his staff had failed to eliminate the need to fit the odd-shaped plates located in the bow and stern of ship hulls. The design of the American ship had begun to change from the sculpted lines that had so distinguished it during the nineteenth century to an engineered structural form. The change that led to this new form earned American shipbuilders worldwide attention once more.[98]

The reason why Henry Morse has been given so much credit as the father of modern shipbuilding is due to his widespread application of new technology and methods at New York Ship. Morse and Henry Lysholm had begun using standardized shipbuilding methods at Harlan and Hollingsworth at the same time these methods were being introduced to other American shipyards. However, their system had been implemented only on a limited scale in a Boston shipyard and such Great Lakes firms as the Chicago Shipbuilding Company, where Washington Babcock oversaw introduction of these techniques.[99]

If anyone deserves credit for successfully implementing the templet system, it would be Henry Lysholm. Lysholm helped work out the use of the templet system at Harlan and Hollingsworth. It worked so well that Morse claimed the greatest production bottleneck occurred at the point of attaching the plates and that his shipyard had to "work overtime to get the material on board in time for the work, it was to a large extent due to the fact that the plates were laid out before the frame . . . [and] . . . 400 or 500 plates had been laid out by templet and were all ready in stock, ready to be raised into position."[100]

When Morse left Harlan and Hollingsworth, he took Lysholm with him as a technical advisor. Lysholm worked on the preliminary layout of New York Ship, and when the first vessel was begun, he took charge of the lofting and templet system employed in the production process. Lysholm remained at New York Ship for the next sixteen years as the superintendent in charge of structural drawing, mold lofting, and plate and angle shops. In essence, he became an expert in reducing the number of steps involved in assembling a ship.[101] The methods employed at New York Ship had not sprung unaided from the genius of only Morse. And, as one historian has noted, the new methods instituted at New York Ship still proved imperfect. A great deal of time-consuming fitting still took place on the shipways even though the templet method had dramatically reduced the fitting process.[102] New York Ship did, however, point the way toward a shipbuilding industry reliant on engineering practices.

A part of shipyard systematization included reforming the way in which American shipyards were organized and operated. As an earlier generation of American naval constructors had reformed the way in which American ships were designed, a second generation of American naval constructors championed this technological transition. Holden Evans led this cadre of naval constructors.[103] Evans was one of an elite group of naval cadets sent overseas to receive training in naval architecture before becoming a naval constructor. Evans began his courses at Glasgow University in 1895. He began serving at the Norfolk Navy Yard in 1901 and was assigned to Mare Island Navy Yard, near San Francisco, shortly thereafter. By 1910, Evans had joined a group of efficiency experts that espoused Frederick Taylor's principles of scientific management. An ambitious man, Evans always carried out his work with a view to the mark he would leave on America's naval establishment. He chose to streamline the process of repairing and constructing ships in whatever way he could and to eliminate waste and inefficiency in American navy yards.[104]

Evans became famous for the reforms he carried out at the Mare Island Navy Yard. These reforms reached all corners of that yard, but they were more systematic than scientific. Evans analyzed the way in which jobs were completed, trying to eliminate all unnecessary and nonrepetitive tasks. In writing Frederick Taylor about the introduction of scientific management to Mare Island, Evans remarked: "I have . . . gotten a number of fundamental principles from my study of your writings and my talks with you. The most important is to analyze the work and find out what is to be done and a better way of doing it."[105] He established a planning department and routing system for the blacksmith shop, and he developed central plants for tool grinding, tool dressing, and leather-belt maintenance. He also instituted a policy of deadlines for intradepartmental jobs and erected blackboards in each department to prioritize important daily tasks.[106]

Evans changed the way in which materials were used and the way labor was managed at the Mare Island Navy Yard. He oversaw repair and construction when portable pneumatic tools were first introduced to field and shop use. He installed fuel oil–powered forges in the blacksmith shop because blacksmiths wasted so much time waiting for their coal-fired forges to heat a metal piece to the right temperature. Evans thereby increased output of the shop by 40 percent, cut the cost of forge fuel in half, and changed the facility from a smoky, sooty environment to a brighter, cleaner one. Due to an incentive pay program introduced by Evans, deck caulkers increased their productivity by using a seat equipped with rollers. This movable stool allowed the caulkers to roll along warship decks and caulk much faster, reducing the number of men necessary to caulk decks.[107]

Evans also changed the way naval vessels were repaired and built by incorporating certain elements of scientific management into navy yard practice. Evans used cost accounting not to track past performance but to control work in progress. For example, he instituted a new system of record keeping in the foundry and machine shop to track expenses. By using this method, he could make judgments concerning the efficiency of measures he put into practice at Mare Island. Based on his experiences at Mare Island, Evans wrote a book entitled *Cost Keeping and Scientific Management*, in which he laid down a five-point formula refining Taylor's cost-keeping methods. In his fifth point, he stressed the importance of keeping "an accurate record of the cost of the work in such detail that the various elements of cost may be quickly determined."[108]

At Mare Island, Evans carried out a number of reforms to cut labor costs. Using time studies, he studied many of the jobs found in the yard and put them on a piecework basis to increase efficiency. He instituted the use of piecework for repair jobs, which caused the yard's union-led workers to strike for the first time. Evans claimed that navy yard workers had established a "Don't give up the ship"[109] principle, because the longer the work took, the longer they would remain employed. Evans convinced the strikers to return to work on a piecework basis, pointing out that the faster ships were repaired, the sooner the yard would enjoy a reputation for quick work and win more private repair contracts.[110] Periodically the yard employed caulkers to caulk the decks of naval vessels. When Evans began his time studies of caulking, the equivalent of 80 to 100 feet of caulking was considered a fair day's work. By coaxing the caulkers on, Evans and his staff managed to get 250 feet per day caulked on average by each man. Next Evans pulled aside the best caulkers and convinced them to work on an incentive plan in which 250 feet would earn them a regular day's pay and any amount beyond that figure would earn them a bonus. This bonus plan increased production figures for the caulkers from 250 feet per day to between 380 and 400 feet per day.[111] Evans applied piecework to the scaling of ship's hulls. He time-studied the work of ten men, including one of his assistant naval constructors, and came up with a rate of about two cents per square foot scaled. The conversion from day rate to piece rate lowered the wages of the men and increased the amount scaled from approximately 60 square feet per day to nearly 200 square feet per day.[112] Evans extended the bounds of piecework beyond its previous confines to all caulking, riveting, hull drilling, chipping, laying off plate, punching, making rivets and bolts, and more. He used other forms of incentive plans common to scientific management but failed to employ them as frequently as piecework.[113]

In addition to job analysis, technical innovation, cost accounting, time studies, and piecework, Evans increased efficiency in other ways. In retubing boilers, he designed a more efficient work flow by sequentially arranging machines "so that the tube went from the door onto the rectifying slab, then to the cut-off saw, then to a grinder where the burrs were ground off, then to the polishing machine, and then to the boiler."[114] Retubing a boiler could be completed in thirteen days at a cost of $400, where it had once taken 120 days and $1,200.[115] Evans replaced his first-class machinists at the lathe with shop helpers trained by his staff. The result was an increase in productivity of 50 percent.[116] In another case, he instilled a sense of competition with other navy yards by challenging his men to build a vessel similar to one in the New York Navy Yard at less cost. The keel of the *Prometheus*, a fleet collier, was laid in the summer of 1907, and the keel of a fleet collier of the same design, the *Vestal*, was laid in New York as well. The collier built in New York should have cost far less than the *Prometheus*, due to the higher cost of materials and transportation costs on the West Coast. The New York Navy Yard had ample shipbuilding facilities, more experience building large naval vessels, and paid wages 25 percent lower than those at Mare Island. By instilling in his men a sense of competitiveness and by instituting his efficiency measures, Evans built the *Prometheus* at a cost of $1,512,828, over $110,000 less than the cost of the *Vestal*.[117]

Evans departed the navy, his mission unfulfilled. Once he had proved the value of scientific management in one navy yard, he would not be satisfied until he had reformed the entire navy yard system. Truman H. Newberry, navy secretary under Theodore Roosevelt, had encouraged Evans in this campaign. He gave Evans every confidence that a sort of Newberry-Evans plan would be installed to reform the navy yards. President Taft came into office before the new plan was instituted, however, and Evans's hopes of reforming the American navy yards became embroiled in politics and a power struggle between line officers on one side and reform-minded naval constructors and Frederick Taylor on the other.

In the end, Evans helped to defeat his own program. Workers in government industrial plants held greater power over politicians in Washington. This was particularly true for politicians whose precincts included navy yards and whose constituents included navy yard employees. Nationwide unions that represented workers at federal industrial plants also opposed the introduction of scientific management at government installations. This was especially so because policies instituted by federal facilities were often later instituted by private industry. Labor groups had been alienated by experiments with scientific management not only at Mare Island but also at the Watertown arsenal, where the U.S. Army produced its ordnance. This opposition led Congress to reject scientific management as official policy in the navy yards.[118] Evans also had alienated many of the powerful line officer faction of the navy. He did this by trying to take away command of navy yards from line officers and give it to trained naval experts, such as naval constructors. Not surprisingly, line officers from lieutenants up to admirals saw the Newberry-Evans plan as a usurpation of their authority. Having the most influence over naval policy of any of the factions in the Navy Department, the line successfully fought and won the battle to prevent the institution of Evans's navy yard reform program.[119]

While his personal experiment met with success, his department-wide crusade to introduce Taylor's principles to the navy proved a failure. Evans's overconfidence and inability to compromise with other elements in the conservative naval establishment doomed him from the start. As a result of his failure to introduce this new system to the navy, Evans quit the service to join the private sector. Evans was welcomed by the civilian shipbuilding industry, and he found himself head of one of the largest shipyards on the East Coast prior to the start of World War I.

In the years after the Evans debacle leading up to World War I, a new breed of engineer began to emerge in American industry. This new kind of engineer became increasingly common because the scale of production and the numerous sources of waste and inefficiency proved too daunting a task for ordinary proprietors. As economist Thorstein Veblen noted in 1914:

> The businessmen in control of large industrial enterprises are beginning to appreciate something of their own unfitness to direct or oversee, or even to control, technological matters, and so they have, in a tentative way, taken to employing experts to do the work for them. Such experts are known colloquially as "efficiency experts."[120]

These experts saw themselves as efficiency engineers or industrial engineers, and they no longer saw their field as scientific management, but as industrial management.[121]

Scientific management met with mixed results in the civilian shipbuilding industry. Shipyards building vessels to meet the needs of the war tried to apply the lessons learned over the previous twenty years. Observers noticed that shipbuilding firms failed to institute scientific management in their yards. In 1917, one observer of the industry complained that "The shipyards apparently have not grasped the fact that these [scientific management] principles are as applicable to their work as to that of others."[122] Industry experts finally realized that scientific management techniques were better applied in industries where there existed more repetition within the production process rather than in the complex nature of building a ship.[123]

For engineers and systematizers, World War I must have seemed like a dream come true. The Emergency Fleet Corporation of the United States Shipping Board filled its administrative ranks with engineers of various kinds to monitor costs and the efficiency of its shipyards. These engineers came equipped with a university degree, and many of them, such as Stephen Rockwell and William Ferguson, received their training at the Naval Academy.[124] Some efficiency measures were used in the shipbuilding industry that had been elements of the scientific management movement while other Emergency Fleet Corp (EFC) measures had been developed independent of scientific management. Industrial engineers focused on three major parts of shipbuilding: labor, materials, and materials handling. Piecework was used extensively in EFC shipyards during World War I. Its use was extended to one-third of the work performed in building EFC ships. In addition to the trades to which Evans applied it, piecework was also used for bolting up plates, pneumatic and oxyacetylene cutting, plate and angle erecting, painting, reaming, tile work, and piping.[125] The "bill of material" was devised to help track materials and keep them coming to the shipyard in proper order. New methods based on cost accounting also helped administrators keep track of materials and equipment. To organize and streamline the shipbuilding process, production engineers used other methods, such as progress charts, flow charts, work boards, instilling production competition between shipyards, and premium and bonus work. A history of the new methods used by shipbuilding management during the early twentieth century would require a volume of its own. Suffice it to say that the realm of management was extended to every aspect of shipbuilding, especially labor, materials, and materials handling.[126]

One of three shipyards established by the EFC, Hog Island was begun in the autumn of 1917, and by February 1918 its first keel was laid. The shipyard cost nearly $70 million and was the largest of its kind erected in the world's history. It covered a mile of Delaware River waterfront just south of Philadelphia and had fifty sets of shipways. At its peak, Hog Island employed nearly 35,000 workers and boasted its own YMCA, a barracks for 6,000 men, a first-class hotel housing over 2,000 men, fourteen eating establishments, a hospital, telephone facilities for 2,000 phones, post offices, a jail, a railroad station, and a bank building for payroll purposes. In essence, Hog Island possessed most of the amenities of a contemporary city of 50,000 inhabitants. Everything made for Hog Island was produced on a grand scale. The shipyard had one of the largest air-compressor plants of any industrial facility in the world. It powered nearly 7,000 portable pneumatic power tools. The yard also had a total of 400 tower derricks to cover its 50 shipways, or eight booms per ship. It also had 80 miles of railroad, with 20 locomotives and 450 railroad cars, and 18 miles of roadways and 165 trucks.[127] One Philadelphia reporter described Hog Island as "a magic city containing everything any other modern city had except a cemetery and a saloon," while a French observer referred to it as the "eighth wonder of the world."[128]

Hog Island was an experiment in improvisation. It not only made use of underemployed structural steel facilities, but it also employed inexperienced workers to build ships. Just as much of the ship steel had been promised to private shipbuilding firms, most all of the experienced shipbuilding labor had been hired on by shipyards during the early stages of the war. Furthermore, Hog Island experienced constant turnover because many of the men it employed were of draft age. Hog Island established its own training school for indoctrinating inexperienced workers. The school's superintendent trained any man who was physically able to do iron work regardless of his background. A survey of the school's attendance records reveals that they included former bartenders, baseball players, chauffeurs, ministers, and students. These men were trained to become riveters, caulkers, drillers, and specialized mechanics. Hog Island also became a training yard for welding, including three instructors and six machines for conducting training sessions. By 1918, Hog Island had approximately sixty men engaged in welding in its facility.[129]

The EFC borrowed the important techniques of fabrication and standardization from New York Ship. The widespread use of these methods during World War I marked the transition between ships designed on the basis of aesthetics and those engineered for rapid manufacture. With the onset of World War I and the need for numerous merchant vessels to counter those lost at sea, new design methods proved useful in ship construction. The EFC took the fabrication principle of New York Ship to a new more successful level than ever before. Where Henry Morse and his associates used the templet method to prefit plates and structural members for all parts of the ship but the stern and bow, the EFC managed to fabricate over 90 percent of the steel parts that entered into their ships. Few of these steel shapes required fitting once they arrived on the shipways.[130]

Many of the methods employed by the EFC at Hog Island originated with New York Ship. In 1916, the American International Corporation (AIC) purchased New York Ship, expanded its facilities in preparation for wartime production, and incorporated the shipyard. Hog Island was also built by

AIC, so New York Ship provided much of the technical support in design matters, and the federal government did not have to employ a large design staff at Hog Island. Even some of New York Ship's staff, such as William Fortune, assisted in the operation of the Hog Island shipyard.[131]

The EFC and New York Ship had to devise a system of precise drawings and paper templets to direct their fabricating shops in the manufacture of steel shapes for the ships. Accuracy became a high priority because the steel pieces shipped from one supplier had to be interchangeable with similar parts from another supplier. The EFC's 7,500-ton "Class A" cargo vessel required 1,300 blueprints, over 300 of which were necessary for the hull alone. Detailed drawings sufficed for all of the straight pieces that had to be fabricated to fit in the ship. Full-size paper templets had to be produced in New York Ship's mold loft, however, to delineate the more difficult pieces, such as the ship's curved shapes. These templets were produced in duplicate, so that New York Ship could retain the master, and a blueprint could be sent to the fabricating yard. This system became so successful that the 30,000 parts that made up a Class A vessel normally fit with few problems.[132]

The EFC took the principle of standardization to a higher level than had any previous shipbuilding concern. Practical shipbuilders had built multiple vessels from one model for hundreds of years, but they had done so not to speed production but to replicate the superior sea-keeping qualities of a successful design.[133] To implement greater standardization, the EFC hired naval architect Theodore Ferris to design a ship that could employ uniform steel shapes and plates for speedy production. Ferris's design was the 7,500-ton vessel generically termed the Class A cargo vessel. Ferris's design incorporated the best shipbuilding and bridge-building practice and called for straight lines and flat surfaces wherever possible. Ferris made the sides, deck, and bottom straight and flat, and the midship section a rectangular shape. This left only the extreme front and rear and bottom corners curved. Tumblehome—the curvature of the hull's side as it rises to deck level—was eliminated from Ferris's ship to reduce the need for the time-consuming process of bending individual frames. Ferris and other EFC naval architects even had to learn the drawing methods and terminology unique to structural steel firms so that they could better understand the size and shape of the parts the firm fabricated for the shipyards. Ship designers learned that straightening the lines of a ship did not increase a hull's hydrodynamic resistance, requiring no more power than an ordinary shipshape hull, and the straight-line form provided greater stability than the hull with curved hull lines.[134] Still, the Class A ships were more of an engineered form that the shapely curved, almost organic, lines of their practically designed predecessors. A member of AIC described the ships as resembling a "steel frame building lying on its side."[135]

Hog Island became the assembly area of a nationwide shipbuilding factory, to which structural steel fabricators shipped parts from all corners of the United States. American bridge-building and structural steel operations had remained relatively idle during early wartime production. The bridge-building industry, particularly the numerous plants of the J. P. Morgan–financed American Bridge Company, provided the expertise and productive capacity to fabricate the parts of ships for the EFC. They made these parts from precise drawings and templets so that laborsaving devices such as multiple punching machines could be employed. Heavy reliance on the multiple punching machine, for example, almost doubled the punching capacity of certain shops.[136]

The steel parts that made up a Hog Island vessel were fabricated in shops and factories hundreds or even thousands of miles from the shipyard. To speed production and maximize railroad capacity, many parts shipped to Hog Island, such as the smokestacks, arrived pre-assembled. One-quarter of each ship's rivets were driven in the subassemblies that came by way of the railroad. As a result, very few of the items received at Hog Island had to be either worked or corrected in the shipyard's plate and angle shop. In fact, the shop erected for the purpose of correcting the shape of fabricated parts proved so useless that it was converted into a storage area. Since most ordinary steel producers were swamped with orders from private shipyards for ship steel, the parts that were shipped to Hog Island originated in thirty-eight mills in Pittsburgh, Youngstown, and Cleveland. Before making their way to Hog Island, the steel parts were transported to eighty-eight fabricating plants as far west as Kansas City and as far north as Montreal.[137] George J. Baldwin, vice president of AIC, described Hog Island as an "assembling floor of a colossal ship factory, whose machinery was made up of all the interrelated wheels of American industry, whose employees were a large part of the entire body of American labor, and whose conveyor belts were the American railways."[138]

Every succeeding vessel built at Hog Island was an exact reproduction of the first, identical to it in most every detail. Standardization prevailed throughout the ships. The Class A model and a modified 8,000-ton version called the Class B freighter represented something of the Model T in the form of a ship. All extraneous gear was eliminated from the decks; wooden decking was eliminated as much as possible; internal fittings were made with standard piping, machinery, and furniture; and all side hull portals were dis-

Figure 24. Parts and subassemblies, such as davits and rudders, are stacked in this World War I shipyard ready to be lifted onto a vessel for assembly. Wisconsin Maritime Museum Collection. By permission of the Wisconsin Maritime Museum, Manitowoc.

pensed with. Over three thousand suppliers and subcontractors nationwide provided such items as standardized hatches, watertight doors, boilers, propellers, and other fittings through mass production. They set up jigs and fixtures so that the products they shipped to the EFC yards met standards of uniformity. The propeller shaft of each vessel was made up of five interchangeable sections to simplify storage and erection.[139] The EFC even set up a branch of its engineering force to standardize practice in the yards under its supervision. Established in 1918, the standard practice branch sent its staff to the shipyards to analyze the methods employed in each yard and then pooled their findings to determine the one most efficient way of fabricating parts for the ships. The results of their analysis were published in the *Emergency Fleet News and Shipbuilders Bulletin* and distributed to the different yards.[140]

By the end of World War I, Hog Island had begun to reach its peak production. When shipbuilding activities ceased in 1921, however, Hog Island had had time to produce only 110 vessels. In 1930, the shipyard property was sold to the City of Philadelphia and later became Philadelphia's airport.[141] Sir Arthur J. Salter, contemporary British expert on shipping, had claimed in his book *Allied Shipping Control* that Hog Island "was a wonderful example of the rapid adaptability of modern engineering skill in a country with ample resources in men and materials, and an adequate incentive to rapid effort."[142] Standardized ship forms proved more efficient to assemble than the one-of-a-kind vessels that had predominated throughout the nineteenth century. Hog Island and the other EFC shipyards had pointed the way toward modern shipbuilding practice. Standardization had proven successful in producing ships rapidly and efficiently. Had there been continued need for these vessels, the cost per vessel probably would have fallen considerably.[143]

By the middle of World War I, Henry Ford pointed the way to modern shipbuilding practice even more by applying mass production methods to American warship construction. By 1918, the United States faced a shortage of small warships capable of carrying out convoy escort duty and submarine warfare. Navy secretary Josephus Daniels asked Ford to consider the possibility of manufacturing warships for the U.S. Navy. Ford saw mass production not just as quantity production but as the "focusing upon a manufacturing project of the principles of power, accuracy, economy, system, continuity, and speed."[144] Many shipbuilding methods and tools developed late in the nineteenth century and early twentieth century had brought shipbuilding closer to that description.

The ultimate expression of the engineered design and rational production of ships came with the Ford Eagle Boat Program in 1918. The 200-ton Eagle Boats represented a factory-built ship in nearly every respect. Ford did not call upon experts in the shipbuilding industry either to plan the layout of his new shipbuilding plant or to help train the men that he hired. The navy provided a design that eliminated as many curves as possible and maximized the use of flat hull plates to simplify the construction process for novice shipbuilders and to speed up production. Some believed the design had been engineered for production to such an extent that seaworthiness had been sacrificed as a result. Industry writers described the new plant as "a combination of bridge shop, automobile works and marine fitting-out yard."[145]

Ford borrowed many design and construction features developed in the previous decades. Use of the templet, or fabricated method, was practiced extensively to preclude the need for fitting. Prefabrication was used wherever possible to speed assembly. Ford also called into use portable pneumatic tools and electric welding to expedite production. The multiple punch machine became the mainstay for the fabrication of plates for the sub chasers. The machines used at River Rouge could punch up to fifty holes at a time if necessary.[146] One reporter writing on the system claimed: "Thus in brief outline is the general method followed of fabricating or manufacturing ship hull components, interchangeable and ready to erect without fitting. When a plate goes into the erecting plant it is finished and ready to erect; no trip back to the fitting shop is necessary."[147]

Ford began the program by assembling a pattern vessel to use as a jig for making patterns and planning the production scheme for the Eagle Boats. He enlarged his production facilities at the River Rouge plant in Michigan so that part of the facility could be devoted to ship production. The new structure, said to be the largest in the world at that time, housed three parallel tracks, each having seven assembly stations. The plant provided for the simultaneous assembly of twenty-one ships.[148] Ford used pressed-steel shapes rather than rolled steel and set up rivet-polishing machines so that rivets could be heated in electric forges. Electric forges assured consistent heating of rivets without the smoke and danger of hot coals. Ford also enlisted the use of newly introduced flame-cutting torches for quick cutting of specialty shapes. Ford was the first individual to employ the assembly line for constructing a class of steel ship, practicing the theory of straight-line movement of material. The Eagles rode on timber cradles supported by twelve four-wheeled trucks. To facilitate the progress of the ships along the assembly line, all staging for riveters and ironworkers was secured to the hulls rather than resting on the floor. After the completed hulls had made their way down the tracks of the assembly plant to the water's edge, they were placed on a hydraulic launching platform very similar to the dry dock built at Union Iron Works in the 1880s. The hydraulic platform expedited the launching process and eliminated the risk of accidents.[149] An industrial reporter wrote about the lack of "sliding down inclined greased ways, breaking of wine bottles and cheering of the crowd." He also wrote that "The movement on wheels which has prevailed throughout . . . the process of erection . . . is here vertical instead of horizontal."[150]

The Eagle Boat Program proved less than successful. It never met the requirements set by Ford for mass-producing items. First of all, the boats were not set on a moving assembly line like the Model T. Instead, they had to be stopped seven times along the assembly line for workstations. Ford and his engineers managed to get fabrication time of the vessels down to ten days per vessel. Fitting-out of the boats proved a process less amenable to rational production methods. Installing the power plant, piping, armament, and other equipment proved time-consuming. One of Ford's requirements

Figure 25. An aerial view of a World War I shipyard shows the influence of mechanization and modern building materials, such as concrete and steel, had on the arrangement of shipbuilding facilities. Wisconsin Maritime Museum Collection. By permission of the Wisconsin Maritime Museum, Manitowoc.

for true mass production was the elimination of fitting parts. The fitting-out process for the Eagle Boats, however, required a good deal of time for the vessels' internal machinery. There were problems with the quality of welding. Ford employed no shipbuilding talent in training his men, a mistake that cost him time and money.[151]

One historian sees Ford's failure to make the Eagle Boat Program a success as a matter of the "difficulty of transferring the methods used to manufacture a high-volume consumer durable like an automobile into an area like shipbuilding, which had its own tradition of knowledge and skills."[152] What Ford failed to do, however, was to extend rational methods to the fitting-out process, a situation that could have been solved given time. Like Hog Island, Ford's shipbuilding program could have fulfilled his expectations had the program not been a stopgap measure designed to satisfy wartime demands. Ships are large and complex machines, and it would take time and experience to develop their manufacture into a mass-production industry. Mass production of ships has not taken place during peacetime because there has never been enough demand for ships to support the investment in such a program.

The late nineteenth century and early twentieth century witnessed the greatest changes in the American shipbuilding industry's history. From the 1880s through World War I, the methods used to manufacture American ships changed from practical to theoretical. Elements of scientific shipbuilding imported by naval personnel were applied to American shipbuilding. Many new efficiency measures and ways to rationalize production were adopted from other American industries where they had proven effective in reducing costs. While chapter 7 described the design methods and institutions ensuring the survival of theoretical design in the United States, this chapter has looked at modern construction techniques developed to improve production in the shops and on the shipways.

In the last two decades of the nineteenth century, American naval personnel brought to the United States a new way of designing ships. A reverse process occurred in the first decades of the twentieth century as Europeans adopted production technology from the United States. Europeans first learned of the changes taking place in the United States when Americans published articles on the success of their methods and American firms began to underbid European ones for shipbuilding contracts. After Washington Babcock presented a paper on portable pneumatic riveters at the Institution of Naval Architects in 1899, British shipyards began to adopt the use of portable pneumatic riveters. The same thing happened after William A. Fairburn submitted papers on American crane technology at the Institution in 1902 and 1903. European shipbuilders envied the equipment available to American shipyards. In 1916, British industrialist Hugh Bell remarked that the horsepower available to workers in the American iron- and steel-working trades was double that for their British counterparts. The Europeans acquired machinery built by American firms, such as millers, lathes, pneumatic riveters, and electric welders. The transfer of American methods and technology to Europe demonstrates that the flow of technology is never one-way.[153]

What the Americans gained in design methods and technology from Europe, they returned in new construction methods and technology. This transfer of American production methods was, in some ways, similar to the transfer of the "American system" of manufactures to England in the mid-1800s. Early in the twentieth century many Europeans came to the United States on fact-finding trips, while others worked in American shipyards to gain experience with the new methods and technology. As Fairburn wrote in one of his papers: "The frequent visits of British and foreign naval architects and engineers to America, having for one of their objects the study of

American methods of handling material in shipyards, has influenced the writer to prepare this extensive paper."[154] The Europeans brought home the templet method of laying off ship plate, prefabrication, standardization of production, and scientific management.[155] In so doing, they not only acquired much of the new technology developed in the United States, buy they also adopted methods that utilized that technology effectively. In this way, European shipbuilders adopted elements of an American style of ship manufacture.

Conclusion

Building an American Ship in the Twentieth Century

It would take a book to hold all one might tell that has occurred while we have encumbered the earth and I am wondering if one gifted as you are with a speaking pen would not find pleasure and profit in letting the present generation know what has gone on before its time in the development of the art and craft of shipbuilding.

Naval architect William A. Dobson to William P. Stephens, 1935

William Dobson's proposition to naval architect William Stephens commends the dramatic changes the American shipbuilding industry experienced during the two men's working lives.[1] Early in the nineteenth century, shipbuilding had been the province of craftsmen whose tools and methods were handed down for centuries. By the early twentieth century, the tools and methods employed in shipbuilding would be unrecognizable to a shipwright a century earlier. Navy support for technological development of shipbuilding methods was responsible for much of this change. American shipbuilders had their own craft-based approach to design and adopted a more theoretical approach after the navy introduced it to the United States. While American shipbuilders resisted the introduction of a new way of designing ships, they did innovate technology in the form of new machines. Labor costs encouraged large manufacturers to adopt new machinery wherever possible. This they did most dramatically in the closing decades of the nineteenth century. Technological development in the shipbuilding industry had continued gradually in a characteristically American way during most of the nineteenth century. By the early twentieth century, however, the American shipbuilding industry had adopted the tools and methods that made it the most advanced in the world.

The object of this work has been to show how American shipbuilding changed from a craft to a heavy industry. The design and construction of wooden ships were the province of highly esteemed craftsmen whose stock of knowledge included an array of hand tools and methods reliant on experience and intuition. The nature of change in the field of ship design and construction in the United States does not lend itself to simplistic theories. During the period covered by this work, numerous factors influenced the development of the trade from a craft—complete with many of the trappings of medieval work methods—to a large-scale heavy industry. This work has covered many, but by no means all, of the factors that influenced the American shipbuilding industry over the course of the nineteenth century. No single event determined the industry's record of change. A myriad of social and economic determinants shaped the course of shipbuilding development.

Over the course of the nineteenth century, the British devised a theoretical approach to shipbuilding. The goal of applying rationalism to design and construction formed the basis of engineering methods that developed in eighteenth-century France and reached Great Britain by the end of the eighteenth century. As with other forms of construction, this theoretical approach influenced shipbuilding. During the nineteenth century, a British profession of naval architecture developed that included research, formal education, and a strong basis of abstract mathematics. The British scientific shipbuilding movement rationalized the process of designing ships and added a layer of elite builders to the hierarchy of an earlier practical shipbuilding establishment.

This work has described a transnational story about the growth of two distinctive approaches to shipbuilding. The comparison of American and British ship design and construction methods bears out the fact that every society adapts technology in its own way. Cultural factors greatly influenced the direction taken by technological development in America and Great Britain. The theoretical approach to shipbuilding seemed elitist and exclusive to Americans, while the practical approach struck them as democratic and available to most any ambitious shipwright. Early on, practical shipbuilders learned everything about their trade, and the path to upward mobility remained open. This would change as American yards grew larger during the rest of the nineteenth century.

A myriad of economic influences helped shape the American shipbuilding industry during the nineteenth century. Raw materials used for shipbuilding, for example, had an impact on the methods employed in each country. By the nineteenth century, wood had been the basis for practical shipbuilding in the United States for centuries. The introduction of iron to the shipbuilding industry did not encourage the application of engineering methods to ship design, however. Instead, American shipbuilders relied on the stock of knowledge handed down from the wood shipbuilding industry, which rested upon skill, experience, and craft knowledge. The early introduction of iron to shipbuilding in Great Britain brought with it civil engineers and engineering methods. British society began to see iron ships as a manifestation of technological progress and the result of applying science to industry.

Urbanization facilitated the growth of the industry. Throughout the history of shipbuilding, the trend has been to build increasingly large ships. As the size of vessels increased, the scale and complexity of the plants that built them increased as well. Small rural shipyards produced coasting vessels and smaller oceangoing ships throughout the nineteenth century. Urban yards built increasingly large sailing vessels and steamers by expanding their workforce and mechanizing to increase efficiency. As urban shipyards grew increasingly large and complex, labor division grew, and control of the production process shifted from skilled workers to managers and engineers. By 1920, most aspects of American shipbuilding had been systematized and mechanized. Shipwrights of 1820 would recognize little, if anything, in the modern shipyard except the form of the ship itself.

During the nineteenth century, American shipbuilding experienced numerous changes. The market for ships varied with historical trends such as immigration and the California Gold Rush. Periodic fluctuations in the market for American ships encouraged the concentration of the industry's capital and labor into fewer yards of larger size. Machinery also made possible increased efficiency and a reduction of the workforce, both skilled and unskilled, necessary to build vessels. The shipbuilding industry became urban-based. The majority of the firms involved in large-scale shipbuilding were situated in urban areas where there existed greater reserves of labor, capital, and readily accessible raw materials. These larger yards led the industry in technological development, and members of the shipbuilding community quickly disseminated technical knowledge between firms.

Political factors played a major role in the way Americans built ships. Political developments hindered the technological development of the American shipbuilding industry. Post–Civil War conditions encouraged shipbuilders to rely on practical methods rather than pursue the theoretical methods developed overseas. Before the Civil War, the federal government began to subsidize American passenger lines to help them compete with the already subsidized British lines. After the war, the federal government turned its back on shipping, choosing to focus its efforts on supporting the construction of a nationwide railroad network. Congress added a tariff to imported iron goods, protecting American iron producers and inflating the cost of American-built iron ships relative to British ones. Fortunately, Congress restricted all domestic shipping to American vessels. Otherwise there would have been little, if any, demand for American-made ships. Congress cut postwar postal subsidies to low levels, and those paid out were often granted to foreign shipping lines. The navy sold off hundreds of surplus vessels at cut-rate prices, thereby depressing the market for newly built ships after the Civil War. British shipbuilders perfected scientific shipbuilding, while the few American iron shipbuilders that survived the antishipping policies of Congress continued to employ the methods of practical shipbuilding.

The development of American shipbuilding methods during the nineteenth century exhibited gradual evolutionary behavior as well as rapid revolutionary change. The shipbuilding industry experienced gradual technological change throughout most of the nineteenth century. Even the changes wrought by the introduction of iron to the industry in the mid-1800s were less than dramatic for shipbuilders. Iron shipbuilders adopted many of the time-honored design and construction methods of their wooden-shipbuilding predecessors.

This distinctively American way of building ships did not hinder the mechanization of processing materials that went into each ship. Wood and iron shipbuilders sought to lower costs wherever possible by reducing the labor force through the use of machines. While iron shipbuilders developed and acquired new machinery, they did not, however, adopt the design and construction methods perfected in Great Britain during the nineteenth century. To the frustration of men like John W. Nystrom, American shipbuilders did not embrace the methods and institutions that an engineering-based profession required. Instead, they continued to develop some of the most technically advanced shipbuilding machinery while taking a decidedly antitheoretical design approach.

The process of gradual development occurring in the nineteenth century would have continued unhindered had not a new system of shipbuilding been introduced from overseas. The transfer of shipbuilding methods from Great Britain changed the course of technological development in the shipbuilding industry. This infusion of new methods and technology came not from the private sector but from the federal government. The need to rebuild the U.S. Navy's post–Civil War fleet spurred the navy into action. The navy began a crash program of acquiring European, in particular British, shipbuilding technology and technical knowledge. The navy transferred from Britain a "scientific" socio-technical system that included formal schools of naval architecture. It also included the use of abstract mathematics and sophisticated mechanical calculators, the publication of trade journals, participation in professional societies, and the establishment and use of experimental facilities such as model ship basins. The British system of scientific shipbuilding eventually supplanted the practical building techniques of American shipyards. The navy established this profession and its supporting institutions on a permanent footing by the early twentieth century, when private shipbuilders began to adopt the profession as a necessary part of the industry. By the end of the century, civilian and naval shipbuilders alike had embraced the trend toward professionalization that resulted in the introduction of this new system of ship design. The British system made possible the development of an engineering-based profession of naval architecture that we see today. The "technology transfer" facilitated rapid technological change in the U.S. shipbuilding industry after the centuries of gradual change that had preceded it.

While the navy imported new design methods to the United States, American shipbuilders devised ways to rationalize ship production. A new breed of industrial experts emerged in the late nineteenth century and early twentieth century who made it their business to systematize American industry. This group included educated engineers and self-trained efficiency experts. They employed all means at their disposal to turn the American factory into a finely tuned machine. During the late nineteenth century, American industry adopted electrical, hydraulic, and pneumatic power and new machines such as materials-handling devices. This new industrial technology aided shipyards in cutting labor costs, streamlining production, and reducing production time. To employ this new production technology more efficiently, engineers introduced such changes as the physical restructuring of shipyards, increased labor division, expanded application of piecework, standardization, prefabricated assembly, and various aspects of scientific management. As the power of engineers over the shipbuilding industry grew, the control of skilled labor over production diminished. By the early twentieth century, American shipyards had become models of efficiency for shipbuilding nations all around the world.

The stock of knowledge comprising tools, methods, and work institutions exerted the greatest influence on the way ships were built. Hand tools remained an important part of hull construction through much of the nineteenth century. The role these tools played in learning and the transmission of skill to raw material diminished as fieldwork became increasingly mechanized and divided among specialized trades. Americans became experts at systematizing the construction of ships by mechanizing the shipyard. The tools, methods, and institutions of ship design experienced their most dramatic transformation with the U.S. Navy's introduction of British naval architecture practices. Naval architecture schools and professional societies replaced the age-old social and educational institutions of apprenticeship, journeymen, and kinship ties within the shipbuilding community. By 1920, the design and construction elements belonging to the craft of shipbuilding had been eliminated in the nation's leading shipyards.

Today most of the major American shipyards have closed. For example, none of the noteworthy shipyards along the Delaware River, the "American Clyde," have survived the 1990s. On the other hand, wooden ship production has recently experienced a revival. Tall ships have become popular as moneymaking ventures and as representatives of their homeports and mother countries. To produce these vessels, wood shipbuilders use power tools and modern design methods as much as possible. The wood shipbuilding industry is far too small to support the institution of apprenticeship or generations of a dynastic shipbuilding family. Visitors to today's wood shipyard, however, can still see some of the same kind of hand tools used by thousands of America's practical shipbuilders. These tools continue to serve their purpose as they did over a hundred years ago despite the development of more modern woodworking technology.

Notes

Chapter 1. The Origin of Practical Shipbuilding Methods

1. Kipling epigraph from "The Wrong Thing: A Truthful Song" in *Rewards and Fairies*.
2. For more on the evolution of technology, see Basalla, *The Evolution of Technology*.
3. Unger, *The Ship in Medieval Economy*, 24–25.
4. In *The Intelligence of a People*, 240–41, Daniel Calhoun makes the distinction between these two forms of shipbuilding.
5. Tudor, *Some memorandums*, 2–5; Chapelle, *The Search for Speed under Sail*, 22; Abell, *The Shipwright's Trade*, 66.
6. Abell, *The Shipwright's Trade*, 34; Lucien Basch, "Ancient Wrecks and the Archaeology of Ships," *International Journal of Nautical Archeology and Underwater Exploration* 1 (1972): 5.
7. For more on the use of molds, see Basch, "Ancient Wrecks and the Archaeology of Ships," 34–39; Arne Emil Christensen Jr., "Lucien Basch: Ancient Wrecks and the Archeology of Ships," *International Journal of Nautical Archeology and Underwater Exploration* 2, no. 1 (1973): 141–44; and Sergio Bellabarba, "The Origins of the Ancient Methods of Designing Hulls: A Hypothesis," *Mariner's Mirror* 82, no. 3 (August 1996): 261–67.
8. Sergio Bellabarba, "The Ancient Methods of Designing Hulls," *Mariner's Mirror* 79, no. 3 (August 1993): 290.
9. Lavery, *Ship of the Line*, 2:10–13; Chapelle, *The Search for Speed under Sail*, 16.
10. Hutchinson, *Medieval Ships and Shipping*, 4–20.
11. Blake, *Lloyd's Register of Shipping, 1760–1960*, 1–5; Higgins, *Annals of Lloyd's Register*, 3–15; H. J. Cornish, "The Classification of Merchant Shipping," *Institution of Naval Architects Transactions* (hereafter cited as *INA Transactions*) 47, pt. 2 (1905): 317–19.
12. Fincham, *A History of Naval Architecture*, 63–75; Frank Fox, "The English Naval Shipbuilding Program of 1664," *Mariner's Mirror* 78, no. 3 (August 1992): 277–92; Chapelle, *History of the American Sailing Navy*, 8–10. For a more complete description of the establishment system, see Lavery, *Ship of the Line*.
13. Blake, *Lloyd's Register of Shipping*, 5–14; Higgins, *Annals of Lloyds*, 16–21.
14. Friel, *The Good Ship*, 43.
15. Abell, *The Shipwright's Trade*, 36–38.
16. John Gardner, "Shipwright's Tools," *Log of Mystic Seaport* 21, no. 3 (September 1969): 94.
17. Goldenberg, *Shipbuilding in Colonial America*, 22.

18. Rorabaugh, *The Craft Apprentice*, 4.

19. Ibid., 9; Hutchins, *American Maritime Industries and Public Policy*, 104, 120.

20. Goldenberg, *Shipbuilding in Colonial America*, 8–9, 122; Kebabian, *American Woodworking Tools*, 143–46; Bishop, *A History of American Manufactures*, 1:37.

21. Goldenberg, *Shipbuilding in Colonial America*, 52–53; quotation Bishop, *History of American Manufactures*, 90.

22. Goldenberg, *Shipbuilding in Colonial America*, 27; Goldenberg, "With Saw and Axe and Auger," in Hindle, ed., *Material Culture of the Wooden Age*, 121; Bishop, *History of American Manufactures*, 41; Chapelle, *History of American Sailing Ships*, 8.

23. Chapelle, *The Search for Speed under Sail*, 6–15.

24. Gardner, "Shipwright's Tools," 91.

25. Goodman, *History of Woodworking Tools*, 9, 40, 123, 188–96.

26. Salaman, *Dictionary of Woodworking Tools and Tools of Allied Trades*, 468; Friel, *The Good Ship*, 59.

27. Friel, *The Good Ship*, 59.

28. Ibid., 55.

29. Salaman, *Dictionary of Woodworking Tools*, 49–50; Jan Bill, "Ship Construction: Tools and Techniques," in Gardiner, ed., *Cogs, Caravels, and Galleons*, 155.

30. Bill, "Ship Construction," 154.

31. Salaman, *Dictionary of Woodworking Tools*, 28–29.

32. Bealer, *Old Ways of Working Wood*, 117–19. For more recent examples of adz injuries, see entries for woodworkers John Carroll, Charles Gingree, W. S. Waltman, J. C. Rogers, and Jacob Harris, in "Accident Reports for Phoenix Bridge Co., 1901–1920," Book 476, Accession 916, Hagley Museum and Library Archives.

33. Goodman, *History of Woodworking Tools*, 143–45; Bill, "Ship Construction," 154.

34. Friel, *The Good Ship*, 63; Bill, "Ship Construction," 154.

35. Friel, *The Good Ship*, 63; Goodman, *History of Woodworking Tools*, 118–31.

36. Bealer, *The Old Ways of Working Wood*, 87–91; Marcil, *The Charley-Man*, 252–53.

37. Goodman, *History of Woodworking Tools*, 165–72; Friel, *The Good Ship*, 59.

38. Unger, *Dutch Shipbuilding before 1800*, 61; Goodman, *History of Woodworking Tools*, 160–64, 175–79; Bill, "Construction Tools and Techniques," 157.

39. Bill, "Ship Construction," 158; Friel, *The Good Ship*, 64; Gardner, "Shipwright's Tools," 92–94.

40. Goldenberg, "With Saw, Axe and Auger: Three Centuries of American Shipbuilding," in Hindle, ed., *America's Wooden Age*, 114; Hutchins, *American Maritime Industries and Public Policy*, 108, 118.

41. Fincham, *History of Naval Architecture*, 77; Laise, "Interpreting the Colonial Shipyard," 244; Harold C. Roberts, "The Old Steam Shed," *American Neptune* 7, no. 3 (July 1947): 196–99.

42. Wood, *Live Oaking*, 111–18; Chapelle, *History of the American Sailing Navy*, 24–25.

43. Keller and Keller, *Cognition and Tool Use*, 61–63 (quotation on page 60).

Chapter 2. The Growth of Scientific Shipbuilding in Great Britain

1. Chatfield epigraph from *Reflections on the State of British Naval Construction in Eighteen Hundred and Thirty One*, 10.

2. See, for example, Blackburn, *Treatise on the Science of Ship-Building*. For more on the definition of science, see Edwin Layton "American Ideologies of Science and Engineering," *Technology and Culture* 17, no. 4 (October 1976): 688–701.

3. Chatfield, *Reflections on the State of British Naval Construction*, 8 (italics in original).

4. Discussion of Charles H. Cramp, "Evolution of Screw Propulsion in the United States," *Society of Naval Architects and Marine Engineers Transactions* (hereafter cited as *SNAME Transactions*) 17 (1909): 161.

5. Robert G. Albion, "The Timber Problem of the Royal Navy, 1652–1862," *Mariner's Mirror* 38, no. 1 (February 1952): 4–22; Albion, *Forests and Sea Power*; Abell, *The Shipwright's Trade*, 92–97; Fincham, *A History of Naval Architecture*, 214–16.

6. Blackburn, *Treatise on the Science of Ship-Building*, v.

7. Clarke, *The Changeover from Wood to Iron Shipbuilding*, 47–49; Abell, *The Shipwright's Trade*, 96.

8. Kirkaldy, *British Shipping*, 33–37; Clarke, *Changeover from Wood to Iron Shipbuilding*, 21.

9. Kirkaldy, *British Shipping*, 33–37; Fairbairn, *Treatise on Iron Ship Building*, 1–2; Grantham, *Iron, as a Material for Ship-Building*, 6.

10. B. Martell, "A Short Account of Some of the Changes which have been Introduced into the Types, Sizes, and Construction of Ships . . . ," *INA Transactions* 42 (1900): 14; Warren, *Steel, Ships, and Men*, 26–39.

11. H. Gerrish Smith and L. C. Brown, "Shipyard Statistics," in Fasset, ed., *The Shipbuilding Business in the United States of America*, 1:74–75.

12. Russell, *The Modern System of Naval Architecture*, xxix.

13. Russell, *Fleet of the Future*, 20.

14. "Memoir of the Late T. J. Ditchburn," *INA Transactions* 11 (1870): 235.

15. Fairburn et al., *Merchant Sail*, 2:1380–81.

16. Grantham, *Iron, as a Material for Ship-Building*, 76 (italics in original).

17. Ibid., 27–28; Corlett, *The Iron Ship*, 26.

18. Corlett, *The Iron Ship*, 25; See, for example, Grantham, *Iron, as a Material for Ship-Building*; Grantham, *Iron Ship-Building: with Practical Illustrations*; quotation Grantham, "The Strength of Iron Ships," *INA Transactions* 1 (1860): 57–70; Grantham, "On the Classification of Iron Ships," *INA Transactions* 2 (1861): 128–40; and Grantham, "Jointing and Riveting Iron Ships," *INA Transactions* 3 (1862): 91–97.

19. Pole, ed., *The Life of Sir William Fairbairn*, 154–55.

20. Ibid., 341–42.

21. Ibid., 335–42; "Fairbairn, William," *Dictionary of National Biography*, 6:987–88.

22. Rosenberg and Vincenti, *The Britannia Bridge*, 70–71.

23. Ibid., 57–58; "Hodgkinson, Eaton," *Dictionary of National Biography*, 9:958–59.

24. Pole, *Life of Sir William Fairbairn*, 144–46, 159–62, 350–60.

25. Ibid., 157 (quotation), 401–22; Fairbairn, *An Experimental Inquiry into the Strength of Wrought-Iron Plates*; Fairbairn, *On the Application of Cast and Wrought Iron to Building Purposes*; Fairbairn, *Useful Information for Engineers*; Fairbairn, *Treatise on Iron Ship Building*.

26. Clarke, *Changeover from Wood to Iron Shipbuilding*, 35.

27. Rolt, *Isambard Kingdom Brunel*, 191–99; Graham Farr, "The Great Western," *Mariner's Mirror* 24, no. 2 (April 1938): 131–52; Fincham, *History of Naval Architecture*, 313–16.

28. Farr, "Great Western," 143–44.

29. Grantham, *Iron, as a Material for Ship-Building*, 47; Basil Jack Greenhill, "The S.S. Great Britain and the Coming of Steam Navigation," quotation 9–10; Rolt, *Isambard Kingdom Brunel*, 203, 218; Graham Farr, "The Great Britain," *Mariner's Mirror* 36, no. 1 (January 1950): 41–44; Fincham, *History of Naval Architecture*, 317–19.

30. Nevins, ed., *The Diary of Philip Hone*, 2:743.

31. E.C.B. Corlett, "The Stranding of the S.S. *Great Britain* in Dundrum Bay," *Mariner's Mirror* 61, no. 2 (May 1975): 117–26.

32. Martell, "A Short Account of Some of the Changes," 13–14; E. F. Kenney, "The Development and Use of Steel in Shipbuilding," in *Historical Transactions, 1893–1943*, comp. Society of Naval Architects and Marine Engineers, 444.

33. Fairbairn, *Treatise on Iron Ship Building*, 9–17, 65–70; Brunel, *The Life of Isambard Kingdom Brunel*, 289–339; Reed, *Shipbuilding in Iron and Steel*, 4–11, 73–97; Russell, *Modern System of Naval Architecture*, xxvii; Clarke, *Changeover from Wood to Iron Shipbuilding*, 33; Rosenberg and Vincenti, *Britannia Bridge*, 56–57; Pollard and Robertson, *The British Shipbuilding Industry*, 132; "John Scott Russell," *Minutes of the Proceedings of the Institution of Civil Engineers*, 87:432–35; Rolt, *Isambard Kingdom Brunel*, 241–47.

34. Corlett, *The Iron Ship*, 215; Pollard and Robertson, *British Shipbuilding Industry*, 132.

35. William H. White, "Address of Sir William H. White, President," *Minutes of Proceedings of the Institution of Civil Engineers* (London: Institution of Civil Engineers, 1904), 21–22; Kenney, "The Development and Use of Steel in Shipbuilding," 445; Emmerson, *The Greatest Iron Ship: S.S. Great Eastern*, 34–50.

36. Baynes and Pugh, *The Art of the Engineer*, 162–63; Emmerson, *The Greatest Iron Ship*, 171–76.

37. Corlett, *The Iron Ship*, 188–210.

38. Emmerson, *The Greatest Iron Ship*, 65; "Brunel, Isambard Kingdom," *Dictionary of National Biography*, 3:143–44.
39. Russell, *Modern System of Naval Architecture*, 301.
40. Clarke, *Changeover from Wood to Iron Shipbuilding*, 35; Mumford, *Technics and Civilization*, 209.
41. Rosenberg and Vincenti, *Britannia Bridge*, 60.
42. For a definition of tools that includes technological knowledge, see Peter F. Drucker, "Work and Tools," in Kranzbert and Davenport, eds., *Technology and Culture: An Anthology*.
43. Clarke, *Changeover from Wood to Iron Shipbuilding*, 35–36.
44. "Lloyd's Rules for the Construction of Iron Ships," *Monthly Nautical Magazine and Quarterly Review* 2, no. 3 (June 1855): 239–40.
45. Clarke, *Changeover from Wood to Iron Shipbuilding*, 35.
46. *New York Times*, November 14, 1859; K. C. Barnaby, *Some Ship Disasters and Their Causes*, 59–67.quotation Fairbairn mentioned the loss of *Royal Charter* again in 1866 in his paper "On the Security of Iron Ships," *INA Transactions* 7 (1866): 30.
47. K. C. Barnaby, *The Institution of Naval Architects, 1860–1960*, 13–21, 580; *INA Transactions* 1 (1860), table of contents.
48. John Grantham, "The Strength of Iron Ships," *INA Transactions* 1 (1860): 1.
49. G. W. Lenox, "On Chain-Cables," *INA Transactions* 1 (1860): 160–83.
50. K. C. Barnaby, *Some Ship Disasters and Their Causes*, 67.
51. Grantham, "The Strength of Iron Ships," 64–69; Discussion of William Fairbairn, "The Strength of Iron Ships," *INA Transactions* 1 (1860): 91–97; K. C. Barnaby, *The Institution of Naval Architects*, 16–17.
52. Higgins, *Annals of Lloyd's Register*, 80–81.
53. Ibid., 81; Blake, *Lloyd's Register of Shipping, 1760–1960*, 41.
54. Higgins, *Annals of Lloyd's Register*, 82.
55. Higgins, *Annals of Lloyd's Register*, 82; Blake, *Lloyd's Register*, 41.
56. Fairbairn, "The Strength of Iron Ships," 99–104; Higgins, *Annals of Lloyd's Register*, 82–85; Blake, *Lloyd's Register*, 42–43.
57. "Lloyd's Revised Rules for the Building and Classification of Iron Ships—1863," *INA Transactions* 4 (1863): 293–302; Joseph H. Ritchie, "Introduction to Lloyd's Revised Rules," *INA Transactions* 4 (1863): 289–302.
58. W. Denny, "On Lloyd's Numerals" *INA Transactions* 18 (1877), 245–50; Bruce, *The Life of William Denny*, 174–87; K. C. Barnaby, *The Institution of Naval Architects*, 109.
59. Griffiths, *Progressive Ship Builder*, 2:252.
60. Fairbairn, "The Strength of Iron Ships," 73–78.
61. Fairbairn, *Treatise on Iron Ship Building*, 9–17, 65–70; Brunel, *The Life of Isambard Kingdom Brunel*, 289–339; Reed, *Shipbuilding in Iron and Steel*, 4–11, 73–97; Russell, *Modern System of Naval Architecture*, xxvii; Clarke, *The Changeover from Wood to Iron Shipbuilding*, 33.

62. Pollard and Robertson, *British Shipbuilding Industry*, 132.

63. A. M. Robb, "Ship-Building," in Singer, ed., *A History of Technology*, 354–55; quotation Sir William H. White, "Notes: The Place of Mathematics in Engineering Practice," *American Society of Naval Engineers Journal* 24 (1912): 1366; White, "Address of Sir William H. White, President," 74.

64. Fairbairn, *Useful Information for Engineers*, 235–39; Russell, Discussion of Fairbairn's "The Strength of Iron Ships," 89; Russell, *Modern System of Naval Architecture*, xxvii; Abell, *Shipwright's Trade*, 119.

65. K. C. Barnaby, *The Institution of Naval Architects*, 279; J. W. Isherwood, "A New System of Ship Construction," *INA Transactions* 50 (1908): 115–37.

66. White, "Address of Sir William H. White, President," 25–26.

67. "John Scott Russell," *Minutes of the Proceedings of the Institution of Civil Engineers* 87:427–40; Fairbairn, "The Strength of Iron Ships," 79, 86.

68. John Scott Russell, "The Wave-Line Principle of Ship Construction," *INA Transactions* 1 (1860): 184–96; Emmerson, *John Scott Russell*, 12–20; Nathaniel Barnaby, *Naval Development in the Century*, 249; K. C. Barnaby, *The Institution of Naval Architects*, 19–20, 66; Buchanan, *The Engineers*, 189.

69. Sir Edward J. Reed, "On the Advances Made in the Mathematical Theory of Naval Architecture during the Existence of the Institution," *INA Transactions* 39 (1897): 92–93.

70. W.J.M. Rankine, "Stream-line Surfaces," *INA Transactions* 11 (1870): 175–81.

71. Rankine, *Shipbuilding, Theoretical and Practical*; Rankine, "Stream-line Surfaces"; quotation Nathaniel Barnaby, *Naval Development in the Century*, 274–76; Buchanan, *The Engineers*, 169.

72. Sir Westcott Abell, "William Froude, M.A., LL.D., F.R.S.," in Duckworth, ed., *The Papers of William Froude, M.A., LL.D., F.R.S., 1810–1879*, xvi.

73. Reed, "On the Advances Made in the Mathematical Theory of Naval Architecture," 93.

74. William Froude, "On Experiments with H.M.S. Greyhound" *INA Transactions* 15 (1874): 51; Pollard and Robertson, *British Shipbuilding Industry*, 133; Bruce, *Life of William Denny*, 194.

75. K. C. Barnaby, *The Institution of Naval Architects*, 293–94; Abell, "William Froude," xiii.

76. Abell, "William Froude," xii–xiii.

77. Ibid., xviii.

78. Froude, "On Experiments with H.M.S. Greyhound," 59.

79. Ibid.

80. Abell, *Shipwright's Trade*, 156.

81. Froude, *On the Rolling of Ships*; Froude, "On the Stability, Propulsion, and Sea-going Qualities of Ships," *Reports of the British Association for the Advancement of Science* (London, 1869); Nathaniel Barnaby, *Naval Development in the Century*, 287–94; Pollard and Robertson, *British Shipbuilding Industry*, 132–33; Buchanan, *The*

Engineers, 164. See also Russell and Goodman, eds., *Science and the Rise of Technology since 1800.*

82. White, "Notes: The Place of Mathematics in Engineering Practice," 1360.

83. Bruce, *Life of William Denny*, 196.

84. Ibid., 195–200; Nathaniel Barnaby, *Naval Development in the Century*, 298–300.

85. Reed, "On the Advances Made in the Mathematical Theory of Naval Architecture," 99.

86. K. C. Barnaby, *The Institution of Naval Architects*, 262; C. H. Peabody, "Personal Impressions of Ship-Model Towing Stations," *SNAME Transactions* 14 (1906): 49; Sidney Pollard, "*Laissez-Faire* and Shipbuilding," *Economic History Review* 1 (1952): 103.

87. Russell, *Modern System of Naval Architecture*, xxiv; Griffiths, *Progressive Shipbuilder*, 2:181. "Turning turtle" is a colloquial term for capsizing.

88. "Moseley, Henry," *Dictionary of National Biography*, 13:1072–73.

89. Sir William H. White, "The History of the Institution of Naval Architects and of Scientific Education in Naval Architecture," pt. 2, *INA Transactions* 53 (1911): 25; "Frederick Kynaston Barnes," *INA Transactions* 51 (1909): 271–73.

90. McGee, "Floating Bodies, Naval Science," 480.

91. Nathaniel Barnaby, "The Relative Influence of Breadth of Beam and Height of Freeboard in Lengthening Out the Curves of Stability," *INA Transactions* 12 (1871): 62–76; W. H. White and W. John, "The Calculation of the Stability of Ships, and Some Matters of Interest Connected Therewith," *INA Transactions* 12 (1871): 77–127; Reed, "On the Advances Made in the Mathematical Theory of Naval Architecture," 81.

92. "Rankine, William John Macquorn," *Dictionary of National Biography*, 16:734; "Francis Elgar," *INA Transactions* 51 (1909): 268; White and John, "Calculation of the Stability of Ships," 78–79.

93. Attwood, *Theoretical Naval Architecture*, 152–53; McGee, "The Amsler Integrator and the Burden of Calculation," 66.

94. Griffiths, *Progressive Ship Builder*, 2:251–52.

95. George Leslie, "Shipbuilding of Yesterday and Today," *Cassier's Magazine* (hereafter *CM*) 36, no. 4 (August 1909): 307; Pollard and Robertson, *British Shipbuilding Industry*, 134; "Elgar," *INA Transactions*; 269; Morrison, *History of New York Ship Yards*, 112–13; McGee, "The Amsler Integrator," 66–67.

96. Ibid.

97. Bruce, *Life of William Denny*, 155–58; A. Denny, "The Practical Application of Stability Calculations," *INA Transactions* 28 (1887): 359–74; Reed, "On the Advances Made in the Mathematical Theory of Naval Architecture," 83; Reed, *A Treatise on the Stability of Ships*; K. C. Barnaby, *The Institution of Naval Architects*, 132.

98. K. C. Barnaby, *The Institution of Naval Architects*, 132.

99. McGee, "The Amsler Integrator," 66–70; Michael Mahoney, "Amsler, Jakob," *Dictionary of Scientific Biography*, ed. Charles Gillespie, 1:147–48.

100. Jones, *Design Methods*, 22.

101. Ibid., 20–22.

102. McGee, "Floating Bodies, Naval Science," 36–40.

103. W. Salisbury, "Navy Board Models," *Mariner's Mirror* 51, no. 1 (February 1965): 70–72; McGee, "Floating Bodies, Naval Science," 59; L. G. Carr Laughton, "The Study of Ship Models," *Mariner's Mirror* 11, no. 1 (January 1925): 12–18.

104. Charles Lamport, "The Problem of a Ship's Form, as Presented to the Practical Builder," *INA Transactions* 6 (1865): 111.

105. For further information on French engineering and naval architecture, see Fairbairn, *Useful Information for Engineers*, 7–11; J. Scott Russell, "On the Education of Naval Architects in England and France," *INA Transactions* 4 (1863): 163–85; Ropp, *The Development of a Modern Navy*; Kranakis, "Social Determinants of Engineering Practice," 5–70.

106. White, "Address of Sir William H. White, President," 2–3.

107. For a complete description of these associations, consult Buchanan, *The Engineers*, 135–36.

108. White, "The History of the Institution of Naval Architects," 15–16; N. Macleod, "Shipwright Officers of the Royal Dockyards," *Mariner's Mirror* 11, no. 4 (October 1925): 366.

109. Quote in Pollock, *Modern Shipbuilding and the Men Engaged in It*, 94.

110. Higgins, *Annals of Lloyd's Register*, 123; Pollard and Robertson, *British Shipbuilding Industry*, 149; White, "The History of the Institution of Naval Architects," 15–16.

111. Reed, "On the Advances Made in the Mathematical Theory of Naval Architecture," 101.

112. E. J. Reed, "Introduction," *INA Transactions* 1 (1860): xv–xvii; Pollock, *Modern Shipbuilding and the Men Engaged in It*, 93; Pollard, "*Laissez-Faire* and Shipbuilding," 101.

113. White, "The History of the Institution of Naval Architects," 25.

114. Ibid., 27.

115. White, "Address of Sir William H. White, President," 15–16.

116. Sir John Somerset Packington, "Inaugural Address," *INA Transactions* 1 (1860): 4.

117. K. C. Barnaby, *The Institution of Naval Architects*, 312–14; McGee, "Floating Bodies, Naval Science," 243–44.

118. Pollard and Robertson, *The British Shipbuilding Industry*, 211–22; D'Eyencourt, *A Shipbuilder's Yarn*, 27–32.

119. Macleod, "Shipwright Officers of the Royal Dockyards," 362–63; Welch, "The Scientific Education of Naval Architects," 181; Fincham, *History of Naval Architecture*, 176.

120. K. C. Barnaby, *The Institution of Naval Architects*, 280; Russell, "On the Education of Naval Architects in England and France," 165–68; Rev. Joseph Woolley, "On

the Education of Naval Architects," *INA Transactions* 5 (1864): 262–63; "The Royal Corps of Constructors," *Brassey's Naval Annual, 1886*, 91; Pollard, *The British Shipbuilding Industry*, 142–43.

121. Macleod, "Shipwright Officers of the Royal Dockyards," 363.

122. John Scott Russell, "On the Technical Education of Naval Architects in England," *INA Transactions* 8 (1867): 223–43.

123. Ibid., 232–36. For a more thorough examination of the naval shipbuilding schools associated with the Royal Navy, see the serialized articles by A. W. Johns entitled "The First British School of Naval Architecture," *Engineering* 121 (March 12, March 26, and April 9, 1926) and "The Dockyard Schools and the Second School of Naval Architecture," *Engineering* 127 (January 18, January 25, February 8, March 1, March 15, and March 29, 1929).

124. W. H. White, "On the Course of Study in the Royal Naval College, Greenwich," *INA Transactions* 18 (1877): 362; W. John, "On the Royal Naval College and the Mercantile Marine," *INA Transactions* 19 (1878): 120–36; Pollard, "*Laissez-Faire* and Shipbuilding," 101.

125. "Royal Corps of Constructors," *Brassey's Naval Annual* 1 (1886): 91; Pollard and Robertson, *British Shipbuilding Industry*, 142–44.

126. Bruce, *Life of William Denny*, 83–84.

127. Fincham, *An Introductory Outline of the Practice of Ship-Building*; Fincham, *On Masting Ships and Mast Making*; Welch, "The Scientific Education of Naval Architects," 181; R. C. Anderson, "Eighteenth-Century Books on Ship-Building, Rigging, and Seamanship," *Mariner's Mirror* 33, no. 4 (October 1947): 221–22.

128. "Moseley, Henry," *Dictionary of National Biography*, 1072–73; Rosenberg and Vincenti, *Britannia Bridge*, 13.

129. Woolley, *The Elements of Descriptive Geometry*; "Woolley, Joseph," *Dictionary of National Biography* 21:903–4.

130. All of these works have been cited in earlier notes.

131. Quote in Pollock, *Modern Shipbuilding and the Men Engaged in It*, 94–95.

132. Reed, "Introduction," *INA Transactions* 1 (1860): xviii.

133. *The Engineer* (London: Morgan Bros., 1856–) and *Engineering* (London: J. A. Dixon, 1866–).

134. *Naval Science: A Quarterly Magazine for Promoting the Improvement of Naval Architecture, Marine Engineering, Steam Navigation, and Seamanship.*

135. Quote found in *Causes of the Reduction of American Tonnage*, 41st Cong., 2nd sess., 1870, H. Rep. 28: 26.

136. Quote from Russell, *Modern System of Naval Architecture*, xxix.

Chapter 3. Practical Shipbuilding Develops in the United States

1. From *Democracy in America*, 455–56.

2. For more on cultural bias and technological style, see Hugo A. Meier, "Technology and Democracy, 1800–1860," *Mississippi Valley Historical Review* 43, no. 4

(March 1957): 618, 640; Edwin T. Layton Jr., "European Origins of the American Engineering Style of the Nineteenth Century," in Reingold and Rothenberg, eds., *Scientific Colonialism: A Cross-Cultural Comparison*, 151–66; Hughes, *Networks of Power*; Kranakis, *Constructing a Bridge*.

3. Hindle, ed., *America's Wooden Age*, 3.

4. For more on the concept of America's "wooden age," see the introduction in Hindle, *America's Wooden Age*, 3–12.

5. Griffiths, *The Ship-Builder's Manual, and Nautical Referee*, 14.

6. Morrison, *History of New York Ship Yards*, 44, 71–84; Cramp, "Sixty Years of Shipbuilding on the Delaware," 177–79; McKay, *Some Famous Sailing Ships and Their Builder*, 9–10.

7. See title page for *The Practical Shipbuilder*, where Lauchlan attaches that appellation to his name. Though his brother Donald always spelled his surname "McKay," Lauchlan's is set on the title page as "M'Kay."

8. Griffiths, *The Progressive Shipbuilder*, 1:246.

9. For more use of the term "practical shipbuilder," see examples in Welch, *An Island's Trade*, 37; John W. Griffiths, "The Value of Calculations in Modelling," *U.S. Nautical Magazine and Naval Journal* 2, no. 2 (April 1855): 10; and *Causes of the Reduction of American Tonnage*, 41st Cong., 2nd sess., 1870, H. Doc. 28: 143.

10. "William Skinner & Sons Record Book, 1852–1927," MS 1485, Maryland Historical Society, 1–2; "Book 3, 1831–1834," James Joseph Williamson Papers, MS 912, Maryland Historical Society, 72–73; "Enoch Moore, 1822–1824," Record Group 2545, Register of Wills-Probates, New Castle County, and "List of the Sales of the goods & Chattles of Nathaniel Lank, 14 March 1868," Record Group 3545, Register of Wills Probates, Kent County, both found at the Delaware State Archives, Dover.

11. Worthington H. Mansfield, "Sparmaking," *Rudder* 57 (August 1943): 17; Kebabian, *American Woodworking Tools*, 39.

12. John Gardner, "Shipwright's Tools," *Log of Mystic Seaport* 21, no. 3 (September 1969): 91–92; C. Drew and Company Trade Catalog, HFM 78, G.W. Blunt White Library, Mystic Seaport, Conn.

13. Hutchins, *American Maritime Industries and Public Policy*, 119–20.

14. Cramp, "Sixty Years of Shipbuilding on the Delaware," 179.

15. Ibid. A "pitching axe" is a type of tree-felling axe.

16. *Biographical and Genealogical History of the State of Delaware*, vol. 1 (Chambersburg, Pa.: J.M. Runk & Co., 1899), 501–3; Scharf, *History of Delaware*, 1:750; Kebabian, "Delaware Apprenticeship Indentures, 1827–1850," 28; *Semi-Centennial Memoir of the Harlan & Hollingsworth Company, 1836–1886*, 212–13; David B. Tyler, *The American Clyde*, 11–12, 119 n. 2.

17. Conrad, *History of the State of Delaware* (Wilmington, Del.: self-published, 1908), 371–72; *Wilmington City Directory*, 1911, Hagley Museum and Library.

18. Taylor, "I Build Men as Well as Ships," 4, 6, 12; Gauer, comp., *Vaughan Shipwrights of Kensington, Philadelphia*.

19. Macdonald, *Mispillion-Built Sailing Vessels*, 10–19; Sarah W. R. Ewing, "The Van Sant Family Shipyards," *Atlantic County Historical Society Yearbook* 8, no. 2 (October 1977): 66–75; Hutchins, *American Maritime Industries and Public Policy*, 120.

20. Buell, *The Memoirs of Charles H. Cramp*, 40; Cramp, "Sixty Years of Shipbuilding on the Delaware," 177–79.

21. Cramp, "Sixty Years of Shipbuilding on the Delaware," 177.

22. Thompson, comp., *General Orders and Circulars Issued by the Navy Department*, 66.

23. Griffiths, *The Ship-Builder's Manual, and Nautical Referee*, 160; McKay, *Some Famous Sailing Ships and Their Builder*, 5–9; Goldenberg, "With Saw and Axe and Auger," 111–12.

24. Griffiths, *The Progressive Ship Builder*, 2:74.

25. Adams and Waters, comps., *English Maritime Books Printed before 1801*, 561–81; Shaw, *Engineering Books Available in America prior to 1830*, 28–61.

26. Rogers, *The Shipwright's Own Book*, iii; Boole, *The Shipwright's Handbook and Draughtsman's Guide*, 7. See also Wiley and Putnam book price list in the back of Sargent, *A Lecture on the Late Improvements in Steam Navigation and the Art of Naval Warfare*.

27. Chapelle, *The Search for Speed under Sail*, 7–8.

28. Rogers, *Shipwright's Own Book*, iii.

29. M'Kay, *The Practical Shipbuilder*, 7. Quote found in Griffiths, *Progressive Shipbuilder*, 1:171.

30. Ibid.

31. Varney, *Ship-Builder's Manual; or Mould Loft Guide*, preface.

32. Griffiths, *Ship-Builder's Manual, and Nautical Referee*, 160; McKay, *Some Famous Sailing Ships and Their Builder*, 5–9; Goldenberg, "With Saw and Axe and Auger," 111–12.

33. Griffiths, *Ship-Builder's Manual, and Nautical Referee*, 160.quotation

34. Goldenberg, "Saw, Axe and Auger," 111.

35. Taylor, "I Build Men as Well as Ships," 13.

36. *Biographical and Genealogical History of the State of Delaware*, 1:501–3; Scharf, *History of Delaware*, 1:750; Kebabian, "Delaware Apprenticeship Indentures," 28.

37. Samuel Eliot Morison, "McKay, Donald," *Dictionary of American Biography* 6:72–3. Notice, for example, Eckford Webb (named for shipbuilder Henry Eckford) and Samuel Hartt Pook (named for naval constructor Samuel Hartt).

38. Murphy, *American Ships and Ship-Builders*, 7–10; William B. Shaw, "Eckford, Henry," *Dictionary of American Biography* 3:4–5; Robert G. Albion, "Webb, Isaac," *Dictionary of American Biography* 10:578–9; Chapelle, *The Search for Speed under Sail*, 321; Chapelle, *History of American Sailing Ships*, 280.

39. Murphy, *American Ships and Ship-Builders*, 10–11; Cramp, "Sixty Years of

Shipbuilding on the Delaware," 178; McKay, *Some Famous Sailing Ships and Their Builder*, 4; Chapelle, *History of the American Sailing Navy*, 120–21; Fairburn, *Merchant Sail*, 2:968–69.

40. Albion, *The Rise of the New York Port*, 302; Hutchins, *American Maritime Industries and Public Policy*, 104, 120.

41. John Stetson to George McNeill, July 19, 1886, in McNeill, *The Labor Movement*, 348. See also Welch, *An Island's Trade*, 36–38; and Hutchins, *American Maritime Industries and Public Policy*, 393–94.

42. Morrison, *History of New York Ship Yards*, 41.

43. Ibid., 44; Albion, *Rise of the New York Port*, 290; "The Old Ship-Builders of New York," *Harper's New Monthly Magazine* 65, no. 386 (July 1882): 228.

44. Hancock and McCabe, eds., *Milton's First Century*, 225, 227, 237; *Milford Peninsula News and Advertiser*, May 8, 1880. See the William Lank Papers, Reference Reel R-135, Delaware State Archives, for correspondence between Lank and his family from 1861 to 1862.

45. U.S. Department of the Interior, Census Office, *Report on the Ship-Building Industry in the United States by Henry Hall, 10th Census of the United States, 1880*, vol. 8, *Special Reports*, 127 (hereafter cited as Hall Report}; "Old Ship-Builders of New York," 231.

46. "Miscellaneous Van Sant Shipyards and Shipbuilders," Accession 79.105a, Atlantic County Historical Society; Ewing, "The Van Sant Family Shipyards," 72. For more examples, see Louis C. Hunter, *Steamboats on the Western Rivers*, 68–69; and the biography in the accession guide for Daniel French Papers and Transcriptions, Indiana Historical Society Manuscript Collections.

47. "A History of the First Century of Steam Navigation," *Nautical Gazette* 74 (March 18, 1909): 237; Finding guide to the Daniel French Papers and Transcriptions, Indiana Historical Society Manuscript Collections.

48. William L. Hanscom Letter Copybook, 1846–1851, Misc. vol. 60, G. W. Blunt White Library, Mystic Seaport; advertisement for Stevenson's firm located at the end of *U.S. Nautical Magazine and Naval Journal* 7 (1858); McNeill, *The Labor Movement*, 349; Philip Hichborn, "Cruise of the Dashing Wave," Entry 46, Record Group 19, National Archives, Washington, D.C.

49. *Causes of the Reduction of American Tonnage*, 41st Cong., 2nd sess., 1870, H. Doc. 28: 174–76; Marcil, *The Charley-Man*, 78–84; Hall Report, 171–72.

50. For Corson, consult *Manufactories and Manufactures of Pennsylvania of the Nineteenth Century*, 394–95. For Burk, see the Burk Papers (Accession 84.12) and accession guide at the Historical Society of Delaware Library, Wilmington.

51. Griffiths, "The Value of Calculations in Modeling," 11.

52. Griffiths, *The Ship-Builder's Manual and Nautical Referee*, 160.

53. Morrison, *History of New York Ship Yards*, 37.

54. Albion, *Rise of the New York Port*, 305; unpublished research by maritime historian Edward G. Brownlee concerning the Samuel L. Tilton Yard in Camden, New Jersey.

55. Griffiths, "The Value of Calculations in Modelling," 11.
56. Frederic Tudor, *Some memorandums*, 3–4; Griffiths, *Treatise on Marine and Naval Architecture*, 204.
57. Between 1830 and 1840, the *Journal of the Franklin Institute* published six articles on fluid resistance of solid bodies. Of that number, one originated in the United States, while the rest came from Britain. See the *Journal of the Franklin Institute* (hereafter cited as *FI Journal*), no. 1 (1832): 271–81; no. 2 (1833): 120–21; no. 1 (1834): 286–87; no. 1 (1835): 56–64, 125–35; no. 2 (1835): 210–11; and no. 2 (1836): 260–61.
58. Nystrom, *A Treatise on Screw Propellers and Their Steam Engines*.
59. David Brown to John W. Griffiths, January 20, 1850, found in Griffiths, *Treatise on Marine and Naval Architecture*, 96.
60. John W. Griffiths, "History of Shipbuilding in New York," *U.S. Nautical Magazine* 6, no. 6 (September 1857): 440.
61. Griffiths, *Treatise on Marine and Naval Architecture*, 96, 208–9.
62. Tudor, *Some memorandums*, 2–5; Murphy, *American Ships and Ship-Builders*, 22; Griffiths, *Progressive Shipbuilder*, 1:195–96, 2:18–19; Griffiths, *Treatise on Marine and Naval Architecture*, 90; Marcil, *The Charley-Man*, 83–84; Chandler, *Philadelphia: Port of History, 1609–1837*, 45. For naval constructor Samuel Humphreys, see "Surveys and Reports of Repairs on Ships, 1834–1845," MS 74–903, Historical Society of Pennsylvania, Philadelphia; and Chapelle, *The Search for Speed under Sail*, 15, 22.
63. Welch, *An Island's Trade*, 40–49; Macdonald, *Mispillion-Built Sailing Vessels*, 15–16; Hutchins, *American Maritime Industries and Public Policy*, 105–6.
64. David Brown to John W. Griffiths, January 20, 1850, found in Griffiths, *Treatise on Marine and Naval Architecture*, 96.
65. Griffiths, "Ship-Building Not Yet a Science," *U.S. Nautical Magazine and Naval Journal* 3, no. 5 (February 1856): 327.
66. Stevenson, *Sketch of the Civil Engineering of North America*, 120.
67. Ibid., 121.
68. Ibid., 119.
69. McKay, *Some Famous Sailing Ships and Their Builder*, 136–40; Chapelle, *The Search for Speed under Sail*, 283–85.
70. For a more complete description of the modeling process, see Griffiths, "Marine and Naval Architecture or the Science of Ship Building," 14–16; and Meade, *A Treatise on Naval Architecture and Ship-Building*, 203–4.
71. Russell, "On American River Steamers," *Institution of Naval Architects Transactions* 2 (1861): 109.
72. Marcil, *The Charley-Man*, 75; Russell, "On American River Steamers," 109.
73. Griffiths, "Marine and Naval Architecture or the Science of Ship Building," 14.
74. Griffiths, "The First Slip Model and Its Inventor," *U.S. Nautical Magazine and Naval Journal* 2, no. 2 (May 1855): 104–5.
75. Charles K. Stillman, "The Development of the Builder's Half-Hull Model in America," *Log of Mystic Seaport* 31, no. 3 (Fall 1979): 91–100.

76. Ibid., 92–93; Cutler, *Greyhounds of the Sea*, 28–29; Morrison, *History of New York Ship Yards*, 56–57.

77. Stillman, "The Development of the Builder's Half-Hull Model in America," 93; Rogers, *Shipwright's Own Book*, 50–51.

78. Stillman, "The Development of the Builder's Half-Hull Model in America," quotation 97; Rogers, *Shipwright's Own Book*, 39–43; Griffiths, "The First Slip Model and Its Inventor," 104–5.

79. "The Building of the Ship," *Harper's New Monthly Magazine* 24, no. 103 (April 1862): 610; Griffiths, *Progressive Shipbuilder*, 1:66; Meade, *Treatise on Naval Architecture and Ship-Building*, 203; Simmons, *Lines, Lofting and Half Models*, 6.

80. Griffiths, *Treatise on Marine and Naval Architecture*, 28–30; *Lines, Lofting and Half Models*, 11–14.

81. Simmons, *Lines, Lofting and Half Models*, 50–53.

82. M'Kay, *The Practical Shipbuilder*, 13.

83. Griffiths, "Marine and Naval Architecture," 18.

84. For examples of using full-scale drawings, see Robert Allison, "The Old and the New," *American Society of Mechanical Engineers Transactions* (hereafter cited as *ASME Transactions*) 16 (1895): 745, 752; Ferguson, ed., *Early Engineering Reminiscences (1815–1840) of George Escoll Sellers*, 38, 49, 170; Cramp, "Evolution of Screw Propulsion in the United States," 149.

85. M'Kay, *The Practical Shipbuilder*, 13; Chapelle, *The Search for Speed under Sail*, 284.

86. Griffiths, "Marine and Naval Architecture," 14.

87. Simmons, *Lines, Lofting and Half Models*, 4–5; Welch, *An Island's Trade*, 30.

88. Israel Smith Diary (1860), Collection 84.39.2, Atlantic County Historical Society, New Jersey.

89. "Walter Bassett Van Sant Papers," vol. I, 79.

90. Gorman and Carlson, "Interpreting Invention as a Cognitive Process," 131–64; Hughes, *American Genesis*, 41–47; Cooper, *Shaping Invention*, 32.

91. Hall Report, 199; Taussig, *The Tariff History of the United States*, 221–23, 236–37; Hutchins, *The American Maritime Industries and Public Policy*, 257–86; Fairburn, *Merchant Sail*, 2:911–57, 2:1495–552.

92. Hall Report, 215–16.

Chapter 4. The Golden Era of Urban American Shipbuilding

1. By G. W. Sheldon, *Harpers Magazine* 65 (June–November 1882), 223–41.

2. Bolles, *Industrial History of the United States*, 577; Morrison, *History of New York Ship Yards*, 54.

3. Bolles, *Industrial History of the United States*, 577.

4. Joseph Whitworth, "Special Report to the House of Commons, 1854" (hereafter noted as Whitworth Report) in *The American System of Manufactures*, ed. Nathan Rosenberg, 361; Cramp, "Evolution of Screw Propulsion in the United States," 155; "The Building of the Ship," 610; "Iron Keelsons, Stronger, Lighter and Cheaper than

Wood," *U.S. Nautical Magazine and Nautical Journal* 2, no. 6 (September 1855): 502–5; "How to Obtain Strength in Vessels," *U.S. Nautical Magazine and Naval Journal* 1, no. 4 (January 1855): 240–44; Chapelle, *The Search for Speed under Sail, 1700–1855*, 269–71.

   5. U.S. Dept. of Interior, Census Office, "Schedule 5. Products of Industry," *U.S. Census 1850*, 11th Ward, City of New York.

   6. Hall Report, 86–87; Morrison, *History of New York Ship Yards*, 93–94.

   7. *Investigation by the Committee on Naval Affairs: Norfolk Navy Yard*, 44th Cong., 1st sess., 1876, H. Misc. Doc. 170, pt. 4: 151; *Investigation by the Committee on Naval Affairs: Brooklyn Navy Yard*, 44th Cong., 1st sess., 1876, H. Misc. Doc. 170, pt. 6: 60; Hutchins, *American Maritime Industries and Public Policy*, 109. The concept of "bastard artisanship" comes from Wilentz, *Chants Democratic*, 108–17.

   8. For more on eighteenth-century American labor practices in shipyards, see Woodwell, "The Woodwell Shipyard," 58–74; Goldenberg, *Shipbuilding in Colonial America*.

   9. James J. Williams, "Time and Waste Book," Maryland Historical Society, 2:128.

   10. William Skinner and Sons Record Book, MS 1485, Maryland Historical Society Manuscripts Collection, p. 27.

   11. Whitworth Report, 194–95; Norman M. Hunter, "Changes in Ship Construction Methods, 1850 to 1950," *INA Transactions* 92 (1952): 209–10.

   12. For a description of subcontracting by a shipwright, see John Stetson to George McNeill, July 19, 1886, in McNeill, *The Labor Movement*, 348.

   13. Woodwell, "The Woodwell Shipyard," 60–62; Robert K. Cheney, "Industries Allied to Shipbuilding in Newburyport," *American Neptune* 17, no. 2 (April 1957): 114.

   14. Whitworth Report, 248; *Investigation by the Committee on Naval Affairs: Norfolk Navy Yard*, 44th Cong., 1st sess., H. Misc. Doc. 170, 1876, pt. 4: 21–22, 151; Carl C. Cutler, "Deering and Yeaton, Ship-Riggers," *American Neptune* 3, no. 4 (October 1943): 289–90; Hutchins, *American Maritime Industries and Public Policy*, 393–94.

   15. Hall Report, 103.

   16. Cramp, "Sixty Years of Shipbuilding on the Delaware," 179; Hutchins, *American Maritime Industries and Public Policy*, 393–94; Ewing, "The Van Sant Family Shipyards," 69–70; entries for John Williams, James Strickland, Somers Snell, Nicholas Smith, Bobby Luke, and Dan Delaney, "Job Van Sant's Timebook," in *Walter Bassett Van Sant Papers*, vol. 1.

   17. "The Ship-Builder and the Apprentice," *U.S. Nautical Magazine and Naval Journal* 4, no. 1 (April 1856): 16.

   18. Ibid., 94–95

   19. Rorabaugh, *The Craft Apprentice*, 4.

   20. George Wallis, "Special Report to the House of Commons, 1854," in Rosenberg, ed., *The American System of Manufactures*, 203.

21. For Westervelt, see *Reduction of American Tonnage*, 40. See also *Investigation by the Committee on Naval Affairs: Kittery Navy Yard*, 44th Cong., 1st sess., 1876, H. Misc. Doc. 170, pt. 1: 44, 47, 89, 102; and Hutchins, *American Maritime Industries and Public Policy*, 393.

22. "The Ship-Builder and the Apprentice," *U.S. Nautical Magazine and Naval Journal* 4, no. 1 (April 1856): 15–16.

23. Robert G. Albion, "Griffiths, John Willis," *Dictionary of American Biography*, 9:626–27.

24. Griffiths, "History of Shipbuilding in New York," *U.S. Nautical Magazine and Naval Journal* 6, no. 6 (September 1857): 438; Griffiths, "Marine and Naval Architecture or the Science of Shipbuilding, September 20th, 1844."

25. "Miscellaneous," *Scientific American* 7, no. 23 (February 21, 1852): 178.

26. John W. Griffiths, "History of Shipbuilding in New York," *U.S. Nautical Magazine and Naval Journal* 6, no. 6 (September 1857): 439.

27. "Introductory," *U.S. Nautical Magazine and Naval Journal* 1, no. 1 (October 1854): 7.

28. "The Ship-Builder and the Apprentice," *U.S. Nautical Magazine and Naval Journal* 4, no. 1 (April 1856): 16.

29. Griffiths, "Early History of Shipbuilding in New York," 443.

30. In *The Craft Apprentice*, Rorabaugh argues that publications on craftwork may have devalued the institution of apprenticeship by broadcasting the "art and mystery" of crafts through publication (33–35).

31. Morrison, *History of New York Ship Yards*, 54; *Report on Steam Engines*, 25th Cong., 3rd sess., 1838, H. Doc. 21: 159–67; Defebaugh, *History of the Lumber Industry of America*, 2:582.

32. Nathan Rosenberg, "America's Rise to Woodworking Leadership," in Hindle, ed., *America's Wooden Age*, 37–62; Hall Report, 103.

33. Hall Report, 86–87; Stephens, *Traditions and Memories of American Yachting*, 47; Hutchins, *American Maritime Industries and Public Policy*, 299

34. "Circular Saw," *Scientific American* 1, no. 47 (August 13, 1846): 2; Goldenberg, "Saw, Axe and Auger, 122; Hall Report, 94–95; Hutchins, *American Maritime Industries and Public Policy*, 108, 394–95.

35. Transcript of Howard Potts, Shipwright of Wilmington, Del.; Accession 2107, Hagley Museum and Library.

36. See advertisement for treenail factory in *U.S. Nautical Magazine and Naval Journal* 7 (1858), at the end of the volume. See also Morrison, *History of New York Ship Yards*, 94; "On Tree-Nails and Tree-Nailing," *U.S. Nautical Magazine and Naval Journal* 5 (February 1857): 356; Stephens, *Traditions and Memories of American Yachting*, 46–47; Hall Report, 87.

37. Hall Report, 87; Albion, *The Rise of the New York Port*, 297; "Beardslee's Planing Machine," *Scientific American* 8, no. 5 (October 16, 1852): 37; Whitworth Report, 344–45; Rosenberg, "America's Rise to Woodworking Leadership," 48–49.

38. "Machinery and Hand Labor," *U.S. Nautical Magazine and Naval Journal* 3, no. 1 (October 1855): 29.

39. "The Old Ship-Builders of New York," 235; Morrison, *History of New York Ship Yards*, 104.

40. *Report on Steam Engines*, 25th Cong., 3rd. sess., 1838, H. Doc. 21: 163; Albion, *Rise of New York Port*, 297.

41. For the most complete history of Blanchard's wood-bending machine, consult Cooper, *Shaping Invention*, 209–36.

42. Griffiths, *Bent Timber Ships and Universal Wood Bending Machinery*. Griffiths publicized this machine in the 1854 pamphlet "Report of the President and Trustees of the Ship Timber Bending Company," but the machinery failed to win recognition until the steam-bent-timber vessel *New Era* won a medal at the Philadelphia Centennial Exhibition. See also Bates, *American Ships*, 83–88; and Hall Report, 236.

43. Morrison, *History of New York Ship Yards*, 51; Hutchins, *American Maritime Industries and Public Policy*, 108–9; Cooling, *Gray Steel and Blue Water Navy*, 27.

44. Morrison, *History of New York Ship Yards*, 53–54, 60–61, 105–6; Albion, *The Rise of the New York Port*, 299.

45. Ibid., 54; Hutchins, *American Maritime Industries and Public Policy*, 107–8.

46. Joseph S. Shultz, "Shipyard Cranes and Their Functions in Marine Construction," *Engineering Magazine* (hereafter cited as *EM*) 29, no. 1 (April 1905): 61–62; W. F. Durfee, "A Power Crane," *ASME Transactions* 5 (1884): 137–38.

47. Hall Report, 87; Morrison, *History of New York Ship Yards*, 94; Albion, *Rise of the New York Port*, 297.

48. Griffiths, *Progressive Shipbuilder*, 1:252.

49. Hall Report, 172.

50. Henry M. Vallette, "History of the Philadelphia Navy Yard," *Potter's American Monthly* 5 (1876): 327–29; *Report of the Secretary of the Navy*, 39th Cong., 1st sess., 1865, H. Exec. Doc. 1, pt. 3: 10.

51. Vallette, "History of the Philadelphia Navy Yard," 264.

52. Ibid., 181, 256, 257, 331; "Navy-Yard," *A Naval Encyclopedia*, 590–607; Whitworth Report, 176.

53. *Niles' Register*, July 6, 1822, 290.

54. Peck, *Roundshot to Rockets*, 81–82.

55. Vallette, "History of the Philadelphia Navy Yard," 257; Whitworth Report, 177, 363.

56. "Navy-Yard," *A Naval Encyclopedia*, 599. See also the annual report of the chief of the Bureau of Yards and Docks in the *Report of the Secretary of the Navy*, H. Exec. Doc. 1, pt. 3, for the years 1860–66.

57. *Report on Steam Engines*, 25th Cong., 3rd sess., 1838, H. Doc. 21: 43–44.

58. *Navy Yards—Board of Navy Officers—Evidence Taken before Them*, 36th Cong., 1st sess., 1860, H. Exec. Doc. 71: 59, 111, 172–73, 191, 203, 239, 260–62; *Report of the Secretary of the Navy*, 37th Cong., 3rd sess., 1862, H. Exec. Doc. 1, pt. 3: 568.

59. *Report of the Secretary of the Navy*, 41st Cong., 2nd sess., 1869, H. Exec. Doc., 1, pt. 3: 230.

60. *Testimony Taken by the Committee on Naval Affairs: Kittery Navy Yard*, 44th Cong., 1st sess., 1876, H. Misc. Doc 170: 44–47.

61. *Manufactories and Manufacturers of Pennsylvania*, 485; Taylor, "I Build Men as Well as Ships," 4; Hutchins, *American Maritime Industries and Public Policy*, 106.

62. Hall Report, 69; Dunbaugh and Thomas, *William H. Webb*, 21–28; Samuel Eliot Morison, "McKay, Donald," *Dictionary of American Biography*, 6:72–73; Hutchins, *American Maritime Industries and Public Policy*, 299.

63. For Pook's skills, consult Laing, *American Ships*. Quote from *Investigation by the Committee on Naval Affairs: Miscellaneous*, 44th Cong., 1st sess., 1876, H. Misc. Doc. 170, pt. 5: 23, 28.

64. Whipple, *The Clipper Ships*, 24–25.

65. *Investigation by the Committee on Naval Affairs: Boston Navy Yard*, 44th Cong., 1st sess., 1876, H. Misc. Doc. 170, pt. 2: 201.

66. Hall Report, 69.

67. M'Kay, *The Practical Shipbuilder*, introduction.

68. Rogers, *The Shipwright's Own Book*; Rogers, *Shipbuilding Made Easy*; Boole, *The Shipwright's Handbook and Draughtsman's Guide*; Chapelle, *The Search for Speed under Sail*, 7.

69. Pook, *A Method of Comparing the Lines and Draughting Vessels*.

70. Murphy, *American Ships and Ship-Builders*, 12; McKay, *Some Famous Sailing Ships and Their Builder*, 356.

71. Griffiths, *Treatise on Marine and Naval Architecture*.

72. Griffiths, *The Ship-Builder's Manual, and Nautical Referee*; Griffiths, *The Progressive Ship Builder*; *United States Nautical Magazine and Naval Journal* (New York: March 1845–May 1846, October 1854–March 1858); *American Ship: Devoted to American Industry, Nautical Commerce, Shipbuilding, Engineering, Navigation, Insurance, Yachting and Naval Interests* (New York: October 1878–September 1882).

73. "Ship-Building Not Yet a Science," *U.S. Nautical Magazine and Naval Journal* 3, no. 5 (February 1856): 328.

74. Laing, *American Ships*, 275–82, 314.

75. Stephens, *Traditions and Memories of American Yachting*, 95–96; McKay, *Some Famous Sailing Ships and Their Builder*, 10.

76. "The Shipbuilders of America: George Steers," *U.S. Nautical Magazine and Naval Journal* 6, no. 4 (July 1857): 242.

77. Griffiths, *Treatise on Marine and Naval Architecture*, 34.

78. Ibid.

79. M'Kay, *The Practical Shipbuilder*, 13; Morrison, *History of New York Ship Yards*, 44.

80. Chapelle, *The Search for Speed under Sail*, 284.

81. Hutchins, *American Maritime Industries and Public Policy*, 383–85; Hall Report, 87, 96–105.

Chapter 5. Building Iron Ships in a Wooden Shipbuilding Culture

1. Epigraph from *The American Maritime Industries and Public Policy*, 449.

2. Tyler, *The American*, 3–9.

3. U.S. Navy Dept., Bureau of Construction and Repair, *History of the Construction Corps of the United States Navy*, 20.

4. Quote from the *Augusta (Ga.) Constitutionalist*, August 15, 1834; found in Alexander Crosby Brown, "Notes on the Origins of Iron Shipbuilding in the United States, 1825–1861," 68.

5. Holbrook Fitz John Porter, "The Delamater Iron Works—The Cradle of the Modern Navy," *SNAME Transactions* 26 (1918): 3. According to Commander W. P. White ("The U.S.S. Michigan, Renamed Wolverine," *SNAME Transactions* 17 [1909]: 47), a crowd gathered at the 1844 launch of the *Michigan* to see whether she would sink.

6. Grantham, *Iron, as a Material for Ship-Building*, 36–37, 74; Brodie, *Sea Power in the Machine Age*, 129, 139–47, 154–57.

7. Grantham, *Iron, as a Material for Ship-Building*, 63–64; United States Shipping Board Emergency Fleet Corporation, "Hearings before the Committee on Commerce . . . on Senate Resolution 170," 617; Brodie, *Sea Power in the Machine Age*, 155.

8. Grantham, *Iron, as a Material for Ship-Building*, 39, 66; Brodie, *Sea Power in the Machine Age*, 151, 157–58; John H. Morrison, "Water-Tight Compartments in Steam Vessels," *CM* 12, no. 6 (October 1897): 711–14.

9. Grantham, *Iron, as a Material for Ship-Building*, 48–52, 55–59, 72–74.

10. Rorabaugh, *The Craft Apprentice*, 64.

11. The article "The American Clyde," in *Harper's New Monthly Magazine* (56, no. 335 [April 1878], 644–45; hereafter cited as "American Clyde"), may have been the first reference made to the American Clyde. See also Hood, "The Clyde of America," 257–61.

12. John Elgar to Dr. Charles Lukens (March 31, 1825), Accession 1366, Hagley Library; Morrison, *Iron and Steel Hull Steam Vessels of the United States, 1825–1905*, 1–2; Tyler, *American Clyde*, 4.

13. For a more detailed account of John Elgar's *Codorus*, see Alexander Crosby Brown, "The Sheet Iron Steamboat *Codorus*," *American Neptune* 10, no. 3 (July 1950): 163–90.

14. Morrison, *Iron and Steel Steam Vessels of the U.S.*, 5–6; Tyler, *American Clyde*, 4–7.

15. Stevens, "The First Steam Screw Propeller Boat to Navigate the Waters of Any Country," 101–30.

16. Charles H. Cramp, "Evolution of Screw Propulsion in the United States, Part

I," *SNAME Transactions* 17 (1909): 145–46; "Ericsson's Patent Steam Propeller," *Naval Magazine* 2, no. 6 (November 1839): 585–86.

17. Cramp, "Evolution of Screw Propulsion in the United States, Part I," *SNAME Transactions* 17 (1909): 146–49, 153–54; John V. Merrick, "Memoirs of John Vaughan Merrick," in Brinton, *Their Lives and Mine*, 26–27.

18. Cramp, "Evolution of Screw Propulsion in the United States, Part I," *SNAME Transactions* 17 (1909): 149–50.

19. Hall Report, 205–6; Swann, *John Roach*, 51–53; Morrison, *Iron and Steel Steam Vessels of the U.S.*, 14–15; Tyler, *The American Clyde*, 7, 14–15.

20. Notebooks kept by Henry Hall for the 10th Census Report on American Shipbuilding, MS 408, Penobscot Marine Museum Library, Searsport, Maine (hereafter cited as Hall Notebooks), 340; Hill, *History of American Shipping*, 77; Hall Report, 208–13; Morrison, *Iron and Steel Steam Vessels of the U.S.*, 6, 10; Tyler, *American Clyde*, 8–9, 13–14.

21. Harlan and Hollingsworth Company, *Semi-Centennial Memoir of the Harlan & Hollingsworth Company, 1836–1886*, 229–30, 251–59; Hall Report, 208–13.

22. *Bangor Whig and Courier*, September 1 and 2, 1845; *Portland Advertiser*, September 2 and 4, 1845.

23. For more on the *Bangor*, see Lawrence C. Allin, "S.S. *Bangor*: Harbinger of Destiny," *American Neptune* 39, no. 3 (July 1979): 218–24; Basil Greenhill and Ewan Corlett, "The Iron Screw Steamship Bangor II," *International Journal of Maritime History* 2, no. 1 (June 1990): 215–26.

24. Contract between Reaney, Neafie, and Co. and Capt. R. F. Loper (November 15, 1847), Palmer-Loper Family Papers, Mss. 18,965, Library of Congress; *Contracts—Navy Department*, 28th Cong., 1st sess., 1844, H. Doc. 72: 8–9; *United States Steamers*, 33rd Cong., 1st sess., 1853, H. Misc. Doc. 2: 2; contract between John Reybold and Brothers and Harlan and Hollingsworth Company for an iron steamer (September 2, 1852), MS 5640, Historical Society of Delaware, Wilmington (hereafter cited as "Reybold Contract").

25. *Steam Navy of the United States*, 33rd Cong., 1st sess., 1854, H. Exec. Doc. 65: 89–92; Hall Report, 198; Reybold Contract; *Contracts of the Navy Department*, 45th Cong., 2nd sess., 1878, H. Rep. 787: 17; *Testimony Taken by the Committee on Naval Affairs*, 45th Cong, 2nd. sess., 1878, H. Misc. Doc. 63: 624; Alexander C. Brown, "Notes on the Origins of Iron Shipbuilding," 122; "Agreement between the Rancocas Steam Boat Co. of Lumberton New Jersey and Reaney, Neafie & Smith of Philadelphia, Feb. 4, 1845," CK 11, Reaney, Neafie, and Company Documents, Mariners' Museum Library and Archives.

26. H. Jasper Cox, "The Application of Electric Welding to Ship Construction," *SNAME Transactions* 26 (1918): 238.

27. Naval engineer Albert Aston, USN, "Ship-Building, Iron," *Naval Encyclopaedia*, 741; "Iron-Clad Vessels," *Harper's New Monthly Magazine* 25, no. 148 (September 1862): 442; Hall Report, 198; J. Humphrys, "On a System of Mechanical Shipbuilding,"

INA Transactions 20 (1879): 232; Lewis Nixon, "The Building of a Ship," *CM* 13, no. 5 (March 1898): 391.

28. Quote from Basalla, *The Evolution of Technology*, 106. See also Pye, *The Nature of Design*.

29. Abell, *The Shipwright's Trade*, 111.

30. Nixon, "Building of a Ship," 392–93; Allen, "Iron Hulls for Western River Steamboats," 274–75.

31. Griffiths, *The Progressive Shipbuilder*, 2:233–34; Chapelle, *Boatbuilding*, 231–34; Hall Report, 198.

32. The quotation comes from Washington Jones, "Some Recollections of Machine Shops in the Early Forties," *American Machinist* 19 (April 30, 1896): 453. See also *Steam Navy of the United States*, 33rd Cong., 1st sess., 1854, H. Exec. Doc. 65: 93–94; Commonwealth of Pennsylvania, *Annual Report of the Secretary of Internal Affairs for the Year 1891. Industrial Statistics, Part III*" (hereafter cited as "Pennsylvania Report") 19:65, 102; Nixon, "Building of a Ship," 393–95; Humphrys, "On a System of Mechanical Shipbuilding," 232–33; *Fifty Years: New York Shipbuilding Corporation*, 15.

33. Cramp, "Evolution of Screw Propulsion in the United States," 157–158 (quotation on 158).

34. House of Representatives, Committee on Naval Affairs, *The Vessels of the New Navy*, 51st Cong., 1st sess. (Washington: GPO, 1890), 11; House of Representatives, Committee on Naval Affairs, *Shipbuilding in Government Yards*, 56th Cong., 1st sess., 29; Hall Report, 219; Henry A. Griffin, "Ship-Building on the Great Lakes," *EM* 4, no. 6 (March 1893): 822.

35. Hennessey, *The Sewall Ships of Steel*, vii–x; Walden Fawcett, "The Ship-Building Yards of the United States," *EM* 19 (1900): 669.

36. "Report of the Board of Naval Officers in the Case of the Iron Double-Ender Ashuelot, December 1893," Entry 187, RG 19, National Archives, p. 3; "Light-Draught Monitors," *Report of the Joint Committee on the Conduct of the War*, 25–32, 41–46; *Report of the Secretary of the Navy*, 37th Cong., 2nd sess., 1861, S. Exec. Doc. 1: 155; White, *A Short History of American Locomotive Builders in the Steam Era*, 59–61; *New York Times*, December 23, 1861, and March 23, 1862; *Scientific American* 7, no. 19 (Nov. 8, 1862): 291, 297; McKay, *Some Famous Sailing Ships and Their Builder*, 333–35, 353–57.

37. Charles Hillman Ship and Engine Company Ledger, Vaughan and Lynn Records, 1853–1896, Accession 1540, Historical Society of Pennsylvania; *Manufactories and Manufacturers of Pennsylvania of the Nineteenth Century*, 485–86; Alexander C. Brown, "Notes on the Origins of Iron Shipbuilding," 234; *Annual Report of the Commissioner of Navigation, 1899*, 56th Cong., 1st sess., H. Doc. 1, pt. 1: 218; Hall Report, 202.

38. Hutchins, *The American Maritime Industries and Public Policy*, 454; Heinrich, *Ships for the Seven Seas*, 45.

39. "American Naval Architecture," *Scientific American* 4, no. 2 (January 12, 1861): 28; Morrison, *Iron and Steel Steam Vessels of the U.S.*, 11; Hall Report, 201.

40. William R. Bagnall, "Sketches of Manufacturing Establishments in New York City" (MS, Baker Library, Harvard University, 1908), 290–91; William N. Still Jr., "Monitor Companies: A Study of the Major Firms That Built the U.S.S. *Monitor*," *American Neptune* 48, no. 2 (Spring 1988): 119; *Relief of Certain Naval Contractors*, 43rd Cong., 1st sess., 1874, H. Rep. 269: 11–13; *Annual Report of the Commissioner of Navigation, 1899*, 56th Cong., 1st sess., H. Doc. 1, pt. 1: 218.

41. David B. Tyler, "Shipbuilding in Delaware," *Delaware History* 7, no. 3 (March 1957): 212–13; Hall Report, 201–2, 218–19; Bishop, *A History of American Manufactures from 1608 to 1860*, 3:68–71.

42. For the low transition rate for woodworkers, see Nathan Lipfert, "The Shipyard Worker and the Iron Shipyard," *Log of Mystic Seaport* 35, no. 3 (Fall 1983): 75–87.

43. According to John S. Kebabian, "Delaware Apprenticeship Indentures, 1827–1850" (MS, Delaware Historical Society, Wilmington, n.d.), 28; and the *Wilmington (Del.) City Directory* for 1881, 1883, and 1891, John Harris's apprentices Enoch Townsend, David Hayes, and John Thomas found work in Wilmington's iron shipbuilding establishments.

44. Hall Report, 198.

45. Testimony of chief naval constructor Theodore Wilson, USN, found in House of Representatives, Committee on Naval Affairs, *On Bill for Increase of Naval Establishment*, 49th Cong., 1st sess., 42.

46. Cramp, "Sixty Years of Shipbuilding on the Delaware," 180–82. Quote from *Testimony Taken by the Committee on Naval Affairs: Boston Navy Yard*, 44th Cong., 1st sess., 1876, H. Misc. Doc. 170: 121.

47. Edward O. Smith, *History of the Newport News Shipbuilding and Dry Dock Company*, 53; Pennsylvania Report, 3:529; "Comparative Statement of Wages Paid and Average Rates," Box 1, MS Coll. 32, William Cramp and Sons Ship and Engine Building Co., Urban Archives, Temple University Library; *The American Carrying Trade*, 67.

48. *Causes of the Reduction of American Tonnage*, 41st Cong., 2nd sess., 1870 H. Rep. 28: 21, 26; House of Representatives, Committee on Naval Affairs, *On Bill for Increase of Naval Establishment*, 49th Cong., 1st sess., 1886, 42; Hall Notebooks, 6; Hall Report, 202; Tyler, *American Clyde*, 8; Cramp, "Evolution of Screw Propulsion in the United States," 157.

49. Hall Notebooks, 6; Hall Report, 202; Tyler, *American Clyde*, 8.

50. Cramp, "Evolution of Screw Propulsion in the United States," 157.

51. Horace See, "The Building of the Steamship in America," *EM* 1 (1891): 374–75.

52. "Pilgrim, August 15th, 1864," MS Accession 435, Microfilm Reel 2, Hagley Museum and Library; Alexander Laing, *American Ships*, 314–16; *Steam Navy of the United States*, 33rd Cong., 1st sess., 1854 H. Exec. Doc. 65: 101.

53. "Loper's Patent Method of Constructing Ships of Metal and Wood," *Scientific*

American 6, no. 13 (December 14, 1850): 100; Lytle and Holdcamper, *Merchant Steam Vessels of the United States*, 160.

54. Contract between Reaney, Neafie, and Co. and Capt. R. F. Loper (November 15, 1847), Container I:11, Palmer-Loper Families Papers, Library of Congress. A bill sent by Reaney, Neafie, and Co. to R. F. Loper (n.d.), found in the same container, indicates John Birely and Son supplied the ship carpenters for assembling the composite vessel.

55. Griffiths, *The Progressive Shipbuilder*, 2:131; Heinrich, *Ships for the Seven Seas*, 26–27.

56. "The American Clyde," *Harper's New Monthly Magazine* 56, no. 335 (April 1878): 645–53; Hall Report, 198; Pennsylvania Report, 19:100; Swann, *John Roach*, 71.

57. For a description of carpentry and joiner departments of a nineteenth-century iron shipyard, see *Semi-Centennial Memoir of Harlan & Hollingsworth*, 320–23. *Eight Hours for Laborers on Government Work* (57th Cong., 2nd sess., 1903, S. Doc. 141: 369–80) includes a departmental breakdown of Cramp workers, including carpentry and joiner departments. See also "The Pusey & Jones Company Organization Chart C, Dec. 1, 1909," in "Book 58: Work Rules, The Pusey & Jones Company," Papers of the Pusey & Jones Corporation, Accession 551, Hagley Library.

58. Buell, *The Memoirs of Charles H. Cramp*, 43; Swann, *John Roach*, 56; United States Shipping Board Emergency Fleet Corporation, "Hearings before the Committee on Commerce . . . on Senate Resolution 170," 1:607, 618.

59. "James Dickie," *SNAME Transactions* 30 (1922): 269–70; Hall Notebooks, 393; "George W. Dickie," *CM* 15, no. 3 (January 1899): 245–47.

60. *Investigation by the Committee on Naval Affairs—Miscellaneous*, 44th Cong., 1st sess., 1876, H. Misc. Doc. 170, pt. 5: 22, 32, 632–33; Laing, *American Ships*, 315–22; William L. Hanscom Letters, VFM 7, Manuscripts Division, G. W. Blunt White Library, Mystic Seaport Museum; "Henry Steers," *National Cyclopaedia of American Biography*, 6:122–3; Swann, *John Roach*, 71.

61. *Semi-Centennial Memoir of Harlan & Hollingsworth*, 182–89, 293–95; Laing, *American Ships*, 204–13.

62. Tyler, *American Clyde*, 14; "Jacob G. Neafie," *Philadelphia Public Ledger*, January 17, 1898.

63. George R. Prowell, *The History of Camden County, New Jersey*, 371–72.

64. Ibid., 233–34; U.S. Department of the Interior, Census Bureau, *Schedule 3: Products of Industry, 1880*, for Wilmington, Hagley Library.

65. *Wilmington City Directory*, 1886–1888, Hagley Library; *Semi-Centennial Memoir of Harlan & Hollingsworth*, 308.

66. U.S. House of Representatives, Committee on Naval Affairs, *On Bill for Increase of Naval Establishment*, 49th Cong., 1st sess., 89; Swann, *John Roach*, 61.

67. For numbers of boys employed at Cramps and other yards, see the Hexamer fire insurance surveys, E. Hexamer, Microform, Camden County Historical Society;

and *Report of the Industrial Commission on the Relations and Conditions of Capital and Labor,* 57th Cong., 1st sess., 1901, H. Doc. 183: 416.

68. *Eight Hours for Laborers on Government Work,* 57th Cong., 2nd sess., 1903, S. Doc. 141: 357–58; *Bulletin of the Bureau of Labor No. 52, May 1904,* 58th Cong., 2nd sess., 1904, H. Doc 343, pt. 3: 550–56.

69. U.S. Department of Interior, Census Bureau, "Schedule 3. Products of Industry," *U.S. Census 1880,* Wilmington, Hagley Library; fire insurance survey for Wm. Cramp and Sons, Ship and Engine Building Company, 1874, E. Hexamer Insurance Survey Co., Hagley Library. For statistics on employment and the physical arrangement of iron shipbuilding firms, consult the fire insurance surveys of the E. Hexamer Company found at the Hagley Library, Camden County Historical Society, and Philadelphia Free Library.

70. U.S. Senate, Committee on Education and Labor, *Report of the Committee of the Senate upon the Relations between Labor and Capital,* 1007, 1038; Swann, *John Roach,* 61.

71. Rubin and Swift, *Negro Employment in the Maritime Industries,* 26–27; U.S. Dept. of Commerce, Census Bureau, *Negro Population, 1790–1915,* 543.

72. For more on the "bastard artisan system," see Wilentz, *Chants Democratic,* 107–42.

73. For division of labor, see *The American Carrying Trade,* 67; and *Hours of Labor for Workmen, Mechanics, etc.,* 55th Cong., 2nd sess., 1898, S. Doc. 318: 37.

74. For numbers of Civil War ironworkers, see naval inspector's report on the monitors *Saugus* and *Napa* on p. 352 of MS Accession 426, microfilm Reel I, Office of the Bureau of Construction and Repair, RG 19, National Archives, Hagley Library. For later division of labor, see Kelly and Allen, *The Shipbuilding Industry,* 279.

75. "On Tree-nails and Tree-nailing," *U.S. Nautical Magazine and Naval Journal* 5, no. 5 (February 1857): 354–56; Kelly and Allen, *Shipbuilding Industry,* 219.

76. David A. Simmons, "'The Continuous Clatter': Practical Field Riveting," *IA: The Journal of the Society for Industrial Archaeology* 23, no. 2 (1997): 7–8; Pennsylvania Report, "Commerce, Navigation, and Shipbuilding," 19 (1981): 103; quotation Kelly and Allen, *Shipbuilding Industry,* 146; Swann, *John Roach,* 69–72. For documentation of injuries suffered by riveters, consult the accident reports for the Phoenix Bridge Company [Book 476 (1901–1910), Accession 916], Hagley Library.

77. Rosenberg, ed., *The American System of Manufactures,* 194. Quotes from *Steam Navy of the United States,* 33rd Cong., 1st sess., 1854, H. Exec. Doc. 65: 93–94.

78. *Journal of the Brotherhood of Boiler Makers and Iron Ship Builders of America* 9, no. 5 (May 1, 1897): 140–41; ibid., 10, no. 12 (December 1, 1898): 376.

79. *Semi-Centennial Memoir of Harlan & Hollingsworth,* 359–60; Swann, *John Roach,* 61.

80. William P. Stephens to William A. Dobson, April 30, 1935, and Stephens to Dobson, May 23, 1935, Stephens Collection; *Report of the Committee of the Senate upon the Relations between Labor and Capital,* 1007; Robert Allison, "The Old and

the New," *ASME Transactions* 16 (1895): 760; *American Merchant Marine in the Foreign Trade*, 51st Cong., 1st sess., 1890, H. Rep. 1210: 113; Watson, "Changes of a Half-Century in the Marine-Engine Shop," 906; Swann, *John Roach*, 61–62.

81. Harrison, *The Mechanic's Tool Book*.

82. Allison, "The Old and the New," 749.

83. Ibid., 754, for use of the term "practical." Iron shipbuilder John Dialogue's business partner referred to him as a "practical machinist" in *Testimony Taken by the Committee on Naval Affairs: Philadelphia Navy Yard*, 44th Cong., 1st sess., 1876, H. Misc. Doc. 170: 93. Machinists used the term to describe themselves during the early twentieth century, as shown by testimony concerning Cramp machinists in *Eight Hours for Laborers on Government Work*, 57th Cong., 2nd sess., 1903, S. Doc. 141: 69.

84. *Semi-Centennial Memoir of Harlan & Hollingsworth*, 306–13; Pusey and Jones Corporation, *A Hundred Years A-Building*, 5–6.

85. Taylor, "I Build Men as Well as Ships," 4–12. The Cramp shipyard executive staff included founder William Cramp; his sons, including Charles H.; his grandsons; and great-grandson H. Birchard Taylor. The Roach shipyard staff included founder John and his sons, Garrett and John Baker Roach.

86. For more on batch production, see Scranton, "Diversity in Diversity," 33–38.

87. S. H. Pook, naval constructor, USN, "Ship, Launching of," *A Naval Encyclopedia*, 744; Griffiths, *Progressive Shipbuilder*, 2:255.

88. Egbert P. Watson, "The Changes of a Half-Century in the Marine-Engine Shop," *EM* 22 (September 1902): 909.

89. James Dickie, "Overhead Cranes, Staging, and Riveter-Carrying Appliances in the Shipyard," *SNAME Transactions* 7 (1899): 189; Pennsylvania Report, 19:101.

90. Ibid. For a thorough description of the frame-bending and punching process, see John W. Nystrom, "On a New System of Shaping Iron Ships' Frames," in his *Treatise on Parabolic Construction of Ships*, 37–40; Swann, *John Roach*, 71.

91. W. J. Macquorn Rankine, "On a Proposed Method of Bevelling Iron Frames in Shipbuilding," *INA Transactions* 6 (1865): 116–18; Nystrom, "New System of Shaping Iron Ships' Frames," 37; "American Clyde," 646; Pennsylvania Report, 19:101.

92. "American Clyde," 645–46, 649.

93. Ibid., 648.

94. S. H. Pook, "Ship, Launching of," *A Naval Encyclopedia*, 744.

95. Dickie, "Overhead Cranes, Staging, and Riveter-Carrying Appliances in the Shipyard," 189; Pennsylvania Report, 19:101.

96. Hexamer Survey.

97. William P. Stephens to William A. Dobson, May 23, 1935, Stephens Collection; "American Clyde," 643; *Chester Times*, March 24, 1883 (before 1882, the *Chester Times* was published as the *Chester Daily Times*); Pennsylvania Report, 3:529.

98. "American Clyde," 651.

99. Ibid., 650; Pennsylvania Industrial Statistics, 1876–77, 646; Swann, *John Roach*, 56.

100. "American Clyde," 647; Cramp, "Evolution of Screw Propulsion in the United States," 157–58; Swann, *John Roach*, 59.

101. *Steam Navy of the United States*, 33rd Cong., 1st sess., 1854, H. Exec. Doc. 65: 93–94; Pennsylvania Report, 19:65, 102; Nixon, "Building of a Ship," 393–95; Humphrys, "On a System of Mechanical Shipbuilding," 232–33; *Fifty Years: New York Shipbuilding Corporation*, 15; Reed, *Shipbuilding in Iron and Steel*, 435–36; Hexamer Survey; Hall Report, 198; Swann, *John Roach*, 59; *Chester Daily Times*, December 7, 1882.

102. "Iron-Clad Vessels," *Harper's New Monthly Magazine* 25, no. 148 (September 1862): 440; "American Clyde," 648–49.

103. Cramp, "Evolution of Screw Propulsion in the United States," 157–58; Reed, *Shipbuilding in Iron and Steel*, 434; *Chester Times*, December 7, 1882; Swann, *John Roach*, 62.

104. A. Campbell Holms, *Practical Shipbuilding*, 294–96; quotation Reed, *Shipbuilding in Iron and Steel*, 435–36.

105. See iron tool inventories of June 16, 1863, and August 15, 1863, in the Papers of Naval Engineer Thomas J. Griffin, USN, American Swedish Institute, Philadelphia; Reed, *Shipbuilding in Iron and Steel*, 341.

106. Kelly and Allen, *The Shipbuilding Industry*, 146, 219; Reed, *Shipbuilding in Iron and Steel*, 340–41, 437; Simmons, "'The Continuous Clatter,'" 7–8; Pennsylvania Report, 19 (1891): 103; Swann, *John Roach*, 67–68. For documentation of injuries suffered by riveters, consult the accident reports for the Phoenix Bridge Company (Book 476 [1901–1910], Accession 916), Hagley Library and Museum.

107. *Journal of the Brotherhood of Boiler Makers and Iron Ship Builders of America* 9, no. 5 (May 1, 1897): 140–41; ibid., 10, no. 12 (December 1, 1898): 376; "Pneumatic Field Riveting in Railway Bridge Work," *Engineering Record* 42, no. 17 (October 27, 1900): 393; Reed, *Shipbuilding in Iron and Steel*, 345.

108. Reed, *Shipbuilding in Iron and Steel*, 340–41, 437; Kelly and Allen, *Shipbuilding Industry*, 146, 219; Simmons, "'The Continuous Clatter,'" 7–8; Pennsylvania Report, 19: 103; Swann, *John Roach*, 69–72. For documentation of injuries suffered by riveters, consult the accident reports for the Phoenix Bridge Company [Book 476 (1901–1910), Accession 916], Hagley Library and Museum.

109. Holms, *Practical Shipbuilding*, 295–96; Reed, *Shipbuilding in Iron and Steel*, 340–41.

110. *Chester Times*, December 31, 1886.

111. Souvenir of Roach's Shipyard, 17.

112. *New York Times*, May 23, 1877; "American Clyde," 648; Hexamer Survey. Quote from *Chester Times*, December 9, 1882.

113. "American Clyde," 650.

114. Ibid., 650; "John Roach of New York," *Scientific American* 47, no. 2 (July 8, 1882): 19; Swann, *John Roach*, 73.

115. *Chester Times*, March 24, 1883; Swann, *John Roach*, 57.

116. Pook, "Ship, Launching of," *Naval Encyclopedia*, 744–45; Pennsylvania Report,

19: 104–5; *Chester Times*, December 6, 1882; William J. Baxter, "Notes on Launching," *SNAME Transactions* 2 (1894): 241–60.

117. Swann, *John Roach*, 58.
118. William Stephens to William Dobson, April 30, 1935, Stephens Collection.
119. Ibid.
120. Ibid.
121. William Stephens to William Dobson, May 23, 1935, Stephens Collection.
122. Ibid.
123. *New York Times*, May 23, 1877; *Chester Daily Times*, June 27, 1877; William Stephens to William Dobson, May 23, 1935, Stephens Collection.
124. For ironworkers' tools, see inventories of June 16, 1863, and August 15, 1863, in the Papers of Naval Engineer Thomas J. Griffin, USN, American Swedish Institute, Philadelphia.
125. Souvenir of Roach's Shipyard, 9; Swann, *John Roach*, 98.

Chapter 6. A Clash of Cultures: The Failure of Theory in a Practical Shipbuilding World

1. Nystrom epigraph from his *Treatise on Parabolic Construction of Ships and Other Marine Engineering Subjects*, 18.
2. For unique national styles of engineering practice, see Kranakis, *Constructing a Bridge*.
3. *Report of the Board on Behalf of United States Executive Departments at the International Exhibition*, 47th Cong., 2nd sess., 1884, H. Misc. Doc. 20, pt. 2: 41–48; Post, *1876: A Centennial Exhibition*, 87–95.
4. Horace See, discussion of Charles H. Cramp, "Evolution of Screw Propulsion in the United States, Part I," *SNAME Transactions* 17 (1909): 161.
5. Ibid.
6. Griffiths, *Treatise on Marine and Naval Architecture*, 96; *Premiums Paid to Contractors of War Vessels for the Navy*, 53rd Cong., 2nd sess., 1894, H. Rep. 407: 104–5; "American Clyde," 643–44; Nixon, "The Building of a Ship," 385.
7. *Testimony Taken by the Committee on Naval Affairs, in Reference to the Administration of the Navy Department*, 45th Cong., 2nd sess., 1878, H. Misc. Doc. 63: 364; *Premiums Paid to Contractors of War Vessels for the Navy*, 53rd Cong. 2nd sess., 1894, H. Rep. 407: 95–96, 126.
8. Hall Report, 202; Hall Notebooks, 6; Tyler, *The American Clyde*, 8.
9. An observer from the Naval Academy briefly described the process in "Report of the Secretary of the Navy, 1880," 72–73; "American Clyde," 644–45; "John Roach, of New York," *Scientific American* 47, no. 2 (July 8, 1882): 19.
10. For Harlan and Hollingsworth's use of models, see Harlan and Hollingsworth Company, *The Harlan & Hollingsworth Co., Ship and Car Builders: Their Plant and Operations*, 8; *Construction of Vessels of War for the Navy*, 47th Cong., 1st sess., 1882, H. Rep. 653: 99; Edward G. Brownlee, "How We Built Ships on Cooper's Point before WW II: A Tribute to George R. Taylor, Shipbuilder," *American Neptune* 56, no. 3

(Summer 1996): 263; D. W. Taylor, "On Ships' Forms Derived by Formulae," *SNAME Transactions* 11 (1903): 244–46.

11. Herreschoff, *Capt. Nat Herreschoff*, 128–40.

12. Ibid., 128–38; "Nathaniel Greene Herreschoff," *SNAME Transactions* 46 (1938): 370–72; *New York Times*, June 3, 1938.

13. "Souvenir of Roach's Shipyard," 9; Swann, *John Roach*, 95–97.

14. Hexamer Survey; William I. Schaffer, Receiver, "Roach's Shipyard: Information as to Plant, Equipment, Etc.," Pamphlet File, Historical Society of Pennsylvania; Swann, *John Roach*, 53, 57.

15. *New York Times*, May 23, 1877; *Chester Daily Times*, April 30, 1877; Hall Report, 207; *The American Carrying Trade*, 67.

16. An observer from the U.S. Naval Academy briefly described the process in *Report of the Secretary of the Navy, 1880*, 46th Cong., 3rd sess., H. Exec. Doc. 1, pt. 3: 72–73; "American Clyde," 644–45; "John Roach of New York," *Scientific American* 47, no. 2 (July 8, 1882): 19; Swann, *John Roach*, 71.

17. "American Clyde," 644–45; Chapelle, *Boatbuilding*, 72–141; Swann, *John Roach*, 71.

18. Boole, *The Shipwright's Handbook and Draughtsman's Guide*, 13–15.

19. Pennsylvania Report, 19:100; "American Clyde," 645; Hall Report, 198; and Swann, *John Roach*, 71.

20. Cramp, "Evolution of Screw Propulsion in the United States," 157–58.

21. Cramp, "Sixty Years of Shipbuilding on the Delaware," 184.

22. Cramp, "Evolution of Screw Propulsion in the United States," 158; Cramp, "Sixty Years of Shipbuilding on the Delaware," 184.

23. A description of the process of laying off plates may be found in naval engineer Alban Stimers to Rear Admiral Francis Gregory, September 22, 1862, Office of the Bureau of Construction and Repair, microfilm reel I, MS Accession 426, RG 19, National Archives, Hagley Library.

24. *Testimony Taken by the Committee on Naval Affairs in Reference to the Administration of the Navy Department*, 45th Cong., 2nd sess., 1878, H. Misc. Doc. 63: 626.

25. Nystrom, *Technological Education*, 31 (italics in original).

26. House of Representatives, Committee on Naval Affairs, *On Bill for Increase of Naval Establishment*, 49th Cong., 1st sess., 87–89, 93–94.

27. For more on Roach's demise, see William Thiesen, "Curse of the *Dolphin*," *American Neptune* 54, no. 1 (Winter 1994): 25–39; Swann, *John Roach*, 235–38.

28. Capt. Elliot Snow, USN, "Model Tank Experiments by Benjamin Franklin," *United States Naval Institute Proceedings* (hereafter cited as *USNI Proceedings*) 49, no. 247 (September 1923): 1469–72.

29. Hindle, *The Pursuit of Science in Revolutionary America*; Bishop, *A History of American Manufactures*, 1:73–74.

30. Frederick D. Herbert, "Robert Fulton's Original Drawings," *SNAME Transac-*

tions 42 (1934): 25; Marestier, *Memoir on Steamboats*, 12–13; Gilfillan, *Inventing the Ship*, 92–93.

31. Henry Howe, *Memoirs of the Most Eminent American Mechanics*, 215; Marestier, *Memoir on Steamboats*, 57–58; Phyllis DeKay Wheelock, "Henry Eckford (1775–1832), an American Shipbuilder," *American Neptune* 7, no. 3 (July 1947): 186.

32. Calhoun, *Intelligence of a People*, 240–41; Nystrom, *On Technological Education and the Construction of Ships and Screw Propellers*, 48.

33. Chapelle, *The History of the American Sailing Navy*, 120–26.

34. *Construction of Vessels of War for the Navy*, 47th Cong., 1st sess., 1882, H. Rep. 653: 78–79, 103–4; William A. Dobson to William P. Stephens, May 13, 1935, Folder 31, Box 2, Collection 91; Blunt White Library, Mystic Seaport.

35. Brief reports summarizing these summer cruises may be found in the "Report of the Naval Academy" in the annual *Report of the Secretary of the Navy* for the years 1872–81.

36. For a list of U.S. Navy contractors employed during the war, see appendix B in Bennett, *Steam Navy of the United States*.

37. Hall Report, 197.

38. Hexamer Fire Insurance Survey, 1874, E. Hexamer Co.; Office of the Bureau of Construction and Repair, microfilm reel I, MS Accession 426, National Archives, RG 19, Hagley Museum and Library Archives, 350–51; *Contracts of the Navy Department*, 45th Cong., 2nd sess., 1878, H. Rep. 787: 68.

39. Office of the Bureau of Construction and Repair, microfilm reel 1, MS Accession 426, National Archives, RG 19, Hagley Museum and Library Archives, 351.

40. Charles W. Pusey, "The History of Pusey & Jones," Folder 43, Box 1, Accession 551, Hagley Museum and Library; Hexamer Fire Insurance Survey, 1874, E. Hexamer Co.

41. "Register of Contracts: Reaney, Son & Archbold; Roach's Shipyard; Merchant Shipbuilding Corporation," 1–2. Quote and physical plant information from Bishop, *A History of American Manufactures from 1608 to 1860*, 3:70; fire insurance survey, E. Hexamer, Microform, Camden County Historical Society.

42. Bishop, *A History of American Manufactures from 1608 to 1860*, 3:134; "Iron Shipbuilding," *Bulletin of the American Iron and Steel Association* 7, no. 54, 1–2; *Causes of the Reduction of American Tonnage*, 41st Cong., 2nd sess., 1870, H. Rep. 28: 177; Herreschoff, *Capt. Nat Herreschoff*, 72; *Investigation by the Committee on Naval Affairs—Brooklyn Navy Yard*, 44th Cong., 1st sess., 1876, H. Misc. Doc. 170, pt. 6: 40; *Harlan & Hollingsworth Company, Memoranda Concerning Foreign Ship-Building, 1881–3*.

43. Byrne, *The American Engineer, Draftsman, and Machinist's Assistant*; Weissenborn, *American Engineering*.

44. Edward O. Smith, *History of the Newport News Shipbuilding and Dry Dock Company*, 79.

45. William P. Stephens to William A. Dobson, May 23, 1935, Folder 31, Box 2, Collection 91; Blunt White Library, Mystic Seaport.

46. W. P. Stephens and J. L. Bogert, "The Roach Shipyard," *SNAME Historical Transactions, 1893–1943*, 233–35; Cramp, "Sixty Years of Shipbuilding on the Delaware," 180; obituaries for Washington I. Babcock (*SNAME Transactions* 25 [1917]: n.p.), Frank S. Martin (*SNAME Transactions* 30 [1922]: 273–74), and William P. Stephens (*SNAME Transactions* 54 [1946]: 477–78); Stephens, *Traditions and Memories of American Yachting*, 148; Swann, *John Roach*, 56–57.

47. Edward O. Smith, *History of the Newport News Shipbuilding*, 17–20, 32–37, 44.

48. Cramp, "Sixty Years of Shipbuilding on the Delaware," 180.

49. William C. Church, "John Ericsson, the Engineer," *CM* 7, no. 37 (November 1894): 8–9; William F. Durand, "Ericsson, John," *Dictionary of American Biography*, 3:171–73; John Ericsson to Navy Secretary Gideon Welles, July 2, 1864, Box 7, John Ericsson Papers, American Swedish Institute, Philadelphia.

50. Cramp, "Sixty Years of Shipbuilding on the Delaware," 180.

51. Church, *The Life of John Ericsson*, 1:18, 1:226–27; John V. Merrick, "Memoirs of John Vaughan Merrick," in Brinton, *Their Lives and Mine*, 26–27; Washington Jones, "Some Recollections of Machine Shops in the Early Forties," *American Machinist* 19 (April 30, 1896): 452.

52. Frank H. Taylor to Amandus Johnson, January 19, 1940, MSS 41, Box 33, Folder 12, Amandus Johnson Papers, Balch Institute, Philadelphia; Egbert P. Watson, "Personal Recollections of Captain John Ericsson," *EM* 21, no. 3 (June 1901): 362–64; "John Ericsson," *Railroad and Engineering Journal* 63, no. 4 (April 1889): 151–52; "The Oldest Railroad Engineer," *American Railroad Journal* 33, no. 22 (June 2, 1877): 710; Bishop, *A History of American Manufactures*, 2:552; "John Ericsson," *ASME Transactions* 10 (1889): 845–50.

53. Church, *Life of John Ericsson*, 2:21.

54. Ibid.; "John Ericsson," *Railroad and Engineering Journal* 63, no. 4 (April 1889): 151–56; William F. Durand, "Ericsson, John," *Dictionary of American Biography*, 3:171–76; *New York Times*, March 9, 1889.

55. Wegner, "Alban C. Stimers and the Office of the General Inspector of Ironclads," 12–14.

56. Walter Millis, "The Iron Sea Elephants," *American Neptune* 10 (January 1950): 19.

57. Ibid., 24; Du Pont, *Rear-Admiral Samuel Francis Du Pont*, 220–21. For the Stimers–Du Pont debate, see *New York Times*, June 11, 1863, and November 8, 1863.

58. "Theodore Allen, M. Am. Soc. C.E.," *American Society of Civil Engineers Proceedings* (hereafter cited as *ASCE Proceedings*) 17 (1891): 240–41; U.S. Senate, *Report of the Joint Committee on the Conduct of the War* (hereafter cited as *Conduct of the War Report*), 94–104.

59. "The Late Isaac Newton," 409–10; "Isaac Newton," *Appleton's Cyclopaedia of*

American Biography, 4:507; "Isaac Newton, M. Am. Soc. C.E.," *ASCE Proceedings* 11 (1885): 128–29.

60. *Conduct of the War Report*, 107, 115; Wegner, "Alban C. Stimers and the Office of the General Inspector," 26, 30, 47–48; Sloan, *Benjamin Franklin Isherwood*, 68.

61. Bennett, *Steam Navy of the United States*, 485; Church, *Life of John Ericsson*, 2:29: Wegner, "Alban C. Stimers and the Office of the General Inspector," 30.

62. Bennett, *Steam Navy of the United States*, 485–86; Wegner, "Alban C. Stimers and the Office of the General Inspector," 51

63. *Conduct of the War Report*, 31.

64. Ibid., 39; Bennett, *Steam Navy of the United States*, 486–91.

65. *Certain Claims for Extra Payments for Vessels Built for the United States Navy*, 56th Cong., 1st sess., 1900, S. Doc. 288: 2; *Conduct of the War Report*, 31; Cramp, "Certain Incidents in the Evolution of the Modern Warship," 118.

66. *Certain Claims for Extra Payments for Vessels Built for the United States Navy*, 56th Cong., 1st sess., 1900, S. Doc. 288: 2; *Conduct of the War Report*, 31; Buell, *Memoirs of Charles H. Cramp*, 82–83.

67. John Ericsson to Navy Secretary Gideon Welles, May 30, 1864, Box 7, John Ericsson Papers, American Swedish Institute, Philadelphia; *Certain Claims for Extra Payments for Vessels Built for the United States Navy*, 50th Cong., 1st sess., 1900, S. Doc. 288: 2.

68. Millis, "Iron Sea Elephants," 26.

69. *Certain Claims for Extra Payments for Vessels Built for the United States Navy*, 50th Cong., 1st sess., 1900, S. Doc. 288: 6.

70. Church, *Life of John Ericsson*, 2:30.

71. "Theodore Allen, M. Am. Soc. C.E.," *ASCE Proceedings* 17 (1891): 240–41; *New York Times*, November 14, 1871, July 15, 1871, July 16, 1871; Wegner, "Alban C. Stimers and the Office of the General Inspector," 53.

72. "The Late Isaac Newton," *Sanitary Engineer* 10, no. 18 (October 2, 1884): 409–10; "Isaac Newton," *Appleton's Cyclopedia of American Biography*, 4:507; "Isaac Newton, M. Am. Soc. C.E.," *ASCE Proceedings* 11 (1885): 128–29.

73. The next major warship construction program, the ABCD Program, took place in the mid-1880s. See chapter 6 for further details.

74. Johnson, "Swedish-American Master Mechanics, Engineers and Inventors, 1638–1947, Part II," *Bulletin of the American Society of Swedish Engineers* 42, no. 1 (Winter 1947–48): 15, 42; Nystrom, *A Treatise on Screw Propellers*.

75. Nystrom, *Pocket-Book of Mechanics and Engineering*; Thure Mansson, "Nystrom, John William," *Svenska män och kvinnor* (Stockholm, 1949), 5:584; Nystrom, *On Technological Education*, 16. See a review of this book in the *New York Times*, April 30, 1872.

76. Nystrom, *A Treatise on Parabolic Construction of Ships and Other Marine Engineering Subjects*.

77. Johnson, "Swedish-American Master Mechanics, Engineers and Inventors, 1638–1947, Part II," 42. A complete list of Nystrom's published work would fill this

page. Please consult the Library of Congress catalog. For Nystrom's articles, see Franklin Institute, *Index to the Journal of the Franklin Institute, 1826 to 1885*, 386.

78. John W. Nystrom, "On a National Academy of Science and Technological Institutions," *FI Journal* 75 (1863): 276; Nystrom, *On Technological Education*, 23–24.

79. Nystrom, *A Treatise on Parabolic Construction of Ships and Other Marine Engineering Subjects*, i.

80. Nystrom, *On Technological Education*, 30.

81. William Barnet Le Van, "John William Nystrom, C.E.," *American Machinist* 8, no. 26 (June 27, 1885): 6–7; Mansson, "Nystrom, John William," *Svenska män och kvinnor*, 5:583–84; *Information in Relation to the Construction of the Iron-clad Monitor*, 40th Cong., 2nd sess., 1868, S. Exec. Doc. 86: 5.

82. See, for example, John W. Nystrom, "Reply to the Remarks of J. V. Merrick, Esq., on Screw Propellers," *FI Journal* 53 (March 1852): 198–201.

83. John W. Nystrom, "Stability of Vessels in Water," *FI Journal* 74 (July 1862): 53–57.

84. Nystrom, *On Technological Education*, 42–43.

85. "Proceedings of the Franklin Institute," *FI Journal* 49 (March 1850): 216; "Nystrom's New Calculating Machine," *Scientific American* 6, no. 35 (May 17, 1851): 1.

86. Nystrom, *Treatise on Screw Propellers*, 114–78.

87. Nystrom, *A Treatise on Parabolic Construction of Ships and Other Marine Engineering Subjects*, 22; M. S. Mahoney, "Amsler, Jakob," *Dictionary of Scientific Biography*, 1:147; W. J. Tennant, "The Planimeter Explained Simply without Mathematics," *Scientific American Supplement*, no. 1427 (May 9, 1903): 22873–74; McGee, "The Amsler Integrator and the Burden of Calculation," 67–68.

88. William T. Powell, "Some Early History Regarding the Double-turreted Monitors *Miantonomoh* and *Class*," *SNAME Transactions* 15 (1907): 205. The quotation may be found in the discussion following the article on page 210.

89. See the more thorough examination of these in chapter 2.

90. See, for example, Nystrom's *Parabolic Construction of Ships*; John W. Nystrom, "Steamship Performance," *FI Journal* 113, no. 2 (February 1882): 139; Nystrom, *Pocket-Book of Mechanics and Engineering*.

91. Nystrom, *Parabolic Construction of Ships*, i, 1; Nystrom, *On Technological Education*, 64.

92. In *On Technological Education* (43), Nystrom describes how chief naval constructor John Lenthall openly disparaged his parabolic method.

93. Professor R. H. Thurston, "Forms of Fish and of Ships," *INA Transactions* 28 (1887): 418–19.

94. "Proceedings of the Franklin Institute," *FI Journal* 49 (April 1850): 216; J. W. Nystrom, "A Few Suggestions as to the Manner of Laying Out a Propeller, When the Dimensions of the Vessel are Given," *FI Journal* 52 (November 1851): 321–32.

95. Nystrom, *Parabolic Construction of Ships*, 18.

96. John W. Nystrom, "On a National Academy of Science and Technological In-

stitutions," *FI Journal* 75 (April 1863): 275–77; "Proceedings of the Franklin Institute," *FI Journal* 75 (April 1863): 284–85.

97. Nystrom's brief history with the Navy Department may be traced through records held by the National Archives, including "Testimonials of Volunteer Officers," Naval Officer Personnel, Vols. 14 and 15, RG 24; "Letters from Volunteer Officers, May 1861 to July 1871," Vol. 25, Entry 78, Office of the Secretary of the Navy, 1776–1890, RG 45; "Letters of Resignation from Officers, March 1803 to June 1877," Vol. 14, Entry 65, Office of the Secretary of the Navy, 1776–1913, RG 45.

98. John W. Nystrom, "On the Elements of Physical Work, Vis-viva, Force, Velocity, Time, Power, and Work," *FI Journal* 78 (November 1864): 325–34; John W. Nystrom, "Work and Vis-viva," *FI Journal* 80 (July 1865): 56–58.

99. Nystrom, *On Technological Education*, 106.

100. See, for example, the exchange between Nystrom and Isherwood in B. F. Isherwood, "Remarks on Nystrom's Screw Propeller," *FI Journal* 52 (1851): 42–48; and John W. Nystrom, "Reply to the Remarks made by B. F. Isherwood, Esq., Chief Engineer, U.S. Navy, on Nystrom's Screw Propeller," *FI Journal* 52 (1851): 138–42.

101. "Letters of Resignation from Officers, March 1803 to June 1877," Vol. 14, Entry 65, Office of the Secretary of the Navy, 1776–1913, RG 45: Nystrom, *On Technological Education*, 85.

102. Nystrom, *On Technological Education*, 41, 50–51, 108–9.

103. Mansson, "Nystrom, John William," in *Svenska män och kvinnor*, 5:584; William Barnet Le Van, "John William Nystrom, C.E.," *American Machinist* 8, no. 26 (June 27, 1885): 6–7.

104. "Proceedings of the Franklin Institute," *FI Journal* 98 (1874): 385.

105. Nystrom, *On Technological Education*, 24–27.

106. John W. Nystrom, "Communication on the Metric System," *FI Journal* 71, no. 6 (June 1876): 386 (italics in original).

107. John W. Griffiths, *Progressive Shipbuilder*, 1:164.

108. Ibid., 56 (italics in original).

109. Merchant Shipbuilding Corporation, "Register of Contracts: Reaney, Son and Archbold, Roach's Shipyard, Merchant Shipbuilding Corporation," 2.

110. Nystrom, *On Technological Education*, 2.

111. Nystrom, *Parabolic Construction of Ships*, 18.

112. Nystrom, *On Technical Education*, 45.

Chapter 7. An American Naval Renaissance and the Introduction of Theoretical Ship Design to the United States

1. Epigraph from "Letter of Captain A. T. Mahan," *USNI Proceedings* 15, no. 48 (1889): 58.

2. Rear-Admiral Stephen B. Luce, "The U.S. Naval War College," *USNI Proceedings* 36 (June 1910): 566–67.

3. In *The Engineer in America* (16–17), Terry S. Reynolds explains how French

military experts had the same effect at West Point in the early 1800s. In this case, U.S. Army personnel learned the aristocratic theoretical model of French engineering.

4. Albion, *Makers of Naval Policy, 1798–1947*, 200; Lance C. Buhl, "Maintaining 'An American Navy,' 1865–1889," in Hagen, ed., *In Peace and War*, 145–46; Frederick S. Harrod, "New Technology in the Old Navy: The United States Navy during the 1870s," *American Neptune* 53, no. 1 (Winter 1993): 5.

5. *Report of the Secretary of the Navy* (hereafter cited as *RSN*), 38th Cong., 2nd sess., 1864, H. Exec. Doc. 1, pt. 6: xxiii; Michael E. Vlahos, "The Making of an American Style," in King, *Naval Engineering and American Sea Power*, 23.

6. *RSN: Report of the Admiral of the Navy*, 49th Cong., 1st sess., 1885, H. Exec. Doc. 1, pt. 3: 290; Sexton, "Forging the Sword" 176; Buhl, "Maintaining 'An American Navy,'" 148.

7. Reprinted in *United States Army and Navy Journal* 21, no. 1055 (November 10, 1883): 295.

8. Kennedy, *The Rise and Fall of the Great Powers*, 196.

9. Harrod, "New Technology in the Old Navy," 5–19.

10. Cooling, *Gray Steel and Blue Water Navy*, 61; Herrick, *American Naval Revolution*, 29.

11. Commodore Foxhall Parker, "Our Fleet Maneuvers in the Bay of Florida, and the Navy of the Future," *USNI Proceedings* 1, no. 8 (1874): 168–69.

12. Lieutenant Charles Belknap, "Prize Essay of 1880: 'The Naval Policy of the United States,'" *USNI Proceedings* 6, no. 14 (1880): 382.

13. Seager, "Ten Years before Mahan," 497; Naval History Division, *Dictionary of American Naval Fighting Ships*, s.v. "*Tallapoosa*," 3:24; Sexton, "Forging the Sword," 8; Shulman, "The Emergence of American Sea Power," 251; Canney, *Old Steam Navy*, 146.

14. Mahan, *From Sail to Steam*, 197.

15. *Increase of the Naval Establishment*, 49th Cong., 1st sess., 1886, H. Rep. 993: 7.

16. For a more extensive analysis of American foreign policy during this period, consult Beisner, *From the Old Diplomacy to the New, 1865–1900*; LaFeber, *The New Empire*; and Sprout and Sprout, *The Rise of American Naval Power*.

17. "John A. Tobin," *SNAME Transactions* 34 (1926): 291. See Bennett, *The Steam Navy of the United States*, appendix A; an alphabetical database of the naval careers of members of the navy's engineering corps.

18. Sloan, *Benjamin Franklin Isherwood*, 5–8.

19. "Theodore D. Wilson," *Dictionary of American Biography*, 10:346.

20. *RSN: Report of the Admiral*, 47th Cong., 1st sess., 1881, H. Exec. Doc. 1, pt. 3: 109.

21. Karsten, *The Naval Aristocracy*, 286–89, 277–325.

22. "Discussion" following J. H. Biles, "Some Recent War-Ship Designs for the American Navy," *INA Transactions* 32 (1891): 57–58.

23. For more on the intellectual regeneration of the navy, see Dorwat, *The Office of Naval Intelligence*, 3–11.

24. "United States Naval Institute, 1873–1891: Origin, Progress, and Object," *USNI Proceedings* 16 (1891): Appendix (iii).

25. Layton, *The Revolt of the Engineers*, 35–37; Calvert, *The Mechanical Engineer in America, 1830–1910*, 46–49, 259.

26. A volume of *Proceedings* typically included the results of experiments, technical articles, and descriptions of new naval technology and typically surpassed five hundred pages in length during the 1880s.

27. Chief constructor Theodore D. Wilson, "Education of Naval Constructors," *United Service* 2 (February 1880): 180–89; Master M. L. Wood, "The Interior Lighting of Steamers, *United Service* 8 (April 1883): 427–36; Lieutenant Commander F. M. Barber, "The Most Efficient Battery for a Despatch-Boat," *United Service* 13 (August 1885): 129–47; Dorwat, *Office of Naval Intelligence*, 13.

28. Reports of civilian fact-finding missions may be found in Farr and Bostwick, *John Lenthall*, 7–9; Dunbaugh and Thomas, *William H. Webb*, 21–28; "Donald McKay," *Dictionary of American Biography*, 6:72–73; Herreschoff, *Capt. Nat Herreschoff*, 72; *Causes on the Reduction of American Tonnage*, 41st Cong., 2nd sess., 1870, H. Rep. 28: 177; *Investigation by the Committee on Naval Affairs—Brooklyn Navy Yard*, 44th Cong., 1st sess., 1876, H. Misc. Doc. 170, pt. 6: 40; Hall Notebook 8:340; and Harlan and Hollingsworth Company, *Memoranda Concerning Foreign Ship Building, 1881–3*.

29. Dorwat, *Office of Naval Intelligence*, 6–8; Theodore D. Wilson, "Report on British Dockyards," Entry 195, RG 45, National Archives; Edward Simpson, "Report on a Naval Mission to Europe, Especially Devoted to the Material and Construction of Artillery"; J. W. King, *The Warship and Navies of the World, 1880*; *Report on Foreign Systems of Naval Education*, 46th Cong., 2nd sess., 1880, S. Exec. Doc. 51; *Improvements in Naval Engineering in Great Britain*, 47th Cong., 2nd sess., 1883, H. Exec. Doc. 48; Hichborn, Report on European Dock-Yards.

30. *National Cyclopaedia of American Biography*, 3:282–83; Coletta, *French Ensor Chadwick*.

31. U.S. Navy Dept., Office of Naval Intelligence, *The United States Navy as an Industrial Asset*, 10; Misa, "Science, Technology and Industrial Structure," 69; Paolo E. Coletta, "The 'Nerves' of the New Navy," *American Neptune* 38, no. 2 (April 1978): 123; Karsten, *Naval Aristocracy*, 293–99; Reynolds, *Famous American Admirals*, 317–18, 349–50; Rear-Admiral C. M. Chester, "The Scientific Work of the United States Navy," *CM* 26, no. 1 (May 1904): 63.

32. *RSN*, 38th Cong., 1st sess., 1863, H. Exec. Doc. 1: xviii–xx; Bennett, *Steam Navy of the United States*, 654–57; Sloan, *Benjamin Franklin Isherwood*, 190–91.

33. Sweetman, *Illustrated History of the Naval Academy*, 109; Brown, "Christopher Raymond Perry Rodgers," 294.

34. Bennett, *Steam Navy of the United States*, 665–72.

35. Ibid., 673.

36. Ibid., 673–74.

37. Soley, *Historical Sketch of the United States Naval Academy*, 170–215.

38. In "Inspection Trips," *Society for the Promotion of Engineering Education Proceedings* 18 (1911): 220–29; William T. Macgruder dated the appearance of this method in engineering schools around 1870, making the Academy one of the first to undertake it.

39. See the annual report for the Naval Academy found in the *Report of the Secretary of the Navy* (H. Rep. 1, pt. 3) for the years 1872–82.

40. United States *Statutes at Large*, 12:285; *RSN*, 49th Cong., 2nd sess., 1882, H. Exec. Doc. 1, pt. 3: 164.

41. "Robert S. Griffin," *SNAME Transactions* 41 (1933): 416; Bennett, *Steam Navy of the United States*, appendix A; "Charles W. Dyson," *SNAME Transactions* 38 (1935): 331–36; "Asa M. Mattice," *Journal of the American Society of Naval Engineers* 37 (1925): 649–61; "William L. R. Emmet," *SNAME Transactions* 49 (1941): 410–12; "Walter M. McFarland," *SNAME Transactions* 43 (1935): 316–21.

42. Bennett, *Steam Navy of the United States*, 732–43; Calvert, *Mechanical Engineer in America*, 50–51; Harold G. Bowen, *Ships, Machinery, and Mossbacks: The Autobiography of a Naval Engineer*, 17; John D. Alden, "Growth of the New American Navy," *Naval Engineering and American Sea Power*, 36.

43. "William F. Durand," *SNAME Transactions* 66 (1958): 749–50. For a more detailed account of Durand's life, see Durand, *Adventures in the Navy*.

44. *RSN*, 45th Cong., 2nd sess., 1877, H. Exec. Doc. 1, pt. 3: 18, 275; *RSN*: Bureau of Construction and Repair, 46th Cong., 2nd sess., 1879, H. Exec. Doc. 1, pt. 3: 310; Rear Admiral William P. Robert, "Formation of the Society of Naval Architects and Marine Engineers," *SNAME Historical Transactions 1893–1943*, 542. See also naval constructor Theodore D. Wilson, USN, "Education of Naval Constructors," *United Service* 2 (February 1880): 180–89.

45. Meade, *A Treatise on Naval Architecture and Ship-Building*; William B. Cogar, *Dictionary of Admirals of the U.S. Navy, 1862–1900*, 107–9.

46. Stephen D. Brown, "Christopher Raymond Perry Rodgers: Mentor of the New Navy," in Masterson, *Naval History*, 297.

47. Wilson, "A Series of Ten Lectures Delivered to the Second Class of Cadet Midshipmen"; Wilson, *An Outline of Ship Building*; *New York Times*, June 30, 1896.

48. *RSN*, 45th Cong., 2nd sess., 1877, H. Exec. Doc. 1, pt. 3: 53.

49. See, for example the *Annual Register of the United States Naval Academy at Annapolis, Maryland* for the years 1872–82, which show that cadet engineers consistently held the top academic standing for their respective classes.

50. U.S. Navy Dept., Office of Naval Intelligence, *United States Navy as an Industrial Asset*, 95–96.

51. *New York Times*, July 29, 1940; "David W. Taylor," *Dictionary of American Biography*, 11:652; U.S. Navy Dept., Office of Naval Intelligence, *United States Navy as an Industrial Asset*, 10; Reynolds, *Famous American Admirals*, 349–50; Shuon,

U.S. Navy Biographical Dictionary, 249–50; *SNAME Transactions* 48 (1940): 392–96; Holden A. Evans, *One Man's Fight for a Better Navy*, 100.

52. Manning, *The Life of Sir William White*, 62; Sir William H. White, "The History of the Institution of Naval Architecture and of Scientific Education in Naval Architecture," *INA Transactions* 53 (1911): 21; Stephens, *Traditions and Memories of American Yachting*, 148.

53. William Francis Gibbs, "William Hovgaard," *Biographical Memoirs* 36, 165; U.S. Navy Department, Bureau of Construction and Repair, *History of the Construction Corps of the United States Navy*, 40–41; S. V. Goodall, "The Naval Construction Corps of the United States Navy," *INA Transactions* 60 (1919): 101.

54. E. L. Attwood, "The Admiralty Course of Study for the Training of Naval Architects," *INA Transactions* 47 (1905): 243; "John Harvard Biles, L.L.D.," *CM* 33, no. 4 (February 1908): 498–500; "Sir John Harvard Biles," *SNAME Transactions* 41 (1933): 413–14; *Dictionary of National Biography, 1931–1940*, 78–79; Hoyt, *Sherman Hoyt's Memoirs*, 44–46; "W. Selkirk Owen," *SNAME Transactions* 72 (1964): 533; Holden A. Evans, *One Man's Fight for a Better Navy*, 90–98.

55. Karsten, *Naval Aristocracy*, 293–99; Tyler, *The American Clyde*, 93.

56. During the 1870s, the navy built 22,868 tons of wooden warships and 5,010 tons of iron warships. In the 1880s, Congress authorized the construction of 149,596 tons of steel warships, but it authorized no more wooden- or iron-warship construction. For details, see *Navy Yearbook: Compilation of Annual Naval Appropriation Laws from 1883 to 1912*, 62nd Cong., 3rd sess., 1912, S. Doc. 955: 764–65; Bennett, *The Steam Navy of the United States*, appendix B.

57. *Report on the Training Systems for the Navy and Mercantile Marine of England, and on the Naval Training System of France*, 46th Cong., 2nd sess., 1880, S. Exec. Doc. 52; Maguire, *French Ensor Chadwick*, i.

58. Maguire, *French Ensor Chadwick*, 50–53, 143, 582.

59. Coletta, "French Ensor Chadwick," 133.

60. William H. White to Captain French E. Chadwick, December 10, 1883, in Manning, *Life of Sir William White*, 124.

61. Coletta, "French Ensor Chadwick," 139–40. For a more comprehensive treatment of Chadwick's contribution to American naval development, consult Coletta's *French Ensor Chadwick: Scholarly Warrior*.

62. Caspar F. Goodrich, "The Founding of the New Navy," *USNI Proceedings* 44, no. 184 (1918): 1267–68.

63. *Improvements in Naval Engineering in Great Britain*, 47th Cong., 2nd sess., 1883, H. Exec. Doc. 48: 3.

64. Ibid., 3–4.

65. Robley D. Evans, *A Sailor's Log*, 230; Swann, *John Roach*, 154–64. Naval Advisory Board member Evans claimed to have first introduced the board to the notion of steel-warship construction, but according to Swann, the records show Mackenzie to be the one who first mentioned it. Lieutenant E. W. Very, "The Type of (I) Armored

Vessel, (II) Cruiser, Best Suited to the Present Needs of the United States," *USNI Proceedings* 7, no. 15 (1881): 43–83.

66. *RSN: Report of the Board*, 47th Cong., 1st sess., 1881, H. Exec. Doc. 1, pt. 3: 38–46.

67. United States *Statutes at Large*, 22:477.

68. Coletta, "'Nerves' of the New Navy," 123–24; Karsten, *Naval Aristocracy*, 298.

69. *Appropriations for the Navy*, 48th Cong., 1st sess., 1884, S. Rep. 405: 4.

70. Commodore Robert W. Shufeldt to William E. Chandler, January 31, 1883, "Report of the Naval Advisory Board, 1882–1884," Box 1, RG 45, National Archives, 9.

71. Manning, *Life of Sir William White*, 126; Maguire, *French Ensor Chadwick*, 23, 34; "Specifications for the Leander," Entry 272, RG 19, National Archives; Dorwat, *Office of Naval Intelligence*, 19–20.

72. "Francis T. Bowles," *SNAME Transactions* 35 (1927): 289.

73. *Additional Steel Vessels*, 48th Cong. 1st sess., 1884, S. Rep. 161: 84–85.

74. For more on political shipbuilding, see Thiesen, "Curse of the *Dolphin*," 25–39.

75. *Reconstruction of the Navy*, 48th Cong., 1st sess., 1884, H. Exec. Doc. 127: 201–4; *Additional Steel Vessels*, 48th Cong. 1st sess., 1884, S. Rep. 161: 25–39; Swann, *John Roach*, 176–77.

76. *Letter from the Secretary of the Navy*, 50 Cong., 1st sess., S. Exec. Doc. 241: 1–4; *In the Senate of the United States*, 50th Cong., 1st sess., 1888, S. Misc. Doc. 33: 1; "Francis T. Bowles," *SNAME Transactions* 35 (1927): 289; *Navy Yearbook: Compilation of Annual Naval Appropriation Laws from 1883 to 1912*, 62nd Cong., 3rd sess., 1912, S. Doc. 955: 760–76; *New York Times*, December 18, 1890.

77. S. B. Luce, "Our Future Navy," *North American Review* 149 (1889): 64.

78. Maguire, *French Ensor Chadwick*, 128–33.

79. "Discussion" following J. H. Biles, "Some Recent War-Ship Designs for the American Navy," *INA Transactions* 32 (1891): 57–58.

80. *In the Senate of the United States*, 50th Cong., 1st sess., 1888, S. Misc. Doc. 33; *Letter from the Secretary of the Navy*, 50th Cong., 1st sess., 1888, S. Exec. Doc. No. 241: 1–4.

81. Heinrich, *Ships for the Seven Seas*, 103.

82. Holden A. Evans, *One Man's Fight for a Better Navy*, 95–96.

83. Seager, "Ten Years before Mahan," 497–98.

84. Sexton, "Forging the Sword," 140–51; Paullin, *Paullin's History of Naval Administration, 1775–1911*, 407; Cooling, *Gray Steel and Blue Water Navy*, 58–65; Davis, *A Navy Second to None*, 44–47; Herrick, *The American Naval Revolution*, 33–38; Hirsch, *William C. Whitney*, 335–36.

85. Hutchins, *The American Maritime Industries and Public Policy*, 458; Cooling, *Gray Steel and Blue Water Navy*, 77.

86. Swann, *John Roach*, 191–99; U.S. Navy Dept., Office of Naval Intelligence, *United States Navy as an Industrial Asset*, 48.

87. Karsten, *Naval Aristocracy*, 176; "Frank Lysander Fernald," *SNAME Transactions* 29 (1921): 379.

88. "Mechanical Engineering Notes," *EM* 8, no. 2 (May 1894): 288.

89. U.S. Navy Dept., Office of Naval Intelligence, *United States Navy as an Industrial Asset*, 37–39, 98–99; Misa, "Science, Technology and Industrial Structure," 77–83; Cooling, *Gray Steel and Blue Water Navy*, 69–74; Karsten, *Naval Aristocracy*, 176–77; Rear-Admiral C. M. Chester, "The Scientific Work of the United States Navy," *CM* 26, no. 1 (May 1904): 63.

90. Hutchins, *American Maritime Industries and Public Policy*, 458; Misa, "Science, Technology and Industrial Structure," 66–67.

91. U.S. Navy Department, Bureau of Construction and Repair, *History of the Construction Corps of the United States Navy*, 40–41; Goodall, "The Naval Construction Corps of the United States Navy," 198–201; *Course in Naval Architecture, United States Naval Academy*, 55th Cong., 3rd sess., 1899, H. Doc. 148: 1–2; *Course in Naval Architecture, United States Naval Academy*, 55th Cong., 3rd sess., 1899, S. Doc. 74: 1–10; "William Hovgaard," *Biographical Memoirs*, 164.

92. "Walter M. McFarland," *SNAME Transactions* 43 (1935): 318.

93. Calvert, *Mechanical Engineer in America*, 46–49, 259; W. P. Stephens, "International Racing and National Supremacy on the Sea," *EM* 10, no. 1 (October 1895): 5.

94. William F. Durand, "Dr. Robert Thurston's Eighteen Years at Cornell," *Science* 90, no. 2346 (December 15, 1939): 550; Durand, *Adventures in the Navy*, 37–39; Rear Admiral George H. Rock, "Education of Naval Constructors and Naval Architects," *SNAME Transactions* 40 (1932): 199; "William Hovgaard," *Biographical Memoirs*, 164–65.

95. *New York Times*, July 9, 1891, July 25, 1897, Sept. 30, 1898, Oct. 1, 1898; Goodall, "The Naval Construction Corps of the United States Navy," 98–101; Henry S. Pritchett, "Technical Training for Shipbuilders," *SNAME Transactions* 10 (1902): 3–14; Munroe, *A Life of Francis Amasa Walker*, 382.

96. Dunbaugh and Thomas, *William H. Webb*, 137–38; *Scientific, Technical, and Related Societies of the United States*, 167–68; *Scientific American* 63, no. 780 (December 13, 1890): 368–69; "Webb's Academy and Home for Shipbuilders, New York, N.Y.," *Seventeenth Annual Report of the Commissioner of Labor, 1902: Trade and Technical Education*, 175–80.

97. Rock, "Education of Naval Constructors and Naval Architects," 196–210; "Herbert C. Sadler," *SNAME Transactions* 56 (1948), 591; W. E. Dalby, "The Training of Engineers in the United States," *INA Transactions* 45 (1903): 47; Gilfillan, *Inventing the Ship*, 262.

98. Alden, "Growth of the New American Navy," in King, *Naval Engineering and American Sea Power*, 36. Established in the early 1890s, the Society of Naval Architects and Marine Engineers became another association greatly influenced by naval personnel. For more information, see the *SNAME Historical Transactions, 1893–1943*.

99. *Scientific, Technical, and Related Societies of the United States*, 79–80, 167–68; *New York Times*, November 16, 17, and 18, 1893; Holden, *Men, Ships, and the Sea*; Robert, "Formation of The Society of Naval Architects and Marine Engineers," 538–44.

100. Morrison, *Admiral Sims and the Modern American Navy*; Morrison, *Men, Machines, and Modern Times*.

101. Captain Elliot Snow, USN, "Model Tank Experiments by Benjamin Franklin," *USNI Proceedings* 49, no. 247 (September 1923): 1469–72; Whipple, *The Clipper Ships*, 24–25; Herreschoff, *Capt. Nat Herreschoff*, 105; Professor C. H. Peabody, "Personal Impressions of Ship-Model Towing Stations," *SNAME Transactions* 14 (1906): 43, 49.

102. Francis T. Bowles to William E. Chandler, April 17, 1884, "Report of the Naval Advisory Board, 1882–1884," Box 4, RG 45, National Archives; F. T. Bowles, "Towing Experiments on Models to Determine the Resistance of Full-Sized Ships," *USNI Proceedings* 9, no. 23 (1883): 81–98; *RSN: Experimental Works to Determine Resistance of Ships*, 48th Cong., 2nd sess., 1884, H. Exec. Doc. 1, pt. 3: 236; U.S. Dept. of Navy, Office of Naval Intelligence, *Navy as an Industrial Asset*, 97.

103. William Hovgaard, "Biographical Memoir of David Watson Taylor," *Biographical Memoirs* 22, 137; D. W. Taylor, *Resistance of Ships and Screw Propulsion*; D. W. Taylor, *The Speed and Power of Ships*; McFarland, "Presentation of the John Fritz Medal," *SNAME Transactions* 38 (1930): 326; Holden A. Evans, *One Man's Fight for a Better Navy*, 100.

104. *Premiums Paid to Contractors of War Vessels for the Navy*, 53rd Cong., 2nd sess., 1894, H. Rep. No. 407: 96, 126; Naval Historical Foundation, *The David W. Taylor Model Basin*, 1.

105. Hovgaard, "Biographical Memoir of David Watson Taylor," 137–39; Walter McFarland, "Presentation of the John Fritz Medal," *SNAME Transactions* 38 (1930): 326; "Discussion" after David Taylor, "U.S. Experimental Model Basin," *SNAME Transactions* 8 (1900): 55; Naval Historical Foundation, *David W. Taylor Model Basin*, 2–3.

106. "Discussion" after David W. Taylor, "U.S. Experimental Model Basin," 53; David W. Taylor, "Simple Explanation of Model Basin Methods," *Scientific American* 97, no. 23 (December 7, 1907): 418.

107. SNAME, *Index to Transactions*, 11–19.

108. Ibid., 138–39, 151–53; "Discussion" after Professor Herbert C. Sadler, "The Experimental Tank at the University of Michigan," *SNAME Transactions* 14 (1906): 59; David W. Taylor, "On Ships Derived by Formulae," *SNAME Transactions* 11 (1903): 243–70. For Nystrom, see Nystrom, *A Treatise on Screw Propellors and Their Steam-Engines*.

109. Goodall, "Naval Construction Corps of the United States Navy," 114.

110. Richard W. Meade, "Some Suggestions of Professional Experience in Connection with the Naval Construction of the Last Ten Years," *SNAME Transactions* 2 (1894): 24.

111. "Francis T. Bowles," *SNAME Transactions* 35 (1927): 287–93.

112. Karsten, *The Naval Aristocracy*, 293–99; Tyler, *The American Clyde*, 93; "Homer L. Ferguson," *National Cyclopaedia of American Biography* 40: 3–4; "Holden A. Evans," *SNAME Transactions* 65 (1957): 885; "John W. Powell," *SNAME Transactions* 62 (1954): 718; *New York Times*, January 30, 1895.

113. Karsten, *The Naval Aristocracy*, xi–xv.

114. For more on technological translators, see Douglas, "The Navy Adopts the Radio," in her *Inventing American Broadcasting, 1899–1922*; and Aitken, *Syntony and Spark*, 330–32.

115. Maguire, *French Ensor Chadwick*, 147.

116. Richardson, ed., *Messages and Papers of the Presidents, 1789–1897*, vol. 9, *1889–1897*, 200.

Chapter 8. The New American Style of Shipbuilding

1. Quoted in J. H. Biles, "The Mechanical Equipment of the Ship-Yard," *EM* 21, no. 2 (April 1901): 187–88.

2. Hoffecker, *Wilmington, Delaware*, 19.

3. Harrison, *The Iron Worker and King Solomon*, 30.

4. See fire insurance maps for the shipyards of John Roach; William Cramp and Sons; Reaney, Archbold, and Son; and Neafie and Levy in the E. Hexamer Insurance Map Collection, Library of Congress Map Collection, Washington, D.C.

5. Charles H. Benjamin, "Electricity versus Shafting in the Machine Shop," *ASME Transactions* 18 (1897): 867.

6. *American Merchant Marine in the Foreign Trade*, 51st Cong., 1st sess., 1890, H. Rep. 1210: 129; Heinrich, *Ships for the Seven Seas*, 45, 136–38, 170–72.

7. Swann, *John Roach*, 49–74.

8. "Iron Shipbuilding: A Talk with Mr. John Roach," *Bulletin of the American Iron and Steel Association* 7, no. 54 (10 September 1873): 426.

9. Swann, *John Roach*, 58; Morrison, *Iron and Steel Hull Steam Vessels of the United States*, 28.

10. R.H.M. Robinson, "Fabricated Ships," *SNAME Transactions* 25 (1917): 140–41.

11. "The Works of the New York Shipbuilding Company," *Marine Engineering* 6, no. 12 (December 1901): 502; quotation Biles, "The Mechanical Equipment of the Ship-Yard," 389–92.

12. Biles, "The Mechanical Equipment of the Ship-Yard," 392; J. Arthur Gray, "Modern Shipbuilding Tools," *CM* 10, no. 1 (May 1896): 461.

13. William S. Aldrich, "Requirements of Electricity in Manufacturing Work," *ASME Transactions* 22 (1901): 1005–7; Sydney F. Walker, "Electric Appliances in Ship-Building Yards," *EM* 22, no. 5 (February 1902): 681; Dugald C. Jackson, "Electrical Power-Equipment for General Factory Purposes," *ASME Transactions* 18 (1897): 1050–54.

14. George Richmond, "Operating Machine Tools by Electricity," *EM* 8, no. 4 (January 1895): 669–70.

15. Biles, "The Mechanical Equipment of the Ship-Yard," 398.

16. George H. Baxter, "Hydraulic Cranes and Wharf Machinery," *EM* 27, no. 2 (May 1904): 187–200.

17. George W. Dickie, "Some Interesting Applications of Hydraulic Power," *CM* 8, no. 2 (December 1897): 138–52; Hugo P. Frear, "History of Bethlehem's San Francisco Yard," *SNAME Historical Transactions, 1893–1943*, 238–39; Edward O. Smith, *History of the Newport News Shipbuilding and Dry Dock Company*, 29–30; Dickie, "Overhead Cranes, Staging, and Riveter-Carrying Appliances in the Shipyard," 190–92; Stuart Smith, "Boiler Shop and Plant at the Union Iron Works, San Francisco, Cal.," *Journal of the American Society of Naval Engineers* 2, no. 1 (1890): 139–43.

18. C. J. Appleby, "On Cranes as Labor-Saving Machines," *ASCE Transactions* 15 (May 1886): 369–80.

19. Erwin Graves, "Hydraulic Travelling Cranes," *ASME Transactions* 12 (1891): 202–20; George A. Goodwin, "The Relative Merits of Working Hoisting Machinery by Steam, Water and Electricity," *ASCE Transactions* 29 (September 1893): 695–717.

20. Whitfield P. Pressinger, "Pneumatic Shop Appliances," *CM* 15, no. 4 (February 1899): 262; W. I. Babcock, "Portable Riveters in Shipbuilding," *SNAME Transactions* 6 (1898): 39.

21. "Haupt, Herman," *Dictionary of American Biography*, 4:400–401; "Haupt, Herman," *National Cyclopaedia of American Biography*, 10:224–25; Ward, *That Man Haupt*, 88–97, 153–54, 172–82.

22. Babcock, "Portable Riveters in Shipbuilding," 30; Robert L. Streeter, "Air Compressors and Compressed Air Machinery," *EM* 46, no. 6 (March 1914): 913–30; Whitfield P. Pressinger, "The Widening Use of Compressed Air," *EM* 6, no. 1 (October 1893): 145–51; Frank Richards, "A Note on Compressed Air," *ASME Transactions* 15 (1894): 703; Curtis W. Shields, "The Rise of the Young Giant, Compressed Air," *EM* 12, no. 4 (January 1897): 657–73; Simmons, "'The Continuous Clatter,'" 8.

23. Pressinger, "Pneumatic Shop Appliances," 264; James Ritchie, "The Construction of the Lorain Dry Dock and Shipyard of the Cleveland Ship-Building Company." *ASCE Transactions* 39 (June 1898): 323–38.

24. Byrne, *Dictionary of Machines, Mechanics, Engine-Work, and Engineering*, 2:529–34; Bruno Jacomy, "The Technological Evolution of Riveting Machines," *IA: The Journal of the Society for Industrial Archaeology* 24, no. 2 (1998): 37–41; Pole, *The Life of Sir William Fairbairn*, 163–64.

25. Ralph Hart Tweddell, "Hydraulic Machine Tools," *CM* 7, no. 37 (November 1894): 63.

26. Ibid., 55–64; E. W. De Russett, "On the Use of Hydraulic Riveting in the Construction of the *Mauretania*," *INA Transactions* 49 (1907): 308–11; Jacomy, "The Technological Evolution of Riveting Machines," 42–43.

27. "Tweddell's Portable Rivetter," *FI Journal* 51 (1876): 256–57; Wm. Sellers & Co., "Hydraulic Rivetting Machines," *FI Journal* 52, no. 5 (November 1876): 305–12; *Report*

of the Board . . . at the International Exhibition, 1876, 47th Cong., 2nd sess., 1884, H. Misc. Doc. 20, pt. 1 (1884): 941–43.

28. Streeter, "Air Compressors and Compressed Air Machinery," 914; Pressinger, "Pneumatic Shop Appliances," 259, 263–64; R. Emerson, "Applications of Pneumatic Power in the Machine Shop," *EM* 30, no. 5 (February 1906): 723.

29. "Allen, John F.," *Dictionary of American Biography*, 1:199; "John F. Allen," *ASME Transactions* 22 (1901): 1149; Jacomy, "The Technological Evolution of Riveting Machines," 44–45; Wright, *Freshwater Whales*, 14; Morrison, *Iron and Steel Hull Steam Vessels of the United States*, 28.

30. Dept. of the Interior, Census Office, "Report on Power and Machinery Employed in Manufactures, by W. P. Trowbridge," 29–30; Morrison, *Iron and Steel Hull Steam Vessels of the United States*, 30; Jacomy, "The Technological Evolution of Riveting Machines," 44–45.

31. Jacomy, "The Technological Evolution of Riveting Machines," 39–40; Morrison, *Iron and Steel Hull Steam Vessels of the United States*, 30.

32. Pressinger, "Pneumatic Shop Appliances," 267–69; "Hurley, Edward Nash," *National Cyclopaedia of American Biography*, 40:8–9; "Hurley, Edward Nash," *Dictionary of American Biography*, vol. 11, Supplement 1, 446–7; *New York Times*, February 26, 1948.

33. *Report of the Commissioner-General for the United States to the International Universal Exposition, Paris, 1900,* 56th Cong., 2nd sess., 1901, S. Doc. 232: 109–58; Simmons, "'The Continuous Clatter,'" 16.

34. Waldon Fawcett, "The Ship-Building Yards of the United States, Part II," *EM* 19, no. 5 (August 1900): 678–79.

35. Edward O. Smith, *History of the Newport News Shipbuilding and Dry Dock Company*, 68–75, 91, 99; Waldon Fawcett, "The Ship-Building Yards of the United States, Part I," *EM* 19, no. 4 (July 1900): 504; William Burlingham, "Experiences with Compressed Air in Ship-Building and Ship-Yard Work," *ME* 2, no. 9 (September 1898): 15–18.

36. Babcock, "Portable Riveters in Shipbuilding," 29.

37. Simmons, "'The Continuous Clatter,'" 13.

38. Ibid., 13, 15.

39. Babcock, "Portable Riveters in Shipbuilding," 35; Biles, "The Mechanical Equipment of the Ship-Yard," 527; Wright, *Freshwater Whales*, 16.

40. Simmons, "'The Continuous Clatter,'" 5, 13; Babcock, "Portable Riveters in Shipbuilding," 31.

41. Simmons, "'The Continuous Clatter,'" 13.

42. Babcock, "Portable Riveters in Shipbuilding," 38; Wright, *Freshwater Whales*, 13–15; "Pneumatic Tools at Home and Abroad," *Railroad Gazette* 32, no. 17 (April 27, 1900): 274; Ewart C. Amos, "Portable Pneumatic Tools," *Compressed Air* 6 (April 1901): 1278.

43. Ibid., 35.

44. "Effect of Air Hammer on Hands of Stonecutters," 5–13; Jacomy, "The Tech-

nological Evolution of Riveting Machines," 50; Babcock, "Portable Riveters in Shipbuilding," 37–38; Simmons, "'The Continuous Clatter,'" 13–14.

45. Aldrich, "Requirements of Electricity in Manufacturing Work," 1007.

46. Ibid., 1009–38; Walker, "Electric Appliances in Ship-Building Yards," 682–92; Jackson, "Electrical Power-Equipment for General Factory Purposes," 1049–62; Benjamin, "Electricity versus Shafting in the Machine Shop," 867–73.

47. Benjamin, "Electricity versus Shafting in the Machine Shop," 888.

48. Louis Bell, "Electricity in the Modern Machine Shop," *EM* 13, no. 4 (July 1897): 579–86; Walker, "Electric Appliances in Ship-Building Yards," 679–92; Wright, *Freshwater Whales*, 14.

49. Richmond, "Operating Machine Tools by Electricity," 670.

50. Ritchie, "The Construction of the Lorain Dry Dock and Shipyard of the Cleveland Ship-Building Company," 333–38.

51. Benjamin, "Electricity versus Shafting in the Machine Shop," 888.

52. Walker, "Electric Appliances in Ship-Building Yards," 679.

53. "The Works of the New York Shipbuilding Company," *ME* 6, no. 12 (December 1901): 502.

54. J. B. O'Hara, "Electricity in a Modern Shipyard," *CM* 22, no. 1 (May 1902): 117–36; "The Works of the New York Shipbuilding Company," 499–509; *Fifty Years: New York Shipbuilding Corporation*, 11–17.

55. William A. Fairburn, "Methods of Handling Material over Shipbuilding Berths in American Shipyards," *INA Transactions* 44 (1902): 266–7.

56. Robert H. Peebles, "Navy Shipbuilders 'Discover' Welding," in Masterson, ed., *Naval History*, 157–64; "First Rivetless Vessel Launched in England," *Iron Age* 102 (September 5, 1918): 610.

57. Wright, *Freshwater Whales*, 13.

58. Biggs, *The Rational Factory*, 50.

59. Towne, "Cranes: A Study of Types and Details," 288.

60. Ibid., 60; Dickie "Overhead Cranes, Staging, and Riveter-Carrying Appliances in the Shipyard," 189–90.

61. Henry R. Towne, "Cranes: A Study of Types and Details," 289–91; Fairburn, "Methods of Handling Material over Shipbuilding Berths in American Shipyards," 229–70; T. Kennard Thomson, "Hoisting Machinery for the Handling of Materials," *EM* 34, no. 6 (March 1908): 1005–28; Charles R. Hanscom, "Descriptions of the Design and Building of the 21,000 Ton Steamships *Minnesota* and *Dakota*," *SNAME Transactions* 11 (1903): 206–8.

62. Henry R. Towne, "Cranes: A Study of Types and Details," 289–91; Frederick A. Waldron, "Mechanical Transportation in the Modern Machine Shop," *EM* 28, no. 4 (January 1905): 490–97; and Graves, "Hydraulic Travelling Cranes," 202–20.

63. Waldron, "Mechanical Transportation in the Modern Machine Shop," 493–95; Dickie, "Overhead Cranes, Staging, and Riveter-Carrying Appliances in the Shipyard," 189–90; Edward O. Smith, *History of the Newport News Shipbuilding and Dry*

Dock Company, 30; Anthony Victorin, "Performance of an Overhead Travelling Crane, Operated by a Single Electric Motor," *ASME Transactions* 14 (1893): 379; Benjamin, "Electricity versus Shafting in the Machine Shop," 879; "An Electric Traveling Crane," *Railroad Gazette* 21 (February 8, 1889): 95.

64. O'Hara, "Electricity in a Modern Shipyard," 119–23.

65. Fairburn, "Methods of Handling Material over Shipbuilding Berths in American Shipyards," 266.

66. S. M. Henry, "Recent Developments in Shipyard Plants," *SNAME Transactions* 26 (1918): 178–82; Biles, "The Mechanical Equipment of the Ship-Yard," 536; Swann, *John Roach,* 59.

67. Homer L. Ferguson, "The Newport News Shipbuilding and Dry Dock Company," in *SNAME Historical Transactions, 1893–1943* (Westport, Conn.: Greenwood Press, 1945), 218; William H. Wiley, "Shipbuilding in America," *CM* 2, no. 9 (July 1892): 163.

68. Charles Day, "The Planning and Building of Industrial Plants," *EM* 37, no. 6 (September 1909): 891–92; Biggs, *The Rational Factory,* 36–37; Gordon, *The Texture of Industry,* 327.

69. John T. Klaber, "Building the Factory," *EM* 51, no. 3 (June 1916): 358; H. I. Crandall and Son Company, Engineers and Contractors, to Edwin S. Cramp, November 8, 1907, and December 17, 1907, Box 1, Cramp Papers, MS 32, Temple University Archives; "The Works of the New York Shipbuilding Company," 502; Biggs, *Rational Factory,* 24–25, 53, 81–85, 91–94.

70. Klaber, "Building the Factory," 362; Henry, "Recent Developments in Shipyard Plants," 183; C. H. Matthews, "Description of the Steam Engineering Plant at the Navy Yard, N.Y.," *Journal American Society of Naval Engineers* 8, no. 4 (November 1901): 875; J.P.H. Perry, "Materials and Methods of Construction for Industrial Buildings," *EM* 37, no. 5 (August 1909): 806–16; Waddell, *Bridge Engineering,* 28: Gordon, *Texture of Industry,* 330–34; Swann, *John Roach,* 58.

71. Fairburn, "Methods of Handling Material over Shipbuilding Berths in American Shipyards," 245; "The Works of the New York Shipbuilding Company," 502; O'Hara, "Electricity in a Modern Shipyard," 119–20; John F. Metten, "Standard Yards," in Fassett, *The Shipbuilding Business in the United States of America,* 210.

72. Fairburn, "Methods of Handling Material over Shipbuilding Berths in American Shipyards," 266.

73. Ibid., 259.

74. Metten, "Standard Yards," 211.

75. See table, "Accidents at Roach's Shipyard, 1877–1882," in Swann, *John Roach,* 70. Also, the "Industrial Chronology," in the *Bureau of Industrial Statistics of New Jersey* for the years 1902–17 indicates that the leading causes of injury and fatality at the New York Shipbuilding Corporation were falls and falling objects.

76. Olsson, *Engineers as System Builders.*

77. Trowbridge, "Report on Power and Machinery Employed in Manufactures," 22.

78. Ward, *That Man Haupt*, 154–55; Haupt, *Military Bridges*, 41–42.

79. Charles E. Fowler, "Some American Bridge Shop Methods," *CM* 17, no. 3 (January 1900): 200–204; Waddell, *Bridge Engineering*, 29; Edwards, *A Record of History and Evolution of Early American Bridges*, 139; DeLony, *Landmark American Bridges*, 90–91.

80. Charles C. Schneider, "The Evolution of the Practice of American Bridge Building," *ASCE Transactions* 54 (June 1905): 223; Thomas C. Clarke, "European and American Bridge-Building Practice," *EM* 21, no. 1 (April 1901): 43–58; Fowler, "Some American Bridge Shop Methods," 200–215.

81. "Death of Henry G. Morse, President New York Shipbuilding Company," *ME* 8 (July 1903): 376; *New York Tribune*, June 3, 1903; *New York Times*, June 3, 1903; *Wilmington Every Evening*, June 3, 1903.

82. "Death of Henry G. Morse, President New York Shipbuilding Company," *ME* 8 (July 1903): 376; *New York Tribune*, June 3, 1903; *New York Times*, June 3, 1903; *Wilmington Every Evening*, June 3, 1903; quotation Morrison, *Iron and Steel Hull Steam Vessels of the United States*, 30.

83. "Death of Henry G. Morse, President New York Shipbuilding Company," *ME* 8 (July 1903): 376; *New York Tribune*, June 3, 1903; *New York Times*, June 3, 1903; *Wilmington Every Evening*, June 3, 1903.

84. "Death of Henry G. Morse, President New York Shipbuilding Company," *ME* 8 (July 1903): 376; *New York Tribune*, June 3, 1903; *New York Times*, June 3, 1903; *Wilmington Every Evening*, June 3, 1903.

85. "Main Office Building of the New York Shipbuilding Co., Camden, N.J.," *ME* 5, no. 5 (May 1900): 193; O'Hara, "Electricity in a Modern Shipyard," 117; "William B. Fortune Dies in Verga at 78," *Camden (N.J.) Courier-Post*, January 17, 1942; *New York Times*, June 3, 1903; "Death of Henry G. Morse," 376; Heinrich, *Ships for the Seven Seas*, 132.

86. "Henry Lysholm," *SNAME Transactions* 29 (1921): 385–87.

87. John F. Metten, "The New York Shipbuilding Corporation," in *SNAME Historical Transactions, 1893–1943*, 229; "Death of Henry G. Morse," 376.

88. Fairburn, "Methods of Handling Material over Shipbuilding Berths in American Shipyards," 266.

89. "Morse, Henry Grant," *National Cyclopaedia of American Biography*, 29:243.

90. Metten, "New York Shipbuilding Corporation," 224–27; Fairburn, "Methods of Handling Material over Shipbuilding Berths in American Shipyards," 248.

91. Metten, "New York Shipbuilding Corporation," 224–27; Metten, "Standard Yards," 207; United States Shipping Board Emergency Fleet Corporation, "Hearings before the Committee on Commerce, United States Senate . . . on Senate Resolution 170," 1:642–43.

92. W. I. Babcock, "System of Work in a Great Lake Shipyard," *SNAME Transactions* 7 (1899): 182–88; Fairburn, "Methods of Handling Material over Shipbuilding Berths in American Shipyards," 270.

93. "Man and His Machines," 329.

94. Olsson, *Engineers as System Builders*, 50.

95. Biles, "The Mechanical Equipment of the Ship-Yard," 195.

96. Fairburn, "Methods of Handling Material over Shipbuilding Berths in American Shipyards," 270.

97. Olsson, *Engineers as System Builders*, 50; Bridenbaugh, *The Colonial Craftsman*, 93; Henry R. Sutphen, "Structural Steel Standardized Cargo Vessels," *SNAME Transactions* 26 (1918): 104–6.

98. United States Shipping Board Emergency Fleet Corporation, "Hearings before the Committee on Commerce, United States Senate . . . on Senate Resolution 170," 2:1401–3, 2:1408–10.

99. Babcock, "System of Work in a Great Lake Shipyard," 174–88.

100. Dickie, "Cranes, Staging, and Riveter-Carrying Appliances," 193.

101. "Henry Lysholm," *SNAME Transactions* 29 (1921): 385–7.

102. Heinrich, *Ships for the Seven Seas*, 135–36.

103. Young naval constructors who followed Evans's lead included G. A. Bisset, Frank Coburn, C. W. Fisher, H. M. Gleason, John E. Otterson, C. S. Radford, James Reed, T. G. Roberts, George H. Rock, and H. F. Wright.

104. *New York Times*, January 30, 1895; Karsten, *The Naval Aristocracy*, 293–99; "Holden A. Evans," *SNAME Transactions* 65 (1957), 885; Holden A. Evans, *One Man's Fight for a Better Navy*, 181. While Evans was little known compared to such men as Carl Barth and Henry Gantt, his correspondence in the Taylor Papers attests to his close relationship with Frederick Taylor.

105. Evans to Taylor (December 20, 1909), Folder 187D, Frederick Taylor Papers, Stevens Institute (hereafter cited as Taylor Papers).

106. Memo: Evans to Commandant (December 8, 1911), Folder 187F, Taylor Papers.

107. Holden A. Evans, *One Man's Fight for a Better Navy*, 199–200, 207.

108. Ibid., 182.

109. Ibid., 203.

110. Ibid., 202–4.

111. Evans to Taylor (January 20, 1912), Folder 187G, Taylor Papers; Holden A. Evans, *One Man's Fight for a Better Navy*, 206.

112. Evans to Taylor (January 6, 1912), Folder 187G, Taylor Papers.

113. H. M. Gleason to Taylor (May 13, 1911), Folder 188B, Taylor Papers.

114. Evans to Taylor (December 20, 1909), Folder 187D, Taylor Papers.

115. Ibid.

116. Holden A. Evans, *One Man's Fight for a Better Navy*, 184.

117. Lott, *A Long Line of Ships*, 148–49; Holden A. Evans, *One Man's Fight for a Better Navy*, 208–9.

118. Taylor to Evans (January 1, 1912), Folder 187G, Taylor Papers; Aitken, *Scientific Management in Action*, 186–242; *Taylor and Other Systems of Shop Management*, 62nd Cong., 2nd sess., 1912, H. Rep. 403: 1–7; *"Taylor System" of Shop Management*, 63rd Cong., 2nd sess., 1914, H. Rep. 1175: 1–13.

119. "Sanity in Naval Organization: Secretary Meyer's Plans for the U.S. Navy Department," *EM* 38, no. 4 (January 1910): 489–96; John R. Edwards, "The Fetishism of Scientific Management," *Journal of the American Society of Naval Engineers* 24, no. 2 (May 1912): 355–416; Holden A. Evans, *One Man's Fight for a Better Navy*, 242–68.

120. Veblen, *Instinct of Workmanship*, 345.

121. Norman Howard, "Industrial Engineering Applied to Shipyard Management," *Industrial Management* 59, no. 5 (May 1920): 372–75.

122. "The Advance in American Shipbuilding," *Iron Age* 99, no. 1 (4 January 1917): 35.

123. Roberts, "An Analysis of the Principles of Industrial Management," 182, 265.

124. "Face to Face with Our Contributors," *Industrial Management* 61, no. 2 (January 15, 1921): 5; Stephen G. Rockwell, "Wage Incentive Plans in Ship Building," *Industrial Management* 59, no. 4 (April 1920): 295.

125. United States Shipping Board Emergency Fleet Corporation, "Hearings before the Committee on Commerce, Sixty-Fifth Congress, Second Session," vol. 2, S. Res. 170, 1389; Rockwell, "Wage Incentive Plans in Ship Building," 296–98; William Kennedy, "Industrial Management Principles in Shipyard Practice," *Industrial Management* 53, no. 6 (September 1917): 816; William B. Ferguson, "Production Methods in Shipbuilding, Part V: How Incentive Systems Increase Output," *Industrial Management* 60, no. 6 (December 1920): 409–12.

126. Rockwell, "Wage Incentive Plans in Ship Building," 295–300; R. E. Roesler, "Keeping Track of Construction Plant at Hog Island," *Engineering News-Record* 82, no. 5 (January 30, 1919): 246–47; William Kennedy, "Industrial Management Principles in Shipyard Practice," 803–17; Roberts, "An Analysis of the Principles of Industrial Management," 229–33; Mattox, *Building the Emergency Fleet*, 57–59.

127. B. K. Price, "Hog Island's Compressed Air System," *Marine Review* 48, no. 8 (August 1918): 331–33; Kelly and Allen, *The Shipbuilding Industry*, 95–96; "Hog Island's Ship-Erection Equipment: Four Hundred Tower Derricks for Fifty Ways," *Engineering News-Record* 81, no. 2 (11 July 1918): 77–80; W. H. Blood, "Hog Island, the Greatest Shipyard in the World," *SNAME Transactions* 26 (1918): 243–54; Keller, *Stone and Webster*, 105–6.

128. *Philadelphia Ledger*, August 6, 1918; Hurley, *Bridge to France*, 82.

129. H. Jasper Cox, "The Application of Electric Welding to Ship Construction," *SNAME Transactions* 26 (1918): 213; Keller, *Stone and Webster*, 106.

130. Kelly, *Shipbuilding Industry*, 94–95; Robinson, "Fabricated Ships," 139–40; Sutphen, "Structural Steel Standardized Cargo Vessels," 106.

131. Kelly, *Shipbuilding Industry*, 96.

132. "Design Steel Ship for Maximum Efficiency of Bridge-Shop Fabrication," *Engineering News-Record* 81, no. 1 (July 4, 1918): 9–10; "Institute Rejoices over War Victory: The Standardization of Ship Materials," *Iron Age* 103, no. 22 (May 29, 1919): 1422–23; Heinrich, *Ships for the Seven Seas*, 186; Sutphen, "Structural Steel Standardized Cargo Vessels," 106–7.

133. E. H. Rigg, "Standardization as Affecting the Shipbuilding Industry in the United States," *SNAME Transactions* 30 (1922): 208–9.

134. H. C. Sadler, "Experiments on Simplified Ship Forms," *SNAME Transactions* 26 (1918): 161; Kelly, *Shipbuilding Industry*, 98; Sutphen, "Structural Steel Standardized Cargo Vessels," 104.

135. Heinrich, *Ships for the Seven Seas*, 184.

136. Hurley, *Bridge to France*, 49–51.

137. Ibid.; Blood, "Hog Island, the Greatest Shipyard in the World," 249; Heinrich, *Ships for the Seven Seas*, 186.

138. Kelly, *Shipbuilding Industry*, 97.

139. Rigg, "Standardization as Affecting the Shipbuilding Industry in the United States," 208–9, 215–16; "Design Steel Ship for Maximum Efficiency of Bridge-Shop Fabrication," 12.

140. Mattox, *Building the Emergency Fleet*, 65–66.

141. Keller, *Stone and Webster*, 106–8.

142. Quote found in Hurley, *Bridge to France*, 87.

143. "New Methods Applied to Shipbuilding," *Engineering News-Record* 81, No. 1 (4 July 1918): 2–3.

144. David A. Hounshell, "Ford Eagle Boats and Mass Production during World War I," in Merritt Roe Smith, ed., *Military Enterprise and Technological Change*, 178.

145. "Submarine Chasers Made by Quantity-Production Methods," *American Machinist* 49, no. 19 (November 7, 1918): 841; J. A. Furer, "The 110–Foot Submarine Chasers and Eagle Boats," *USNI Proceedings* 45, no. 5 (May 1919): 765; Frank A. Cianflone, "The Eagle Boats of World War I," *USNI Proceedings* 99, no. 6 (June 1973): 76.

146. Cianflone, "The Eagle Boats of World War I," 76; Furer, "The 110–Foot Submarine Chasers and Eagle Boats," 765; "Submarine Chasers Made by Quantity-Production Methods," 841–44; Fred E. Rogers, "Ford Methods in Ship Manufacture—II," *Industrial Management* 57, no. 2 (February 1919): 121–23; Rogers, "Ford Methods in Ship Manufacture—V," *Industrial Management* 57, no. 5 (May 1919): 370.

147. Rogers, "Ford Methods in Ship Manufacture—II," 124.

148. Rogers, "Ford Methods in Ship Manufacture—I," *Industrial Management* 57, no. 1 (January 1919): 4; Rogers, "Ford Methods in Ship Manufacture—III," *Industrial Management* 57, no. 3 (March 1919): 190.

149. Furer, "The 110–Foot Submarine Chasers and Eagle Boats," 766; "Submarine Chasers Made by Quantity-Production Methods," 844; Rogers, "Ford Methods in Ship Manufacture—IV," *Industrial Management* 57, no. 4 (April 1919): 295; Rogers, "Ford Methods in Ship Manufacture—V," 368–69.

150. Rogers, "Ford Methods in Ship Manufacture—VI," *Industrial Management* 57, no. 6 (June 1919): 458.

151. Cianflone, "The Eagle Boats of World War I," 77; Furer, "The 110–Foot Submarine Chasers and Eagle Boats," 765.

152. Hounshell, "Ford Eagle Boats and Mass Production during World War I," 201.

153. W. I. Babcock, "Portable Pneumatic Riveters in Shipbuilding," *INA Transactions* 41(1899): 121–27; Fairburn, "Methods of Handling Material over Shipbuilding Berths in American Shipyards," 229–70; William A. Fairburn, "Fitting-Out Wharf Crane Service in American Shipyards," *INA Transactions* 45 (1903): 153–82; Alexander Murray, "The Introduction of Cranes in Shipyards," *INA Transactions* 48 (1906): 179–95; George W. Dickie, "Can the American Shipbuilder under Present Conditions Compete with the British and German Shipbuilders...?" *SNAME Transactions* 8 (1900): 185–87; Pollock, *The Shipbuilding Industry*, 108–10; Norman M. Hunter, "Changes in Ship Construction Methods, 1850 to 1950," *INA Transactions* 94 (1952): 209–12; Warren, *Steel, Ships, and Men*, 177; Olsson, *Engineers as System Builders*, 49–55.

154. Fairburn, "Methods of Handling Material over Shipbuilding Berths in American Shipyards," 260.

155. Olsson, *Engineers as System Builders*, 49–55; M. Lavallée, "Results Obtained by Applying Scientific Management in a French Ship Yard," *Industrial Management* 60, no. 3 (September 1920): 240–44; ibid. 60, no. 4 (October 1920): 287–89.

Conclusion: Building an American Ship in the Twentieth Century

1. William A. Dobson to William P. Stephens, April 26, 1935, Folder 31, Box 2, Collection 91; Blunt White Library, Mystic Seaport.

Bibliography

Primary Sources

Archival Collections and Personal Papers
American Swedish Institute, Philadelphia
    John Ericsson Papers
    Thomas J. Griffin Papers
Atlantic County Historical Society, Somers Point, New Jersey
    Israel Smith Diary
Balch Institute, Philadelphia
    Amandus Johnson Papers
Camden County Historical Society, New Jersey
    Cramp Shipyard Scrapbook
    E. Hexamer Insurance Maps, Microform
    New York Shipbuilding Corporation Papers
    Sanborn Fire Insurance Company (maps of Camden)
Delaware State Hall of Records, Dover
    Apprentice Indenture Papers
    Register of Wills-Probates, Kent County, Record Group 3545
    Register of Wills-Probates, New Castle County, Record Group 2545
    William Lank Papers
Hagley Museum and Library, Wilmington, Delaware
    J. Crosby Brown Papers
    Harlan and Hollingsworth Company Papers
    Iron Vessel *Codorus*
    Jackson and Sharp Company Papers
    Phoenix Bridge Company Collection
    Howard Potts Oral Interview
    Pusey and Jones Corporation Papers
    Stockly Family Papers
    Wilmington City Directories, 1845–1900
Historical Society of Delaware, Wilmington
    Burk Papers
    Shipbuilding Papers
Historical Society of Pennsylvania, Philadelphia
    Edgar M. Levy Papers
    Vaughn and Lynn Papers, Charles Hillman and Company Collection
Independence Seaport Museum, Philadelphia
    William Cramp and Sons Ship and Engine Company Papers

Harlan and Hollingsworth Company Collection
New York Shipbuilding Corporation Papers and Shipyard Publications
Pusey and Jones Company Collection
Reaney and Neafie / Neafie and Levy Collection
John Roach Collection
Library of Congress, Washington, D.C.
Palmer-Loper Family Papers
Mariners' Museum, Newport News, Virginia
Charles E. Emery Letters
Reaney, Neafie, and Company Records
Maryland Historical Society, Baltimore
William Skinner Papers
James J. Williams Papers
National Archives, Washington, D.C.
Bureau of Ships, Record Group 19
Bureau of Naval Personnel, Record Group 24
Naval Records Collection, Record Group 45
Stephen Phillips Memorial Library, Penobscot Marine Museum, Searsport, Maine
Henry Hall Collection
Rutgers University Library, Special Collections and Archives
Leaming M. Rice Papers
Stevens Institute, Hoboken, New Jersey
Frederick W. Taylor Papers
Urban Archives, Temple University Library, Philadelphia
William Cramp and Sons Ship and Engine Building Company Papers
G. W. Blunt White Library, Mystic Seaport Museum
C. Drew and Company Trade Catalog
William L. Hanscom Letters
Captain R. F. Loper Papers
Neafie and Levy Records, Howard E. Cornell Papers
William Skinner and Sons Papers
William P. Stephens Papers
Wilmington Institute, Delaware
Delaware Collection

GOVERNMENT PUBLICATIONS

Annual Register of the United States Naval Academy at Annapolis, Maryland. Washington: Government Printing Office (hereafter cited as GPO), 1872–82.
Hichborn, Philip. *Report on European Dock-Yards.* Washington: GPO, 1886.
Naval History Division. *Dictionary of American Naval Fighting Ships.* 8 vols. Washington: GPO, 1964.

Pennsylvania, Commonwealth of. Internal Affairs, Bureau of Industrial Statistics. *Annual Report of the Secretary of Internal Affairs for the Years 1874–75. Part III: Industrial Statistics.* Vol. 3. Harrisburg: B. F. Meyers, 1876.

———. *Annual Report of the Secretary of Internal Affairs for the Years 1876–77. Part III: Industrial Statistics.* Vol. 5. Harrisburg: Lane S. Hart, 1878.

———. "Commerce, Navigation and Ship-Building on the Delaware River, by Edward P. Cheney." *Annual Report of the Secretary of Internal Affairs of the Commonwealth of Pennsylvania for the Year 1891. Part III: Industrial Statistics.* Vol. 19. Official Document No. 10. Harrisburg: Edwin K. Meyers, 1892.

Richardson, James D., ed. *Messages and Papers of the Presidents, 1789–1897.* Vols. 7–9. Washington: GPO, 1898.

Simpson, Edward. *Report on a Naval Mission to Europe, Especially Devoted to the Material and Construction of Artillery.* Washington: GPO, 1873.

Soley, James R. *Historical Sketch of the United States Naval Academy.* Washington: GPO, 1876.

U.S. Commissioner of Agriculture. "Ship Timber in the United States, by William W. Bates." *Report of the Commissioner of Agriculture for the Year 1866.* Washington: GPO, 1867.

U.S. Commissioner of Labor. *Seventeenth Annual Report of the Commissioner of Labor, 1902: Trade and Technical Education.* Washington: GPO, 1902.

U.S. Commissioner of Navigation. "Iron Ship Construction in the United States, by William M. Lytle." *Annual Report of the Commissioner of Navigation, 1899.* Washington: GPO, 1899.

United States Congressional Documents. *Report on Steam Engines in the United States.* 25th Cong., 3rd sess., 1839. H. Exec. Doc. 21.

———. *Contracts—Navy Department.* 28th Cong., 1st sess., 1844. H. Doc. 72.

———. *United States Steamers.* 33rd Cong., 1st sess., 1853. H. Misc. Doc. 2.

———. *Steam Navy of the United States.* 33rd Cong., 1st sess., 1854. H. Exec. Doc. 65.

———. *Annual Report of the Secretary of the Navy.* H. Exec. Doc. 1, 1860–1920.

———. *Navy Yards—Board of Navy Officers—Evidence Taken before Them.* 36th Cong., 1st sess., 1860. H. Exec. Doc. 71.

———. *Information in Relation to the Construction of the Iron-clad Monitor.* 40th Cong., 2nd sess., 1868. S. Exec. Doc. 86.

———. *Report of the Select Committee (chaired by John Lynch) on the Causes of the Reduction of American Tonnage.* 41st Cong., 2nd sess., 1870. H. Rep. 28.

———. *Relief of Certain Naval Contractors.* 43rd Cong., 1st sess., 1874. H. Rep. 269.

———. *Investigation by the Committee on Naval Affairs: Testimony Taken by the Committee on Naval Affairs.* 44th Cong., 1st sess., 1876. H. Misc. Doc. 170, pt. 4.

———. *Investigations of the Navy Department (by the Naval Affairs Committee).* 44th Cong., 1st sess., 1876. H. Rep. 784.

———. *Contracts of the Navy Department.* 45th Cong., 2nd sess., 1878. H. Rep. 787.

———. *Testimony Taken by the Committee on Naval Affairs.* 45th Cong., 2nd sess., 1878. H. Misc. Doc. 63.

———. *Report on Foreign Systems of Naval Education.* 46th Cong., 2nd sess., 1880. S. Exec. Doc. 51.

———. *Report on the Training Systems for the Navy and Mercantile Marine of England, and on the Naval Training System of France.* 46th Cong., 2nd sess., 1880. S. Exec. Doc. 52.

———. *Construction of Vessels of War for the Navy.* 47th Cong., 1st sess., 1882. H. Rep. 653.

———. *Improvements in Naval Engineering in Great Britain.* 47th Cong., 2nd sess., 1883. H. Exec. Doc. 48.

———. *Report of the Board on Behalf of the United States Executive Departments at the International Exhibition, 1876.* 47th Cong., 2nd sess., 1884. H. Misc. Doc. 20.

———. *Report of the Joint Select Committee on American Ship-building on American Shipping, by Mr. Nelson Dingley.* 47th Cong., 2nd sess., 1882. H. Rep. 1827.

———. *Reconstruction of the Navy.* 48th Cong., 1st sess., 1884. H. Exec. Doc. 127.

———. *Additional Steel Vessels.* 48th Cong., 1st sess., 1884. S. Rep. 161.

———. *Appropriations for the Navy.* 48th Cong., 1st sess., 1884. S. Rep. 405.

———. *Increase of the Naval Establishment.* 49th Cong., 1st sess., 1886. H. Rep. 993.

———. *In the Senate of the United States.* 50th Cong., 1st sess., 1888. S. Misc. Doc. 33.

———. *Letter from the Secretary of the Navy.* 50th Cong., 1st sess., 1888. S. Exec. Doc. 241.

———. *American Merchant Marine in the Foreign Trade.* 51st Cong., 1st sess., 1890. H. Rep. 1210.

———. *Premiums Paid to Contractors of War Vessels for the Navy.* 53rd Cong., 2nd sess., 1894. H. Rep. 407.

———. *Course in Naval Architecture, United States Naval Academy.* 55th Cong., 3rd sess., 1899. S. Doc. 74.

———. *William Cramp and Sons Ship and Engine Building Company.* 54 Cong., 1st sess., 1895–96. H. Doc. 68.

———. *Course in Naval Architecture, United States Naval Academy.* 55th Cong., 3rd sess., 1899. H. Doc. 148.

———. *Annual Report of the Commissioner of Navigation, 1899.* 56th Cong., 1st sess., 1899. H. Doc. 1.

———. *Certain Claims for Extra Payments for Vessels Built for the United States Navy.* 56th Cong., 1st sess., 1900. S. Doc. 288.

———. *Report of the Commissioner-General for the United States to the International Universal Exposition, Paris, 1900.* 56th Cong., 2nd sess., 1901. S. Doc. 232.

———. *Report of the Industrial Commission on the Relations and Conditions of Capital and Labor.* 57th Cong., 1st sess., 1901. H. Doc. 183.

———. *Eight Hours for Laborers on Government Work.* 57th Cong., 2nd sess., 1903. S. Doc. 141.

———. *Bulletin of the Bureau of Labor No. 52, May 1904.* 58th Cong., 2nd sess., 1904. H. Doc. 343, pt. 3.

———. *Taylor and Other Systems of Shop Management.* 62nd Cong., 2nd sess., 1912. House Report 403.

———. *Navy Yearbook: Compilation of Annual Naval Appropriation Laws from 1883 to 1912.* 62nd Cong., 3rd sess., 1912. S. Doc. 955.

———. *"Taylor System" of Shop Management.* 63rd Cong., 2nd sess., 1914. H. Rep. 1175.

U.S. Department of Commerce. "Shipping and Shipbuilding Subsidies, by J. E. Saugstad." Trade Promotion Series 129. Washington: GPO, 1932.

———. Census Bureau. *Negro Population, 1790–1915.* Washington: GPO, 1918.

U.S. Department of Interior. Census Office. "Products of Industry," *U.S. Census 1850*, 11th Ward, New York.

———. "Products of Industry," *U.S. Census 1880*, Wilmington, Delaware.

———. Fitch, Charles H. "Manufacture of Engines and Boilers." *Tenth Census of the United States, 1880.* Vol. 8, *Special Reports*. Washington: GPO, 1884.

———. Hall, Henry. "Report on the Ship-Building Industry of the United States." *Tenth Census of the United States, 1880.* Vol. 8, *Special Reports*. Washington: GPO, 1884.

U.S. House of Representatives. Committee on Naval Affairs. *Investigation by the Committee on Naval Affairs: Testimony Taken by the Committee on Naval Affairs.* 3 vols. Washington: GPO, 1876.

———. *On Bill for Increase of Naval Establishment.* Washington: GPO, 1886.

———. *The Vessels of the New Navy.* Washington: GPO, 1890.

———. *Shipbuilding in Government Yards.* Washington: GPO, 1900.

U.S. Navy Department. Bureau of Construction and Repair. *History of the Construction Corps of the United States Navy.* Washington: GPO, 1937.

———. Office of Naval Intelligence. *The United States Navy as an Industrial Asset: What the Navy Has Done for Industry and Commerce.* Washington: GPO, 1923.

U.S. Senate. *Report of the Joint Committee on the Conduct of the War.* Washington: GPO, 1865.

———. Committee on Commerce. *United States Shipping Board, Emergency Fleet Corporation: Hearing before the Committee on Commerce, United States Senate, Sixty-Fifth Congress, Third Session, on Senate Resolution 170 . . .* 8 vols. Washington: GPO, 1919.

———. Committee on Education and Labor. *Report of the Committee of the Senate upon the Relations between Labor and Capital.* Washington: GPO, 1885.

U.S. Shipping Board Emergency Fleet Corporation. *Hearings before the Committee on Commerce, United States Senate . . . on Senate Resolution 170.* 6 vols. Washington: GPO, 1918.

———. *Report to the United States Shipping Board, Emergency Fleet Corporation on Electric Welding and Its Application in the United States of America to Ship Con-*

struction. Philadelphia: United States Shipping Board Emergency Fleet Corp., 1918.

CONTEMPORARY BOOKS AND MANUSCRIPTS

Bates, William W. *American Ships: Their Past and Future, and the Question of Wood or Iron for Their Construction, Reviewed.* Chicago: self-published, 1870.

Bennett, Frank M. *The Steam Navy of the United States: A History of the Growth of the Steam Vessel of War in the U.S. Navy, and of the Naval Engineer Corps.* Pittsburgh: W. T. Nicholson, 1896.

Bishop, J. Leander. *A History of American Manufactures from 1608 to 1860.* 3 vols. Philadelphia: Edward Young and Co., 1868.

Blackburn, Isaac. *Treatise on the Science of Ship-Building; with Observations on the British Navy.* London: James Asperne, 1817.

Boole, Leonard H. *The Shipwright's Handbook and Draughtsman's Guide: Containing Directions for the Mold-Loft, Explanation of Lines, Bevelings, Cants, Stern Frame, etc.* Milwaukee: Ben Franklin Printing House of Burdick and Treyser, 1858.

Brunel, Isambard. *The Life of Isambard Kingdom Brunel: Civil Engineer.* Rutherford, N.J.: Fairleigh Dickinson University Press, 1971.

Buell, Augustus C. *The Memoirs of Charles H. Cramp.* Philadelphia: J. B. Lippincott, 1906.

Byrne, Oliver. *Dictionary of Machines, Mechanics, Engine-Work, and Engineering,* 2 vols. New York: D. Appleton and Co., 1851.

———. *The American Engineer, Draftsman, and Machinist's Assistant.* Philadelphia: C. A. Brown and Co., 1853.

Chapman, Fredrik Henrik af. *Treatise on Shipbuilding.* Stockholm: John Pfeffer, 1775.

Chatfield, Henry. *Reflections on the State of British Naval Construction in Eighteen Hundred and Thirty One.* London: Sherwood, Gilbert, and Piper, 1832.

Clark, Victor S. *History of Manufactures in the United States, 1860–1914.* Washington, D.C.: Carnegie Institution of Washington, 1929.

William Cramp and Sons Ship and Engine Building Company. *William Cramp and Sons Ship and Engine Building Company of Philadelphia.* Philadelphia: self-published, 1894.

———. *Cramp's Shipyard: The William Cramp and Sons Ship and Engine Building Company, 1830; the I. P. Morris Company, 1828; the Kensington Shipyard, ca. 1900.* Philadelphia: self-published, 1910.

———. *Cramp's Shipyard Founded by William Cramp, 1830.* Philadelphia: self-published, 1902.

Defebaugh, James E. *History of the Lumber Industry of America.* 2 vols. Chicago: American Lumberman, 1906–7.

Delaware's Industries: An Historical and Industrial Review. Philadelphia: Keighton Printing House, 1891.

Desmond, Charles. *Wooden Ship-Building.* 1919. Reprint, New York: Vestal Press, 1984.

D'Eyencourt, H. W. Tennyson. *A Shipbuilder's Yarn*. London: Hutchinson and Co., 1951.

Diderot, Denis. 1751. *A Diderot Pictorial Encyclopedia of Trades and Industry*. New York: Dover Publications, 1959.

Duckworth, A. D., ed. *The Papers of William Froude, M.A., LL.D., F.R.S., 1810–1879*. London: Institution of Naval Architects, 1955.

Durand, W. F. *Adventures in the Navy, in Education, Science, Engineering, and in War*. New York: American Society of Mechanical Engineers, 1953.

Evans, Holden A. *Cost Keeping and Scientific Management*. New York: McGraw-Hill, 1911.

———. *One Man's Fight for a Better Navy*. New York: Dodd, Mead, and Co., 1940.

Evans, Robley D. *A Sailor's Log: Recollections of Forty Years of Naval Life*. New York: D. Appleton and Co., 1908.

Fairbairn, William. *An Experimental Inquiry into the Strength of Wrought-Iron Plates and Their Riveted Joints, as Applied to Ship-Building and Vessels Exposed to Severe Strains*. London: R.&J.E. Taylor, 1850.

———. *On the Application of Cast and Wrought Iron to Building Purposes*. London: John Weale, 1854.

———. *Useful Information for Engineers*. London: Longmans, Brown, Green, Longmans, and Roberts, 1856.

———. *Treatise on Iron Ship Building: Its History and Progress*. London: Longmans, Green, and Co., 1865.

Ferguson, Eugene S., ed. *Early Engineering Reminiscences (1815–1840) of George Escoll Sellers*. Smithsonian Institution, Washington: Government Printing Office, 1965.

Fincham, John. *An Introductory Outline of the Practice of Ship-Building*. Portsea, England: W. Woodward, 1825.

———. *On Masting Ships and Mast Making; Giving Some of the Principles on which the Masting of Ships Depends*. London: Whittaker, Treacher, and Arnot, 1829.

———. *A History of Naval Architecture*. London: Whittaker, 1851.

Foden, James. *The Boilermakers' and Iron Shipbuilders' Companion*. London: E. and F. N. Spon, 1869.

Freedley, Edwin T. *Philadelphia and Its Manufactures*. Philadelphia: Edward Young and Co., 1858.

Froude, William. *On the Rolling of Ships*. London: Parker, Son, and Bourn, 1862.

Gause, J. Taylor. *Memoranda Concerning Foreign Shipbuilding, 1881–1883*. Wilmington, Del.: James and Webb Printing Co., 1883.

Grantham, John. *Iron as a Material for Ship-Building; Being a Communication to the Polytechnic Society of Liverpool*. London: Simpkin, Marshall, and Co., 1842.

———. *On Iron Ship Building, with Practical Examples and Details*. London: J. Weale, 1858.

———. *Iron Ship-Building: with Practical Illustrations*. London: J. Weale, 1859.

Griffiths, John W. "Marine and Naval Architecture or the Science of Ship Building, Condensed into a Single Lecture, and Delivered before the Shipwrights of the City of New York, in the Rooms of the American Institute, September 20th, 1844." New York: J. M. Marsh, printer, 1844.

———. *A Treatise on Marine and Naval Architecture or Theory and Practice Blended in Ship Building.* New York: D. Appleton and Co., 1853.

———. "Report of the President and Trustees of the Ship Timber Bending Company." New York: Pudney and Russell, printers, 1854.

———. *The Ship-Builder's Manual, and Nautical Referee.* New York: self-published, 1856.

———. *The Progressive Shipbuilder.* 2 vols. New York: self-published, 1875.

———. "Bent Timber Ships and Universal Wood Bending Machinery." New York: self-published, 1876.

Harlan and Hollingsworth Company. *Memoranda Concerning Foreign Ship-Building, 1881–1883.* Wilmington, Del.: James and Webb Printing Co., 1883.

———. *The Semi-Centennial Memoir of the Harlan and Hollingsworth Company, Wilmington, Delaware, 1836–1886.* Wilmington, Del.: self-published, 1886.

———. *The Harlan & Hollingsworth Co., Ship and Car Builders: Their Plant and Operations, Wilmington, Delaware.* Philadelphia: Armstrong and Fears, 1898.

Harrison, Joseph. *The Iron Worker and King Solomon.* Philadelphia: J. B. Lippincott & Co., 1868.

Harrison, W. B. *The Mechanic's Tool Book with Practical Rules and Suggestions for the Use of Machinists, Iron Workers, and Others.* New York: D. Van Nostrand, 1868.

Haupt, Herman. *Military Bridges: With Suggestions of New Experiments and Constructions for Crossing Streams and Chasms. Including, also, Designs for Trestle and Truss Bridges for Military Railroads.* New York: D. Van Nostrand, 1864.

Hill, Charles S. *History of American Shipping, Its Prestige, Decline, and Prospect.* New York: American News Company, 1883.

Holms, A. Campbell. *Practical Shipbuilding: A Treatise on the Structural Design and Building of Modern Steel Vessels; the Work of Construction, from the Making of the Raw Material to the Equipped Vessel, Including Subsequent Up-keep and Repairs.* London: Longmans, Green, and Co., 1904.

Howe, Henry. *Memoirs of the Most Eminent American Mechanics also, Lives of Distinguished European Mechanics; Together with a Collection of Anecdotes, Descriptions, etc., Relating to the Mechanic Arts.* New York: A. V. Blake, 1844.

Hurley, Edward N. *Bridge to France.* Philadelphia: J. B. Lippincott, 1927.

Kelly, Roy W., and Frederick J. Allen. *The Shipbuilding Industry.* Boston: Houghton Mifflin, 1918.

King, J. W. *The Warship and Navies of the World, 1880.* Annapolis: United States Naval Institute, 1881.

MacFarlane, Robert. *History of Propellers and Steam Navigation with Biographical Sketches of the Early Inventors.* New York: G. P. Putnam, 1851.

Maguire, Doris D. *French Ensor Chadwick: Selected Letters and Papers.* Washington: University Press of America, 1981.

Mahan, A. T. *From Sail to Steam: Recollections of Naval Life.* New York: Harper and Brothers, 1907.

Manufactories and Manufacturers of Pennsylvania of the Nineteenth Century. Philadelphia: Galaxy, 1875.

Marestier, Jean B. *Memoir on Steamboats of the United States of America.* Paris: Royal Press, 1824.

McNeill, George E. *The Labor Movement: The Problem of Today.* New York: M. W. Hazen, 1887.

Meade, Richard, Comm. (USN). *A Treatise on Naval Architecture and Ship-Building.* Philadelphia: J. B. Lippincott, 1869.

Merchant Shipbuilding Corporation. "Register of Contracts: Reaney, Son and Archbold, Roach's Shipyard, Merchant Shipbuilding Corporation." Chester, Pa.: self-published, n.d.

M'Kay, L. *The Practical Ship-Builder, Containing the Best Mechanical and Philosophical Principles for the Construction of Different Classes of Vessels, and the Practical Application of Their Several Parts, with the Rules Carefully Detailed.* New York: Collins, Keese, and Company, 1839.

Murphy, John M. *American Ships and Ship-Builders.* New York: Charles W. Baker, printers, 1860.

Naval Encyclopedia. Philadelphia: L. R. Hamersly, 1881.

Neafie and Levy Ship and Engine Building Company. *The Neafie & Levy Ship and Engine Building Company, Penn Works, Philadelphia.* New York: U. G. Duffield, 1896.

Nevins, Allan, ed. *The Diary of Philip Hone.* 2 vols. New York: Dodd, Mead, and Co., 1927.

New York Shipbuilding Corp. *Fifty Years, New York Shipbuilding Corporation, Camden, N.J.* Camden, N.J.: self-published, 1949.

Nystrom, John W. *A Treatise on Screw Propellers and Their Steam Engines with Practical Rules and Examples How to Calculate and Construct the Same for Any Description of Vessels, Accompanied with a Treatise on Bodies in Motion in Fluid, Exemplified for Propellers and Vessels; also a Full Description of a Calculating Machine.* Philadelphia: Henry Carey Baird, 1852.

———. *Project of a New System of Arithmetic, Weight, Measure and Coins: Proposed To Be Called the Tonal System with Sixteen to the Base.* Philadelphia: J. B. Lippincott and Company, 1862.

———. *A Treatise on Parabolic Construction of Ships and Other Marine Engineering Subjects.* Philadelphia: J. B. Lippincott and Company, 1863.

———. *Pocket Book of Mechanics and Engineering, Containing a Memorandum of Facts and Connection of Practice and Theory.* Philadelphia: J. B. Lippincott and Company, 1864.

———. *On Technological Education and the Construction of Ships and Screw Propellers, for Naval and Marine Engineers.* Philadelphia: Henry Carey Baird, 1866.

———. *Principles of Dynamics.* Philadelphia: J.P. Murphy, 1874.

———. *A New Treatise on Steam Engineering, Physical Properties of Permanent Gases, and of Different Kinds of Vapor.* New York: Putnam, 1876.

———. *On the French Metric System of Weights and Measures.* Philadelphia: J. B. Lippincott and Company, 1876.

Pole, William, ed. *The Life of Sir William Fairbairn.* London: Longmans, Green, and Co., 1877.

Pook, Samuel M. *A Manual of Comparing the Lines and Draughting Vessels, Propelled by Sail or Steam, Including a Chapter on Laying Off on the Mould Loft Floor.* New York: D. Van Nostrand, 1866.

Preble, George H. *A Chronological History of the Origin and Development of Steam Navigation, 1543–1882.* Philadelphia: L. R. Hammersly and Co., 1883.

Prowell, George R. *The History of Camden County, New Jersey.* Philadelphia: L. J. Richards and Co., 1886.

Pusey and Jones Company. *Fiftieth Anniversary of the Founding of the Pusey and Jones Company, 1848–1898.* Wilmington, Del.: John M. Rogers Press, 1898.

———. *The Pusey and Jones Company, Builders of Iron Vessels, Steam Engines, and Boilers.* Wilmington, Del.: self-published, 1900.

———. *A Hundred Years A-Building.* Wilmington, Del.: self-published, 1948.

Rankine, W.J.M. *Shipbuilding, Theoretical and Practical.* London: William Mackenzie, 1866.

Reed, Edward J. *Shipbuilding in Iron and Steel: A Practical Treatise, Giving Full Details of Construction. Processes of Manufacture, and Building Arrangements.* London: John Murray, 1869.

———. *A Treatise on the Stability of Ships.* London: Charles Griffin and Co., 1885.

Roach, John. "Iron Steamships: Shall We Build Them of Our Own Material, or Buy Them, or the Material to Build Them, Abroad? A Practical Answer to the Above Important National Question." Washington, D.C.: Gibson Brothers, printers, 1872.

Roach Shipyard. *Souvenir of Roach's Shipyard, the Delaware River Iron Shipbuilding and Engine Works, Chester, Pa.* New York: Ulysses G. Duffield, 1895.

Rogers, George W. *The Shipwright's Own Book.* Pittsburgh: J. M'Millin, 1845.

———. *Shipbuilding Made Easy.* St. Louis: R. P. Studley, 1865.

Russell, John Scott. *Fleet of the Future: Iron or Wood?* London: Longmans, Green, Longmans, and Roberts, 1861.

———. *The Modern System of Naval Architecture.* London: Day and Son, 1865.

Sargent, John O. *A Lecture on the Late Improvements in Steam Navigation and the Art of Naval Warfare.* New York: Wiley and Putnam, 1844.

Schaffer, William I. Receiver, "Roach's Shipyard: Information as to Plant, Equipment, Etc." Chester, Pa.: Wm. Schaffer, 1907.

Scharf, J. Thomas. *History of Delaware, 1609–1888.* 2 vols. Philadelphia: L. J. Richards and Co., 1888.

Scharf, J. Thomas, and Thompson Westcott. *History of Philadelphia, 1609–1884.* 3 vols. Philadelphia: L. H. Everts and Co., 1884.
Smiles, Samuel. *Lives of the Engineers.* 3 vols. London: John Murray, 1861–62.
Stevenson, David. *Sketch of the Civil Engineering of North America.* London: John Weale, 1838.
Taylor, D. W. *Resistance of Ships and Screw Propulsion.* New York: Macmillan and Co., 1893.
———. *The Speed and Power of Ships.* New York: John Wiley and Sons, 1910.
Taylor, Frank H. *Philadelphia in the Civil War, 1861–1865.* Philadelphia: Dunlap, 1913.
Thompson, M. S., comp. *General Orders and Circulars Issued by the Navy Department, from 1863 to 1887.* Washington: GPO, 1887.
Tocqueville, Alexis. *Democracy in America.* Translated by George Lawrence. Edited by J. P. Mayer. New York: Doubleday Anchor, 1966.
Tudor, Frederic. *Some memorandums, by which it is attempted to be shewn that an improved model may be adopted in the construction of ships, by a new application of well-known principles.* Boston: n.p., 1812.
"Valuable Ship Building Plant and Other River Front Properties of John H. Dialogue." Philadelphia: Samuel T. Freeman and Co., 1915.
Varney, William Henry. *The Ship-builder's Manual, or Mould Loft Guide: A Practical and Theoretical Treatise on the Various Operations of Drafting and Designing of Ships and Boats.* New York: T. Holman, printer, 1877.
Weissenborn, Gustavus. *American Engineering, Illustrated by Large and Detailed Engravings Embracing Various Branches of Mechanical Art.* New York: self-published, 1861.
White, William H. *A Manual of Naval Architecture.* London: John Murray, 1877.
Wilmington and Its Industries. Philadelphia: J. B. Lippincott and Co., 1873.
Wilson, Theodore D. *A Series of Ten Lectures Delivered to the Second Class of Cadet Midshipmen in the Practice of Building, Launching, Docking, and Fitting Out of U.S. Naval Vessels.* Annapolis, Md.: U.S. Naval Academy, 1872.
———. *An Outline of Ship Building, Theoretical and Practical.* New York: John Wiley and Sons, 1878.
Woolley, Joseph. *The Elements of Descriptive Geometry.* London: J. W. Parker, 1850.

CONTEMPORARY ARTICLES

Cramp, Charles H. "Certain Incidents in the Evolution of the Modern Warship." *Proceedings of the Numismatic and Antiquarian Society of Philadelphia for the Years 1904–1906* (1907): 105–28.
———. "Sixty Years of Shipbuilding on the Delaware (Read to the Numismatic and Antiquarian Society of Philadelphia, April 5th, 1906)." *Proceedings of the Numismatic and Antiquarian Society of Philadelphia for the Years 1907–1909* (1910): 175–88.

Croasdale, W. T. "Iron Ship-Building: Wilmington's Distinguishing Industry." *State Normal School Advocate* 5, no. 1 (June 1871): 11.

Denny, Archibald. "Fifty Years' Evolution in Naval Architecture and Marine Engineering." *Nature* 116 (September 16, 1925): 468–71.

Goodrich, Arthur. "The Expansion of the American Shipyard." *World's Work* 3 (1901–2): 1933–50.

Hood, Sheridan. "The Clyde of America." *Our Continent* 2 (Sept. 6, 1882): 257–61, 2 (Sept. 13, 1882): 289–93.

"The Late Isaac Newton." *Sanitary Engineer* 10, no. 18 (October 2, 1884): 409–10.

Roach, John. "Mr. John Roach on Ship-Building (interview in the *New York Herald*)." Washington, D.C.: Gibson Brothers, printers, 1877.

Stevens, Francis B. "The First Steam Screw Propeller Boat to Navigate the Waters of Any Country." *Stevens Indicator* 10 (April 1893): 101–30.

Valette, Henry M. "History and Reminiscences of the Philadelphia Navy Yard." *Potter's American Monthly* (1876). Philadelphia. 6–7.

Welch, J. J. "The Scientific Education of Naval Architects." *Transactions of the North-East Coast Institution of Engineers and Shipbuilders* 25 (1909): 177–98.

Wilson, Theodore D. "Education of Naval Constructors," *United Service* 2 (February 1880): 180–89.

CONTEMPORARY PERIODICALS

Augusta (Ga.) Constitutionalist
Bangor Whig and Courier
Brassey's Naval Annual
Bulletin of the American Iron and Steel Institute
Cassier's Magazine
Chester (Pa.) Times
Engineer
Engineering
Engineering Magazine
Harper's New Monthly Magazine
Harper's Weekly
Industrial Management
Iron Age
Journal of the American Society of Naval Engineers
Journal of the Brotherhood of Boiler Makers and Iron Ship Builders of America
Journal of the Franklin Institute
Marine Engineering
Marine Review
Minutes of the Proceedings of the Institution of Civil Engineers
Nation
Naval Magazine

New York Daily Graphic
New York Times
New York Tribune
Niles' Weekly Register
North American Review
Philadelphia Evening Bulletin
Philadelphia Inquirer
Philadelphia Public Ledger
Portland Advertiser
Proceedings of the American Society of Civil Engineers
Railroad and Engineering Journal
Railroad Gazette
Scientific American
Transactions of the American Society of Mechanical Engineers
Transactions of the Society of Naval Architects and Marine Engineers
   (*SNAME Transactions* and *Historical Transactions*)
United States Army and Navy Journal
United States Nautical Magazine and Naval Journal
Wilmington Every Evening

Secondary Sources

BOOKS

Abell, Sir Wescott. The Shipwright's Trade. Cambridge: Cambridge University Press, 1948.
Adams, Thomas R., and David W. Waters, comps. *English Maritime Books Printed before 1801*. Providence: John Carter Brown Library, 1995.
Aitken, Hugh G. *Syntony and Spark—The Origins of Radio*. New York: John Wiley and Sons, 1976.
———. *Scientific Management in Action: Taylorism at Watertown Arsenal, 1908–1915*. Princeton: Princeton University Press, 1985.
Albion, Robert G. *Forests and Sea Power: The Timber Problem of the Royal Navy, 1652–1862*. Cambridge: Harvard University Press, 1926.
———. *The Rise of the New York Port*. New York: Charles Scribners' Sons, 1939.
———. *Makers of Naval Policy, 1798–1947*, edited by Rowena Reed. Annapolis: United States Naval Institute, 1980.
The American Carrying Trade. New York: H. B. Grose and Company, 1880.
Appleton's Cyclopaedia of American Biography. 6 vols. New York: D. Appleton & Co., 1888–89.
Attwood, Edward L. *Theoretical Naval Architecture*. London: Longmans, 1953.
Baker, William A. *A History of the First 75 Years*. Dept. report no. 69-3. Cambridge: MIT Dept. of Naval Architecture and Marine Engineering, 1969.

Barnaby, K. C. *The Institution of Naval Architects, 1860–1960*. London: Royal Institution of Naval Architects, 1960.

———. *Some Ship Disasters and Their Causes*. South Brunswick, N.Y.: A. S. Barnes and Company, 1968.

Barnaby, Nathaniel. *Naval Development in the Century*. London: W.&R. Chambers, 1904.

Basalla, George. *The Evolution of Technology*. New York: Cambridge University Press, 1988.

Bauer, K. Jack, and Stephen S. Roberts. *Register of Ships of the U.S. Navy, 1775–1990*. New York: Greenwood Press, 1991.

Baynes, Ken, and Francis Pugh. *The Art of the Engineer*. Woodstock, N.Y.: Overlook Press, 1981.

Bealer, Alex W. *Old Ways of Working Wood*. Barre, Mass.: Barre Publishers, 1972.

Beisner, Robert L. *From the Old Diplomacy to the New, 1865–1900*. New York: Thomas Y. Cromwell, 1975.

Biggs, Lindy. *The Rational Factory: Architecture, Technology, and Work in America's Age of Mass Production*. Baltimore: Johns Hopkins University Press, 1996.

Bijker, Wiebe E., Thomas P. Hughes, and Trevor Pinch, eds. *The Social Construction of Technological Systems*. Cambridge: MIT Press, 1987.

Biographical and Genealogical History of the State of Delaware. Vol. 1. Chambersburg, Pa.: J. M. Runk, 1899.

Blake, George. *Lloyd's Register of Shipping, 1760–1960*. London: Lloyd's Register of Shipping, 1960.

Bolles, Albert S. *Industrial History of the United States*. Norwich, Conn.: Henry Bill, 1879.

Bowen, Harold G. *Ships, Machinery, and Mossbacks: The Autobiography of a Naval Engineer*. Princeton: Princeton University Press, 1954.

Bridenbaugh, Carl. *The Colonial Craftsman*. New York: Dover Publications, 1990.

Brinton, Mary Williams. *Their Lives and Mine*. Philadelphia: by the author, 1972.

Brodie, Bernard. *Sea Power in the Machine Age*. Princeton: Princeton University Press, 1941.

Brown, John K. *The Baldwin Locomotive Works, 1831–1915: A Study in American Industrial Practice*. Baltimore: Johns Hopkins University Press, 1995.

Bruce, Alexander B. *The Life of William Denny, Ship-Builder, Dumbarton*. London: Hodder and Stoughton, 1889.

Bruchey, Stuart. *The Roots of American Economic Growth, 1607–1861: An Essay on Social Causation*. New York: Harper and Row, 1965.

Buchanan, R. A. *The Engineers: A History of the Engineering Profession in Britain, 1750–1914*. London: Jessica Kingsley Publishers, 1989.

Burgess, Robert H. *Coasting Schooner, The Four-Masted* Albert F. Paul. Newport News, Va.: Mariners' Museum, 1978.

Calhoun, Daniel. *The Intelligence of a People*. Princeton: Princeton University Press, 1973.

Calvert, Monte. *The Mechanical Engineer in America, 1830–1910: Professional Cultures in Conflict*. Baltimore: Johns Hopkins University Press, 1967.
Canney, Donald C. *Old Steam Navy: Frigates, Sloops, and Gunboats, 1815–1885*. Annapolis: Naval Institute Press, 1990.
Chandler, Charles L., Marion V. Brewington, and Edgar P. Richardson. *Philadelphia: Port of History, 1609–1837*. Philadelphia: Philadelphia Maritime Museum, 1976.
Chapelle, Howard I. *The History of American Sailing Ships*. New York: Bonanza Books, 1935.
———. *Boatbuilding: A Complete Handbook of Wooden Boat Construction*. New York: W. W. Norton, 1941.
———. *The History of the American Sailing Navy: The Ships and Their Development*. New York: W. W. Norton, 1949.
———. *The Search for Speed under Sail, 1700–1855*. New York: W. W. Norton, 1967.
Church, William C. *The Life of John Ericsson*. 2 vols. New York: Charles Scribner's Sons, 1891.
Clarke, J. F. *The Changeover from Wood to Iron Shipbuilding*. Newcastle-upon-Tyne: Newcastle-upon-Tyne Polytechnic, 1986.
Cochran, Thomas C. *Frontiers of Change: Early Industrialism in America*. New York: Oxford University Press, 1981.
Cogar, William B. *Dictionary of Admirals of the U.S. Navy, 1862–1900*. Annapolis, Md.: Naval Institute Press, 1989.
Coletta, Paolo E. *French Ensor Chadwick: Scholarly Warrior*. Lanham, Md.: University Press of America, 1980.
Conrad, Henry C. *History of the State of Delaware*. Wilmington, Del.: self-published, 1908.
Constant, Edward W. *The Origins of the Turbojet Revolution*. Baltimore: Johns Hopkins University Press, 1980.
Cooling, Benjamin F. *Gray Steel and Blue Water Navy: The Formative Years of America's Military-Industrial Complex, 1881–1917*. Camden, Conn.: Archon Books, 1979.
Cooper, Carolyn C. *Shaping Invention: Thomas Blanchard's Machinery and Patent Management in Nineteenth-Century America*. New York: Columbia University Press, 1991.
Corlett, Ewan. *The Iron Ship: The History and Significance of Brunel's* Great Britain. New York: Arco Books, 1975.
Cutler, Carl C. *Greyhounds of the Sea: The Story of the American Clipper Ship*. Annapolis, Md.: Naval Institute Press, 1984.
Davis, George T. *A Navy Second to None: The Development of Modern American Naval Policy*. Westport, Conn.: Greenwood Press, 1940.
DeLony, Eric. *Landmark American Bridges*. Boston: Little, Brown, and Co., 1993.
Dictionary of American Biography. 10 vols. New York: Charles Scribner's Sons, 1927–36.

Dictionary of National Biography. 22 vols. London: Oxford University Press, 1921–22.

Dictionary of Scientific Biography. Edited by Charles Gillespie. 18 vols. New York: Charles Scribner's Sons, 1970–90.

Dorwat, Jeffrey M. *The Office of Naval Intelligence: The Birth of America's First Intelligence Agency, 1865–1918.* Annapolis, Md.: Naval Institute Press, 1979.

Douglas, Susan J. *Inventing American Broadcasting, 1899–1922.* Baltimore: Johns Hopkins University Press, 1987.

Dunbaugh, Edwin L., and William duBarry Thomas. *William H. Webb: Shipbuilder.* Glen Cove, N.Y.: Webb Institute of Naval Architecture, 1989.

Du Pont, H. A. *Rear-Admiral Samuel Francis Du Pont.* New York: National Americana Society, 1926.

Edwards, Llewellyn N. *A Record of History and Evolution of Early American Bridges.* Orono, Me.: University Press, 1959.

Emmerson, George S. *John Scott Russell: A Great Victorian Engineer and Naval Architect.* London: John Murray, 1977.

———. *The Greatest Iron Ship: S.S.* Great Eastern. London: David and Charles, 1981.

Fairburn, William A. *Merchant Sail.* 6 vols. Center Lovell, Me.: Fairburn Marine Educational Foundation, 1945–55.

Farr, Gail E., and Brett F. Bostwick. *John Lenthall, Naval Architect.* Philadelphia: Philadelphia Maritime Museum, 1991.

Fassett, F. G., Jr., ed. *The Shipbuilding Business in the United States of America.* 2 vols. New York: Society of Nautical Architects and Marine Engineers, 1948.

Friel, Ian. *The Good Ship: Ships, Shipbuilding, and Technology in England, 1200–1520.* Baltimore: Johns Hopkins University Press, 1995.

Gardiner, Robert, ed. *Cogs, Caravels, and Galleons: The Sailing Ship, 1000–1650.* Annapolis: Naval Institute Press, 1994.

Gauer, David W., comp. *Vaughan Shipwrights of Kensington, Philadelphia.* Decorah, Iowa: Anundsen, 1982.

Gilfillan, S. Colum. *Inventing the Ship: A Study of the Inventions Made in Her History between Floating Log and Rotorship.* Chicago: Follett, 1935.

Goldenberg, Joseph A. *Shipbuilding in Colonial America.* Newport News, Va.: Mariners' Museum, 1976.

Goodman, W. L. *The History of Woodworking Tools.* London: G. Bell and Sons, 1962.

Gordon, Robert B. *The Texture of Industry: An Archaeological View of the Industrialization of North America.* New York: Oxford University Press, 1994.

Greenhill, Basil J. *The Evolution of the Wooden Ship.* New York: Facts on File, 1988.

Habakkuk, H. J. *American and British Technology in the Nineteenth Century.* New York: Cambridge University Press, 1962.

Hagan, Kenneth J., B. Franklin Cooling, Jacob W. Kipp, Bruce Swanson, and A. Michael McMahon. *Naval Technology and Social Modernization in the Nineteenth Century.* Manhattan, Kans.: Military Affairs, 1976.

Hagan, Kenneth J., ed. *In Peace and War: Interpretations of American Naval History, 1775–1978*. Westport, Conn.: Greenwood Press, 1978.
Hancock, Harold B., and Russell McCabe, eds. *Milton's First Century, 1807–1907*. Milton, Del.: Milton Historical Society, 1982.
Hasslöf, Olof, Henning Henningsen, and Arne Emil Christenson Jr. *Ships and Shipyards, Sailors, and Fishermen*. Copenhagen: Rosenkilde and Bagger, 1972.
Heinrich, Thomas R. *Ships for the Seven Seas: Philadelphia Shipbuilding in the Age of Industrial Capitalism*. Baltimore: Johns Hopkins University Press, 1997.
Hennessey, Mark W. *The Sewall Ships of Steel*. Augusta, Me.: Kennebec Journal Press, 1937.
Herreschoff, L. Francis. *Capt. Nat Herreschoff: The Wizard of Bristol*. Dobbs Ferry, N.Y.: Sheridan House, 1953.
Herrick, Walter R., Jr. *The American Naval Revolution*. Baton Rouge: Louisiana State University Press, 1966.
Higgins, George. *Annals of Lloyd's Register*. London: Lloyd's Register of Shipping, 1934.
Hindle, Brook. *The Pursuit of Science in Revolutionary America, 1735–1789*. Chapel Hill: Institute of Early American History and Culture, 1956.
———, ed. *America's Wooden Age: Aspects of Its Early Technology*. Tarrytown, N.Y.: Sleepy Hollow Restorations, 1975.
———. *Material Culture of the Wooden Age*. Tarrytown, N.Y.: Sleepy Hollow Press, 1981.
Hirsch, Mark D. *William C. Whitney: Modern Warwick*. New York: Dodd, Mead, and Company, 1948.
Hoffecker, Carol. *Wilmington, Delaware: Portrait of an Industrial City, 1830–1910*. Charlottesville: University Press of Virginia, 1974.
Hounshell, David A. *From the American System to Mass Production, 1800–1932*. Baltimore: Johns Hopkins University Press, 1984.
Hoyt, C. Sherman. *Sherman Hoyt's Memoirs*. New York: D. Van Nostrand, 1950.
Hughes, Thomas P. *Networks of Power: Electrification in Western Society, 1880–1930*. Baltimore: Johns Hopkins University Press, 1983.
———. *American Genesis: A Century of Invention and Technological Enthusiasm*. New York: Penguin Books, 1989.
Hunter, Louis C. *Steamboats on the Western Rivers*. New York: Dover Publications, 1977.
Hutchins, John G. B. *American Maritime Industries and Public Policy, 1789–1914*. Cambridge: Harvard University Press, 1941.
Hutchinson, Gillian. *Medieval Ships and Shipping*. Rutherford, N.J.: Fairleigh Dickinson University Press, 1994.
Jeremy, David J. *Transatlantic Industrial Revolution: The Diffusion of Textile Technologies between Britain and America, 1790–1830s*. Cambridge: MIT Press, 1981.
———. *International Technology Transfer*. Brookfield, Vt.: Aldershot, 1991.

Jones, J. Christopher. *Design Methods: Seeds of Human Futures*. London: Wiley-Interscience, 1970.
Karsten, Peter. *The Naval Aristocracy: The Golden Age of Annapolis and the Emergence of Modern American Navalism*. New York: Free Press, 1972.
Kasson, John F. *Civilizing the Machine: Technology and Republican Values in America, 1776–1900*. New York: Penguin Books, 1976.
Kauffman, Henry J. *American Axes: A Survey of Their Development and Their Makers*. Brattleboro, Vt.: Stephen Greene Press, 1972.
Kebabian, Paul B. *American Woodworking Tools*. Boston: New York Graphic Society, 1978.
Keller, Charles M., and Janet D. Keller. *Cognition and Tool Use: The Blacksmith at Work*. New York: Cambridge University Press, 1996.
Keller, David Neal. *Stone and Webster, 1889–1989: A Century of Integrity and Service*. New York: Stone and Webster, 1989.
Kennedy, Paul. *The Rise and Fall of the Great Powers: Economic Change and Military Conflict from 1500 to 2000*. New York: Random House, 1987.
King, R. W. *Naval Engineering and American Sea Power*. Baltimore: Nautical and Aviation Publishing Co., 1989.
Kipling, Rudyard. *Rewards and Fairies*. London: Macmillan and Co., 1910.
Kirkaldy, Adam W. *British Shipping: Its History, Organisation, and Importance*. London: Kegan Paul, Trench, Trübner, and Co., 1914.
Kranakis, Eda. *Constructing a Bridge: An Exploration of Engineering Culture, Design, and Research in Nineteenth-Century France and America*. Cambridge: MIT Press, 1997.
Kranzberg, Melvin, and William H. Davenport. *Technology and Culture: An Anthology*. New York: Schocken Books, 1972.
Kuhn, Thomas S. *The Structure of Scientific Revolutions*. Chicago: University of Chicago Press, 1970.
LaFeber, Walter. *The New Empire: An Interpretation of American Expansion, 1860–1898*. Ithaca, N.Y.: Cornell University Press, 1963.
Laing, Alexander. *American Ships*. New York: American Heritage Press, 1971.
Lavery, Brian. *Ship of the Line*. 2 vols. Annapolis: Naval Institute Press, 1984.
Layton, Edwin T. *The Revolt of the Engineers: Social Responsibility and the American Engineering Profession*. Baltimore: Johns Hopkins University Press, 1971.
Lindstrom, Diane. *Economic Development in the Philadelphia Region, 1810–1850*. New York: Columbia University Press, 1978.
Lott, Arnold S. *A Long Line of Ships: Mare Island's Century of Naval Activity in California*. Annapolis: United States Naval Institute, 1954.
Lytle, William M., and Forrest R. Holdcamper. *Merchant Steam Vessels of the United States, 1790–1868*. Staten Island, N.Y.: Steamship Historical Society of America, 1975.
Macdonald, Betty Harrington. *Mispillion-Built Sailing Vessels, 1761–1917*. Milford, Del.: Milford Historical Society, 1990.

Manning, Frederic. *The Life of Sir William White*. New York: E. P. Dutton and Company, 1923.
Marcil, Eileen Reid. *The Charley-Man: A History of Wooden Shipbuilding at Quebec, 1763–1893*. Kingston, Ontario: Quarry Press, 1995.
Masterson, Daniel M., ed. *Naval History: The Sixth Symposium of the U.S. Naval Academy*. Wilmington, Del.: Scholarly Resources, 1987.
Mattox, W. C. *Building the Emergency Fleet*. Cleveland: Penton, 1920.
McKay, Richard C. *Some Famous Sailing Ships and Their Builder, Donald McKay*. New York: G. P. Putnam's Sons, 1928.
Montgomery, David. *Workers' Control in America: Studies in the History of Work, Technology, and Labor Struggles*. New York: Cambridge University Press, 1979.
Morison, Elting E. *Admiral Sims and the Modern American Navy*. Boston: Houghton Mifflin and Co., 1942.
———. *Men, Machines, and Modern Times*. Cambridge: MIT Press, 1966.
Morrison, John H. *History of American Steam Navigation*. New York: W. F. Sametz, 1903.
———. *History of New York Ship Yards*. New York: W. F. Sametz, 1909.
———. *Iron and Steel Hull Steam Vessels of the United States, 1825–1906*. Salem, Mass.: Steamship Historical Society of America, 1945.
Mumford, Lewis. *Technics and Civilization*. New York: Harcourt, Brace, and Co., 1934.
Munroe, James Phinney. *A Life of Francis Amasa Walker*. New York: Henry Holt and Co., 1923.
National Academy of Sciences. *Scientific, Technical, and Related Societies of the United States*. Washington, D.C.: National Academy of Sciences, 1971.
National Cyclopaedia of American Biography. 63 vols. New York: James T. White, 1898–1984.
Naval Historical Foundation. *The David W. Taylor Model Basin: A Brief History*. Washington: Naval Historical Foundation, 1971.
Nelson, Daniel. *Managers and Workers: Origins of the New Factory System in the United States, 1880–1920*. Madison: University of Wisconsin, 1975.
Noble, David F. *America by Design: Science, Technology, and the Rise of Corporate Capitalism*. New York: Alfred A. Knopf, 1977.
North, Douglass C. *The Economic Growth of the United States, 1790–1860*. New York: W. W. Norton, 1961.
Olsson, Lars O. *Engineers as System Builders*. Gothenburg, Sweden: Chalmers University of Technology, 1995.
Paullin, Charles Oscar. *Paullin's History of Naval Administration, 1775–1911*. Annapolis: United States Naval Institute, 1968.
Peck, Taylor. *Roundshot to Rockets: A History of the Washington Navy Yard and U.S. Naval Gun Factory*. Annapolis, Md.: United States Naval Institute, 1949.
Pollack, David. *Modern Shipbuilding and the Men Engaged in It*. London: E. & F. N. Spon, 1884.

Pollard, Sidney, and Paul Robertson. *The British Shipbuilding Industry, 1870–1914*. Cambridge: Harvard University Press, 1979.

Post, Robert C. *1876: A Centennial Exhibition*. Washington: Smithsonian Institution Press, 1976.

Pye, David. *The Nature of Design*. New York: Reinhold Publishing, 1964.

———. *The Nature and Art of Workmanship*. London: Cambridge University Press, 1968.

Reingold, Nathan, and Marc Rothenberg, eds. *Scientific Colonialism: A Cross-Cultural Comparison*. Washington: Smithsonian Institution Press, 1987.

Reynolds, Clark G. *Famous American Admirals*. New York: Van Nostrand Reinhold, 1978.

Reynolds, Terry. *The Engineer in America*. Chicago: University of Chicago Press, 1991.

Ridgely-Nevitt, Cedric. *American Steamships on the Atlantic*. Newark: University of Delaware Press, 1981.

Rolt, L.T.C. *Isambard Kingdom Brunel: A Biography*. New York: St. Martin's Press, 1959.

Ropp, Theodore. *The Development of a Modern Navy: French Naval Policy, 1871–1904*. Annapolis: Naval Institute Press, 1987.

Rorabaugh, William J. *The Craft Apprentice: From Franklin to the Machine Age in America*. New York: Oxford University Press, 1986.

Rosenberg, Nathan, ed. *The American System of Manufactures*. Edinburgh: Edinburgh University Press, 1969.

Rosenberg, Nathan, and Walter G. Vincenti. *The Britannia Bridge: The Generation and Diffusion of Technological Knowledge*. Cambridge: MIT Press, 1978.

Roysdon, Christine. *American Engineers of the Nineteenth Century: A Biographical Index*. New York: Garland, 1978.

Rubin, Lester, and William S. Swift. *Negro Employment in the Maritime Industries*. Philadelphia: Wharton School, University of Pennsylvania, 1974.

Russell, C. A., and D. C. Goodman, eds. *Science and the Rise of Technology since 1800*. Bristol, England: Open University Press, 1972.

Salaman, R. A. *Dictionary of Woodworking Tools and Tools of Allied Trades, ca. 1700–1970*. Newtown, Conn.: Taunton Press, 1990.

Schatzberg, Eric. *Wings of Wood, Wings of Metal: Culture and Technical Choice in American Airplane Materials, 1914–1945*. Princeton: Princeton University Press, 1999.

Scranton, Philip. *Proprietary Capitalism: The Textile Manufacture at Philadelphia, 1800–1885*. New York: Cambridge University Press, 1983.

Shaw, Ralph R. *Engineering Books Available in America Prior to 1830*. New York: New York Public Library, 1933.

Shuon, Karl. *U.S. Navy Biographical Dictionary*. New York: Franklin Watts, 1964.

Simmons, Walter J. *Lines, Lofting, and Half Models*. Lincolnville Beach, Me.: self-published, 1991.

Singer, Charles J., ed. *A History of Technology*. 6 vols. Oxford, England: Clarendon Press, 1958.

Sloan, Edward William, III. *Benjamin Franklin Isherwood: Naval Engineer*. Annapolis, Md.: United States Naval Institute, 1965.

Sloane, Eric. *A Museum of Early American Tools*. New York: Funk and Wagnalls, 1964.

Smith, Edward O. *History of the Newport News Shipbuilding and Dry Dock Company*. Newport News, Va.: Mariners' Museum, 1965.

Smith, Merritt Roe. *Harpers Ferry Armory and the Challenge of Change*. Ithaca, N.Y.: Cornell University Press, 1977.

———, ed. *Military Enterprise and Technological Change: Perspectives on the American Enterprise*. Cambridge: MIT Press, 1985.

Society of Naval Architects and Marine Engineers. *Historical Transactions, 1893–1943*. Westport, Conn.: Greenwood Press, 1945.

Sprout, Harold, and Margaret Sprout. *The Rise of American Naval Power*. Princeton: Princeton University Press, 1939.

Stephens, William P. *Traditions and Memories of American Yachting*. Brooklin, Me.: Wooden Boat Publications, 1989.

Swann, Leonard A., Jr. *John Roach: Maritime Entrepreneur*. Annapolis, Md.: United States Naval Institute, 1965.

Sweetman, Jack. *Illustrated History of the Naval Academy*. Annapolis, Md.: United States Naval Institute, 1979.

Taylor, George R. *The Transportation Revolution, 1815–1860*. New York: Holt, Rinehart, and Winston, 1951.

Taussig, F. W. *The Tariff History of the United States*. New York: G. P. Putnam's Sons, 1914.

Temin, Peter. *Iron and Steel in Nineteenth-Century America: An Economic Inquiry*. Cambridge: MIT Press, 1964.

Tyler, David B. *The American Clyde: A History of Iron and Steel Shipbuilding on the Delaware from 1840 to World War I*. Newark: University of Delaware Press, 1958.

Unger, Richard W. *Dutch Shipbuilding before 1800*. Amsterdam: Van Gorcum, 1978.

———. *The Ship in Medieval Economy*. London: Croom Helm, 1980.

Veblen, Thorstein. *Instinct of Workmanship and the State of the Industrial Arts*. New York: Macmillan, 1914.

Waddell, J.A.L. *Bridge Engineering*. New York: John Wiley and Sons, 1916.

Wallace, Anthony F. C. *Rockdale: The Growth of an American Village in the Early Industrial Revolution*. New York: W. W. Norton, 1972.

Ward, James A. *That Man Haupt: A Biography of Herman Haupt*. Baton Rouge: Louisiana State University Press, 1973.

Warren, Kenneth. *Steel, Ships and Men: Cammell Laird, 1824–1993*. Liverpool: Liverpool University Press, 1998.

Welch, Richard F. *An Island's Trade: Nineteenth-Century Wooden Shipbuilding on Long Island*. Mystic, Conn.: Mystic Seaport Museum, 1993.

Whipple, A.B.C. *The Clipper Ships*. Alexandria, Va.: Time-Life Books, 1980.
White, John H. *A Short History of American Locomotive Builders in the Steam Era*. Washington, D.C.: Bass, 1982.
Whitehurst, Clinton H. *The U.S. Shipbuilding Industry, Past, Present, and Future*. Annapolis: Naval Institute Press, 1986.
Wilentz, Sean. *Chants Democratic: New York City and the Rise of the American Working class, 1788–1850*. New York: Oxford University Press, 1984.
Wood, Virginia Steele. *Live Oaking: Southern Timber for Tall Ships*. Annapolis: Naval Institute Press, 1981.
Wright, Richard J. *Freshwater Whales: A History of The American Ship Building Company and Its Predecessors*. Kent, Ohio: Kent State University Press, 1969.

ARTICLES AND PAPERS

Bernstein, Mike. "Then and Now: The William Cramp & Sons Shipyard in World War I and the Site Today." Nautical Research Journal 37, no. 1 (1992): 44–57.
Brown, Alexander C. "John Elgar, America's First Iron Shipbuilder." *United States Naval Institute Proceedings* 76, no. 9 (September 1950): 990–95.
Cochran, Thomas. "Did the Civil War Retard Industrialization?" *Mississippi Valley Historical Review* 48 (1961): 197–210.
Crowther, Simeon J. "The Shipbuilding Output of the Delaware Valley, 1722–1776." *Proceedings of the American Philosophical Society* 117 (1973): 90–104.
Dobson, William. "The Early History of American Shipbuilding." *Journal of the Engineers' Club of Philadelphia* 35, no. 10 (October 1918): 455–66.
"Effect of Air Hammer on Hands of Stonecutters." *Bulletin of the U.S. Bureau of Labor Statistics* 236 (July 1918): 5–13.
Egan, Robert S. "Two Hundred Years of Naval Shipbuilding in the Delaware Valley." *Spring Meeting Papers*. Paper presented before the annual meeting of the Society of Naval Architects and Marine Engineers, Philadelphia, June 2–5, 1976.
Gorman, Michael E., and W. Bernard Carlson. "Interpreting Invention as a Cognitive Process: The Case of Alexander Graham Bell, Thomas Edison, and the Telephone." *Science, Technology, and Human Values* 15, no. 2 (Spring 1990): 131–64.
Graham, Gerald S. "The Ascendancy of the Sailing Ship, 1850–1885." *Economic History Review* 9, no. 1 (1956): 74–88.
Harley, Charles K. "On the Persistence of Old Techniques: The Case of North American Wooden Shipbuilding." *Journal of Economic History* 33 (1973): 373–91.
Hutchins, John G. B. "The American Shipping Industry since 1914." *Business History Review* 28 (1954): 105–27.
Johnson, Amandus. "Swedish-American Master Mechanics, Engineers, and Inventors, 1638–1947, Part II." *Bulletin of the American Society of Swedish Engineers* 42, no. 1 (Winter 1947–48): 14–86.
Kranakis, Eda. "Social Determinants of Engineering Practice: A Comparative View of France and America in the Nineteenth Century." *Social Studies of Science* 19 (1989): 5–70.

Laise, C. Stevens. "Interpreting the Colonial Shipyard." *Spring Meeting Papers*. Paper presented before the annual meeting of the Society of Naval Architects and Marine Engineers, Philadelphia, June 2–5, 1976.
"Man and His Machines." *World's Work* 36 (July 1918): 329–32.
McGee, David. "The Amsler Integrator and the Burden of Calculation." *Material History Review* 48 (Fall 1998): 57–74.
Scranton, Philip. "Diversity in Diversity: Flexible Production and American Industrialization, 1880–1930." *Business History Review* 65 (Spring 1991): 27–90.
"Shipbuilding in the Delaware Valley Spans Three Centuries of Achievement and Progress." *Mariner* 2, no. 6 (June 1955): 10–20.
Snow, Ralph L. "Introduction to Wooden Shipbuilding." *Wooden Shipbuilding and Small Craft Preservation: Papers from the Symposium on the American Wooden Shipbuilding Industry*. Washington, D.C.: Preservation Press, National Trust for Historic Preservation in the United States, 1976.
Woodwell, William H. "The Woodwell Shipyard, 1759–1852." *Bulletin of the Business Historical Society* 21, no. 3 (June 1947): 58–74.

OTHER PERIODICALS

American Machinist
American Neptune
Atlantic County (N.J.) Historical Society Yearbook
Compressed Air
Delaware History
Economic History Review
Engineering News-Record
Engineering Record
IA: Journal of the Society for Industrial Archaeology
Industrial Management
International Journal of Maritime History
International Journal of Nautical Archeology and Underwater Exploration
Log of Mystic Seaport
Nautical Gazette
New Jersey History
South Jersey Magazine
Technology and Culture

UNPUBLISHED MATERIAL

Arrison, John G. "Wilmington Shipbuilding: Needs and Opportunities for Historical Research and Education." Typescript, Independence Seaport Museum, 1991.
Bagnall, William R. "Sketches of Manufacturing Establishments in New York City." Typescript, Baker Library, Harvard University, 1908.
Brown, Alexander C. "Notes on the Origins of Iron Shipbuilding in the United States, 1825–1861." Master's thesis, College of William and Mary, 1951.

Carter, John S. "Delaware's Civil War Shipbuilding: A Survey of the Harlan and Hollingsworth and Pusey and Jones Companies of Wilmington." Historical Society of Delaware, n.d.

Doerrfeld, Dean A., David L. Ames, Bernard L. Herman, and Rebecca J. Siders. "The Delaware Ship and Boat Building Industry, 1830–1940+/–: An Historic Context." Newark, Del.: Center for Historic Architecture and Engineering, University of Delaware, 1994.

Greenhill, Basil J. "The S.S. *Great Britain* and the Coming of Steam Navigation." Lawrence F. Brewster Lecture in History 9 (November 1990).

Hinsley, Jacqueline. "Wilmington, 1876: A Bicentennial Exhibit at the Hagley Museum, opening May 10, 1976." Wilmington, Del.: Eleutherian Mills-Hagley Foundation, 1976.

Hutchins, John G. B. "The Rise and Fall of the Building of Wooden Ships in America, 1607–1914." 2 vols. Ph.D. diss., Harvard College, 1937.

Kebabian, John S. "Delaware Apprenticeship Indentures, 1827–1850." Typescript, Delaware Historical Society, Wilmington, n.d.

McGee, David. "Floating Bodies, Naval Science: Science, Design and the *Captain* Controversy, 1860–1870." Ph.D. diss., University of Toronto, 1994.

Misa, Thomas J. "Science, Technology and Industrial Structure: Steelmaking in America, 1870–1925." Ph.D. diss., University of Pennsylvania, 1987.

Ritter, A. R., comp. "A Brief History of the Philadelphia Navy Yard from Its Inception to December 31, 1920." Typescript, Independence Seaport Museum, 1921.

Seifeddine, Richard. "Scientific Management at the Boston Navy Yard." Senior honors thesis, Harvard University, March 20, 1987.

Sexton, Donal James. "Forging the Sword: Congress and the American Naval Renaissance, 1880–1890." Ph.D. diss., University of Tennessee, 1976.

Shulman, Mark Russell. "The Emergence of American Sea Power: Politics and the Creation of a U.S. Naval Strategy, 1882–1893." Ph.D. diss., University of California, 1990.

Taylor, H. Birchard. "I Build Men as Well as Ships." Philadelphia: Cramp Shipbuilding Co., 1941.

Wegner, Dana M. "Alban C. Stimers and the Office of the General Inspector of Ironclads, 1862–1864." Master's thesis, State University of New York, Oneonta, 1979.

Index

Aaron Manby (iron steamer), 18
ABCD Warship Program (*Atlanta, Boston, Chicago,*and *Dolphin*), 153, 155, 156
Abrams, James, 99
Account of the Construction of the Britannia and Conway Tubular Bridges, An (1849), 20
Admiralty (British), 31, 32, 34, 38, 39
Aesthetics, use of in practical ship design, 54
African-American workers, 95
Airey, George, royal astronomer, 22
Alabama, CSS (commerce raider), 142
Aldus, George, 90
Alert, USS (iron gunboat), 147
Alexander Stephen and Sons Shipyard, 34
Allen, John F., 179
Allen, Theodore, 128, 129, 131
American Bridge Company, 206
American Institute, 65
American International Corporation (AIC), 204
American Society of Mechanical Engineers (ASME), 144
American Society of Naval Engineers (ASNE), 161
"American system" of shipbuilding, 62
America's Cup, 77, 117
Amsler integrator, 35
Amsler planimeter, 133, 134
Anglo-American shipbuilding, 5
Apprenticeship, 6, 48, 49, 65, 97
Archimedes (steamer), 21
Armstrong, William, Sir, 175
Armstrong College, 40
Associations, professional, 36
Atlanta, USS (cruiser), 156
Austral (passenger vessel), 34

Babcock, Washington I., 124, 125, 181, 182, 211
Bacon, Daniel, 5
Baird, George W., 161

Baker family (English), 5
Baldwin, George, 206
Baltimore, USS (cruiser), 156
Bancroft, George, secretary of the navy, 81
Bangor (iron steamer), 86
Barber, Francis M., Lt., 158
Barnaby, Nathaniel, Sir, 33, 39
Barnes, Frederick K., 32, 33
Barton Company, D. R., 46
Bayeau Tapestry (1085), 10
Belcher, Ambrose, 111
Bell, Jacob, 90
Bending slab, 99
Bennett, John, 84, 93
Bensen, Nathaniel, Captain, 94
Bergh, Christian, 50
Bergh family and New York shipbuilding, 47
Bethlehem Iron Company (later Bethlehem Steel), 158, 159, 166
Betts, Mahlon, 86
Beveling machines, 174
Biles, John H., Sir, 39, 151
"Bill of material," 203
Birely, John, and Son Shipyard, 90, 92, 116
Birely and Van Duesen Shipyard, 68
Birely family and Philadelphia shipbuilding, 47
Birkenhead (passenger vessel), 25
Black family and Delaware shipbuilding, 47
Blanchard, Thomas, 69
Bland, Joseph, 110
Board of Trade (London), 6
Bogert, John L., 125
Bolting ship plates, 106
Books, shipbuilding, 48
Boole, Leonard H., 48, 76, 77, 93, 118
Boston, 81
Boston, USS (cruiser), 156
Bowles, F. T., Admiral, chief naval constructor, 156, 161, 163, 165, 166; education of, 151, 155

Boys, as workers, 95
Bridge-building industry, 192
Britannia Bridge, 19
British Association for the Advancement of Science, 19–20, 31
Brotherhood of Boiler-Makers and Iron Ship Builders, 97
Brown, David, 53, 137
Brown, Noah, 67
Brown and Bell, 53, 71
Brown family and New York shipbuilding, 47
Brunel, Isambard K., 21, 22, 23, 36
Buckley Patent Dryer, 73
Buildings, shipyard, 189, 190. See also Shiphouses
"Bull riveter," 173
Burk, Joseph, 51
Byrne, Oliver, 124

Cadet Engineering Program, U.S. Naval Academy, 146, 147; graduates from, 147–49; and inspection trips, 122, 147
Camden, N.J., 50
Camden and Amboy Railroad, 84
Cammel-Laird shipyard, 38
Campbell Axe Company, 46
Canadian shipbuilders, 51
Canonicus, USS (light draft monitor), 128
Capps, Washington, Admiral, chief naval constructor, 151, 161
Captain, HMS (iron warship), 33–34, 35
Carlisle family and Delaware shipbuilding, 47
Ceiling, description of, 14
Centennial Exhibition at Philadelphia (1876), 114, 178
Center, Robert, 77
Center of flotation, 56
Central School of Mathematics and Naval Architecture, 39
Chadwick, French Ensor, 145, 162, 167; and intelligence gathering, 152, 155, 157, 158
Chapman, Fredrik Henrik af, 41, 134
Charles Hillman Ship and Engine Company, 90
Charleston, USS (cruiser), 156, 157
Chatfield, Henry, 16
Chester Rolling Mill, 172

Chicago, 180
Chicago, USS (cruiser), 155, 156
Chicago Engineering Congress (1893), 181
Chicago Pneumatic Tool Company, 180
Chicago Shipbuilding Company, 181
Chimo, USS (light draft monitor), 130
Clark, William, 100
Clermont (river steamboat), 54, 121
Cleveland, Grover, President, 157
Cleveland Pneumatic Tool Company, 180
Cleveland Shipbuilding Company, 184
Codorus (river steamer), 83, 171
Collins Axe and Tool Company, 46
Columbia University, 121, 161
Commission on Ordnance and Gunnery, 158
Committee on Designs of Ships of War, 33
Committee on Machinery, 63
Comparison, as design technique, 52
Composite ship, 92
"Conduct of the War" investigation, 130
Connaught (passenger vessel), 25
Constitution, USS (frigate), 53
Continental Iron Works, 90
Cooley, Mortimer E., 148
Cornell University, 159, 160, 164
Corson, David, 51
Cort, Henry, 18
Cost Keeping and Scientific Management (1911), 200
Cramp, Charles, 47, 49, 120, 123; and iron shipbuilding, 89, 91, 92; as ship designer, 92, 116, 119; and wood shipbuilding, 47, 88
Cramp, William, and Sons Shipbuilding Company, 90, 95, 125, 172, 181
Cramp family, 47, 98
Crandall, H. I., and Son Company, 188
Crane, Clinton H., 151
Cranes, 186, 187. See also Lifting devices
Crimean War, 38, 60
Cuba, 142

Daphne (iron steamer), 34
"Dark Ages" (aka "dark years," "doldrums," "days of our humiliation"), 141, 142, 143, 167
"Dead fingers," 182
Delaware, shipbuilders move away from, 50

Delaware River Iron Ship Building and Engine Works (aka Roach shipyard), 85, 120, 158, 191; and technological advances, 172–73, 179
Delaware Valley, 81, 83
Delmarva Peninsula, 50
Demand for American ships, before Civil War, 60
Denny, Archibald, 185, 188, 190, 195
Denny, William, 32
Denny Shipyard, 40
Deputy family and Delaware shipbuilding, 47
Deskilling, 64, 65, 95, 182
Dialogue, John H., 90
Dickie, George W., 169
Dickie, James, 94
Displacement, 56
Disston, Henry and Sons, Philadelphia, 46
Dobson, William A., 122, 125, 213
"Dolly bar," 106
Double bottom, benefits of in iron hulls, 83
Double-planking wooden hulls, 61
Drafting, 35, 77, 120, 196
Drew, C., and Company, Kingston, Mass., 5, 46
Drew shipbuilding family (English), 5
Dry dock, 69, 71, 74
DuPont, Samuel F., Admiral, 128
Durand, William F., 148, 160, 164, 165
Dyson, Charles W., Admiral, 148

Eagle Boat Program, 208, 209
E. and A. Sewall Shipyard, 89
Eckford, Henry, 49, 53, 55, 76, 121; as migrant shipbuilder, 50, 122
Ecolé Politechnique (Paris), 149
Edge Moor Bridge Company, 193
Electric lighting, 173
Electric machines, 183–84, 185, 187–88
Elements and Practice of Naval Architecture, The, cost of in 1844, 48
Elgar, Francis, 33, 34
Elgar, John, 83
Eliza (ketch), 56
Emergency Fleet Corporation, United States Shipping Board (EFC), 203–8
Emmet, William L. R., 148, 165

Engineer Magazine, 42, 141
Engineering Magazine, 42
Englis, John, 50
Ericsson, John, 84, 125–27, 141
Evans, Holden, 151, 166, 199–201
Evans, Robley D., 153
Evolution of wood shipbuilding, 1

Fairbairn, William, Sir, 19–20, 23, 36, 178; papers and publications of, 20, 25, 28
Fairburn, William A., 211
Family networks, 47, 48, 94
Faron, Edward, 118
Ferguson, Homer, 151, 166
Fernald, Frank L., 158
Ferris, Theodore, 205
Fincham, John, 41
Fiske, Bradley A., Admiral, 145, 155, 158
Fitting out wharf, colonial, 11
Fluid resistance of hulls, 29, 53
Folger, William, 158
Ford, Henry, 208, 209
Fore River Ship and Engine Building Company, 166, 167
Fortune, William B., 194
Fountain, John, 93, 103
Fox, Gustavus V., 136, 146
Fox, Josiah, 50, 122
Fragments of Ancient Shipwrightery, 2
Frames, 2–3, 13
Framing, an iron vessel at Roach shipyard, 104
Franklin, Benjamin, 121
Franklin Institute, 161, 185
Fraser, James, 111
Frazee, Andrew, 94
Freeboard, 33
Freighter (EFC), 205
French, Daniel, 51
Frick, Henry, 194
Froude, Robert E., 32
Froude, William, 22, 29–31, 113
Fulton, Robert, 54, 121
Futtocks, 13

Gangs, subcontracting of, 64
Garboard plank, 13

Gardner, William, 125, 150
Garry Owen (iron steamer), 18
Gatewood, Richard, 155, 156
Gatling Gun Company, 158
Gause family, 98
George E. Weed (yard tugboat), 109
Gibbons, William, 123
Glasgow University, 40, 149, 199
Gloucester Iron Works, 132, 136
Gold rush, California, 60
Graham, James, Sir, First Lord of Admiralty, 39
Grantham, John, 18, 19, 20, 25, 36
"Greasers," 146
Great Britain (iron passenger steamer), 21, 22
Great Eastern (iron passenger steamer), 22, 23, 28, 29
Great Lakes, migration of American shipbuilders to, 50, 51
Great Western (wooden passenger vessel), 21
Green, Bill, 108
Greyhound, HMS (steam gunboat), 31
Griffin, Robert S., Admiral, 148
Griffiths, John W., 27, 34, 64, 69, 73, 76; and education of shipbuilders, 48–49, 52, 65, 66, 76; lectures and publications of, 65, 66, 76; on practical and theoretical shipbuilding, 46, 48, 137–38; and ship design, 52–53, 55, 57, 75, 77, 134
Guiler, James, 94, 104, 118

Haeseler, C. H., Company, 180
Half-hull model, 44, 55, 56, 57, 58
Hall, Henry, 64, 67
Hanscom, Isaiah, chief naval constructor, 94
Hanscom, William, 51, 94
Harlan, Samuel, 86
Harlan and Hollingsworth Company, 86, 90, 116, 193; development and expansion of, 86, 123, 191; employment trends at, 94, 95
Harris, John, 91
Harris family, 47, 49
Harrison, Benjamin, President, 168
Harrison, Joseph, 171
Harrison, W. B., 97
Harvard University, 146

Haswell, Charles H., engineer-in-chief, 161
Hathorne, William, 77
Haupt, Herman, General, 177, 192
Henry Disston and Sons, Philadelphia, 46
Herreschoff, John, 117, 123
Herreschoff, Nathaniel, 116–17, 123, 162
Herreschoff Manufacturing Company, 117
Hichborn, Philip, Admiral, chief naval constructor, 51, 91, 145, 165, 166; and the Naval Advisory Board, 153, 156
Hillman, Charles, Ship and Engine Company, 90
Hobson, Richmond P., 159
Hodgkinson, Eaton, 19–20
Hog Island shipyard, 203–8
"Hogging," 82
Hollingsworth, Elijah, 86
Hollingsworth and Tees, 171
Hollis, Ira N., 148, 158, 161
"Hollow girder" theory, William Fairbairn's, 28
Hone, Philip, 21
"Hoosier," 64
Hotchkiss, Benjamin, 141, 158
Hovgaard, G. William, 150, 160, 165
Hoyt, C. Sherman, 151
Hudson River steamboats, 54
Humphreys, Joshua, 53, 122
Humphreys, Samuel, 53
Hunt, William H., secretary of the navy, 152
Hurley, Edward N., 180
Hutchins, John G. B., 80
Hydraulic machines, 175, 176, 177, 178, 183, 187

Immigrant labor, 95
Immigration, and demand for American ships in antebellum America, 60
Injuries, of workers in modern American shipyards, 190
Inman, James, 41
Institution of Civil Engineers, 31, 37, 41
Institution of Engineers in Scotland, 37
Institution of Engineers and Shipbuilders in Scotland, 37
Institution of Naval Architects, 33, 37, 39; founding of, 25, 37, 38; members of, 38,

161; papers presented to and published by, 20, 31, 33, 41, 42
Iron parts in wooden vessels, 61
Iron ships, 83, 89
Iron shipbuilding, 83, 88, 95; early, 86, 93, 119; in Great Britain, 15, 18, 25; in the U.S., 80, 81, 82, 83, 112
Isherwood, Benjamin F., engineer-in-chief, 136, 143, 153, 161
Isherwood System of longitudinal supported hulls, 29

Jacques, William, Lt., 158, 162
Jenkins, Peter, 150
Jersey City Treenail Factory, 68
"Job 169" (the steamer *Niagara*), 99, 118
"Job 170" (the steamer *Saratoga*), 99, 109, 118
Job work, 61–62, 63
Joggling machine, 173, 174
John, William, 33, 156
John Birely and Son Shipyard, 90, 92, 116
John Randolph (iron vessel), 81
Joiner work, 14
Jones, Christopher J., 35
Jones, John, 85
Journal of the Franklin Institute, 53, 135
Journeymen, 50
Julia Robbins (bark), 63

Kaemerling, Gustave, Admiral, 148
Keel, laying of the, 12
Keelson, 13
Kelly, Alexander, Captain, 94
King, James W., engineer-in-chief, 135, 145, 146
Knowledge, spread of shipbuilding, 6, 7, 36, 40, 49, 50

Labor, 61, 62
Labor division and specialization, 61–62
Laird, John, British shipbuilder, 18
Lank, William, 50
Lank family and Delaware shipbuilding, 47
"Law of comparison," 31
Lawrence, George W., 90
Lehigh University, naval architecture program at, 161

Lenox, G. W., 26
Lenthall, John, chief naval constructor, 53, 94, 153
Lesseps, Ferdinand de, 142
Levy, John P., Captain, 85, 94
Lewis, David, 109
"Lift" model, 56
Lifting devices, 71, 74. *See also* Cranes; Materials handling technology
Light Draft Monitor Program, 125, 127, 129, 130, 131
Lincoln, Abraham, President, 146
"Liners," 106, 173, 174
Liverpool University, 40
Livestock, 12, 72
Lloyd's of London, 26–27
Lloyd's *Register of Shipping*, 3–4
Lofting, 99
Long, Josh, 107
Longitudinal framing, 87
Loper, Richard F., Captain, 85, 92, 94, 132
Loper propeller, 85, 132
Lorain, Ohio, 184
Lord Dundas (iron steamer), 19
Lucas, Theodore, 194
Luce, Stephen B., Admiral, 156
Lukens, Charles, Dr., 83
"Lumper," 64
Lynn, John, 93
Lynn family and Philadelphia shipbuilding, 47
Lysholm, Henry, 194, 198

Mackenzie, M.R.S., Lt., 153
Magowan, Joseph, 101
Mahan, Alfred Thayer, Captain, 140, 142
Maine, 78
Mare Island Navy Yard, 51, 74, 199–201
Marine Engineering, 185
Marine railway, 69
Martin, Frank S., 125
Massachusetts Institute of Technology (MIT), 160, 161
Master shipwright, 5
Materials handling technology, 61, 71, 74; early, 71, 99; by man and/or animal power, 72, 103; modern, 186, 188. *See also* Cranes; Lifting devices

Mattice, Asa M., 148
Mayflower, USS (navy steamer), 147
McFarland, Walter M., 148, 165
McKay, Donald, 46, 50, 55, 75, 76; education of, 49, 77; shipyard, 67, 78, 89
McKay, Lauchlan, 46, 48, 50, 51, 57
McKay, Nathaniel, 90
Meade, Richard W., III, Commander, 148, 161
Mechanic's Magazine, 42
Mechanization, 171, 181, 211; in American shipyards, 61, 66, 172–73, 188
Meigs, John F., Lt., 159
Mellon, Andrew, 194
Melville, George W., engineer-in-chief, 161
Merrill, Orlando, 56
Metropolis (passenger vessel), 25
Mexican War, 60
Midwest, migration of shipbuilders to, 51
Migrant shipbuilders, 6, 49–50
Mills, Joseph, 101
Models, 58
Model ship basins, 32, 76, 116, 121, 162, 164; in Great Britain, 31, 32; campaign for first American, 133, 163, 164
Mold loft, 73, 99
"Molds," 88, 99
Molton, Robert, 6
Monitor, USS (monitor), 127, 128
Moore family and Wilmington, Delaware, shipbuilding, 47
Morgan, J. P., 151, 166, 206
Morgan Iron Works, 117, 158
Morris, William, 23
Morse, Henry G., 192–93, 194, 195, 198
Morse, Henry G., Jr., 194
Morse Bridge Works, 193
Moseley, Henry, 32, 33
Multiple hole punching machine, 173, 209

Nashua Steel and Iron Works, 158
Natural forms, for hull design, 2, 57
Naval Advisory Board, 153, 155, 156
Naval architecture, 24, 197
Naval architecture education: in American colleges and universities, 121, 159, 160–61; in dockyards, 39, 41; in Great Britain, 39,
40, 159; as a medium for spreading shipbuilding knowledge, 36, 40
Naval constructors (U.S.), 143, 150
Naval engineers (U.S.), 143, 148
Naval industrial complex, 38, 158
Naval Science, 42
Navy yards, 48, 60, 73, 74, 75
Neafie, Jacob, 85
Neafie and Levy Company, 85, 91, 191
Nessenthaler, George "Coppersmith," 109
Newbury, Truman H., secretary of the navy, 201
New England, colonial shipbuilding centers of, 6–7
"New Navy, the," 158
Newport News Shipbuilding and Dry Dock Company, 166, 176, 187, 188, 190; staff of, 95, 124, 125, 181
Newton, Isaac, 128, 131
New World (steamboat), 54
New York, decline of iron shipbuilding in, 81
New-York Historical Society, 56
New York Navy Yard, 59, 74, 201
New York Shipbuilding Company, 185, 190, 194, 195, 196; and technology, 181, 185, 187, 188, 195; and efficiency, 189, 196, 197
New York Times, 142
Niagara (passenger liner), 111
Nile's Register, 74
"Ninety Day gunboats," 53
Nixon, Lewis, 151, 166, 165
Norfolk Navy Yard, 75
Northeast Coast Institution of Engineers and Shipbuilders, 37
North River Steamboat (river steamboat), 121
Novelty Iron Works, 179
Nystrom, John W., 132–37; criticism of shipbuilding in the United States, 113, 120, 132, 137, 138, 216; technical treatises and publications of, 53, 124, 131, 133, 134

Offsets, 56, 118–19
Ogden, Francis B., 126
Ohio, USS (74-gun warship), 77
"Old navy," 166
Olympia, USS (cruiser), 176
Oregon, USS (battleship), 176

Packet ships, construction of, 61
Packington, John S., Sir, 38
Palmer, Nathaniel B., Captain, 94
Panama Canal, 142
"Parabolic method," 134
Paris International Exposition (1900), 181
Parker, Foxhall, Commodore, 141
Patton, Leslie, 95
Paul, John, 99–100, 101, 105
Pawnee, USS (gunboat), 93
Peabody-Essex Museum, Salem, Mass., 55
Pennsylvania Railroad, 193
Perseverance, HMS (British warship), 33
Pett shipbuilding family (English), 5
Philadelphia, 50, 83
Philadelphia, Wilmington and Baltimore Railroad, 86
Philadelphia and Reading Railroad, 103
Philadelphia Pneumatic Tool Company, 180
Piecework, 61, 63, 96, 203
Pilgrim (tugboat), 92
Pittsburgh, Pa., 58
Planer, steam-powered, 68
Planimeter, Amsler, 133, 134
Plank, garboard, 13
Planking, 13, 14, 61
Plate mill, 101
Plating gang, 104, 105–6
Pneumatic tools, 178, 182, 183; manufacturers of, 179, 180–81; promotion and benefits of, 177, 181; shipyards using, 173, 177–78, 181, 203
Pole derrick, 71, 99
Pook, Samuel H., 75, 77, 94
Pook, Samuel M., 76
Pook family and Boston shipbuilding, 47
Porter, David D., Admiral, 143
Porter, Hugh Fitz John, 124, 125
Portsmouth Advocate, 65
Portsmouth Dockyard, 39
Portsmouth Navy Yard, 74
Powell, Joseph W., 167
Practical Shipbuilder, The (1839), 48
Practical shipbuilding, 44, 46, 47, 51, 52, 80; and design, 44, 52, 53, 54, 55; training for, 48, 49
President, USS (1797), 53

Princeton, USS (sail- and steam-powered warship), 84, 127
Productivity, in modern wooden shipyards, 73
Prometheus, USS (navy collier), 201
Propeller shafts, problems caused by wooden hulls, 82
Publication, 36, 40–42, 76, 144
Purvis, F. P., 32
Pusey, Joshua L., 85
Pusey and Jones Company, 85, 90, 91, 123, 180, 191
Pusey family, 98

Q and C Company, 180
Queen Elizabeth, 5
Queen Elizabeth (passenger vessel), 25

Railway networks, in the navy yards, 74
Rankine, William J. M., 28–30, 33, 41
"Rational shipyard," 170
Reaney, Neafie and Company, 85, 90–92, 94, 123
Reaney, Son and Archbold, 85, 130
Reaney, Thomas, 85
Red Jacket (clipper ship), 77
Reed, Edward J., Sir, 31, 37, 39, 41
Register of Shipping, Lloyd's, 3–4
Rensselaer Polytechnic Institute, 192
Riveting gang, 95, 96, 106, 181, 182
Riveting machines, 173, 175, 178–80, 182
Rivetless ship, 185
"Rivet passer," or "rivet boy," 106
Roach, John, 85, 117, 120, 123, 172
"Roach boys," 124
Roach family, 98
Roach shipyard. *See* Delaware River Iron Ship Building and Engine Works
Robb, W. L., 194
Robeson, George M., secretary of the navy, 146
Rogers, George W., 76
Ross, Josiah, 108
Rowland, Thomas, 42, 123
Rowland, William, 93, 107
Royal Charter (passenger vessel), 25
Royal dockyards, 5, 39

Royal Navy, 17
Royal School of Naval Architecture and Marine Engineering, 33, 39, 40, 149, 150, 159
Royal Society (British), 20, 33
Russell, John Scott, 22, 35, 36, 39, 41, 43; on iron shipbuilding, 23, 88; theories of, 29–30, 134

Sadler, Herbert, 151, 161, 165
Samuel Sneeden and Company, 90
Saratoga (passenger liner), 99
Sawmills, steam, 67
Sawyer, as specialized trade, 9
Saylor, John B., 95
"Scheming," 115
"Scientific management," 199–202, 216
"Scientific shipbuilding," 16, 17, 113
Scott, William "Scotty," 108
Scottish Shipbuilders Association, 37
Screw dry dock, 69
Screw propeller, 21, 84
"Sectional half-hull models," 56
See, Horace, 115
Select Committee on Ordnance and Gunnery, 157
Selkirk, Owen W., 151
Sellers, William, 193
Sermons, John, 63
Sewall, E. and A., Shipyard, 89
Shaft, propeller, 82
Shear leg derrick, 71, 109
Shipbuilder's Assistant, The, 5
Shiphouses, 71, 73, 190
Ships, growth in size (1830–50), 61
Shipways, 11, 98, 103, 190
Shipwrights, 6
Shipyard, 11, 172, 189
Silliman's Journal, 53
Simonds Rolling Machine Company, 158
Simpson, Edward, Admiral, 145, 155
Skinner, William, 63
"Slip" model, 56
Smith, A. Cary, 77
Smith, Francis Pettit, 21
Smith, Israel, 57
Smith, Oberlin, 184
Smith, Stephen, 49, 77

Smith, Sommers N., 93
Smith, William, 85
Sneeden and Lawrence Shipyard, 90
Sneeden and Rowland Shipyard, 90
Sneeden, Samuel, and Company, 90
Society for the Improvement of Naval Architecture, 36
Society of Naval Architects and Marine Engineers (SNAME), 161–62, 164
Soley, James R., 145
Spangler, Harry W., 148
Spanish Armada, 5
Sparrow's Point, Md., 166
Spear, Lawrence Y., 151, 159
"Specification book," 119, 120, 130
"Spiling," 88
Spiegelhalter family, 98
Sprague, Frank J., 145
Stability, ship, 29, 32–35, 133
Standardization, 3–4, 52, 207
Standard Pneumatic Tool Company, 180
Standish, USS (navy steamer), 142
Stanley Rule and Level Company, 46
Starr, Jesse W., 84
Steamboats, river, 54
Steam box (aka steam trunk, steam chest), 11, 68
Steam power, 68, 73, 74, 171, 172, 174
Steam sawmill, 67
Steers, George, 77
Steers, Henry, 94, 123
Stephen, Alexander, and Sons Shipyard, 34
Stephens, William, 6
Stephens, William P., 103, 111, 125, 213
Stephenson, Robert, 19
Stevens, John L., 84
Stevenson, David, 54
Stevenson, George K., 51
Stimers, Alban C., 127–29, 131
"Stock of knowledge," 14
Stockton, Robert F., 126
Stokes, William, 109
Stone, C. A., Lt., 159
Strike, labor, 182
Subcontracting, 61, 64, 65
Swallow (river steamboat), 54
Sylvester Hull (colonial frigate), 55
"System builders," 191, 192, 202

Taft, William H., President, 201
Tallapoosa, USS (naval gunboat), 142
Taylor, David W., chief naval constructor, 149–51, 161, 163–65
Taylor, Frederick, 199, 201
Technology transfer, 157, 211, 212
"Templet" system, 197–98
Tennyson D'Eyncourt, Charles, Sir, 38
Texas, USS (battleship), 156
Thatcher, W. and A., Shipyard, 91–92, 116
Thomas H. Dallett and Company, 180
Thompson, Elihu, 185;
Thurston, Robert, 135, 144, 159
Tibbels, E. W., 107
Timber, ship, 12, 17, 73
Timber bending machine, 69
Titanic (passenger liner), 24
Tobin, John A., 143, 145, 153
Tools, hand, 7, 9–10, 46, 47, 57, 111
Top timber, 13–14
Towne, Henry R., 186, 187
Transactions, Society of Naval Architects and Marine Engineers journal, 164
Treatise on Mills and Millwork (1861–62), 20
Treatise on Shipbuilding (1775), 41
Treenail making machine, 67
Treenails (or trunnels), 13, 14, 67
Trial (canal boat) (1787), 18
Trowbridge, W. P., 192
Tunxis, USS (light draft monitor), 130
Turkey, Henry Eckford, 122
"Turning turtle," 32
Twedell, Ralph H., 178
Tyler, David B., 80

Union Iron Works, 157, 158, 175, 176, 184, 187
United Service, 144
United States, USS (frigate), 53
United States Metallic Packing Company, 180
United States Nautical Magazine and Naval Journal, 68
United States Naval Academy, 122, 143, 145, 146, 159
United States Naval Institute, 144
United States Navy, 53, 149, 167
United States Shipbuilding Company, 151, 166

University of California, 161
University of Michigan, 161, 164
University of Washington, 161
Unskilled labor, 64
Upward mobility, 65, 95
Urban American shipbuilding, 59, 78; and employment, 61, 63, 64, 67, 75; and technology, 61, 67, 71–73
Urban ship designers, 75, 76
Useful Knowledge for Engineers (1856), 20

Van Duesen, Carter, 51
Van Sant, John W., 51
Van Sant, Samuel, 51
Van Sant, Walter Bassett, 57
Van Sant family, 47, 51
Varney, William, 48, 77, 94
Vaughan family and Philadelphia shipbuilding, 47
Veblen, Thorstein, 202
Very, Edward W., Lt., 153
Vickers Shipyard, 38
Victor Emmanuel (passenger vessel), 25
Vinsinger, Francis, 95
Virginia, CSS (ironclad), 128
Virginius (American gun runner), 142
Voyageur de la Mer (passenger vessel), 92
Vulcan (iron sailing vessel), 18

Wages, 91
Walker Board, 156
Wallis, George, 65
W. and A. Thatcher Shipyard, 91–92, 116
Warner, Henry, 51
War of 1812, 50, 58
Washington, USS (armored cruiser), 195
Waterman, Robert, Captain, 94
Watertight bulkheads, 83
Watt, Richard M., chief naval constructor, 151, 165
Watts, Philip, Sir, 38
"Wave line" model, 56
Webb, Isaac, 49, 55, 77
Webb, William, 49, 68, 71, 75, 160, 162
Webb Academy and Home for Shipbuilders, 160, 161
Webb family and New York shipbuilding, 47
Welding, 181, 185, 204

West, migration to the, 51
Westervelt, Jacob, 50, 65
Westinghouse, George, 144
White, I. J., 46
White, L., 46
White, William H., Sir, 32, 38, 41, 165; as educator, 150, 151; and the Institution of Naval Architects, 33, 37, 38, 42; and intelligence gathering by the U.S. Navy, 144, 152, 156, 157
White oak, 50
Whitney, William, secretary of the navy, 157
Whitworth, James, 63
Whitworth Works, 158
"Whole molding," 2–3
William Armstrong and Company, 38, 156
William Sellers and Company, 178, 180, 187

Williams, James J., 63
Wilmington, Delaware, 50, 83
Wilson, Theodore D., chief naval constructor, 91, 143, 145, 166; and the Naval Advisory Board, 153, 156; papers and publications of, 149, 165
Wood, influence on shipbuilding of, 45
Wood, Richard, 109
Wood to iron shipbuilding transition, 86, 87, 90–93
Woolley, Joseph, Dr., 39, 41
Worden, John L., Admiral, 146
Wrought Iron Bridge Works, 193

Yantic, USS (naval gunboat), 141
"Young turks," 143

Zebley, Jonathan, 51

William Thiesen has served as Curator and Director of Operations for the Wisconsin Maritime Museum since 2001. He has worked in the wood shipbuilding industry and has taught college students the subject of ship design and construction. He earned a master's degree in maritime studies from East Carolina University and a doctorate in the history of technology from the University of Delaware's Hagley Program in the History of Technology and Industrialization. He has published articles on shipbuilding in several journals, including *The Mariner's Mirror, The American Neptune, The Naval War College Review*, and *The International Journal of Maritime History*.